Speeding to the Millennium

THE SUNY SERIES IN
POSTMODERN CULTURE
Joseph Natoli, Editor

Speeding to the Millennium

Film & Culture 1993–1995

Joseph Natoli

State University of New York Press

Published by
State University of New York Press, Albany

© 1998 State University of New York

For information, address State University of New York Press, State University Plaza, Albany, N.Y., 12246

Production by Diane Ganeles
Marketing by Patrick Durocher

Library of Congress Cataloging-in-Publication Data
Natoli, Joseph, 1943–
    Speeding to the millennium : film & culture,
  1993–1995 / Joseph Natoli.
        p.   cm. — (SUNY series in postmodern culture)
    Includes index.
        ISBN 0-7914-3727-2 (hc : alk. paper). —
    ISBN 0-7914-3728-0 (pb : alk. paper)
        1. Motion pictures—Social aspects—United States.
    2. Motion pictures—Political aspects—United States.
    I. Title.   II. Series.
    PN 1995.9.S6N38 1998
    302.23'43'097309049—dc21   97-26977
                                                 CIP

10 9 8 7 6 5 4 3 2 1

For Amelia and Brenda

Contents

Preface

To the Reader at the Outset of the Journey

Speeding to the Millennium is that different kind of book that definitely has to begin defensively and with an *apologia.* Defensively because this is a postmodern journey toward the millennium—which I'll try to explain in this preface—and depending upon which side of the "culture wars" and the "science wars" (and all the "theory" wars before that) you're on, you'll either want to take the journey in this way or won't want to; you'll either be upset by the postmodern style of journeying or you won't; you'll either pick up on the "vibe of my voice" or wonder what ever happened to the "passive voice." And so on. *Apologia* because *Speeding* probably winds up offending a lot of protocols of social history writing, or film critique, or political journalism, or sociological analysis, or personal memoir, or philosophical argument, or rhetorical exhortation, or economic analysis, or stand-up comedy. And so on. I say I'm doing a variation on cultural studies, but that admission, in today's climate, is in need of an *apologia,* too. So, I risk beginning *Speeding* with a style that is not the style of *Speeding* but only because the nature of the times compels me to theorize at the outset my sins.

What We Are About

In *Hauntings: Popular Film and American Culture 1990–1992* I set out to comment in a postmodern way about the intersections of headline *events* and popular film during the first years of this last decade of the twentieth century. I continue that project in *Speeding to the Millennium* and, from a certain perspective, I suppose I am engaged in a sort of postmodern social history of this millennial decade. And since most of the scenes from the culture

1

that I write about seem to have been filmed in the "abyss," one might also, from a certain perspective, think I am on the "moral decay of our culture at a millennial moment" wagon.

This last decade of the century and the millennium is more anxious about fixing moral grounds than rational ones, yet anyone attempting to describe the anxieties of the decade—what inevitably becomes a sort of "history of social anxieties at a millennial moment"—seems bound, under modernist protocols, to connect the moral and the rational. I can update the file, but in principle I should be positioning myself somewhere near Kant's transcendental connection of the moral and rational agent or Rousseau's appeal to a valid and binding social contract between men and women of natural goodwill and fair-mindedness. Now, I could forgo the rational/moral link altogether and align myself with the Christian Coalition or Michael Lerner's Judaism-inspired "politics of meaning" or even the more secular ethics of William Bennett's *The Book of Virtues,* or, some brand of New Age spiritual reawakening, or, some mystical faith in the humanitarian effects of "browsing the Web," or "surfing the Net," or, much more prevalent, some mystical faith in a Global New World Order compliments of the transnationals operating globally without speed limits.

Rather than do any of this, including appealing to some self-grounding notion of Reason, I offer observations from a postmodern point of view of our culture "speeding" toward the millennium. But, oddly, rather than showing us in such forward directed accelerated motion, the scenes I focus on have us at various stages of breakdown at the side of the road. Another, equally depressing way of putting this, is to say these scenes show us wandering through a cultural labyrinth of many roads. Without maps, or, only the nomadic, mazy Deleuzian variety. Now the postmodern lens is giving us a view of what many consider the cultural devastation and wreckage being wrought by postmodernity itself. My approach, in their view, is the very cause of a breakdown in what John Searle calls our Western Tradition of Rationality and Realism. Apparently, in a lot of quarters, postmodernity is ripping a big hole in this Tradition's defensive barricade against the abyss and its minions, chaos and anarchy. I take up the approach, obviously, because I think there's as much sense in demonizing postmodernity as in demonizing the underclass and homeless, or in demonizing our own entitlement programs and the federal employees administering them. I take up the postmodern approach because it enables me to narrate across our culture's multiple and diverse struggles to create values and meanings without pretending I'm reconciling them or sorting through them via some miraculous methodology. I am not delving down, examining root causes of moral decay or societal disintegration or loss of civility, but narrating a journey across our culture during a particular period of time.

Most specifically, I ask "If we have created a renewed sense of the abyss for ourselves during this time, how is this variously narrated throughout the culture?" "If we are no longer speeding down the Golden Road to One Reality and its Truths, are we then heading toward—because we are now constructing—multiple millennial realities?" Through this sort of narrative immersion, we work our way into the present culture not as language-users—repeating imposed connections of meaning and value, and thereby gaining a reproducible yet thievish mastery—but language-players, working to write and re-write ourselves into a culture in motion which we are always constructing and which is always at the same time constructing us.

The book is made up of scenes on which I focus, as if I were Tarantino or Lynch behind a camera. In the time I was writing the cultural studies scenes for *Speeding*, I was also trying to write paralleling scenes which gave the cultural observations their thrust and focus. I was all along writing the fictional scenes to help me grasp the way I was responding to things on the more discursive level. I wasn't after a structured analysis or critique. What I wanted to do was put us into our culture's performance of its millennial fears, seductions, and repressions during these years. In brief, I have been consuming and responding to these times in both imaginative and critical ways. Only toward the end of my writing did I realize that in these days in which we are speeding to the millennium, "we" are not simply to be found in the headlines nor in the movies but in our own imaginations, in our "cultural imaginary." The fullness of the moment, of the present, of these years before the millennium are somewhere in the interstices of scenes that made the headlines and scenes that live only in our imaginations. I haven't captured "our" imaginations nor pretend to represent our "cultural imaginary" but I represent my own to mark their place.

I can argue that American culture during this time set up all the scenes in this book. I never know beforehand—for the most part—what the culture will serve up. For instance, at the outset of writing *Hauntings* I knew only, that the 1992 Presidential election would fall within the span of years the book was covering. Likewise, in *Speeding,* I knew that in 1994 there would be Congressional elections, but I certainly had no idea that the infamous "Contract with America" was in the cards. In order to find out what's going on in the culture, I do what every American does: I watch TV, listen to the radio, read the newspapers and magazines, and ponder headline events with a lot of head shaking, listen to the different "takes" on things from the people I run into, listen to their stories, ponder, dream, make connections and distinctions, critique, gripe, yell out the window "I can't take it anymore!" and imagine. Since in my pursuit of the "cultural imaginary," I'm not out to understand these events in themselves but only in the way our culture responds to them, indeed makes mountains or molehills out of them, I don't turn my nose up at tabloid TV, or the talk shows; I touch base now and then with the soaps, count down with MTV, follow the O.J. trial avidly, admit to being a C-SPAN "junkie," channel surf Letterman and Leno, stay up with Conan, wisecrack with Tom Servo and Crow, never miss all the "hottest" shows from *Friends* to *X-Files* and *Seinfeld, Beavis and Butthead, Simpsons* and *Frasier.*

Headline issues, of course, will come to the news media and the talk shows. I join in the conversation from home. All of this becomes a sort of horizon to my viewing of popular film—everything that critics truly hated or truly loved, everything that generated a moral uproar, everything whose subject matter crossed the headlines. What I look for is a crisscrossing of popular film and headline concerns. Popular film can tap into what electrifies the culture and yet eludes its full understanding. While market forces doubtlessly have commodifying/collusionary effects upon popular culture, as Fredric Jameson asserts, those same forces propel popular culture toward making a buck anyway and anywhere it can. Finally, postmodern theory is the lens that enables me to jump disciplinary fences, narrates me off a Golden Road to the Truth onto a Borgesian garden of forking paths, and puts my own cultural positioning up front rather than continue the charade that particularly keen argument has given it the slip.

When I started *Speeding to the Millennium,* I had no idea that Newt's "revolution" and the now legendary "Contract with America" were on the horizon, but it was not difficult to see a crisscrossing of Newt Gingrich's own rewriting of the American "counter-culture" of the '60s as "a wrong turn away from the

American dream" and Robert Zemeckis' film, *Forrest Gump,* (a film which sets out to do the same thing.) The whole country was being contemporaneously "Newted" and "Gumpized." I also could never fully anticipate the whole culture's "tough love" campaign—one retrofitted with what I thought were outworn notions of genetics, intelligence and criminal pathology. Who could have anticipated the O.J. Simpson trial? And, most crucial, in its wake amid the "pundit analyses" of what it all "means," who could deny that at this moment—February 1996—there is a silence of response that is most meaningful *on an unsayable level?* The Unabomber rises at this millennial moment like a voice from the abyss. Violence and the violent come to the TV screen as a degenerate underclass for whom the rest of us must build prisons and more prisons. But in Quentin Tarantino's *Reservoir Dogs* and *Pulp Fiction,* they appear on the Big Screen undemonized, their violence wrapped up in personal stories that are themselves wrapped up in larger cultural stories and *all* stories are clearly of our own continuous fabrication. Tarantino shows us a postmodern way in which we are weaving our world on different looms but whose threads can accidentally run into each other, a commonality not of product—the same world for everyone—but of the weaving, the narrating itself. As we all share the same warping and woofing mode of mediating the world, we are all in the same designing union.

Most of what I wound up writing about in both the earlier *Hauntings* and in *Speeding to the Millennium* were accidental events: there was no anticipatory logic; they just happened. I believe that since we are not slowly erecting truths on a foundation of absolute truth-making, we must face the fact that we reality-build within the abyss of contingencies as well as within our narratives of order, and that the latter is not in charge of the former. Sometimes a whole life, like Jeff Dahmer's, defied our logical grasp. Minds swirl out of the abyss and torment a culture intent on rebuilding its hold on sanity as well as truth. Friends and I have long, exasperating, closure-less arguments over what motivated Susan Smith, the mom who sent her two babies tied in their car seats to the bottom of a lake. We switch effortlessly into talking about Woody Harrelson's eerie portrayal of "natural born killer" Mickey in Oliver Stone's film, and Linda Fiorentino's mesmerizing sociopath in *The Last Seduction.* Sexuality in the age of AIDS; new and haunting hook-ups between love, romance, sexuality and death. Are we crawling toward our own end beyond the horizon of the New Millennium? Do our new positions in cyberspace give us a new beginning on the face of this planet? We seek the screen to supplement the headlines, to give some framing to the disturbingly contingent, to the seemingly senseless. We wander back to O.J. and object to the attention we are paying it. A fragmented, contingent-laden, haunted journey to a new millennium, a decade of crosswirings, fatal intersections, undecidable beginnings and endings, speeding toward our own xanadus of virtualization while hoping to restore a dream of reality "as we all once knew it." We're all in each and every scene, if not then, now.

How We Journey

First and foremost, *Speeding* is a postmodern journey through these years. All the coordinates are on a postmodern mapping of the world, or, more precisely, we in this last decade of the millennium are conceiving new configurations of the world and the way we are in the world and attending to the world. We are in the process of shifting from a modernist mapping to a postmodern one, a mental journey that we have been on for the last twenty-five years that has been making steady alterations in the "geography of mind," of consciousness, and that mental mapping is being projected onto a real, spatial, worldly geography. We are Blakean mental travelers, but ones whose imaginations are shaped by all prior journeys that we have taken, by all prior mappings of our worldly attendance. We are making conceivable to ourselves a way of being and being in the world that all past and existing ways of being in the world have made possible.

I am on a journey, speeding or not, to the millennium that our American culture is already on, the reader is already on, and it is a postmodern form of travel, a form I try to capture in the very form and style of *Speeding.* When the manuscript was sent out for review by SUNY Press, one anonymous reviewer referred to it as "prophetic collage," an assembly of film criticism, headline events, postmodern theory, politics, economics, clinical diagnosis, philosophical musings, and fictional interludes. In the first installment of this chronicling of the "cultural imaginary" of the '90s—*Hauntings*—I theorized connections between headline events, popular culture, "formal" discourse, mostly concerned with the market and politics, and my own positioning during those years. Now, if we as a culture were only on an Enlightenment journey, (and all variations of that mapping), I would be bound to restrict my attention to some domain of scholarly expertise—entering that domain because I had an original contribution to make and armed with some methodology of approach that would bear the argument and deliver the thesis. I would also be bound to vaporize my own positioning, my own perceptual frame at that time and at that place—rather like a magician curtaining an elephant, saying some magic words and then vaporizing the elephant.

The American "cultural imaginary" in this decade did not and does not allow me to journey into it in that enlightened, solely discursive fashion. Like you, the reader, I can no longer be sedentary within that mental mapping, nor confidently objective and disinterestedly observant in one place, outside and untouched by the cultural flux—a culture in motion in this last decade of the millennium, in very particular, very unsettling and yet very fascinating ways. In *Hauntings* I made the choice to tell a story of American culture during this decade without pretending to write my own narrative frame out of it because quite clearly the culture has already "framed" me toward conceiving and representing—that is, telling a story of the culture—within not only cultural ways already in play but in personal ways. The entanglement, or crisscrossing, of a cultural imaginary, a social order arising out of it and attempting to put a lid on it, and the individual at once defined and describing from within that entanglement, represents a big chunk of what I have called a "postmodern mapping" of things. I am true to it because '90s American culture has been true to it before me.

We have not been journeying in this decade "discursively," by which I mean either guided by some empirical or rational methodology or producing a world that can only be grasped in an analytical-rational way. I realize that since the Enlightenment we have been able to mark clear boundaries between fictional, poetic, artistic attempts to reveal the non-discursive—reaching toward "affect," or "subliminal desires," the "sublime," laughter, pleasures and holidays of fantasizing—and the serious stuff of "critical reasoning." I call that distinction, that polarity, an overlay, an imposition upon everyday life, upon the cultural turmoil, upon the "stuff" of the world, upon the contingencies, desires, hauntings, and imaginings of what Heidegger calls the "world's worlding." Boundaries between "structured, critical" renderings of American culture and solipsistic, chaotic, or inchoate ones are clearly marked only on modernity's mapping of our journey. We are in the '90s still taking that "Enlightened" journey but it has nevertheless intersected a different form of journeying. And that collision of two differing form of mental traveling fills the days and nights of our American '90s and augments a fear and anxiety regarding the future. We press harder on the gas pedal as we head toward the millennium, perhaps in the same way Oedipus sped to Thebes to avoid his fate, or, perhaps, we push it in the way David Koresh pushed himself and his followers toward a fiery Armageddon.

The future does not lie before us in any particularly discursive way, nor does the present play itself out in any particularly discursive way. The headlines and our "pundit" responses to them reveal only that we are mostly haunted by what is unthought, by anxieties, desires, memories, phantasms, bitter battles, fears and traumas, seductions and repressions that produce the world we give shape to and in turn shape the way we know the world. We cannot restrict that "knowing" to a form of knowing that has no map coordinates for all of this. I can't constrain my performance of our "cultural imaginary" in the '90s to a "geography of mind" that is no longer the only geography we project upon the world.

Another anonymous reviewer referred to *Speeding* as a "cultural diary" structured as a critique. I think this captures the mixing of modes here in an attempt to reflect how our world entwines the personal, social and cultural. But if this work were purely a "cultural diary," that is *my* encounter with American culture during a particular period, I wonder if the interest would extend beyond family and friends. I do not use Samuel Pepys as a model or consider myself a Pepys drawn to the headlines and box office film. I intrude myself into this "cultural imaginary" not to update the reader on my personal life but because my "I" is like your "I"—it's a player in the drama, it's framed in some way that tells us more about the culture than about the "I," and it is both imagining and caught in what has already been imagined. On the other hand, if I am structuring a critique here, why muddy it with personal engagements and thus risk a dismissal of the critique as "too subjective"? My point is that once you begin to identify *Speeding* with anything other than a postmodern trot or dictionary in hand, you fall into attaching certain meanings and valuing in certain ways that yearn for what *Speeding* is trying mightily to resist. But you don't need that postmodern dictionary in hand in order to read and enjoy *Speeding*. In a very notable way, you, the reader have already done your part in creating that dictionary, that postmodern mapping of the world. You are already a postmodern traveler on a postmodern journey to the millennium. You have already imagined our culture into being in these years. Every reader is my accomplice.

I don't know what a "cultural imaginary" history, if you will, would look like before a postmodern way of looking at things developed. Probably no one would conceive of such a phrase or such a project. I do know, however, that a postmodern perceptual change now envelops you as well as me because it envelops the culture. And though we may still want to represent that change within older ways of representation, I find myself pushed toward writing in a style and format that will not appear alien to the reader precisely because the horizon or staging of your reading is the same American culture in the '90s that is the horizon of my writing. If the postmodern mapping that I follow here in developing style and format, interspersing fictional vignettes with diary pieces, critical discussions, philosophical theorizing and so on, was only available to *cognoscenti* of postmodernity and not already a notable, lived and experienced part of the terrain of our American culture, then the reader would have no means to engage the culture through the writing. Therefore, I have written this chapter in the history of the '90s in a postmodern way without feeling compelled to restage the entire debate between modernity and postmodernity, most recently breaking out in the "science wars," (a topic I take on, among numerous others, in *A Primer to Postmodernity*.)

So, I am neither structuring or pursuing a critical argument here, nor taking a walk down memory lane. I am trying to write in such a way as to make the cultural furor during these years resonate on the page and in the mind of a reader, who has also lived these years in a culture speeding to the millennium and who has configured, tacitly or explicitly, the world in both modernist and postmodernist ways at the same time. Inevitably, my encounter with our American culture during these years both shared the experiences of others and also re-oriented other experiences in personal ways. The lens of my seeing has a certain prescription as does the reader's. Inevitability extends to this situation also. But by putting myself forward as a "player" in the drama, I allow the reader to make his or her adjustments to my seeing, rather than confound things by pretending to be a transparent observer. By putting a "diary-like" quality or personal tenor into the writing, I also mark the inevitable consorting of the personal with the cultural. By supplementing critique with fiction, I mark the place of the imaginary in the creation of our times and our world. And all these adjustments from a modernist to a postmodernist format, enable me to come closer than isolated discursive and fictional accounts to consuming and responding to a "cultural imaginary" of a decade.

My intent throughout *Speeding* has been to capture some of the dramatic energy of the numerous conflicts America has experienced in the '90s, in film, in the headlines, on TV, in our personal lives. I have tried to move the camera in close on particular lives in particular conversations—the fictional vignettes—and panned back to capture the headlines, the "culture wars," the political battles, and the play of global market "logic" behind those headlines. We are not only doubtlessly speeding toward a millennium of our own making but we are doing so down postmodern super-highways, postmodern maps in mind and in hand.

Speeding to the New Millennium

August 20, 1994

"It seems reasonable at millennium's end that things and beings might fall (or rise) out of sight in the blink of an eye, that the wheel of fortune should accelerate to spin at a blinding speed."

Hillel Schwartz, *Century's End*

"[O]ne might suppose that the acceleration of modernity, of technology, events and media, of all exchanges—economic, political and sexual—has propelled us to 'escape velocity,' with the result that we have flown free of the referential sphere of the real and of history."

Jean Baudrillard, *The Illusion of the End*

Is the action-packed film *Speed* in any possible way a *fin de millenaire/fin de siecle* film?

Let me talk about "vibe." These are the vibrations that we are currently emitting into our environment and which in turn are producing a *fin de siecle* atmosphere that is affecting us. The approach to the end of a millennium begins imperceptibly at the head of the runway, and then gradually we build up speed, enough speed to lift off, to jump clean from one millennium into another. As we get closer and closer to lift-off we envision ourselves hovering above a Miltonian "vast immeasurable abyss . . . dark, wasteful, wild."[1] And despite all our brave technological progress, a Third Economic Revolution promising a "restoration of our American dream," we find ourselves not on a well-charted main road to the new millennium but detoured, pathless. Despite Newt Gingrich's declaration that except for "a generation spent in the counterculture . . . things were on the right track," we are at this moment harboring a fear of being propelled toward our own destruction.[2]

11

The fear crosses class lines; it propels the wealthy toward only short term investment "play" interspersed with playing hard and fast with all the distractions money can buy. It propels the remaining eighty percent of the population toward nothing more than the horizon of the wealthy. Lives minus a teleological dimension are not into anything for the "long haul." The "Contract With America" promise to "renew American civilization" links a golden but shadow-filled past with the present. But what we face—the new millennium—is in front of us, next stop or two down the road.

We are staring straight ahead then, hoping to link present with future. There's the rub, especially for a short-term dedicated society that has been running down the road "burning daylight and never mind the consequences." Spirit of renewal is countered by suspicion of disintegration. We are the transition team that will link this century, this millennium, with the next, carry the dream forward. But we are also a fractured society haunted by the fear that we have exhausted a future that was never ours to exhaust. The closer we come to the millennium the greater our sense of heading not into dream but into an abyss. And in the abyss we go faster and faster, while everybody has a take on what this "dark, wasteful, wild" is and how we can best reach "escape velocity."[3]

When we reach fifty miles an hour, we can neither stop nor slow down. Nor can we get off. Otherwise we will blow up. Dennis Hopper has arranged this. He's doing it for money. He wishes he had a great political cause or a great philosophical desperation but he doesn't. A year later, in the film *Waterworld*, Hopper will have a destination—land. In fact it will be more than a destination for Hopper and his post-apocalyptic, waterbound followers. It will be their destiny. But here in *Speed*, he has no vision. He's just rigged our bus so that once we reach fifty miles an hour we can't go slower or stop or the bomb he's affixed to the underside of the bus will go off. Shades of a *coming* apocalypse. It finally does go off at the movie's end. And guess what? It mushrooms up to A-bomb proportions. Or almost. The bus hits a plane being fuelled and the conflagration is apocalyptic. The camera pans the faces of the rescued passengers behind the glass windows of the rescue vehicle. Their faces are contorted like the faces in Dante's burning river. This could have been their end. Our end. The world's end. The Soviet Union threat is gone but we now discover we are still hurtling toward doom, extinction, our own prodigiously labored annihilation. Not only the market has gone global, stretching out beyond a nationalism nurtured by our cold war mentality. Now our fears have globalized. We worry less about "making the world safe for democracy" than about technologically skewering the whole planet out of its "natural" sync. We are falling further and further behind in identifying, monitoring and therefore controlling what we concoct.

When the camera pans down to Sandra Bullock's foot on the gas pedal—as it does repeatedly, furtively almost—our first reaction' is to get off the pedal, slow down, stop. But she can't. And it's our foot on the pedal. She's an innocent bystander, like us. Her license has been revoked for speeding so she's forced to take public transportation. She isn't in any way connected to the madness that connect Keanu Reeves and Dennis Hopper in their game of revenge. She's like us: we didn't put the planet in the mess it's in but it's our foot on the gas pedal nonetheless. We've all been caught speeding before. We've violated the natural speed of things with our synthetic, technicized order of things. Our internal clock and the planet's have been out of sync for a long time. Too long? Is the new millennium a fresh start, a fresh winding of the clock? Or, is it more what we fear it is: a painful reminder of what might have been, of a time when future time was hopeful and not already wearied, redundant, bearing more of what has already been packaged than what is new and inconceivable. The future is already a re-presentation, a re-play. In Baudrillard's view we have escaped the linear space of the Enlightenment and entered "our non-Euclidean *fin de siecle*" in which "the future no longer exists." "Are we condemned," Baudrillard wonders, "in the vain hope of not abiding in our present destruction . . . to the retrospective melancholia of living everything through again in order to correct it all, in order to elucidate it all . . . do we have to summon all past events to appear before us, to reinvestigate it all as though we were conducting a trial?"

We run history over again, Baudrillard suggests, "like a film played backwards."[4] Recall in the film when the scene of passengers is taped for about a minute or so and that minute is looped so as to trick Dennis Hopper into thinking he is watching present action. The minute ends and then begins again. Everybody looks frightened, eyes glued to the road ahead as the bus exceeds the fifty miles an hour doom limit. The feel of what the future is for us lies in this substitution of the tape loop for real life, dead time for living time, real, vibrant lives for taped simulacra. But unlike Dennis Hopper, who is deceived for a time, we are not deceived. We are both the perpetrators of the simulated reality and the partakers of it. The real millennium is not only anticipated, it is already co-opted, depleted, worn out. That there is thus nothing ahead but re-runs becomes itself our special twentieth century contribution to the vibe of *fin de siecle*. We have constructed a global life-world for ourselves in which time and the natural, seasonal world which so expresses itself—at least until Carson's "silent spring"—has nothing to offer us. And we fear retaliation. Hell, we're expecting it.

The film *Speed* allows some time to reflect, although it keeps the pressure on us. Time is running out. We can't hold this speed forever. We're bound to hit something, or our fuel will run out, or, most frighteningly, the conflagration will come even though we think we still have time. What are we to think about? Well, this is a popular film, a full dip into the pool of naive realism. It is not constructed to put us into this doomsday downer I am talking about. It is directed *against* allowing us time to think about what terrible nightmares fuel the film's hold on us. We cannot have it any other way: we must be excited afresh in order to attend at all. Ironically, what generates our excitement is a subliminal dread of the course our endless simulations in the service of our always to be renewed excitements has put us on. I mean the road to ruin, brother.

The tensions are all here. Consider the inexplicable mania of Dennis Hopper, the mad bomber whose mania overspills his reasoning: "I'm just doing it for the money." Unlike our present real-world Unabomber, Hopper doesn't have a sixty-two page manifesto he wants to broadcast.[5] Three and a half million dollars and not ideology motivates Hopper. Nonetheless, we're more comfortable with Hopper's motivation than with our Unabomber's, in spite of the great lengths the Unabomber has taken to explain what he's up to. The problem is the more he appeals to a common court of reason, the more aware we become of just how obligingly serviceable that court is. On the other hand, Hopper is a known commodity. He's a sort of entrepreneur playing "hard ball" just a wee bit too hard. He's in the arena to win, let the bodies fall where they may. Of course, he's not competing in the free play of the market. Or is he? The law is there to protect what the winners have won, but it is also there to be tested for holes, outflanked and outmaneuvered, stonewalled, slipped by, circumvented, legislated in *your* best interest, thrown up as an obfuscation in *your* best interests, detoured away from the regulation of how you do business and what profits you glean.

I am saying that Dennis Hopper is a "player" in this film and his disparagement of Keanu Reeves's intelligence ("Don't start growing a brain on me now" Hopper tells Reeves) clearly marks Reeves as a "loser." We are told by others that Reeves has "more guts than brains" and that his partner is the "brains of the two." We are heading at fifty miles an hour toward certain tragedy and the villain in the piece is *us* for in 1994 we have all attended to the global drive toward being a "winner." "We can all win again." The whole country can. We can compete and win. We can all get the three and a half million dollars. And guys like Keanu? Gordon Gecko in Oliver Stone's *Wall Street* puts it succinctly: "If you're not a player, you're a nobody. You're nothing." Following the money has put us on this doomed bus at the century's end. We may not reach the New Millennium. We're running out of fuel and Dennis Hopper's going too far. Nothing is valued but getting the money. That's was the '80s signature and this is the '90s. Have things really changed?

We circle the airport in the end, as we try to save ourselves, keep time going, keep everything from exploding. This is a sort of purgatory we are in, circling until we can . . . repent? If this word sounds totally out of place here it is only because our rush to the New Millennium has no eschatology, no contemplation of "last things." We are approaching in our minds neither hope of immediate redemption or, like David Koresh and his followers, a thousand year rule of Christ on earth. We're in this bus and we're sapped of teleology, of intent, hope, purpose, meaning, understanding, vision, values, or heart.

Heart? Follow Sandra Bullock, who is exuberant, fresh, vital. It's a Hollywood way out; a naive realist exit. But is there something more here? She is finally doomed but Keanu won't leave her. He faces her fate with her. And they survive. Is this just the reproductive urge, the biological drive that will get us to the New Millennium, get us safely out of this century and into the next? Surely, that foundational clash of Eros and Thanatos is played out in this film. But also surely we have Eros *and* Thanatos, and the Eros is almost subtextual, a footnote, a remote possibility. It is not hard to figure out that we take AIDS with us to the century finish line, that it has thrown us into a rush to reconceive love and sexuality. *Amour* is no longer *toujours;* abstinence is advised. Even Hollywood can't do its sex scenes without feeling the shadow here.

All this film does is back away from where our desire will take us because that desire is not the heart's but the eye's—the world is nothing more than an endless display of products, resplendent colors, shapes, movements, spaces, surfaces. We construct the desires that construct us.

At one point in the film, the speeding bus faces a fifty foot gap, a portion of unfinished elevated highway. Can we jump it? Can we reach "escape velocity" and return to "the way things were"? There is applause everywhere when the bus flies across this empty space, this unexpected absence on the road we have been hurtling down. We may, in this postmodern world, have lost our sense of continuity and connection, of coherence and progress, but that only seemed to be the case. Here in this popular film *Speed* we are able to leap over the abyss. And—this is most important—we have not "flown free of the referential sphere of the real and of history."[6] Our century and the next are not incommensurable—we are not heading toward a nose dive into that emptiness but will rise phoenix-like onto the other side. We can take our presence and present into the future, into the New Millennium.

This is very upbeat—at the same time the film reveals us as already lost in that absence, that gap, that abyss it ironically shows us spanning. If we have been building bridges between ourselves and the world, ourselves and others, ourselves and the past and the future, this film fails to show us. Rather, it shows us speeding away from all the ways we have connected ourselves. I like to think we are speeding toward postmodern connections. But if the film were about that, the bus would not be forced to keep speeding but rather forced to stop and detour, detour every time it came to a new fork in the road.

Precisely the postmodern itinerary of *Speeding to the Millennium.* Let's begin with two scenes from opposite sides of the road: *Forrest Gump* and *Pulp Fiction.*

Notes

1. John Milton, *Paradise Lost,* Book VIII.

2. Maureen Dowd, "GO.P.'s Rising Star Pledges to Right Wrongs of the Left," *New York Times* November 10, 1994, p. A1.

3. Talk of the "abyss" increases as we approach century and millennium end, links with postmodernity often being made. Gertrude Himmelfarb's *On Looking into the Abyss*, New York: Alfred Knopf, 1994, accuses the postmodern ethos of being the abyss creator of our time. Hers is an academic's indictment, but nonetheless she stands on the same sort of implacable foundation of reality and truth as do the Republicans in their *Contract With America* and *Restoring the Dream.* Gingrich's attack on the '60s counterculture is in effect his attack on postmodern roots. But all manner of events seem daily to be viewed as coming out of the abyss that looms closer and closer to us: the civil war in Rwanda (Joshua Hammer, "Deeper into he Abyss," *Newsweek* April 25, 1994); political struggle in Russia (James Sherr, "To the Abyss and Back," *National Review* Nov. 1, 1993); American economic decline (Robert Kuttner, "The Abyss: Does America Have a Parachute?" *The New Republic* Oct. 29, 1990); elections in Haiti ("Sliding Toward the Abyss," *Time* Sept. 24, 1990); the Gulf War (Lisa Beyer, "Pausing at the Rim of the Abyss," *Time* Sept. 10, 1990); Assisted suicides (John Garvey, "Extraordinary Means: Approaching the Abyss in Michigan," *Commonweal* August 10, 1990); national health care (Ronald Bronow, "A National Health Program: Abyss at the End of the Tunnel," *JAMA, Journal of the American Medical Association* May 9, 1990); post-cold war (Evan Thomas, "From Abyss to Brink" *Newsweek* Jan. 8, 1990); Latin American political struggle (Frank Smyth, "Salvadoran Abyss," *The Nation* Jan. 8, 1990). We are at century and millennium's end certainly not obsessed with renewing a dream. I think we're having nightmares.

4. Jean Baudrillard, *The Illusion of the End,* Stanford: Stanford University Press, 1994, 10–11.

5. See the *Washington Post* supplement, "FC," "Industrial Society and Its Future," September 19, 1995, 8 pp. for the Unabomber's manifesto.

6. Baudrillard, p. 1.

Running with Gump

August 19, 1994

"Obviously, nothing anyone writes will keep the film from soaring toward $200 million or prevent the Gumpization of the '96 election."
Amy Taubin, "Plus Ça Change,"
Voice August 3, 1994, 53
"We spent a generation in the counterculture laughing at McGuffey Readers and laughing at Parson Weems's vision of Washington."

Newt Gingrich

Where are we running to with *Forrest Gump?* I think it's pretty clear that we're running just behind him through the second half of the century. Toward the new century and the new millennium. It's a film, then, about making sense of where we've already been so we can be clear about where we're going. For those alive now in 1994 it's important to "lay to rest," to "come to terms with, "to make sense of" the turbulence of . . . of the '60s! Not just the decade beginning with the New Frontier and John XXIII—both investing their constituencies with a renaissance fervor—but the mark of the '60s that the culture still bears.

And who is making these observations? Or, more meaningfully, what counter-countercultural "spirit of renewal" is making these observations? Let's call it the Gumpish spirit. We saw it at work at the 1992 Republican Convention. You can read it in the letters to *Fortune* protesting the government's treatment of a true American entrepreneurial hero—Michael Milken. It beat back ERA. It has a secret love affair with the Avenger AIDS and an ambivalent response to drug entrepreneurship. It's swarming right now all over China, distributing free Coke, Dr. Pepper, and Pepsi on streetcorners, until they're hooked, until Marxist "utopianism" is replaced by a "rush to consume," one nightmare with another.

Gump is running as fast as he can to re-write history, to narrate the last fifty years in a populist way, a winning way. We're involved here not only in 1996 election politics but end of the millennium politics. We are involved in that most important issue, a struggle for meaning and value. What meaning will the road we have just been on have for the majority of those who will come to vote in 1996? What values will they extract from the cataclysmic events American society has been through in this second half of the century? Recall, we never did make sense of Vietnam although there has been much talk of "lessons learned." It was clear however in the Persian Gulf War that someone could come forward and say "We can win this as a vindication for our poor performance in Vietnam"—say this and win the support of millions of cheering Americans. Is it at all clear that a multicultural nation that is yet a community without imposing one concept of unity upon that community is something, in bell hooks phrase, "to be yearned for"? Or, are we more attracted to unrivalled meanings and values, Blakean "single vision" wherein difference, whether it be political, sexual, racial, ethnic, class or gender, is "reconciled," "resolved," "unified," "civilized," "identified"? Have we in any way clearly asserted an egalitarian, socially just, ecologically sound counterstatement to "global market values"? And, most relevant here to the success of *Forrest Gump,* have we retrieved our own past in any commonly shared fashion? Can we connect the images and words of the past on one big stage of cultural literacy?

On one hand, *Gump* is all about the staging of certain preferred connections of word and world—this event means this, or, this way of attending the world is *not* to be valued. On the other hand, its adeptness at staging its own constructions of our American past gives away the game. I mean *history is being constructed here;* it is being shaped, interpreted, narrated. Nothing that happens or has happened bears unambiguously within it what meaning it will have for us and what value we will place upon it. In fact, the whole audience is already painfully aware that what connotes our own recent American history is this very battle over the meaning and value of every person (from Reagan to Arafat), event (from 'Nam to Chiapas), and idea (from the play of the free market to liberalism). That which is most desired—a clear, determinate representation of things—is absent. But every representation holds out the promise of satisfying that desire. Everyone in the audience eagerly anticipates such satisfaction, especially now at this millennial moment when the whole culture is taking account of itself. At the same time we have the experience of failure, of only a momentary stay against confusion and then a return to conflict, chaos, indeterminacy, undecidability, uncertainty, incommensurability. Some "Other" always shows up and points out *other* connections to images up there on the screen that we once thought were self-evidentially "real" and "true."

The film, in fact, bears its own Otherness—it has to. It can't keep it out. Consider this: here we are running through the second half of the century with a young white male with a 75 IQ. Now while Selma, the Kennedy assassinations, the Woodstock generation, Vietnam, Nixon and Watergate, the Wallace and Reagan shootings, the opening of China and so on are all observed through the eyes of Gump, we *are* him in our viewing and *not* him at the same time. In order to narrate the past in a certain way, that past has been re-imaged up there on the screen. That representation can be controlled, can be shaped so that it appears to be just a re-presentation of what actually occurred. But this film itself undermines that by using a postmodern trick or two. We know for sure that Tom Hanks wasn't back there standing behind George Wallace or shaking hands with JFK, Nixon, and Johnson. So the film subverts its own bid for re-presentation. This has all been cleverly constructed. Just as Hanks is distanced from Gump, we too are distanced from both and from the film. And from that distance we are free to observe the events the film depicts in ways other than those the film attempts to orchestrate.

The film has to provide such openings for other ways of attending to its images and words because it cannot contain us or the events within the gaze of Gump, because the history it relates does not have one universal meaning tagged to it but is already full of different ways of looking at it, because the audience has already made various linkages to this history (consider the Vietnam vet in the audience, or the shrimp boat captain who was bought out by a large cartel), and because, in order to appear positioned in a hip present, the film bites into some self-destructive gambits of postmodernity. All this bears closer examination.

While the film is trying to Gumpize history (fix it within a fixed frame of meaning and value), its techniques are clearly showing that history is in motion in terms of the present. Gump is literally running in and out of the great events of the recent past. He's like Woody Allen's Zelig—he's showing up in the most unlikely places. The present puts itself into any picture of the past; it frames the past within its own lens. Zemeckis takes us once again back to the future where we find the present's future and when we go back to the past we find the present's past. It's all present. We're like Gump—we've never really gone anywhere. You leave home and you take yourself with you.

We have then a postmodern view of history. All of history is eternally available to us—not as it was because even when it was, no one knew its meaning, or its meaning was overdetermined. There were too many offers of "true meaning." We cannot remain fixed in the present because the present only comes to us within narratives floating around in the present—everything from the story of little Buddha to the story of Lt. Dunbar out west, from J. Edgar Hoover's crossdressing to how Columbus really "discovered" America. We are all filming the present and there is no way that our cameras are moving forward from mark to mark. Time is a narration that does not follow the hands of a clock or the progress of digits.

Our culture at millennium's end wants to put itself back into the past and replay its role, revisit its connections, before it can go ahead. I suppose this need to regroup before going ahead is an Enlightenment need. After all, we are on a Golden Road to the Truth, but if that yellow brick road has gotten hard to follow, is clouded over, seems to be there and not here, then perhaps we took the wrong turn after all? We need to retrace our steps, go back and re-interpret our actions and our words. It is not surprising then that Gump's face and figure perforate our recent past. We're in that theatre doing the same thing. The whole American culture is re-introducing itself into past scenes. Disastrously, however, the present popping up in past scenes doesn't give us much hope of settling the tensions of the past in a Gumpish way. Disastrously because you can't show the past "as it really was"—a Gumpish promise—by showing how easily the present rewrites/revises that past. I mean you can't focus a camera on the last half of this American century without rekindling bad memories, salting old wounds, overwhelming any consciousness with a flood of undecidables.

Any consciousness? What if it were possible to get this audience to travel the back roads of American memory with a sweet and innocent guy like Gump? Won't the audience be gumpized and in this fashion the revisionist history that the film presents could stand in for the present refractory image of our own recent past? As the film soars toward $200 million it is obvious that the audience has been gumpized. I say this only because if it were transparent that Gump was no more than an angling device, the latest avatar of a High Romantic faith in innocents, fools, madmen, Cumberland beggars and idiot savants, and that as such he was less able and not more able to make sense of the messiness of the recent past, then the film would be painful to us. Doubly painful because it was putting all those past irresolvables and animosities before our eyes once again *and* because it was making a crude and cynical attempt to seduce us into a gumpish mode of awareness and thus a gumpish take on the recent American past. And from this entrapment, the hope is that we could be launched into the new millennium. The film wants Gump leading the way with us behind him running from one century into another. It's arguing for commensurability in a postmodern age of incommensurability. It has to. A global marketplace must be full of commensurables, from people to ideas, but most importantly the movement of time must be the movement of commensurables. A gap, a fissure, a black hole separating our entrepreneurship in the present from our profits and goals in the future, or separating past efforts from present realization would indeed be abysmal. Even short-term players demand continuity.

Although the film clearly does gumpize us, the film also makes a mockery of its own gumpish attempt—history is there to be looted and exploited, to be refigured and remodeled, rehearsed and re-shot, by any film company passing through. Or any pair of eyes in a theatre looking back. Our turbulent American past is not a solid chunk of Golden Age legacy we could all re-grasp, as Reagan narrated things, but a melee of meanings and values that always come out looking strangely like our present melee of meanings and values. The past is being pushed like product. And *Forrest Gump* not only treats the past like a modifiable commodity but it exposes its own hucksterism.

The film then winds up in the same fix Dan Quayle did when he tried to stabilize family values by attacking Murphy Brown. His attempt wound up educating more people regarding the sheer numbers of alternative family structures in this country than any efforts made by the nontraditional families themselves. Claims to the privileged status of the heterosexual couple, indeed to heterosexuality itself, and to the traditional roles of "fathering" and "mothering" all came to the attention of a mass market audience.

Thanks to Quayle, doubts as to the legitimacy of such privileging were given headline play. Of course, Quayle didn't want to have such privileging questioned but rather was after a reconfirmation of something he thought could bring back to George Bush's camp the Democrats who had voted for Reagan in 1980 and 1984. He thought family values were a rally–round–the–flag cross party issue. But instead it blew up in his face, as did the whole Republican Convention. Rather than re-etch more deeply a firm ground of American values and the indisputable meaning of things past, present and future, the Republicans only succeeded in putting on view the shakiness of those grounds and the disingenuousness of their representations.

So too with *Forrest Gump.*

It's a cynical act to put a character like Forrest Gump before us because while reason has clearly been a pawn used for various purposes in our past, there is no one on the face of this wide world who will gain from a loss of his or her critical faculties. There is, however, profit and gain in transmuting folks from ends in themselves to mere instruments of purchase, i.e. consumers. Critical thinkers are not especially welcome as jurists by impaneling attorneys nor are they especially welcome as consumers by advertisers. Gump's "unexamined life" makes him vulnerable to the loudest rift of hype. Unless of course he has an inner light of goodness and innocence and wisdom that shines upon the world, distinguishing the real from the hype. And here is the very heart of the cynicism I see: a person who would normally be the most victimized in the sort of "play of the free market" ethic we have established, a vicious competitiveness in an entrepreneurial arena that denies identity to "non-players," is here represented as somehow standing above it all, making his way, and indeed making sense of all the horrors of the recent past.

The idiot whose idiocy somehow transcends its own limitations—or perhaps by virtue of them—and touches the true heart of wisdom and goodness is, at its grandest level, an archetype, as formulated by Jung. The youthful Christ teaching in the temple, the Doestoevskian idiot who aspires to recapture the pure innocence of Christ, the naif of High Romanticism, a parade of Dickensian simpletons of pure heart, the cloistered, uncorrupted innocence of Jerzy Kosinki's Chauncey Gardener in *Being There,* the fascinating, potent innocence of the idiot savant in *Rainman*—all representations of a desire to connect the uncanny with the sacred, to reconnect word and world in a transparently

clear and naive, unmediated way. We are all too canny raison-
neurs; the true meaning of words and events is revealed to the
innocent eye, the eye unveiled by vanity's experiences.

I could go on. The point is that Forrest Gump is running in
Good Company. In a corrupt world, he is untainted. He is pure.
Especially of AIDS. Which his "girl friend" Jenny gets and dies
from. She's not so pure. But with her we turn from archetype,
from desire for the transformation of base flesh into purity and
innocence, to . . . base flesh. While it's a relief, it's also meant to
be an admonition. Do we want to run with Forrest, run out of the
century that swallowed Jenny, into a drugfree, safe sex (or no
sex), successful shrimp entrepreneurship? So while Gump is
running in Good Company, it's a nebulous lot he's running with.
Endlessly differing and deferring signifiers these: "innocence,"
"goodness," "wisdom," "purity." As Dostoevski discovered in writing *The Idiot*. Gump cannot hook up with anything but other signifiers in search of hook-ups. *If* he is really in motion. If he were
really in search of word/world connections—the connections between what anyone *says* about the world and what the world *really* is—his heart would be hollow, an empty place in search of
connection, a place of absence and not grounding presence.
Therefore, there is to be no growth, no movement in his non-
awareness—he is at once perfectly formed in his inattentiveness.
It's the only way he can be saved as our wise guide through history. When you run with Gump (and it is clear by the present
apotheosis of Newt Gingrich that many wish to do so), you are
not moving at all.

Somebody in this film has to be in motion because this is a
run through the last half of the century. Gump must be steadily
supplemented by the Jenny-world. It is this need that draws
Gump and the whole film into the devilishly difficult circuitry of
the last fifty years of American history. And while Zemeckis
shows us Gump running through this history, and then passing
on the baton to his son (or a feather or a box of chocolates), he
never gets out of that history alive. He gets swallowed. And
strangely, Jenny re-emerges. Jenny and love and desire and sex
and AIDS. And dissent. We must not forget that like many in the
'60s generation, Jenny dropped out. Of what? The "cash nexus."
Any way you look at it, it was this nexus that was being unplugged, the one connection that at the end of the century we
wind up privileging to such a degree that a film like *Forrest Gump*
has to be made to insure that the past is buried in the correct way.

But it's Forrest whom I lose interest in while Jenny haunts me. And Bubba. Bubba never did get his entrepreneurship, not in the film, nor did his counterparts ever get theirs in real life. Although it has been promised. And Lt. Dan. I like to think that every Vietnam vet who lost his legs or his soul or his mind in that "conflict" got a trim haircut, put on a clean suit and married a Vietnamese woman, as a sort of symbolic spiritual reconciliation of our two countries. And this woman greets Forrest with bright, smiling, unhaunted eyes. As if Forrest had the miraculous power to cleanse us of all our hurt, wipe away the dark madness of 'Nam, of AIDS, of racism, of poverty and hopelessness, of molesting fathers, of the disenfranchised, disinherited, of relentless market values that fix a winner/loser order of things that only a miracle can amend or dissolve. We should all like to think that we were perfect fools in the '60s because if we weren't fools then, we are surely fools now. We want to feel that we have made progress since then, that progressive entrepreneurship made possible by technological advancements will create a New World Order in which love, peace, social justice, egalitarianism, and ecological harmony are natural byproducts of a global market free play.

But the film itself disabuses us of this fantasy. If *Forrest Gump* is out to settle the postmodern furor of clashing wills, values, and meanings, it does so by re-asserting old truisms, cliches, divisions, unities, realities, continuities, impositions, blindnesses. Gump is an excellent *raisonneur* here because he literally makes no observations. He reacts in a Pavlovian manner. But we are led to think that these reactions are *natural,* that he is not the man of artifice but of natural purity and goodness. Gump is free of observation and therefore focus, which means we cannot haggle over the particular way he marks the unmarked space of the world. Indeed, that unmarked space is also between his ears. The trade off here is that in order to create an unoffending Gump, he must initiate no observations but merely react to a world made by the observations of others.

When the Berkeley SDS president slaps Jenny hard, Gump is there to tackle him. When the strip joint enthusiasts get to enthusiastic over Jenny's naked body, Gump is there to tackle them. When the war in Vietnam is about to waste all of Gump's platoon buddies, he picks them up one by one and races them to safety. When Lt. Dan has lost all respect for himself and is destroying himself with booze and whores, Gump says "No" to sex and resets a moral standard for the legless lieutenant. When Jenny's molesting Dad haunts Jenny's adult life, Gump goes out there with a bulldozer and razes the Dad's house. He literally wipes out the evils of the past. When whites line up to protest integration, Gump comes forward and picks up a fallen book and returns it to a young black girl. He calls the police on the Watergate burglars. Just by accident he sees something. When the whole country is trying to work itself out of an entrepreneurial slump, Gump continues to cast his nets upon the waters until finally the bounty of the sea fills those nets. It fills his nets because every other shrimper has been wiped out of existence— not by Gump's superior shrimping style, but by a natural disaster. Contingency drops a million bucks in his nets.

This last reactiveness takes us to the heart of a contingency that can never be pre-empted and most certainly discretion must rule when we make no effort to construct a relationship with the world. This is an impossible affair—to be inattentive to the world in any way, to be purely buffeted by the winds. But in order to have a Gump that is pure and natural and can offend no one, it is necessary to make a miraculous creature of him—a man without attendance. At the same time, contingency—one of the winds that blow in the abyss of postmodernity along with power and the unconscious—is too clearly represented as perforating our lives at every turn. Attentiveness does not master contingency, but inattentiveness of the gumpish variety surrenders all reality constructiveness to contingency.

What sort of stable base for economic growth is this—an acceptance of the overwhelming power of chance in the determination of our cultural values and meanings? The casino logic of free market play is not only acceptable, it is a religious dogma. Paradoxically, the culture must establish firm, immoveable, universal values and meanings. It must build a barrier between its constructions and the force of contingency. In fact, contingency must always be re-interpreted as "that which was not factored in due to faulty methodologies." Contingency is an anomaly—an expected, allowable deviation from the norm. Modernity tries mightily to pass this nonsense off, but this film shows us history as a fabrication of present whim and human life as a feather blowing in the winds of chance. "Life's like a box of chocolates," Gump's mother tells him. "You never know what you're going to get." Now, I think that is a big hunk of the postmodern abyss that on first viewing we thought this film had avoided or filled in.

Of course, if we do accept our lives as being like feathers blowing in the wind, we may just decide to float along, sit back, turn on the Information Superhighway and its five hundred advertising messages, and see how our lives get shaped. Contingency, however, which the film has only revealed as a trade–off for a non-narrating and therefore non-constructing Gump, remains lethal to the gumpizing aspirations of the film. If any order of things, say Gump's order of pure goodness, corresponded precisely to both what that order marks and what it leaves unmarked (in other words corresponds to the whole unmarked space of the world), then there could be no intrusions of contingency. Contingencies, indeed, would be always already there within the order of things. However, since no society, nor any contesting culture out of which that society is formed, both establish distinctions and boundaries and dismiss them, contingencies are always reminders of what has been left out. They are the absence that pops up to unravel what we grant presence. Put blankly, Gump isn't providing us with a solid foundation upon which to view the past, project the future, make firm decisions regarding social issues, unambiguous verdicts in the courtroom, clean separation of good and evil, victims and heroes and so on. He is and has always been constructing a contingency-free metanarrative which is at once perforated by contingencies.

What is the Gump order of things that exposes itself as being as vulnerable to contingencies as any of the narratives it exposes? Let's take the women—they roamed in the '60s and continue to roam today. But where are they running to? Clearly, Jenny is running on empty, winds up exhausted, as exhausted as the dissident counterculture of desire and misrule. Her path and Gump's intersect a couple of times and each time she declines what he is offering her and runs off again. Finally, AIDS afflicted, she comes "home." The whole roaming, discordant, clashing culture has to finally come "home." Come back to basic values, family values, moral values, economic values—all clear and indisputable. She and her whole counterculture generation stop laughing at Newt's Parson Weems.

But if Gump's home values are as groundless and floating, as tension and contradiction filled, as unable to defend themselves against their own repressions and suppressions, as unravelled by contingencies as Jenny's (and here Jenny is representing the whole cacophony of the last fifty years), then we don't have a clear choice here. We've got another undecidable to add to our growing pile of undecidables. The film does nothing more than turn us yet again toward a postmodern condition. In fact, if we follow through logically here, we should be going back to our recent past not to claim a cheap victory by slippery means, but to regain what was conceivable then and no longer conceivable to us now.

What might that be? Well, certainly not a society grounded in a global market crap shoot trying to diminish our attentiveness to a gumpish level. The notion that "we construct the reality that constructs us" became conceivable during the same period of time that *Forrest Gump* traverses. But when we run with Gump we run in place, crisscrossing nothing, intersecting nothing—all we have to do is do what Gump does; float inanely in the market winds, follow their course blindly and in so doing follow the path of Reality and Truth. It can take you on a clearsighted tour of the past. Once you return you're ready to continue the course—cleanly and without a postmodern fuss into the next millennium.

Reality as Pulp Fiction

November 1994

"So much of what inundates us these days—in film, in various kinds of pop music—is calculated grunginess, of climate and temper. So much of what goes on in (what I hear of) rock music revels in the lower end of every kind of spectrum, grungy ideas and diction delivered by grungy people. So much of modern film seems to compete in grunginess."
Stanley Kauffman, "Shooting Up," *The New Republic*
November 14, 1994
"I kind of like the idea that everybody makes up their movie."
Quentin Tarantino

Accommodating Reality

In 1992 Siskel and Ebert gave Quentin Tarantino's *Reservoir Dogs* two thumbs down, and reviewers in *The Village Voice* reported that director Tarantino was a new Scorcese on the horizon. Although the film and Tarantino connected negatively in Siskel and Ebert's minds, it connected positively with the *Voice* reviewers. Tarantino made the movie but the reviewers make it too—in this case they make it up in diametrically opposed ways. For a postmodernist, everything—novel, film, headline story, rock video, TV show, Internet and so on—that is made up by its audience in contrary ways represents a cultural aneurism, a societal glitch, a rip, however small, in the fabric of the social order. Here in this place, at this time, our construction of this "whatever" stands before us as undecidable.

Overwhelming "thumbs down" verdicts on films also draw me. I want then to know how this failure, this trash, is being made up by those who advise me not to see it. If I hear fear and anger in the stories they tell me, if I sense that the film has unsettled their "sense of realism," of what is true and what is false, what is right and what is wrong, I run to see the film. *Pulp Fiction* has received overwhelming "thumbs up" responses. Do I refuse to see it? I mean do I assume that the film is made up in the same welcoming way by everyone and therefore represents, culturally speaking, the old "same old-same old," connects with the majority framing of reality and truth in the same way a good politician does? I believe that even those popular films that seem to be acknowledged by all as pure entertainment and escapism, as totally devoid of any cultural or individual ontologically upsetting elements, cannot draw us to them unless they tap into what defies or eludes our common grasp. Defending against such a tapping into the abyss, as in *Forrest Gump*, only succeeds in revealing what it fears. The abyss is not popular, but it fascinates.

Undecidables in popular film are quoted and then erased. Fears are elicited and then buried. Everything surfaces where we are seated; the cracks and fissues lie under our seats in the darkened theatre. Sometimes the play of the surface is so lively, so filled with crackling conversation—endless stories that grab us like a con man on a street corner, energy on the screen that draws us in and makes us one with it—that when all this happens, we are enchanted. In some way the inscrutables and unsettlings that lie on that surface do not stop our engagement; strangely they add to it. We do not stop to reconcile, to assess the damage to our moral sensibilities, our ways of "real-izing," our truth-stories. The rush of the film, which seems always ahead of us and wide of where we are, pulls us along. We enjoy the ride. Maybe we say "I am escaping; this is only a movie. My hand goes into the popcorn box, my eyes are riveted on the screen. Afterward, I will be back in the 'real world.'" Maybe we say this because we need to tell ourselves something, to reassure ourselves that even though we are not in control we are yet fascinated and that fascination will not harm us. When we leave the theatre our way of making up the world, other people, and ourselves will go on as before. We remain ontologically secure; our being-in-the-world remains as we know it. And it will remain our being-in-the-world as long as we continue to know it in that way.

In this postmodern climate, we already know that the smooth surface of a likeable film is smooth because of something called the "classic or naive realism formula." Postmodernists try to break the spell of that formula. What are the tensions the film produces in us; the cracks in the sense of realism we come in with? If an abiding sense of realism is being played with here, being challenged, being subverted and teased out of countenance, how can this happen, how is it being done? The cracks in the surface proliferate: our observation of alien linkages with the world, of effects whose causes we are not sure of, of contingencies that we hope and pray *we* could have anticipated and avoided, of "grungy ideas and diction" that still won't be dismissed by our superior ideas and diction, of constructions of reality that refuse to be subsumed within our overiding sense of Reality.

In short, the "we are only being entertained" alibi collapses and the film, in all its unsettling crisscrossing of characters, stories, events, time, us and American culture now in the '90s, still awaits what we are to make of it. And recall Tarantino's own words: he wants us to make up the movie ourselves, as if reality were nothing more than pulp to be shaped and reshaped, as if every time we encountered a story about reality, we responded with a story, as if reality were brought to us through our fictionalizing. But what if we enter the movie believing that reality is hard and unchangeable, distanced from us and standing there clearly as reference points against which our stories can be judged? What if we are already producing that sort of reality by knowing it in that way? What if we know it not in a reality-is-pulp way, but in a reality is *not* pulp way? What if reality is so objectively determinable that we can clearly distinguish when we are constructing it—when we are telling stories about it—from when we are telling the truth about it? What if when we walk into a viewing of *Pulp Fiction* our being-in-the-world is already nestled comfortably in a sense of realism that allows us to real-ize only within the frame of that sense of realism? What if out of that sense of realism we know what the truth is, or, we know we have the means to uncover the true meaning of anything? What if out of that sense of realism we know what is to be valued and what is not to be valued? What if our sense of realism has already shaped for us a hierarchy of meanings and values? Of sense and nonsense? Of discordancy and harmony? Of disruption and continuity? Of order and disorder? Of intelligence and stupidity? Of wisdom and ignorance? Of sanity and insanity? Of good and evil? Of justice and injustice? Of beauty and "grunge"?

Why then *Pulp Fiction* is going to do us violence. My feeling is that when Tarantino's film loses its mesmerizing hold on us, it will haunt us. It will haunt the rational-realistic in which we attend to the world. The unsettling effect will slowly creep in, if it hasn't already begun to do so. That effect unsettled our response to Tarantino's first film, *Reservoir Dogs*. That film found its way into our present cultural fixation on violence and the violent. *Pulp Fiction* also swims in blood, but Tarantino mediates the swimming in a seductive way. He "quotes" it if you will within other Hollywood bloodbaths and thus distances it from us. Imagine a direct confrontation with a drunk at a bar. Face to face. Something is bound to happen. Tarantino is like the friend with a lot of the right words who comes in between. Anger turns to laughs.

A film that enacts reality as pulp fiction at a time when conservative Republicans have won a majority in both houses of Congress for the first time in forty years will ultimately not be a film that is laughed off. The 1994 election returns have been interpreted variously. Everyone is engaged in making up stories as to what they mean. My story is this: these election returns connect to an overriding desire in this country since Reagan in 1980 to return to a once firm, indisputable, reason based bed-rock Reality. If one Reality can be established, then notions of truth and falsehood, along with all other either-or propositions, are determinable. Truth reproduces the reality; reality determines what is true. Our sense of realism then is not a construction but emerges from this determinate Reality and responds to our calibrations of truth and falsehood.

Let's listen to Newt Gingrich on the majority view of truth and values:

> If, by moral tone, you mean voluntary school prayer, the bulk of Americans are for it; if, by moral tone, you mean punishing violent criminals the first time they're violent, the majority of Americans are for it; if, by moral tone, you mean teaching the truth about American history, teaching about the Founding Fathers and how this country came to be the most extraordinary civilization in history, the vast majority of Americans are for it.[1]

The certitude necessary to legislate morality and truth can only come from an absolute certitude that what one is representing about reality corresponds to reality itself. Once one is certain that the sense of realism and real-izing that one possesses is grounded in reality itself, then the ways in which that sense of realism is confirmed and reproduced are at hand. A progressively closer correspondence with reality can indeed be legislated.

Differing values and meanings are seen for what they are: deviations from the majority sense of realism, false and misguided detours from truth, perverse machinations of "counterculture McGovernicks," the enemies of truth, morality and reality in the words of Gingrich. And indeed Gingrich is very much aware that his claim to the truth rests on his grasp of reality. When asked whether the Clinton administration would accept the proposed legislation or veto it, Gingrich responded that the White House can "either decide to accommodate reality or they can decide to repudiate reality. That's their choice."[2]

Gingrich's reiteration of an early Enlightenment faith in the capacity of humankind to tell stories about the world that correspond exactly to what was going on in the world contests a postmodern-based "politics of meaning."[3] We are, within this "politics of meaning" view always engaged in a struggle to construct meanings and values as rival representations of what is real and what is true clash. Reality then is always in process, always in a state of being constructed, not on one path or within one sense of realism but on many paths and within many reality frames. If there were a means of determining once and for all whose construction of reality was The Reality, then the struggle would not be needed. Reality would not be a process construction nor would meanings and values have to emerge from a clash of narrative frames. Of course, the struggle might go on because of the totally unrelated dispositions of power. But only such power could keep us from pointing to a fixed, commonly shared Reality and the absolute, universal and unchanging truths and values that we all could hook up with within this shared Reality.

While a postmodern "politics of meaning" brings us into a social construction of reality, and therefore of meanings and values as negotiated entities always culturally and temporally relative, both Newt Gingrich's and Michael Lerner's *Tikkun* "politics of moral tone", (though supporting different meanings), connect their politics with Reality as it is. Therefore truth and morality are graspable and need only be legislated. Beneath the politics of representation, then, are divergent ontologies and therefore divergent epistemologies. In a postmodern politics of meaning, reality is always inevitably, for humans, *human reality* and that reality is inevitably a self/social/cultural construction. We live in our own inseparable constructions of self and world, within dynamic landscapes in which our biological structures respond to our social practices, and since we do not live in just one belief or value system but in many over different periods of time, we do not construct one reality but multiple realities. And people live in these many constructed reality frames. They are in essence our pathways to the world, and what is in the world must always be modulated across these pathways.[4] How the truth is pursued, how one's reality is known is a function, then, of the reality frame itself. Reality then *is* pulp fiction. In Gingrich's politics of meaning, we have humans who can free themselves of their values and divest themselves of their beliefs (be theory-neutral and value-free), observe a reality outside themselves and erect a foundation of truths in agreement with that observed reality. Reality *is* this solid foundation. In *Tikkun's* politics of meaning, a value-free context is replaced with ethical and spiritual values that provide a foundation of truth out of which reality emerges.

Pulp Fiction doesn't even pay lip service to a one Reality ontology but plunges us into as many social constructions of reality as it can in two hours and thirty minutes. It makes no attempt to establish a firm point of reference for us so that we distinguish good from bad, true from false, stupid from intelligent. Tarantino lays down no metanarrative thread that ties everything together while promising to return us to one determinate Reality. While the whole country it seems is rushing back to bedrock Reality and its truths, Tarantino is acting as if we are all already in the postmodern flux, in Borges's garden of forking paths—that we've all acknowledged that there are multi-layers of pulp fictions between us and reality. As if we may all continue the quest for reality *beyond and outside* human artifice but that quest is always already being carried on *from within* human artifice. And we're really into it in a duplex way: the whole world comes to us through our fictions which we live in; *and* judging by the historical record and our actions in the present, we are and have obviously been very into our fabrications, our constructions, our fictionalizings.

How could we be anyplace else? When was there ever anyplace else but these multiple worlds and multiple narratives for human beings? Even during Attila the Hun's time, there had to be folks treating reality as pulp—as not just what Attila said it was, but what they could make of it. Even when reality is imposed upon us viciously we can't stop making up our movie. I mean our reality. You might say it's the human plight—the real human condition. But it's not so bad, not as bad as all of us living in one story about what the Founding Fathers *really* meant. Or one story about family values. Or one story about religion.

There is no doubt that the imposition of one interpretation of the Constitution, one interpretation of what is meant by a family and what is meant by values, one interpretation of a spiritual world and so on—all this would doubtlessly end gridlock, drown dissent, replace struggles with protocols, culture wars with a social order of things. Julius Caesar and Napoleon achieved this, as did Queen Elizabeth and Frederick II, Adolph Hitler and Chairman Mao, Louis XIV and Ghengis Khan, Ayatollah Khomeini and Saddam Hussein, to name a few. And the world has yet to see an "order of things" as clearly etched and efficiently executed as Henry Ford's assembly line and Hitler's extermination camps.

From a postmodern perspective, these fictions of order have constructed reality in the most inhumane and horrific ways. In Tarantino's *Pulp Fiction* we do not fail to run into reality being shaped in such ways. But it clear that these ways are fictions among other fictions, that there are weak narratives of reality and truth and strong ones. And the weak are not weak according to market criteria: losers; and the strong are not the strong according to market criteria: winners. Rather, strength comes in not tyrannizing, not imposing, and weakness lies in not struggling against such tyrannizing. Ezekiel provides the pulp for the reality/fictionalizing of Samuel L. Jackson's Jules: "You're the weak, and I'm the tyranny of evil men. But I'm trying, Ringo, I'm trying real hard to be the shepherd." In other words, Jules is trying to alter a fiction of hierarchy and polarization. Reality can't become pulp fiction until we engage in a postmodernist de-centering—a movement from a vertical, hierarchical plane of reality and unreality, sense and nonsense, right and wrong to a horizontal plane that circumvents hierarchy. In terms of fictions what we have then is a displacement: fiction A/fiction B. Once the tyranny of an absolute truth grounded in a universal foundation is revealed to be nothing more than an Emperor without clothes, the continuum of horizontal displacements is there not only to be observed, but now the process of creating meanings and values goes on in and between these interrelationships. And interrelationships are what we get in *Pulp Fiction*, fictions from A to Zed.

Pulping Time and Order

The film begins with Tim Roth and Amanda Plummer in a diner. Talk about robbery turns to a robbery of the diner. The robbery action is frozen and then returned to in the last scene of the film. We have not, we discover, begun with first scene but with the last. Time is pulpy here. In that last scene we are no longer in the petty thieves' fiction but in Jules's fiction. There is no linear clock time; only pulp fiction time. When we are in Jules's narrative fiction, which at this moment is one of spiritual awakening, the diner thieves become moments within Jules's journey to spiritual awakening—his wrestling with the Devil. Time, like reality, is pulp—soft stuff that is shaped by fictions. Lives intersect in the present but each life may be within a different story where time is running at story pace. Roth and Plummer, for instance, are brought into Jules's spiritual awakening narrative. They are swallowed up by the moment of crisis in Jules's narrative—will he blow them away as he has the preppy crooks in a scene that happens plot-wise before the opening diner scene or will he convert Roth into a man who breaks out of one narrative and into another? Roth and Plummer go free—they escape the sure destiny that we recognized in the gun in Jules's hand. Perhaps Jules too can free himself of the fiction he is in—shape the pulp of reality into something else, himself into someone else. The film doesn't reveal what happens to him, but as he and Vincent Vega leave the diner, we know that Vincent is going to accidentally run into Butch and get blown away.

Let's follow accidents in this film, the contingencies that any order of things fears and tries to hide, and when forced to recognize, calls anomalies. Vincent's narrative is the most abruptly terminated. Permanently. Mia, who is the wife of the man Vincent and Jules work for, Marsellus Wallace, accidentally finds some heroin in Vincent's jacket, snorts it like cocaine, and goes into cardiac arrest. Instead of rushing her to a hospital, Vincent rushes her to Eric Stoltz and Rosanna Arquette, the dealers who sold him the heroin. And their fictions pulp reality into almost pure chaos. Mia's chances of being saved seem slim indeed. Reality's order is nothing more than a fiction that washes away and all of a sudden all is contingencies—the search for where her heart is, the search for a marker to indicate where the heart is, the warning that unless the needle punctures the sternum the adrenaline won't reach the heart, the needle held above Mia's body looking like something out of a cartoon, an illustration in pulp fiction.

The most extended sojourn in reality as a maze of narratives in which we have no way of keeping from bumping into each other involves Butch, a boxer who has double-crossed Marsellus. The sequencing here is a pure unsettling of our narrative of order and control. First, Butch jumps out a back window of the fight arena, one step ahead of Marsellus's men. He hails a cab and makes his unplanned escape. The taxi driver turns out to be a woman who has heard the fight, heard that Butch has killed his opponent and is aroused by the act. Butch is inspiring to her—she won't tell anyone where she has taken him. We are aware that things could easily have been otherwise. As Butch and his girlfriend Fabienne play out the love-fiction they are in, we anticipate a sudden intrusion of Marsellus's men. But this does not occur. Instead, Fabienne has failed to pack Butch's watch and now he will go back to his apartment to get it.

Why? Because of a watch-fiction, which Tarantino runs for us to make us fully aware of how this watch figures powerfully in Butch's life—powerfully enough for him to risk his life to go back and find it. We flash back to when Butch was a boy and Christopher Walken tells him a story about his father in a prisoner of war camp. Butch's father had been given the watch by his father who had been given the watch by his father. The watch in each case was tied to the ancestor's life story. Butch's own father had stashed the watch up his ass for five years so that it wouldn't be taken from him. Suddenly narratives of suspense and fear, of anger and daring, of nostalgia and sorrow turn into farce. The watch-fiction is a joke. At the heart of the story that propels Butch into danger is this picture of his father and his watch. Why can't we stay within some consistent story-line, a reality with some order and integrity to it? Can reality pulp so easily?

Butch is careful in approaching his apartment—everything is going well. (He hasn't had breakfast; pop tarts in a toaster; he sees a semi-automatic weapon on the counter; he picks it up; Vincent comes out of the bathroom; surprise; Butch pulls the trigger.) Once again Butch escapes. Everything looks clear. He is getting back into his money-girl-escape narrative. Chance intrudes. Marsellus is crossing the street; Butch runs into him, his car is hit by another and Butch crashes. The chase is gripping. We expect Butch will once again escape, and he does—into a pawn shop. Marsellus pursues him into the store. They fight, both men bleeding. We know the fictions here, Marsellus's and Butch's. But there is no way that their fictions can subsume the reality of the guy behind the counter, who knocks Butch out, calls a friend and in the next scene has both Marsellus and Butch tied to chairs and gagged. They even have red balls that look like apples stuck in their mouths, bleeding and sweating, eyes bulging—no longer in control, their fight no longer of consequence. They have intersected a world that has its own values and meanings. And these boys make up a movie that no one wants to be in. This is screen fiction—reality's fictions aren't so sensationalistic, so weird, until we think of those many young men lured into Jeffrey Dahmer's apartment—the young men who became part of Jeff's movie. The movie Marsellus and Butch are suddenly in is a behind-closed-doors movie, a guy in black leather-and-chained-in-a-box movie. Ultimately, fortunes reverse once again and Marsellus has the opportunity to impose his movie on his tormentors, *his* tyranny on the tyranny of these evil men. "I'm gonna get medieval on your ass," Marsellus tells the rapists.

What's the message? Reality is like so much pulp that you can mold into the shape of your own life-fiction but that doesn't give you control over *other* people's fictions *plus* it doesn't give you control over that reality that is out there which we just haven't included in our fictions. We can make a story out of the world and live in it but the world hasn't agreed to acknowledge or respect that story. When something happens that isn't in our story outline and therefore is outside our order of things, our sense of realism, we call it chance, pure contingency, accident. Maybe we wrap contingency up in a story of Fate or Destiny. Or maybe in an Enlightenment story that says reason just hasn't gotten to this yet. Or, this chance event is really an anomaly in an order of things that we have already mapped out. We statistically anticipate these anomalies so therefore they are really *not* out of our story of the order of things. Anomalies are potentially always corrigible—pure contingencies remind us that the unmarked surface of the world has no obligation to correspond to our markings of it, our fictionalizing.

If I had to place the violence in Tarantino's films, as well as in David Lynch's, somewhere I would place it here in the postmodern view of chance. We say "No" to drugs, to rape, to gun violence, to sexual harassment, to abuse of all kinds. We concoct "No" fictions that we seek to impose on the world. We seek to make these "No" fictions the reality that everyone will concoct for themselves. There is no way that we can point to our "No" fictions as external points of reference in reality. They remain constructions, albeit constructions that we seek to impose on the world as universal and absolute. When Butch and Marsellus run into rape and violence, they run into a postmodern way of acknowledging the gap between reality and representation, world and fiction, what stories we seek to impose upon the world and how the world remains indifferent to our stories. We can detour off our story road onto another and there is no universal foundation of reality and truth that can prevent this from happening. In order to drive this postmodern point home, both Lynch and Tarantino have us drive into some very strange stories indeed. From our own side of the street, such collisions are "freaky," chance happenings. Along with Gingrich we ask, "Why haven't these people accommodated reality?"

Along with Stanley Kauffman we object to being led into grungy lives filled with grungy ideas expressed with grungy diction. Why can't we stay in a fiction of high moral tone that the majority of Americans want? It's clear from this 1994 midyear election, that we are all sooner or later going to be shepherded into that fiction.

Vincent & Mia

But for now let's stay in Tarantino's reality as pulp fiction. Let's return to a diner scene, not the classic realist diner that the film opens with but Jack Rabbit Slim's, a movie-prop diner, a postmodern diner where a '50s vibe and fiction runs the clock for us. It's the '50s and the stories we walk in with clash, fall in with, and re-write both the '50s and the '90s. I mean by re-write that our fictions, our ways of tying ourselves to the world, are affected by this simulation of the '50s. And since the '50s we are in *is* a simulation, clearly Jack Rabbit Slim's is staged—it already filters the '50s through the '90s. Was the '50s really like this? And also we ask: "What happened to this or that vibe? We've kind of lost that." Or, in seeing the fictional frame of the '50s we become aware of our own '90s framing. We are not out of the frame, frameless, looking back. We, too, are living in a "symbolic mediation" of the world. And it becomes clear that one of the layers of mediation we're living in *is* the '50s. An interesting question is, "Why is the '50s fiction interpenetrating the '90s now? Why not the '60? Or the 70s?

The '70s in fact are there. In the '50s, or, in Tarantino's staging of the '50s in Jack Rabbit Slim's. John Travolta brings the

'70s into Jack Rabbit Slim's. He's Vincent Vega but he's also Tony Manero of *Saturday Night Fever* and we are especially aware of this when the dance contest begins and Mia urges him to dance with her. But we are also aware that he is Vincent Vega in the '90s when the waiter, a Buddy Holly simulacrum, comes to take their order. The *faux* Buddy is '50s cool and flip—"What's yours, Peggy Sue?" But inside his own heroin-laced, '90s cool, Vincent declares the waiter "not very good." He's not as good as the *faux* Marilyn Monroe. When Mia states that they are all Marilyns, Vincent shows us that he knows his '50s. "No, that's Mamie Van Doren over there. Not Marilyn Monroe." It's not that the '50s aren't already part of who he is. It's just that this Jack Rabbit Slim simulated '50s can't touch his own use of the '50s. And it is clear when he gets up to twist with Mia on a *Saturday Night Fever* type dance floor that wherever he is, he has also transmuted the '70s into his present '90's self.

Vincent Vega lives in a self-contained reality frame. No movement on the surface. Everything from without runs headon into the story: Vincent Vega. Contrastingly, we see some movement in Jules's frame as his frightening professionalism is riddled by a sudden spiritual awareness that comes when a preppie fires point blank several times at Jules and Vincent but the bullets don't hit them. It's a miracle Jules testifies. An intervention of the Almighty. The miracle bounces off Vincent's cool and heads back to the Almighty. It doesn't matter one way or another to Vincent. It has no consequence. It doesn't touch the still center of his being where Vincent's story is filled with the protocols of survival and maintaining his cool. You might say he has a buffer zone of cool in which emotions and responses are filtered. For instance, as he sits across from Mia in Jack Rabbit Slim's we sense the romance story we are in—will Vincent take a chance and make a play for his gangster boss's wife? As he sits there rolling joints, with pulpy face and succinct, measured conversation, we sense that he is not only an enigma to us but to Mia as well. There is a powerful "fatal attraction" tone to this scene but Vincent's cool finesses it out of the realm of explicit behavior, everyday reaction. Even love and sexual attraction get bounced off Vincent's cool frame and get "handled." Like the way he handled the preppie drug dealers who tried to cheat Marsellus. Vincent won't do a square thing here and melt for Mia. And when he gets up on the dance floor and we anticipate the flamboyant Tony Manero of

Saturday Night Fever what we get is Vincent Vega in a quiet, laid back twist out of a zone of cool that covers Vincent like a cloud.

I want to end with this scene (only to pick it up again later in Tarantino style),[5] between Mia and Vincent because they do a bit on the clash between modernity and postmodernity. I'm referring to the continuation of the story about Mia's masseur getting thrown out of a window by Mia's husband, Marsellus. We first heard the story when Vincent and Jules were on their way to execute the preppie drug dealers. While Vincent argued that a foot massage was a very sexual thing and that the masseur should have anticipated Marsellus seeing it as such, Jules argued that in no way could the masseur have anticipated Marsellus's wrath over such an innocent thing. This sort of banal conversation leads to the highly tense scene with the preppies. What sort of people are Jules and Vincent? They casually and coldly go from a tightly reasoned argument over an inane subject—the sexual aspects of a foot massage—to the execution of some thoroughly frightened preppies, who certainly look frightened enough to amend their ways totally. The fact that all sorts of people living in all sorts of stories cross in and out of everyday conversation and gossip escapes us here. We have heard stories of the heart surgeon joking at surgery; the CEO going out for a round of golf after firing several thousand employees; the president of the United States heading back to the ranch after escalating a war; cops using "deadly force" and then going for coffee and donuts, and so on. We are constantly going in and out of story frames. In most cases society has fabricated categories or niches for these shiftings so they become part of our sense of real life—the normal flow of everyday life. But these shiftings remain story-driven and volatile regardless of our putting labels on them. When someone else's everyday rhythms clash with our own, they are in need of correction, of getting back to the way everything should be going on. We want to put their feet to the fire of a commonly shared social reality—not one that is constructed but one that survives because it meets the standards of judgment that rationality and realism provide.

On this note, we get back to Mia and Vincent and the foot massage story. Mia wants to know how in the world Vincent could have ever believed this story. You mean, she says to him, somebody tells you that my husband threw a man out of a window because he was massaging my feet and you believe that story? To which Vincent responds that yeah, he could believe it when he heard it. What would get you to believe such a crazy, illogical, unreal story like that, Mia insists? Her point is clear. And right out of the Enlightenment. Here's what Mia is asking: Don't you have any reasoning faculties that would enable you to judge the truth or falsehood of this story? Vincent blows off this kind of aloof reasoning capacity. In the scene with Jules, he's already revealed that he finds the sex and foot massage connection quite real. Once you're in a story of reality, a pulp fiction, reason plays out the meanings and values of the story. We already know that in his argument with Jules over whether the mis-shooting was a miracle or not, Vincent has stayed with an "it doesn't matter if it's a miracle or an accident" story while Jules has taken the same event and is using it as the basis for a total rewriting of the pulp fiction of his life. In the end, Mia's reason could not anticipate Marsellus and Butch running into the perverts in the second-hand store, nor she could believe that Butch would have run into Marsellus on the street, nor could she believe that Vincent would have come out of the john with a copy of *Modesty Blaise* in his hand and run into a shotgun blast. How are stories believable to us? Certainly not because of some standard of reasonable judgment, but rather because of the sense of realism we are in, the believing and disbelieving mode of our own pulp fictions. And while Mia lives in a modernist fiction, Vincent lives in a postmodern one.

Maybe he's postmodern because he can't reason, because he has grungy ideas expressed with grungy diction? We know Stanley Kauffman thinks what we have in *Pulp Fiction* is grunge—an entertaining, escapist sort but nevertheless grunge. It's a white trash movie, in other words. And maybe these people have grungy ideas ill-expressed because they have low IQs. They lack intelligence. Maybe all the people living grungy, white trash lives don't have the intelligence to live any other kind of life. They've reached their level. Should society tax itself in any way to educate these people? This would appear to be an impossible task if the root problem is an innate incapacity to think on levels that would enable them to succeed in a competitive world, a world whose hierarchy is determined by market competitiveness. Why support the foundationally flawed? Wouldn't a more economic course be to tax ourselves for only one purpose: in order to control the possible deleterious effects of low IQ, of grungy ideas and grungy people, of white trash? Quick apprehension of criminals, expeditious sentencing, one appeal, three strikes and you're out, capital punishment. That's a movie Pete Wilson is shooting in California and the Omnibus Crime Bill of 1994 is re-running. Let's return to *Pulp Fiction*. Is Jules stupid? Is Vincent? Is Mia, Butch, Marsellus, Wolf, Jimmy or any of the others? It doesn't seem the issue; it's not clear; it's not brought out. Rather, what we see is an energy and intensity coming out of their pulp fictions. Vincent and Jules know the world in a certain way, a way that they have mastered. And up until Jules's conversion and Vincent's death, they reproduce a reality that conforms to that way of knowing it. I don't know how intelligent it is to say that, for instance, from Rosanna Arquette's "piercing" reality frame, her pulp fiction, that Jules and Vincent are stupid for attending to the world in the way that they do. Or, for that matter, for somebody to go to Jack Rabbit Slim's and decide that the whole '50s style was stupid, that Ricky Nelson's music was stupid, that our obsession with Monroe was stupid, and so on.

Clearly, however, these evaluations go on all the time. Eventually you can't be too intelligent if you refuse to see that economic values are the most important. You can't be too intelligent if you think the counter-cultural '60s are not a loss of values but a renaissance of values. Your intelligence is questioned if you insist upon knowing the world in a way other than what has been declared "foundational." A foundational, objectivist reality, however, can only be confirmed and reproduced if it is known in that foundational, objectivist way of knowing. If, on the other hand, reality is pulp and is shaped by the fictions we construct, then there are innumerable ways of knowing. And for each way of knowing, there is a companionable intelligence.

We are lightyears yet from seeing this in our social order. But it is there to be seen and heard in *Pulp Fiction*, a film in which we enter the postmodern abyss while its companion, *Forrest Gump*, leads us into a politics of concealment. In a way, Tarantino's *Reservoir Dogs* and *Pulp Fiction* are both from the abyss of a postmodern *film noir*. I want to get deeper into that abyss before engaging a politics of concealment.

Notes

1. Maureen Dowd, "G.O.P. Rising Star Pledges to Right Wrongs of the Left," *The New York Times* November 10, 1994.

2. Ibid., B3.

3. This postmodern politics of meaning is not about replacing one meaning with another, as Michael Lerner, editor of *Tikkun*, does in replacing the market's "ethos of selfishness and cynicism" with an "ethos of caring and idealism." See *"Tikkun's* Politics of Meaning" in *Tikkun* May/June 1995; and the exchange between Hilary Clinton and Lerner in *Esquire* April 1995, p. 16. Meanings multiply and contest in a postmodern politics of meaning; replacement is arbitrary or imposed, never sanctioned by an authorizing metanarrative of Truth.

4. I am here referring to Francisco Varela's theory of *autopoesis,* a biologist's view of the interpenetrating relationship between world or culture and human biology. We "pulp" reality in an always already attached way: reality has already shaped our "self-building," the ways in which we "pulp." Those ways are, however, themselves "pulped" within a self shaped by a long "history of internal validations of interactions." Reality therefore does not adapt to the pulper (total subjectivity) nor does the pulper adopt reality (total objectivity). Reality inevitably for humans is a mutually interactive, dynamic pulping process; a work of artistic creation, a fictionalizing whose product is fiction. See my discussion of *autopoesis* in "Science's Interplay with Disorder," J. Natoli, *Mots d'Ordre,* SUNY Press, 1992, pp. 49–57.

5. See "Is a Foot Massage Sexual—On the Internet?"

The Abyss of the Postmodern *Film Noir*

Spring 1995

"'Inside He Wasn't Like Anybody'"

The *angst* of twentieth century modernism appears in the crack of *film noir*. When Orson Welles wants to bring film out of naive realism and Enlightenment optimism, he turns to *film noir*. *Citizen Kane* is our dark, difficult journey out of the sinewy shadows, over hurricane fence barriers between ourselves and reality—wandering from path to path, searching for pieces of a puzzle that we are destined to do again and again because we can't be quite sure we've got all the pieces or whether we're putting them together in the right way. What Welles does is give us a new slant on *film noir* by bringing out a "tragic vision," the tensions and anxieties already expressed in twentieth century literature, painting, and music. By so doing he brought the *film noir* out of a simple romantic dualism that Hollywood naive realism could saturate even this dark product with. A postmodern slant to *film noir* samples both naive realist and late modernist *film noir*. "Fear and trembling, sickness unto death is" at once in touch with a sly, witty parodying of the mood, a gleeful immersing in dark *film noir* waters, a rush onto all paths and possibilities without fear of getting back, without an ontological need of finally winding up *someplace* where there is a bit of light, a place to rest. It's a ride for the hell of it—a ride that we have to take, that we may think we're not taking but we're taking nonetheless. It's an unravelling, deconstructive journey—a nomadic wandering that has no clear beginning or end. One person's exit is another person's entrance—one person's high is another's low. Who is better than whom, what is better than what is all in motion. We land someplace, we team up with someone, we pursue a thread of sense. At the same time, we are set in motion again or waiting to take off again. We connect with the extreme precariousness and arbitrariness of connecting. We pursue one thread of sense into another, catch the dialogue, play the parts, construct our answers, develop a style. And parody the sense that comes out of the part we play.

In the film *Romeo is Bleeding,* we go on a dark carny ride that like all the best carny rides suddenly explodes into sunlight, takes all the turns you see coming but hope won't be taken, rushes downward until we're ontologically exhilarated . . . Ontologically exhilarated? I have this idea that when we get thrown out of one reality frame and into another, or when we collide with another, we are struck deeply and our being-in-the-world is swept over by an urgency to get going, to get with it, to re-fashion itself along new lines. We are "being" shoppers, shopping for realities—a savvy and adventurous audience to new and other truths emerging from new and other realities.

Yes, Romeo is bleeding but it's *Romeo* who is bleeding—the legendary, ill-fated lover whom reality has oft copied but never quite captured. When we are Romeo we are both cruel destiny and romantic illusion. Gary Oldham's Jack Grimaldi, who both at film's beginning and film's end assumes the name Jim Dougherty, is also a Romeo—a man living in a story of love and lovers, of sexual fantasy and amorous ambitions. Jack/Jim/Romeo is already taking parts, living in stories, plugging into the world through the stories. The darkness of this *film noir* is mediated, narrated, and therefore darkness and ill-fated tragedy has a spin to it, a cinematic spin that puts all manner of darkness at a distance, twice-removed. In that space, a postmodern, parodying space, we can neither affiliate ourselves totally with Jack's "reality" or his "fictionality," his "Jack/Jim" and his "Romeo." We're not touching reality-in-itself but only various send-ups. Even though Jim Dougherty provides voice-over narration, that voice is just another role player, another narrative player. Caught in a tizzy of parts, Jack/Jim/Romeo is more of a way of narrating than a narrator; he's more of a way of attending to this world that spills the beans on its own fractured way of attending than a somebody we identify with. And since he is good theater, so to speak, we attend to how he stages his scenes, how the scenes are staged by others, in confrontation with our own staging, by some metanarrative of design, by chance, outside anyone's staging, and in the world here in 1994.

Take a look at Dick Powell in *Murder, My Sweet* and Robert Mitchum in *Out of the Past,* both classic *film noir.* Total absence of a theatrical, fictional, narrative dimension in both "dark he-roes" and therefore there is no space for us to be free of their lead, their dark trek. We can't fork off the paths, no matter how maze-like they get. Both Powell and Mitchum are set upon, are playing it by ear in worlds without centers, are choosing in a dark flux with uncertain outcome. Yet they are not multiple—they don't live in stories of themselves; but somehow, in spite of the vagaries of the world they are in, they are not in motion, not ontologically. Their life-worlds are buffeted but they are not violated by the buf-fetings—surely they are played with by the goddess Fortuna, not able to make their paths straight by their own will and under-standing. Yet, they are always separated from their trials—true narrators able to observe the circuitries of their dark journeys. No roles being played—the blood they spill is supposed to be real.

"Inside," it could be said of either Mitchum or Powell, "he wasn't like anybody." The self is a discrete entity, having trouble with that identity and with the reality it's dealing with, but nev-ertheless, a self that has a true center. Some place. "Inside he wasn't like anybody" Jim says of Jack in *Romeo is Bleeding* but what we observe is that inside he could be anybody. Jack Grimaldi constructs Jim Dougherty who constructs Jack Grimaldi and Jack Grimaldi constructs Romeo and Jim Dougherty constructs a Juliet-Natalie who will return to him, who will return to her role in his life. And this Natalie, Jack's wife, fills a scrapbook with photos of all the parts Jack has taken, all the Romeo scenes he has done with other women in the course of the marriage. Now this Juliet-wife cooks *chicken francese* for a husband who wants meat and potatoes. She cooks for one hus-band she has narrated for herself and lives with another. Jack is Ricky Ricardo ("Honey, I'm home" he announces at the film's be-ginning), and Juliet-wife has a picture of that part too. Juliette Lewis, another Juliet to Jack's Romeo, plays the role of Marilyn Monroe playing the role of a dumb blonde who wants to play the role of an intelligent woman like "Madame Curry." And while Juliette is all these, Jack wants to be Hud. He wants to be Paul Newman who played Hud. But Jack also wants to be the old rich guy he spies on, the old rich guy in a steady state of orgy with a harem of young women. "What's he got that old Jack ain't got?" Jack asks. He's got the part is what he's got, but that doesn't stop Jack from rehearsing for it. No, "inside he could be anybody."

Reality here is filled with constructions and every Jack and Jim, every Natalie and Mona, are "always already" shaped within those constructions and in the process of shaping others. The postmodern *film noir* protagonist shows up dark not because of the unsteady state of his reality and of reality itself, the loss of control, the glitch between observed and observed. Rather, he shows up dark because he shows up only in stories spread out all over reality, and reality shows up in endlessly proliferating stories and nowhere else. The fear and angst has switched from loss of contact, loss of correspondence between self and world, to fear of the nature of contact, the invariable mediation of self and world through narrative constructions. But this is only a new guise for an old Enlightenment fear. From a postmodern pluriverse of narratives, there are stories of fear and of blind faith, of control and riot, of order and disorder, of sorrow and joy, of routine and dream, of true love and this can't be love. The *film noir,* which is already focused on the uncertainties of focus, entranced by deep, unconscious compulsions, by dangerous desires, by the play of contingency and purpose, of identity and alien otherness, is for the postmodernist a genre focus whose every adjustment will mark the shift from modernist angst to postmodern plenitude and parody. The postmodern *film noir* is no longer on the fringe, a shadowy edge to a centered reality, a lucid truth. All of reality has turned *noir.* Or the *noir* is at the center. Reality is narrated as *noir.* Perhaps this is what those who equate postmodernity with an abyss of chaos conceive as the reality that replaces the reality of modernity's sweetness and light. Contesting these notions, is the notion that there is neither margin nor center and no ultimate legitimacy in representing a loss of Enlightenment focus with fear and trembling. We enter the dark side of popular film in the postmodern *noir* but since we are at the same time entering a labyrinth of not only *noir* narrative of reality but reality through a variety of narratives, we lose the genre and enter the broader postmodern world.

You will notice that in *Out of the Past,* Robert Mitchum has tried to escape his past, from what he was, and live in a small town, pump gas, and court a local girl. In *Murder, My Sweet,* Dick Powell just tries to get to the bottom of things as a detective. Both get caught in dark whirlpools that drag them under. Mitchum loses his life and Powell is drugged into the nether regions. The point is clear: we are subject to dark forces not of our own making. The medievalist would cite Satan as the force behind this collapse of the social order. The *lumiere* cites the irrational, contingency, the unconscious. There is then a preservation of man's privileged positioning, only here man is not distanced, observant and dominant but distanced, blind, and victim.

Jack Grimaldi, however, is neither in complete control nor pure victim. He is packaged already into the world. And that world is made up of not only his packagings or self-constructions but others. All the characters in *Romeo is Bleeding* live in a high cycle whirlpool of their own making. What the world is outside these constructions is not within Jack's capacity to observe or ours. Jack is a strong player then and not just an "unlucky guy," as he says, but an unlucky guy "who fell in love with a hole in the ground." In other words, a guy with a story to spin—a story that spins the guy. And it's not the only story that he concocts. Jack constructs the reality that constructs him. Mitchum and Powell, the modernist *film noir* protagonists, discovered and reacted to a dark reality that the modernist project, if you will, cannot calibrate, cannot theorize, cannot enlighten.

If, then, Jack is responsible for the mess he's in, have we returned to the sort of clear-cut moral judgments that twentieth century modernism (in the *film noir*, for instance), felt it had lost? One gets the sense throughout the whole of *Romeo is Bleeding* that Jack is out of control, that he deserves what he gets, that he has no will, that he sees what must be done but he drifts the other way, that he has choices but always makes the wrong choices. We get down on Jack and I think one of the reasons the critics get down on this movie is for a classic reason: the center, Jack will not hold and the rest of the movie neither moves to fill in the center nor makes decentering its center, its focus. We get annoyed with Jack: toe cut off, limping through half the movie, strangled, tied up hand and foot by the sadistic woman who has just tricked him into killing his own girlfriend, forced to bury another man alive, always willing to make love to the sadist one more time, never knowing when to stop, when to go home. He's his own worst enemy.

I want to distinguish a Jack inevitably caught within other people's stories as well as his own and a Jack who has the capacity to decouple himself from both and prove his worth, earn his redemption. The first is a postmodern Jack, a self in the flux of constructions; the second is a modernist Jack, a self pulling itself out of the flux, out of the shadows. That this was seen to be a more and more impossible task is the essence of twentieth century modernism's tragic vision and the soul of the modernist *noir*. What about the postmodern Jack? Now, I grant that Jack-Romeo is a strong artificer of self-fabrications and labyrinthine involvements, but by saying that we construct the world that constructs us, am I then forced to say we should construct tepidly, within norms of concoction, constrained by protocols of fabulation? I think not. Jack's narrative self-organizations cannot fail to collide with and shape itself within *other* worldly fabulations but it is precisely this flux of interractions that comprise a postmodern reality-making. There are no outside-any-narrative constraints or notions of freedom. Jack's in love with a hole in the ground, *his* story of freedom, *our* story of constraint.

Regardless of this postmodern take on things, maybe our problem with Jack remains this: that he should exchange his desires for societal shackles on those desires. Maybe we'd like to see him more affected by societal constraints. But just maybe our own desire here is to see constraints placed on our global desires. Let's run it through: Jack is in love with a hole in the ground and in that hole is a whole lot of money. Is not our whole American society experiencing the same sort of love affair? Isn't the whole global market free play boldly contemptuous of any sort of constraints upon the desire to fill private holes in the ground with a whole lot of money? Maybe it's not that Jack is too immersed in stories of his own making, but that those stories reveal too much about our own love affairs and the terrible things they lead us into. Maybe, just maybe, our love affair with a private hole in the ground filled with money is a constraint upon our humanity?

Jack's life is messy, sloppy and the film catches the virus. But in the end that messiness is in the world, in a world unknowable in itself but only through and in the stories we concoct and that in turn spin us. Jack is not caught in a solo spin; there is not the angst of an individual consciousness here facing contingencies indifferent to that consciousness. Postmodern Jack is in a mess because he knows the world in a certain greedy, ravenous way and the world remains that way as long as he knows it in that way. And because it is a world that we know too, it is a world that we are constructing along similar lines. Jack's weakness, his vulnerability, his compliance, his refusal to learn from experience, his persistent greed, his undeterred lust, his roach-like survivalism, his moral slovenliness—all this annoys us, sets us against Jack and the film. This has to be our reaction. We are, you see, totally complicitous.

Things were a far sight less messy with the modernist *noir* where some reality stuff on the periphery had broken lose and threatened to decenter us. Late modernism was always moments away from vanquishing the threat at the same time that it was moments away from being overwhelmed by it. When the reality studio is finally stormed we lose hold of that detached but dominating relationship with an objective reality. Reality rushes in to meet us, to interpenetrate us. When we talk, we construct reality. When we do something, we construct reality. We're not observing it, we're doing it. Contingencies, the unconscious, inconceivables, and power therefore are byproducts of our doing reality. All this "unthought" that plagued twentieth century modernism is relative to our reality building, our real-izing and not "reality stuff" from the abyss. If Jack-Romeo's world seems messy, it's the world we're making and that is not just making Jack but making all of us.

Dead Kiss

The 1995 remake of the 1947 *Kiss of Death* draws the postmodern *noir* back to modernist roots but it winds up not *film noir* but *film blanc*. The film *wants* to have been made in 1947; the film *wants* to be seen as if it were not 1995 but 1947. And in this desire to trade our postmodern carnival with old fashioned malaise, to trade a political and social order without foundation for a political and social order *with* a foundation but one that *also* has dark roots, the new *Kiss of Death* is in the spirit of Gingrich's *Contract with America*. The abyss of the postmodern *noir* is here resisted; give us the old-time abyss which yawns only at the darkest hours and only for those whose lives "are not our fault." The postmodern turn was a wrong turn. We go back and take the proper fork in the road. *Noir* has been *gumpized*.

The world of the new kiss is not already wrapped in stories. Rather people make choices in a world that is responsive and comprehensible if one makes the effort. David Caruso's world is what he has made of it—he confesses to having wanted nothing more than to boost cars, get some quick money in his pocket and live above the "8 to 5" horde. There is a way, then, for us in the audience to distance ourselves from his plight—we watch as the world gets darker and darker for him and at the same time it gets lighter and lighter for us because here dark and light, good and evil, right and wrong, are distinguished, made visible. If Caruso were floating in an anchorless world, as is Jack, Romeo—filli-brating as it were within countless stories of meaning and value—political, social, moral, psychological—he would be drift-ing inevitably into us, into the constructions we live within. The abyss contained on the screen would swallow us in the audience.

The film is designed to prevent this from happening. If it were filmed in 1947, I would say that that setting would inspire angst but not a sense of postmodern drift. The 1947 film, in other words, is not concealing by design what the culture already is aware of. That film is modernist *noir* because it expresses an awareness of what Western foundational notions of reality and rationality cannot contain. Chance cannot be really kept at bay, minds spin in a subjectivity that troubles objectivity, reality con-stantly threatens to proliferate. The dark side is being fingered—the audience feels the danger, is consumed by the risk, caught up in the threat to their own stability as well as the world's.

Because the new kiss is designed to distance the viewer from his or her own milieu and place him or her within a world that cannot therefore be unsettling in ways that resonate with the present, the new kiss is, in essence, a deadened kiss. The *film noir* cannot cast its spell if it is only designed to reproduce the features of the *noir* without enacting that twisting of film and world that the viewer is already within. The *noir* characters and the viewers must share nightmares; swing and twist in the same dark winds, see the same abyss. That a man like Tommy Udo, played by Richard Widmark, could really exist, could really laugh maniacally while throwing a wheelchair-confined woman down a flight of stairs, might only resonate in 1947 with the atrocities of the Nazis. How to reconcile this conscience-free, cause-free be-havior with notions of order and civilization? Junior, in the new kiss, played by Nicholas Cage with a great deal of varied inflec-tions, is caught in a mental miasma that is frightening but doesn't leak out into the world and therefore cannot reach us. The thing to do with an evil that can be distanced from us is to throw a net on it and put it in jail. Thank God for capital pun-ishment. Cage plays Junior as weird—it's Cage's forte. Jack, Romeo—you recall, has a "hey, buddy, let me tell you all about it" style that draws us in and convinces us that he is like us—as his life and fascinations go, so do ours. Not so with Junior, a freak of nature who might have had a 1947 audience wondering how one of their own kind got that way. Not a 1995 audience—they aren't seeing resemblances with their own lives. Junior's different and they know what to do, or should know what to do, with his kind. He's a nightmare of depravity, a scene from the abyss in human form.

Junior belongs in jail, without parole. Actually, he should be executed without too much *habeas corpus* delay. The film then is politically tagged. First of all, this conservatively revisionist *Kiss of Death* hides any resemblances between these characters and ourselves and therefore protects us from thinking that their world seeps into ours. A politics of a common plight is put aside—we in the audience are privileged observers and more. We are in a position to judge the lives of those who are making a mess of their own lives. The film becomes one about losers—all *film noir* you might say is about losers. But in a post World War culture when the whole social order was still reverberating from a horrific wounding, feelings of displacement, of something having been lost were common feelings. The whole world had lost something, a great deal. Smack in the midst of victory, the *film noir* pitched its camp because, bottom line, there was a pervading sense of loss and not victory or gain deep within the mid-twentieth century psyche. If their *film noir* were about losers, the word was never attached in the way it is now. Now we have market winners and losers, and the losers, in an increasingly widespread view, cannot fault the winners for their loss. They had a fair and equal chance to win, and they failed.

When they fail and go awry, threaten the stability needed for free, unimpeded competition to take place, then they must be apprehended and brought to justice. So now we have a film aping *film noir* which not only does not darken the horizon of the viewer, but leads the viewer into a certain way of handling what is on the screen. This sort of didacticism in unknown in both the classic *film noir* and in the postmodern one I have been describing. Junior is not in jail because Big Government in the form of the FBI gets in the way of State and local government. Both federal and state government have taken into their hands what properly belongs to the individual. If David Caruso has personal problems that a wiser man could have solved, he does have a problem that all of us have—he's wedged between government forces fighting over what is none of their business.

The scene: FBI and local officials screaming at each other while Caruso has to finally blow a car horn to get the attention back to where it belongs. Phil Gramm and Bob Dole can fight over which one is going to use this scene on TV in his 1996 presidential campaign. It might work there—it doesn't here in this pseudo-*film noir.* Maybe if there were a sharply curtailed federal government with power devolving to the states, David Caruso's life would not so closely resemble a ping pong ball's. That is conjectural; what the film doesn't hold as conjectural is Caruso's power of self-determination and therefore self-responsibility. He has a ping-pong ball life because, like many others, he has celebrated self-indulgence and irresponsibility. That was the deadly climate that swallowed Jenny in *Forrest Gump,* a film where Forrest is not the ball but the man who controls the spin of the ball. I would also add that what isn't conjectural is the fact that if the federal government and the Supreme Court had not intruded into local law enforcement, Junior would have been hung before he had a chance to develop his muscles.

In the end, Caruso becomes something of a shrewd player and works his own escape from the clutches of government. Are there deeper, ontological troubles here that are not resolved? Is there a darkness that creeps outward and into our souls that no manner of artful dealing in the arena of life can put off? Darkness is deep and disturbing but it is also powerful and poetic; chance drags us out of our ruts, against the order of things we impose; desires such as Romeo Jack has come out of us and in turn lead us; power with a bureaucratic face is not the only and probably the least significant power we crash against. None of this kisses our faces in this film. It is not ours and we are not it. It's just part of the contract.

This film does not come out of the abyss of a postmodern *film noir* but out of our new "politics of concealment" where the visible darkness of *film noir* is given a spin.

You're on the Air with Dr. Joy

Day After Thanksgiving
WKZB

"Hello, you're on the air with Dr. Joy."

"Hullo?"

"You're on the air. What's your question, Cleo?"

Silence.

"Cleo? Are you there?"

Silence.

"Okay. Slight synaptic break there. Hello, you're on the air with Dr. Joy. Is this, Jake?"

"Former Sheriff Jake Wilcox."

"Is there a question in there?"

"There were some weird murders perpetrated out behind the County Mental Facility more than thirty years ago. I was a young deputy then on my first case. Tom Sizemore was sheriff then. Maybe some of your listeners will recall Old Tom."

"Define for me what you mean by weird here, Jake."

"They was all strangers. Never identified. And they was all dressed like you seen in photographs hundred years ago."

"They were shot, stabbed, drowned, what, Jake?"

"They all had a small burn hole through the chest. Pandymatty, who was the coroner, swore it wasn't a bullet or a knife wound. Never seen anything like it. Brought the FBI in, too, and they took one look and swore everybody to silence. Case closed. They was gonna handle it from then on. I tried to get in touch with them over the years, but alls I got back were letters saying no such case in their files. Then Pandymatty disappeared

57

all of a sudden and folks said he went back to Bombay but I knew
that wasn't true because one thing Pandymatty was fond of saying was thank Harry Krishy he weren't in Bombay no longer. And
I guess you know what happened to Old Tom Sizemore."

"Tell us, Jake."

"He had a shootout with the FBI about a year or so after the
Mental Facility murders. Over on Crary Island where Tom was
following up a lead."

"And the FBI shot the sheriff because he was following up a
lead?"

"Self-defense they said. Said Old Tom started to open up on
them with both Colts. Tom got them Colts from his Dad who was
one of the first sheriffs this town ever had. That was the original
Old Tom Sizemore. And he wore them Colts at Bull Run."

"How did the original Old Tom die?"

"Why he died in Saint Louey the King Sanitarium. Which
they tore down just before the Big One and built the County
Mental Facility. They still got some Saint Louey the King patients
out there. In comas and such."

"Okay, here's what I think, Sheriff."

"Former Sheriff."

"Former Sheriff. The men you found out behind the Mental
Facility? Probably Columbian drug dealers. Thirty years ago they
were dressing way behind the style in South America. And they
were killed by rival drug dealers in some weird voodoo way that
your Coroner wasn't hip to. The FBI took the case away from you
because one of the dead men was an undercover agent or something like that. Anyway, they were already deeply involved and
Old Tom was just in the way. The shootout on the island? Old
Tom went nuts the same way his father had. Something
snapped. Probably his impulse control wiring rusted out. It happens. The clockwork is in the genes. It's like a warranty except
it's on your cranial arteries. Some people are good for fifty thousand miles, some two hundred and fifty and some five thousand.
And some people are like cars you take out for a trial spin and
break down. You see what I'm saying, Former Sheriff?"

"What about Pandymatty disappearing all of a sudden?"

"Obviously he was in on the drug deal and they Jimmy Hoffaed him."

This was greeted by silence.

"Nothing weird here by '90s standards," Dr. Joy said. "Former Sheriff?"

"What about me?" Jake finally said. "It's why I called up. Why didn't anything weird happen to me?"

"It did."

"It did?"

"You made what happened go weird in your mind and you've carried it around in your mind so long that it's like a rusty tangle of wire that all your other thoughts have been corrupted by. Get the picture, Former Sheriff Jake Wilcox?"

"The unsolved crimes perpetrated out there ain't weird?"

"What's weird is your holding on to them for thirty years."

"Old Tom had rusty wiring and I got rusty wiring is what you're telling me? After all them years as Sheriff doing all I done for this town you telling me I was crazy in the head all them years? I say there's a goddamn cover up going on and this town ain't gonna survive if it don't find out what happened out there. That's how crazy I am!"

"Ouch! Never been hung up on so vehemently. Hello, you're on the air with Dr. Joy."

"Hullo?"

"Is that you Cleo?"

"I'm calling up for my father."

"Who doesn't want to call up himself?"

"He don't know I'm calling. He's a prominent citizen in this town."

"How are you calling for him then, Cleo?"

"Cause I have to."

"Why do you have to, Cleo?"

"Cause he's in a whole lot of trouble but he won't be asking anybody for help."

"What kind of trouble, Cleo?"

"He's been in the entrepreneur business in a really big way and now he's got all these houses built you know and ain't nobody buying them because they was built on the old chemicals that they used to use in the old paper mill."

"Ah, the Nouveau Noire Chateau Estates. Not selling like hotcakes are they?"

"Not since the riot you know. Which made everything racist so now white folks are afraid to move into the Nouveau Noire Estates."

"I don't have any advice to give you, Cleo."

"But here's my question, if folks is getting good value for their money out at the Nouveau Noire and a lot better than elsewhere then ain't that all that counts? Money ain't black or brown. It's green."

"Cleo, let me ask you something. Do you really want us to get to a place where money is what we value most?"

"If it drives folks more than hate does, I do."

"Maybe having only money values drives the hate. Did you ever think of that, Cleo?"

"Think it and heard it. My father is a reverend. A man of the cloth. A man of the Bible. I grew up hearing that mammon was on one side and God on the other."

"But your father is entrepreneurial?"

"He turned entrepreneurial right after Reagan got in. He said the moral majority have money and the liberal Democrats were loose with money and morals."

"Maybe money drives the morals, Cleo."

"That's what my father says."

"No, I mean if you have money you can legislate the values, from civic to moral. And the hate shows up because it's needed when only a few can have what everybody wants. Hate works for the firm of divisiveness but love works for the firm of sharing."

"What they feel like doing is hating. Jealous we are going to get someplace. Frightened we're climbing up that mountain."

"I think there's no room at the top for everyone, Cleo. Hate is just what shows up when everybody wants everything. No sharing. Isn't it pretty clear by now that only a very small percentage can make a profit and the rest have to go begging? Hate and violence are on the scene to preserve an economics of greed and a terribly, terribly unequal distribution of the world's natural wealth. And I'm starting right at ground level with food, air, water, shelter."

"Well, I was just calling for my father. He ain't ever going to be a communist, especially when they're all broke up anyway."

"I'm not a communist, Cleo. I just want us to have other values beside making money. There's no love in our new global capitalism."

"I hear you," Cleo said as Dr. Joy heard her hang up.

"Hello, you're on the air with Dr. Joy."

"You've heard of Lobster Boy?"

"Is that a fish franchise?"

"No, it's me. I'm Lobster Boy. Instead of being born with two hands I was born with two lobster claws and a lobster tail. My body is reddish all over. I'm in a carny passing through this area."

"So what's your problem, Lobster Boy?"

"I think somebody is trying to kill me."

"Why would someone be trying to kill you?"

"You know."

"I do?"

"For my tail. I've got close to a hundred pound lobster tail. Lobster tail retails for over twelve bucks a pound."

"Hello, you're on the air."

"You remember the night of the living dead, Dr. Joy?"

"The movie?"

"No, last week when Joe Nat told the City Council the dead would be walking that night."

"What's your question?"

"I saw one."

"One what?"

"Dead guy. I talked to him in front of Whipple's for over an hour."

"Hello, you're on the air with Dr. Joy."

"The live alien that had been taken from the 1949 Roswell crash was named Ebe."

"Lobster boys, zombies, aliens. Doesn't anybody out there have a normal psychological problem? Okay, I give up. Tell me about Ebe."

"Ebe is an insect-like being but his system was chlorophyll-based and he processed food into energy just like plants. When he became ill, his doctor was a botanist who sprayed him first with Rotenone for sore throat then Sevins for fever."

"How long have you been seeing Ebe?"

"Ebe belongs to a technologically superior race."

"When does he flower?"

"What?"

"Never mind. Are you seeing a psychiatrist?"

"Today cities exist on Mars populated by specially selected people from places like Utah."

"Okay . . . Hello, you're on the air with Dr. Joy."

"This is Frank Coletti. About what you told Sheriff Wilcox. I seen things suddenly open up back there behind County Mental."

"How did you see things suddenly open up back there, Frank?"

"It's hard to put into words."

"Like flowers opening up? Or opportunities? Or suddenly you saw things clearly . . . "

"Like that. Suddenly I saw things clearly. Things that hadn't been there for a long, long time. Like the murders Jake was talking about."

"So you saw the past suddenly appear. Is that it?"

"Yeah. But in bits and pieces. One minute I'm there involved like it was now and the next minute I'm just looking and nobody seems to know I'm there and I'm even looking at me and my Dad when I was young and he was still alive."

"Are you seeing a psychiatrist?"

"I seen Fatima too."

"Who's Fatima?"

"Dog I had when I was a kid that disappeared the night of them murders."

"Now that you've told me all this, Frank, what do you want me to tell you?"

"Things open up is what I wanted to tell you. Just that. Things all of a sudden open up and you can see what ain't here no more."

"Thank you, Frank. For that. It's now eleven twenty five. Fast approaching the bewitching hour. Hello, you're on the air with Dr. Joy."

"I just accidentally tuned in, Doctor. I think I know you."

"But you don't know you, is that it?"

"I guess so. I mean I know I'm Mark Pinsky but I don't know why I'm here. Where I am. Or how I got here. I don't think I was Mark Pinsky a little while ago. And then I heard your voice on the radio and it sounded familiar and all of a sudden I was Mark Pinsky. Am I Mark Pinsky?"

"Mark, do you know I've been looking for you? You have a dissociative disorder which means that you experience a sudden disruption in the usually integrated functions of consciousness, memory, identity, and perception of the environment. You have what's called dissociative fugue."

"Fugue? You mean like in music?"

"No, like in a fugue state. A trance state. It's like sleepwalking. You get up unexpectedly and travel away from home and can't recall your past and you're confused about your identity. In really bad cases of this kind of fugue, you might even assume a new identity."

"Somebody's calling me. A woman. A woman I've never seen before."

"Mark, have you assumed a new identity?"

"She's not calling me Mark. Who's Rico?"

"Mark, where are you?"

"I think she's from the fugue. Goodbye, Doctor Joy."

"Mark? Okay. So be it. Hello you're on the air with Dr. Joy."

"Hullo, Dok-tor. Guess who this is?"

"What do you want, Rick?"

"I'm calling in. This is a call-in show, ain't it? So I'm calling in."

"You've got another thirty seconds, Rick."

"Lobster Boy and that fugue guy and all them other nuts get all the time they need, but Rick, your court appointed case load, gets the bum's rush. I read what you wrote about me. Antisocial personality disorder. I got nothing but disregard for the rights of others and when I get a chance I violate them. Now after all them talks we had is that what I came off as?"

"You're a classic case, Rick. Do you want me to preview your test results?"

"Sure. It says in this report here that I'm indifferent to what other people think, so shoot."

"You use aliases . . . "

"Maybe I got that I-forgot-who-I-am fugue."

"You con others . . . "

"Losers deserve to lose. I picked that up in the Harvard Business Review. I took a course in getting a killer instinct."

"You're a malingerer."

"I'm guilty. Deep inside, I'm not a type A personality. I like to hang out."

"You're deceitful and manipulative in order to obtain what you want. And you don't consider the consequences."

"And what do I want?"

"Whatever you desire at the moment. Money, sex, power."

"Sounds like a Fortune 500 personality to me, Doc. Let's face it. You can label me anti-social because I don't have any money or power. If I did, I'd be one of the people deciding who's social and who's anti-social. And you know who I'd pick for being anti-social? All the people I feared were gonna take my goodies away. People that ain't swallowing all this shit about who's social and who's anti-social. People who see through the bullshit. People like me."

"You'll hurt somebody, Rick, and then they'll put you away for a long time. It's three strikes and you're out now."

"I'll be a political prisoner then, Doc. Most everybody we got in prison now in this country are political prisoners only we say they got anti-social personality disorder. And smart asses like you with big degrees put the stigmata on us."

"Time's up, Rick."

"You're mortal too, Doc," Rick said, hanging up.

"If that was a threat, you all heard it. Rick Monte is the man's name. Hello, you're on the air with Dr. Joy."

"We got cut off about the dead guy I spoke to?"

"Thirty seconds for you and the dead guy. Go."

"Okay, he was a famous swimmer that lived in this town in the last century when there weren't any swimming pools in town and everybody swam out at the Dam. His name was Fred Ferris but everybody in town called him Fish Ferris' cause he swam like a fish. He only had to come up for air every twelve strokes cause he invented a special kind of swimbreathing on account of his lungs. Every chance he got he was down at the Dam swimming. He cut school so he could swim and in the winter when the water froze over he went into a sort of hibernation. When he got older he had a hard time keeping a job what with his sneaking out to go swimming in the good weather and his sleeping on the job in winter . . . "

"But now he's dead and he came back to tell you all this. Why? Did he want something from you?"

"He wanted to tell me we were all going back into the water. Soon."

"Devolutionist."

"Hun?"

"Reverse evolution."

"He passed his swimbreathe technique on to me over at the swimming pool at the Bones estate. I can stay in the water for hours now and swim miles without getting cold or tired."

"Hello, you're on the air with Dr. Joy."

"If I told you I had Elvis's voice on a Cadillac steering wheel and could play it and anything else with the right kind of surface with a laser beam, would you say I was crazy, Dr. Joy?"

"Did anyone else hear Elvis's voice coming out of that steering wheel?"

"Yeah, but if I mention his name on the air he'd be real mad. I just want to know if you think I'm into technology here or a fruitcake."

"What does Elvis tell you to do?"

"He doesn't tell me anything. It's his voice from back then talking to some other people. You can hear their whole conversation almost. Voices somehow get worked into the things around them and the laser beam finds them. You know what linear and rotary voice coil actuators are, Dr. Joy?"

"I'm not up on new technology, I'm afraid."

"Well, the technology is there. The thing is it's spooky to think the whole human drama is sunk into all the stuff around us. The older the stuff and the more it was handled, especially what was said when it was being made, the more we're talking about history coming to life. Energy from sound and motion gets wrapped up in what's being made."

"I've got a painting that my grandmother did the year before she died. Do you think you could laser her voice out of that?"

"I'm not the guy who has the computer and the laser and the program and all that."

"Look, Woad . . . "

"How did you know it was me?"

"Because hi-tech and spaced out equals Mike Woad. Do me a favor, Woad, get over to the National Archives and run that laser computer stuff on Nixon's missing eighteen and a half minutes. Now that conversation would make a fitting Nixon testimonial. Hello, you're on the air with Dr. Joy."

"Hi, Dr. Joy, this is Lucy Powell. Remember me?"

"You're unforgettable, Lucy. And besides, you call in every night. What's up?"

"Certain types of guys when they're in love with me, say certain things, you know?"

"Give me a for instance."

"Virtual Jack says: 'I'd like to mimic your movement.'"

"Virtual Jack? Are you still carrying on with him?"

"He belongs to my synthetic-conversation group. Want to hear another?"

"I'm still digesting the first but go ahead."

"It took a thousand years for me to work my way out of the earth just to be with you. That's a rock in love with me."

"A rock in love with you? What does that mean?"

"Teach me how to love. A very, very, very serious young man in love with me. If you take this pill right now, you can sleep. A nurse in love with me. Your eyes drew me from across the room. An opthamologist in love with me. You are more profound than all the books in the world. A librarian in love with me. Take this dish to your mother with my compliments. A famous chef in love with me . . . "

"Good night, Lucy. Don't forget to take your pill. Hello, your on the air with Dr. Joy. Two minutes before midnight. A cold, wintery day in a lot of people's souls. Who's speeding to the new millennium out there?"

"I saw Further Cooper the other night. You know the kid that Rick Monte run down? It was the same night that other caller said was the night of the living dead."

"I'm tired of Further Cooper sightings. Why don't we all just let the poor kid rest in peace?"

"That's the point, Doc. He obviously ain't resting in peace, otherwise he wouldn't be popping up all over the place."

"You want my advice? Carry a camcorder around and get some tape on Further. Can you do that? Then call me. Hello, you're on the air with Dr. Joy."

"Patti wants to say goodnight, Dr. Joy."

"What's Patti doing up so late, honey?"

"Things."

"Does your Mommy and Daddy know that Patti is up so late?"

"Goodnight, Dr. Joy. That was Patti."

"Good night, Pancakes."

"Patti says Patti too?"

"And Patti too."

"Hello you're on the air with Dr. Joy."

"You must tell your listeners that there is no laser reading of voices in objects."

"Okay. There is no laser reading of voices in objects. Hello, you're on the air with Dr. Joy. Last call."

"We're experiencing a sudden opening up down here behind Neelye's Target Range, Doctor Joy, and we thought you might like to come by after the show."

"Sorry, I've got a date with Virtual Jack."

"Is he gonna mimic your movement?"

"A dirty ending to a show I've got to analyze. Thanks to all of you who took time out of your busy town lives to call in and tell us how you are defeating life. Maybe we're a step closer to each other tonight. At least that's what I hope. Sayonara."

All the Virtues: The Films and Politics of Concealment

Spring 1995

"Without Contraries is no progression."

William Blake

"CHANDLER: You heard what Phil Gramm said at breakfast this morning: the poor have lost the will to hunt . . . gotten used to turning their food stamps for fancy condoms and gourmet cheese.

HOWELLS: If the poor regain the will to hunt, Toby, who do you think they'll come looking for?"

"Entr'acte," Lewis Lapham

Legends of the Lost

Brad Pitt is a sort of '90s version of James Dean, which I guess means that he looks a lot like Dean and seems to be attracting a cult following. I went to see him in *Legends of the Fall*, (based on the novel by Jim Harrison), mostly because I wanted to connect Pitt, the '90s to the James Dean I had waited in long lines to see at the old Fortway in Brooklyn in the late '50s.[1] What did The Dean mean to us back then? How did *he* connect with the times? How did that young and troubled, beyond verbal articulation screen presence become the spokesman for my teenage years? I had already seen Pitt in Robert Redford's fine 1992 film *A River Runs Through It* where Pitt was the wilder of two brothers. Shades of Dean in *East of Eden*.

It turned out that Pitt was once again the younger and wilder brother in *Legends*. And like Dean, he played his best moments on the edge of speech. After all, language is the tool of the Fathers, and Youth therefore employs it reluctantly, peevishly, looking away. Fathers forge meanings while sons rebel without causes because only language can iterate causes. The beauty of Dean's performances lay in his restless gropings beyond meanings—a promise of making true and real connections with people and things, self and society. He registered youth's perennial disappointment in what passed as authenticity in the adult world. It was a long-playing Western rift: rebellion by Hal, revolt by Hotspur, patricide by Blake's Orc, revenge by Heathcliffe, murder by Raskolnikov, dissent and departure by Stephen Daedalus, a brooding, caffeinated Monty Clift, an atavistic Marlon Kowalski, a semi-audible rebellious James Dean. In one way of looking at this youthful lot it is possible to see the constraints, the chains and shackles, the covering nets, becoming more and more effective. Action gives way to speech which in turn gives way to silence peppered with outbreaks of crippled articulation.

Sure enough there is a lessening of both angst and rebellion in both Pitt films, although in *A River* he is clearly meant to be the youth too wild to live long, and in *Legends,* he is clearly meant to be an embodiment of the wild spirit of the American West—the legend America today lives within regarding its own youthful and wild beginnings. *A River,* however, is a tension-free film—it has a much better handle on the order and harmony of poetic memory, (Norman Maclean's and Robert Redford's), than on the disorder and wild exuberance that the brother who died too young, (Pitt's role), is meant to display. That Dionysian energy is now only recollected by an Apollonian memory. The film is starving for more of what drives Pitt to the extreme, to the edge of everything. But it is all told from a calm, discerning center and no matter how good the fly fishermen are here, no one casts far enough to the outlying rebellion nor deep enough into its disruptive energy. "As a film," Adam Mars-Jones writes in the *Independent,* "it has all the virtues except tension, which is unfortunately like saying that a watch would be a good timekeeper if the mainspring wasn't bust." "The trouble is, it's more or less what we expect," Stanley Kauffman writes in *The New Republic.* "We feel that we've seen it before we go."[2]

The notion that youthful rebellion ain't what it used to be, at least in films and in rock (where all the rebel posturing is too transparently a marketing ploy), didn't last the night. The screen was still showing the collision of youth and the social order. Black, Hispanic, gay and women's films pitch their battle in the realm of innocence. The boyz in the hood are angry, the homeboys in the barrio are just as angry. Perhaps it is only the rebellion of white youth that seems now enervated on the screen—they seem to have given up the fight, succumbed already in the womb to the market order of things. They've lost their edge. They've exchanged rebellion for dollars and bonus gifts. They are as adrift in regard to any values but market values as the nation is. If they can't buy it or dream about buying it, they don't know what to make of it. I am thinking of the blank gazes of youth in *River's Edge*, the emptiness of the Heathers in *Heathers*, the passiveness of the high schoolers before Christian Slater pumps them up in *Pump Up the Volume*, youth as material dregs in *Less Than Zero*.

Our youth are becoming painful reminders of how we have shortchanged them. We live in a society that is willing to see its youth make it or break it according to the casino logic of the market. They have become as expendable as the working class, immigrants, minorities, the poor and homeless, the unemployed, the old and feeble, the imprisoned, the poets and philosophers, the vagabonds and dreamers. After all, the investment in youth is long–term and we are now a society of short-term players. Nor is the market especially interested in extending expensive entitlements to them, from schooling and apprenticeship to medical coverage. There is, of course, a discourse of concern—how could there not be? But we are as concerned here as we have been with the former Soviet Union and the former Yugoslavia. It is all a nominal concern—when push comes to shove, the youth of today represent the workers of tomorrow, a resource the global market has no shortage of. Why would we expect the market to extend more concern to future workers than it does to workers now?

If white, hetero, middle-class youth appear washed out on the screen, all their energies already sapped, it is because they know their presence is unheralded. They have too great an awareness of the numbers who have gone before them who remain a burden to the society we have created. They are, in essence, filled with a sense of defeat before the battle of life has even begun. They stare blankly at the insecurity of those who go before them. They are transfixed by what Edward Luttwak calls "the central problem of our days: the completely unprecedented personal economic insecurity of working people, from industrial workers and white-collar clerks to medium-high managers."[3] And the rebellion that should erupt from this is presently being side-tracked at a feverish pace into all manner of market distractions—from the promises of the Net to automobile "culture," sports obsessions, up-scale cataloguing of simply everything by the already endebted, "services" dependency and all manner of "top of the line" dependencies. It seems clear that since drug dependency is one of the all-time most successful—marketwise—dependencies and that the price of, say, pot will drop to the price of corn if it is legalized, drugs will remain, purely for market reasons, illegal. If all vegetables were made illegal, the price of an ear of corn or a brussel sprout on the street would be astronomical. Our market-created dependencies distract us from our plight—we are being consumed while at a feast of consumption.

So my thinking about Brad Pitt in *Legends* left me here—while there is a desire to show youthful energy and rebellion on the screen, there is a disconnect present. This energy cannot be shown without facing the abyss from two different directions. We would either be facing the scrunched and lifeless youth we are nurturing or the seething clamor of the minority youth we have disenfranchised. A film like *Legends* wants to conceal those views so it settles for a literary rendering, a small variation on the classic rift of youthful rebellion. And it removes the action to the past, a safe distance, which of course, depending upon the mood and mania of the present, may or may not be safe. In working to make the film safe from the youth anxieties of the present, the film in effect disconnects itself from the present. Pitt samples Dean but not in an explicit, postmodern way in which we would be aware of the distance and thus re-see both Pitt and Dean and consequently the differing cultural waters youth have swum in. The sampling is to be concealed—the attempt is to clone but without context, or, hopefully only the context the film itself creates. Since this context cannot exist uncoupled from the present, and that coupling is concealed, this film floats somewhere in space—one of a number at this moment in American culture. What does it mean?

If the film is as disconnected from the present as I suggest, how then is it succeeding? How are we relating to it? There is great reliance on what Brad Pitt brings to this film from other films, from interviews and gossip columns and so on. He is young—posing rebelliously on magazine covers, representing an image of youth that radiates desires of all sorts—he is youth-as-commodity of the moment. There is no way really to separate that presence from the character he plays in the film. The screen youth is alluring, charismatic. Casting and marketing conceal both the failure to show youthful rebellion close-up or impart the sense that the filmmakers knows what such rebellion is. I think they know what it is, where it is and, most painfully, what it now amounts to. I slowly became aware that I hadn't just come upon a film trying to make a buck on the legend of a wild, free, and young spirit while concealing our present uneasy relationship with our youth. I had seen a film that had managed to disconnect itself from our present postmodern abyss. It was a good, old-fashioned film with all the virtues of those old films. It managed to focus the resonance of filmic rebellion to real world rebellion on its lead, on Brad Pitt. Any other intersections between America in the '90s and this film are blocked off.

I was both surprised and not surprised by *Legends of the Fall*. I was surprised that such a successful film here in the '90s succeeded in blocking off a culture seething with so much turmoil. However, I was not suprised to find a film that attempted to do so. What this tells me is that there is now as much or greater marketability for films that turn away from our societal clash of values and meanings as there is for films that tap into this clash. In the first two years of the decade, virtually no popular film that attracted wide and sustained attention from the media was not somehow grounded in something troubling American culture. Our attention and our concern has been and continues to be easy to spot. I turn to today's headlines: Dr. Kevorkian has assisted at another suicide. The death toll of the Oklahoma City bombing reached closure today: 167 killed. A witness for the prosecution continues to try and explicate the matter of DNA to the jury in the O.J. Simpson trial. Senator Pete Domenici wants to cut Medicare in order to give a tax break to those making over $100,000 a year. And so on.

In *Hauntings: Popular Film and American Culture 1990-1992*, I argued that we cannot help attending the screenings of what haunts us in our culturally war-torn society. Now, in the spring of 1995, it seems we are more than ready to escape what haunts us, to see our hauntings concealed on the screen. While many would applaud the return to traditonal family values—good solid stories with moral tags, a steady sense of realism, old fashioned plot and character development, clear closures and a sense of well-being on the way out—I fear the worst. These are my nightmares and they are not what Bob Dole calls "nightmares of depravity."[4] I fear that we're ready to close down the cultural dissent for the sake of a unified, harmonious society. And I think that such social stability is not being engineered by a moral and religious right—which is merely helping to provide an alibi discourse—but by market forces. It seems clear to me that, if the officers of the Chase Manhattan Bank can write to the president of Mexico and tell him to either impose order on Chiapas through military means or lose American investments, there must be the same efforts being made to close down our own cultural wars.[5] The South Central L.A. revolt and resulting riot could not have been evaluated as anything more than a Chiapas-like event.

Let's Put the Lid On: Violence, I.Q., Honor, Elitism, and Virtue

For what Luttwak calls the Republican/Tories, the abyss we face is a result of a failure of a cultural dissensus of heterogeneity—that is, an American culture of ever increasing numbers of narratives battling each other over who is to determine societal meanings and values—to be subsumed totally within market values, to be grounded peaceably in corporate Darwinism and its notions of unimpeded competition, self-interest, and the supreme virtues of the maximization of profits. Now, the question is, who's on the other side? Surely there is no organized, observable "postmodern" response along the lines that I have been making. For the postmodernist, on the lookout for a reigning master narrative, the abyss we fear must be tied to the metanarrative force of our "turbo-charged capitalism." Such a force is engaged in a usurpation of all other values and meanings. And regardless of whether or not we perceive any worthy challengers to it, the postmodern observation is that we fabricate its dominancy and consume its configurations of the total unmarked space of the world. We accept that what such a master narrative leaves out or dismisses is justifiably and legitimately left out and dismissed. We accept that what it privileges is also privileged by the same light.

Perhaps this postmodern discourse is on the rise, or, perhaps because of its reputed connection to the cultural divisiveness we face, it is on its way out. Nevertheless, that cultural divisiveness represents the challenging view to unimpeded competitiveness grounded in self-interest. Such a fury of contesting narratives *are* the abyss from one point of view, and yet there are dissenting narratives that speak of a rising out of misrepresentation or no representation, or still worse, inconceivability, into the light of identity. Their values and meanings will find a place in society. The culture will voice their voices, connect with their words. They see themselves as rising from an abyss of neglect, disenfranchisement, non-identity, non-being, the abyss of invisibility. Contemporaneously, there have been a number of popular films in 1994 and 1995 that have engaged in a 1950's sort of politics of concealment. Films such as *The Shawshank Redemption, Kiss of Death, Little Women, Love Affair, It Could Happen To You, Rob Roy, Blue Sky, I.Q., Quiz Show,* and *Legends of the Fall* could easily have been made in 1954 or '55. Or could they? Such detachment from our present narrative-rich cultural milieu refers to an "art" of concealment as well as a politics of concealment. And yet because of this artfulness there does indeed remain a contemporary connection, rather like a latent set of prints you hope to find by dusting the scene thoroughly. The connection you might say is definitely in the cultural milieu, the *mis en scene* of our viewing. No viewer in the '50s would pick out *our* hot spots, nor could we discern theirs.

Of all the contemporary films of concealment, *Forrest Gump* most directly engages our times and most artfully conceals that engagement. Why the "directest" engagement? Because it attempts to rewrite the past, namely the '60s, in line with our present mid-'90s view of progress and retrogression. Most "artfully" concealing? Because it seems all-fashioned apolitical while serving a conservative *Contract with America* view of our past. *Gump*'s success at the box office, its *legerdemain* in concealing its politics, becomes a new model for other popular films to follow. The present, with all its seething clash and furor, can be seduced. There must be once again in the land a *marketable* desire to escape the postmodern abyss—a mandate from the people to once again make invisible what has become too visible in our culture. Let's put the lid on.

I have already begun this piece with some words on *Legends of the Fall* and how it trades in rebel youth—a contemporary sore spot—and yet packages that rebellion before it reaches our eyes and ears. Getting the violent off our streets and into our prisons for lengthy stays is another contemporary hot spot. *Shawshank* avoids it: the film attaches itself to a Count of Monte Cristo narrative and we wind up applauding Tim Robbins' masterful escape and his clever tactics in financing a prosperous retirement in a tropical clime. The film glosses over the fact that he was an innocent man found guilty. Could it be that in our present lust for putting people in prison without parole, keeping the violent off our streets as it were, we have overlooked the fact that justice is an interpretation and our interpretations change over time? The romance of bold escape and a cunning, resourceful, Ulysses-like hero overwrites other crossings with the present. Cheap labor and artful bookkeeping make a financial success of the warden. Robbins becomes the E. F. Hutton of the prison, etching in every viewer's mind the utter transcendence of "business" over all matters, including matters of justice. Morgan Freeman is finally paroled after he trades a pretense at having been "rehabilitated" for a candid denunciation of the rehabilitation expectation itself. It's a charade. Is it his refreshing honesty that finally earns him the parole? Or does his rehabilitation lie in the fact that he is willing to recognize that he has been there for punishment and not rehabilitation? The goal of imprisonment is not to move one from a lower moral plane to a higher one, for that involves proof of moral superiority. Such proof is infinitely contestable. Freeman bows to simple power—the power to punish and incarcerate, to keep him there until he dies. Letting him go when he does bow to it becomes then nothing more than a confirmation that he has finally guessed right. But, as I say, this very hot issue of the intent of imprisonment is swaddled in this film within the mythos of countless prison movies where the hero finally makes his escape. Paul Muni in *Fugitive from a Chain Gang* more tellingly connected with the quandaries of guilt and innocence that perplexed his day than does this 1995 film.

I.Q. is not about *The Bell Curve* controversy in intelligence but it is a film that came out in the midst of that controversy.[6] It slips by it. There are no blacks in this movies, only a working class stiff, (Tim Robbins again), an auto mechanic who falls in love with Einstein's granddaugher, Meg Ryan. For her to love him, he has to prove he's got a high I.Q. In our present market mentality, the winners are just plain smarter than the losers. The best and the brightest will accumulate wealth and power. The fittest will survive in the market. The sort of intelligence a theoretical physicist such as Albert Einstein has—well, that's a *different* sort of intelligence. In fact, our American legend of intelligence has Einstein right at the heart of it—an unworldly, abstract intelligence that doesn't extend to matters like opening an umbrella in the rain. The sort of intelligence we want to pursue has more to do with Michael Milken and Ivan Boeg, Bill Gates and John Malone than with Einstein. Ross Perot's qualifications for the American presidency was a non-issue precisely because he had proven himself at a transcendent level—he had already become a billionaire.

A film with the title *I.Q.* comes out at a time when American culture ponders nervously whether its poor are poor because they are losers and are losers because they don't have the "right stuff" to compete. If a free market means that everyone has an equal opportunity to compete, but competition is a contest of differences, then the question as to what difference is the telling or winning difference is *the* question. Is the difference in the genes, as *The Bell Curve* implies? Do we ultimately have not only rich and poor, but a class society because this is the way the market arena sorts us all out? Are egalitarianism and free market competition reconcilable? Can you have a political democracy based on class division? And at the heart of all this is the question of I.Q. What sort of intelligence does market competitiveness require? And does this requirement construct our societal sense of what intelligence is? The unsettling question is not whether intelligence is culturally or genetically shaped, but what sort of intelligence does our society privilege? While we have been debating the first question, our society has gone ahead and constructed a very definite notion of what intelligence ought to be. It ought to be the sort of thing that enables one to be a successful market player—the sort of intelligence needed to get in the arena, compete and win.

I think we are back to the matter of education that I broached in regard to the market's treatment of youth in this country. Within the market metanarrative, education is not so much a means to successful competition but rather another possession that one must compete for. And why? Again, not so much because there is a direct link between education and market success (*Corporate Lives* profiles market winners who invariably have had lackluster college careers)[7] but because we live in a society that has constructed a link between the two. To play the game well is to first know the rules of the game. Since no one can spell out the substantive link between any curriculum and market success, the education-success linkage is best achieved on a nominal level, on the level of the signifier—Harvard, Hopkins, Oxford, Brown, Wharton School and so on. Patent leather signifiers.

What sort of intelligence does Tim Robbins have in the film *I.Q.?* A car mechanic's intelligence? And he wants to have a theoretical physicist's intelligence? Only to win the heart of Meg Ryan, of course. And what sort of intelligence does the majority, if not all, of the audience want? Only to win a fortune, of course. We have clearly constructed a notion of intelligence for ourselves which fulfills our desires. And desire here is the desire of the global market which extends no further than the bottom line—maximization of profits. The question then that the film, like our society, puts out of sight is this: what manner of intelligence does this or that person display? To question the amount of intelligence a person has—a measurement of I.Q.—is to assume that there is only one kind of intelligence. While we are measuring Einstein's I.Q. and imposing that sort of measurement universally, we are at the same time totally perplexed as to what sort of intelligence measures well in the market arena.

The hegemony of computer technology has put forward a new sort of intelligence, best displayed by Bill Gates of Microsoft. He is a combination of technological inventiveness and shrewd business skill. His intelligence goes beyond cloning and redundancy to creativeness, although this creativeness does not hinder him from closely attending to worldly affairs. But his intelligence is everywhere acknowledged to be eccentric, out of the mainstream. If the soul of intelligence is the capacity to create anew, to break the mold of redundancy, then the rote of education hardly serves us well.

In the end, Tim Robbins cannot learn what Einstein and his colleagues have, he can only ape it. But he remains creative in his own right—he creatively pursues Meg Ryan and wins her in the end. He has been intelligent in a different way. But it is *cherchez la femme* and not our capacity to be intelligent in different ways that the film itself pursues. Meg Ryan's bouncy, cutsey, impulsive ways are the film's ways—we bounce over and down the bell curve that has our society transfixed. One law of intelligence for the ox and the lion is oppression but it is an oppression the film conceals. The alibi discourse that the bell curve provides our market mentality—the vast number of global "losers" in the market game lose by virtue of their genes not by the inherent inequities and injustices of the game itself—prepares us for the film's tactic: there is no profit in this film scanning, in a postmodern way, the subject of "intelligence."

In a society in which no one really knows how to achieve what the whole society nevertheless is intent on achieving, namely material prosperity or market success, chance has a growing fascination. Maybe I'll win the lottery. Nicholas Cage does in the film *It Could Happen To You*. While the film sets Cage up as a man of good heart whose values transcend the material, and also sets Rosie Perez up with the ontology "I shop therefore I am," the best thing that could happen to you remains victory at the crap table. The Western Tradition of Rationalism and Realism winds up here. It's already happened to us.

What Nicholas Cage has is moral integrity—call it honor which is what Liam Neeson in *Rob Roy* calls it over and over again. "Are you a man of honor?" Neeson asks an English lord, played by John Hurt. And when asked by his son what honor is, Neeson replies that it is what holds a man's life together, the grounding force, the *sine qua non* of human existence. The remarks are telling—we in the audience get the sense that while something rather nebulous called honor existed "back then," it hardly connects in the present. Is President Clinton an honorable man? Donald Trump? Ross Perot? Newt Gingrich? David Duke? Richard Nixon? Michael Milken? Ollie North? Colin Powell? Phil Gramm? How and why have we substituted notions of personal honor with the market view that "good guys finish last"? The question almost makes its way to our lips but is stifled by the film's own effort to romanticize itself. Tim Roth, the bastard son of nobility, is unhindered by honor. When confronted by the young serving girl he has ruined he declares that he is a crowing cock on a dung hill which she calls love. And Neeson calls honor. Out to make his fortune unencumbered by any allegiances either to God or Man, Roth is a player and entrepreneur before his time, a Gordon Gecko out to liquidate others in pursuit of his own aggrandizement. Honor seems no match for his villainy but the film would have it otherwise. Roth is smote with a mighty stroke of Neeson's sword. Honor prevails. At least in popular film.

In a way, Robert Redford's film *Quiz Show* is a lament for lost honor, but only if you necessarily attach honor with the well-bred. When tested, Charles Van Doren, played by Ralph Fiennes, proves not to possess a sustaining honor. He agrees to cheat. Why? Because he has lived in the shadow of his famous father for too long and desires some fame of his own. Regardless, however, of the psychology here, Charles agrees to dirty his conscience and jump into the competitiveness arena. He'll compete and win—he'll remain in the spotlight at any cost. What is this all about? I think we are back to the "best and the brightest" syndrome, back to the idea that a certain sophistication and civilization resides with the "better families" in America. There is more "breeding" there, a more well defined sense of honor, a more genetically unflawed intelligence there. More than what or who? Well, more than the unappealing Jew played by John Tuturro who has an intelligence honed on rote memorization, whose wife is obscenely vulgar, whose home life is without any trace of grace. And Tuturro is not above revenge—he both recognizes Fiennes's social superiority assumed to be a natural superiority and seeks to destroy it. Rob Morrow plays the part of another Jew, a young lawyer "on the make" with the Justice Department, who has been to Harvard law school, graduating first in his class as he tells anyone who will listen. He recognizes breeding—it is what he and Tuturro do not possess. It is the '50s and all of America is drifting into that miasma ruled by the lowest common denominator, the lowest standards and sensibilities that de Toqueville had predicted would be the upstart of democracy. The love of fame and fortune has forced everyone into the arena. No one is too honorable to enter—no manner of intellectual sophistication can hold the line with the low and vulgar cunning of making a buck. The film is a lament for the deeper and richer culture we as a nation have lost and for those purveyors of that culture who remained "uncommodified." When Charles Van Doren is so commodified, the dark tragedy of a democracy that levels in every way begins. De Toqueville had jumped the gun.

At the moment the film is released the working class and the underclass in this country are moving from the margins to the land of "not being costed in." And an oligarchic elite is thriving.[8] But *Quiz Show* is absorbed only in the tragedy that comes in the wake of egalitarianism. Public education has put Tuturro through City College, but this education has lost the *je ne sais quoi* of a proper gentleman's education. Quality has been hopelessly distilled in this franchise extension. It little matters here whether that franchise is now being threatened by a privatization mania.[9] The film conceals every bit of politics that interferes with its indulgence in a tragedy that the market itself is now "correcting." We are now much closer to an acceptance of privileged classes in America and the dissolution of that spirit of the "common man" and "common sensibility" which *Quiz Show* finds so destructive.

In many ways *Quiz Show* is a variation on *Forrest Gump's* aversion to the turbulent '60s. What was the counter-cultural revolution but a sudden voicing of hordes hitherto voiceless? When I rewrite the '60's, I see it as an explosion of the Whitmanian impulse to level all humanity to grass level. Whitman threw his arms around the scattered refuse piles of a latent nineteenth century class society, a Whartonian age of innocence in which good families bred proper sensibilities and refined taste. In every way, the '60s were a playing out of Whitman and not Wharton or James, who both mourned more deeply than they critiqued the inanities and superficialities of those supposedly bred to observe value and quality. Instead of concealing and filming over the renewed "democratic vistas" of the '60s, which is what *Forrest Gump* does, *Quiz Show* goes back to the '50s and focuses on the moment before this counter-cultural, egalitarian outbreak—the moment when class and breeding, culture and sophistication, were seduced and then trampled by the atavistic genes of democracy. The fact that it is the play of market forces, of competitive capitalism, that is creating that political paradox—an oligarchic democracy— is, as I say, left alone by the film. The Jeffersonian impulse to educate all in the services of democracy is found to be destructive but the battle is not engaged. Perhaps such engagement is in bad taste, something John Tuturro would welcome but surely not the Van Dorens.

I want to end on the subject of virtue and concealment with the film *Blue Sky*, for which Jessica Lange earned the 1994 Best Actress Oscar. Again we are back in the '50s, a temporal/spatial disengagement with our own catastrophic times. *Rob Roy*, *Forrest Gump*, *Quiz Show*, *Little Women*, *Legends of the Fall* and *The Shawshank Redemption* also distanced us from today's headlines. As in these films, *Blue Sky*, we can easily say, is an escape from the present—an old-fashioned film to be enjoyed and not taken apart to reveal political biases, sexism, racism, homophobia and so on. Of course, if the film truly escaped the present rather than just selectively suppressed it, it would also escape our perceptions. Lange's performance both reveals and conceals the hot spots of the film. We want to see it as a vehicle for an academy award performance, reduce it to a fine actress' full engagement with a good part. The part is itself contained in an old-fashioned moral fable—monogamy is led to the abyss by a distracted woman who falls and then rises magnificently to redeem monogamy. Family values, you might say, dissolve then recombine on another level. While divorce would be the simple '90s solution to such difficulties, it is here implicitly not a solution but another difficulty. We are to see how marriages can be made to work, how families stay together. But unlike *Little Women,* a film in which the "pure being" of family forestalls tension and dilemma, *Blue Sky* distracts itself from family and monogamy and in the end these distractions linger.

The film's dilemma is simply put: it shows us a woman whose energies and desires cannot be constrained by "all the virtues" and yet must, in the end, show her to us as so constrained. She submits in the end to loyalty to her husband and responsibility for her children. She once again agrees to play act within the realities that his choices create. She does this at the film's beginning and continues with it at the film's end, substituting an Elizabeth Taylor role for a Brigitte Bardot one. The stereotypic constraints of military life are replaced with the stereotypic liberalities of academic life. But the point remains the same: Nora hasn't left her doll's house. What is on view for a '90's audience— women especially take note—is a woman full of passion and whim, a woman without self-restraint, a woman of cinematic billboard "unbridled passion!" who yet checks herself and returns to the family fold.

The latest avatar of the liberated woman rises out of the ashes of the '60s. But, under the guidance of this film, under the blue skies it arranges, if we go back to the '50s and focus the camera on a woman unpoliticized, a pre-'60s woman, a woman trying to make her marriage work and at the same time enjoy the delights that a working husband provides, we can see that women took a wrong turn in the '60s—just as the love of Forrest Gump's life did. Breaking out of this conservative overlay, however, is the frenetic desperation that Lange reveals in her performance—the outbursts of revolt, the wild blows against house arrest, the bitter and angry declarations of rebellion. It is as if she is fighting against the strait jacket of a plot that ensnares her performance, that she is unable to break through. But she tries and the attempt is exhilarating. This woman was meant to dance freely and no Tommy Lee Jones can grab her off the dance floor and carry her out kicking and screaming.

Wynona Ryder's performance in *Little Women* stops breath. It has all the virtues without the contraries—the virtues suppress the contraries. Thus, there is no life, neither in the film, nor in her performance. The sap has not run out of Jessica Lange's performance however. Virtue here cannot conceal the breathing, tension–filled life beneath. Nevertheless, *Blue Sky* clearly adheres to our new filmic politics of concealment, our new contract with ourselves and our past.

I want to consider the widely popular *Schindler's List* in this light and end this section with a view of what we are concealing— the "nightmares of depravity."

Notes

1. As I revise this piece in the fall of 1995, the Museum of Television and Radio is screening Dean's TV appearances, "James Dean on Television: A Myth in the Making."

2. Adam Mars-Jones, *The Independent;* Stanley Kauffman, "Fall Round-up," *New Republic,* November 16, 1992, p. 28.

3. Edward Luttwak, "Why Fascism is the Wave of the Future," *London Review of Books,* April 7, 1994, p.6.

4. See Bernard Weinraub, "Senator Moves to Front of Conservative Critics," *New York Times* June 1, 1995, A1.

5. See Alexander Cockburn and Ken Silverstein, "The Demands of Capital," *Harper's,* May 1995, 66–67.

6. Charles Murray and Richard J. Herrnstein, *The Bell Curve* New York: The Free Press, 1994. See the October 31, 1994 issue of *The New Republic* for an apologia by Murray and Herrnstein as well as a variety of responses to that apologia.

7. *Corporate Lives* New York: Van Nostrand, 1976.

8. See Michael Lind, *The Next American Nation: The New Nationalism and the Fourth American Revolution* New York: The Free Press, 1995.

9. See Louis Menand, "Keep CUNY Whole," *The New York Times* May 12, 1995, A19.

The Bottom Line of Schindler's List: The Player is a Savior

December 1993

I went to see Stephen Spielberg's *Schindler's List* after three *Village Voice* critics, Georgia Brown, Amy Taubin, and J. Hoberman, kept it off their list of the ten best movies of the year. I saw it after Terrence Rafferty in the *New Yorker* put it at the top of his list for all time great movies. At this moment, the film was in the "undecidable" category, like at least two of its contemporaries, *Philadelphia* and *Age of Innocence*. The word was out— Spielberg was taking on the Holocaust like a thrilling serial adventure of the '40s. The *other* thrilling Saturday matinee serials that held us spellbound, Spielberg had already resurrected spectacularly in the Indiana Jones films. The *Voice's* verdict— *Schindler* was strictly for the *goyim*.

As for *Philadelphia*, Michael Musto in the *Voice* was a voice crying in the wilderness. Sure, it wasn't a film that covered all the bases on AIDS, gays and the power-bloc, but it was more than Hollywood had given gays previously. *Philadelphia* was another message to the straights to wear a condom.

And *Age of Innocence?* Amy Taubin summed it up when commenting on her list of the best films of 1993: "I'll have to ponder this film for a couple of years." Here, the undecidability could be traced to the suspicion that Dan Quayle would probably have liked the film's display of family values. Newland Archer doesn't run away with the Countess, he stays home, puts his kids through school and so on. In another words, he and May are spitting images of Dan and Marilyn. Those of us who didn't think the film was about family values or had anything to do with Dan and Marilyn were nonetheless stopped cold by the suggestion of a Quayle approbation. It threw me headlong into undecidability.

I went into *Schindler's List* with this horizon of expectation— there was a chance that Spielberg had reduced the unreducible, the Holocaust, to a naive realist pattern. I had an eye out for this. Would there be, for instance, someone I could immediately identify with? Someone that would take me into the film? Someone I didn't at all mind being? Would there be a guiding discourse, implanted by Spielberg, that would enable me to sort things out? Even the unsortable things like an entire society giving itself over, mind, body and soul, to genocide, to the systematic, bureaucratized extermination of the Jews? Would the haunting problem of this sort of "state of mind" be solved?

Good guys and bad guys—an easy moral dualism—is not a problem here. Or is it? Why the urgency placed on not forgetting this particular Holocaust? The further we get from it in time, the more urgent its retrieval seems to be. We must keep its image in our minds lest we forget and repeat. But beyond this there is something that is peculiar to our postmodern moment and it is this—the Third Reich and its Final Solution engrave within history firm, non-intersecting categories of good and evil. They are discrete, fully determinate entities; a clear-cut dualism. No blurring on the edges, no forking onto each other's path. Never the twain shall meet. And if we in 1994 have forgotten what firm moral categories are, we need but recall the Third Reich and its Final Solution.

This is the first need of the present that I see the film serving. Part of my postmodern horizon of seeing any representation of the past made by the present is this—the past gets mediated by the stories of the present. What about an objective, disinterested historical retrieval, one with full foundational footnoting and extant letters and a warehouse full of documentation, all primary source material? Doesn't all this lead to the true, reliable representation of what went on back then? Of course it does. It leads to several true, reliable representations. Or, truth be told, an undisclosed number. Who does the looking, the sorting through, the selections? I mean a personal/cultural "who." Does timing matter? I mean the time and place this sorting through goes on—say, a review of Medgar Evers's murder: 1964 or 1994? Does the who, when and where narrate and mediate our representations of the past?

I have not yet seen the film but these already resident questions make me uneasy about historical "retrievals." I am in the theatre but they haven't run the film yet. I'm watching assorted commercial messages and quiz questions running on the screen, but I'm prepping for the film. Now the classic realist formula will always set up a clear-cut, easy moral dualism. The guy with the white hat and so on. But this clear-cut moral dualism has to be in this film about the Holocaust so its presence won't necessarily mean Spielberg is packaging the Holocaust for easy digestion. Or, am I really saying that in order for Spielberg to package the Holocaust for easy digestion, we must have an easy moral dualism? I perceive an urgency in this last decade of the millennium that has more to do with the future than the past. And that urgency is to reduce the Holocaust horror to something that will not shadow our gaze at the road ahead. We want a packaged version that we can connect to the Ascent of Man in such a way that we can continue ascending without fear that we might suddenly fork off—yet again—and use the Modernist Project to gas a certain projected number of people a day. Meet the quota so to speak, just as years later GM and Toyota would be battling it out over who would be able to meet an ever expanding quota. Worldwide cultural belief that a universal, objective, absolute Truth can be established has made us all gullible and therefore vulnerable. Just before mid-century that vulnerability was brought home to the entire world, but I think it is only now that postmodernity is observing the framing of that vulnerability—modernity.[1]

You must think I'm crazy to say so much about a film I haven't seen. But of course as I am writing this I have already seen the film and you will just have to believe me when I say that everything I have written so far was thought prior to seeing the film. The reviews, of course, mobilized me, but I am already in the world in a certain way, attend to the world in certain ways, and want to attend to this film in certain ways, so that my story doesn't have to wait for the film. I even suggest that the film is waiting for my story, my framing. Follow: I can only attend to it from within my way of attending to things. The film only comes through to me, hooks up with me, through my frame of realizing, my way of making sense of things, my way of seeing that produces that sense. It is not then ludicrous or inane to write about how I am going to, how I can, engage the film. Let me say that those who choose not to see the film, who are as aware of all the media fuss about the film as I am, have already, in effect, seen the film. How so? They have already gone through what I am going through now—running through their possible connections with the film, with the history the film attempts to represent, with Spielberg and his other films, with the commentary, with all the reasons we in the present resurrect this historical moment now.

And after seeing the film in this way, they choose not to see it. Of course, both those who choose to see it and those who choose not to see it are as much constructed already by the film as they are already constructing it. And this is so because film, world, viewer, and non-viewer intersect, interpenetrate. The film waits for me to see it, but both film and I have already met in stories in the world, stories that I live in and the film lives in. We've already seen each other before I take a seat in the theatre. Or, because of that same acquaintance, choose not to take a seat.

Let's resurrect the moral categories. You see, I think that *not* running a naive realist scam on good and evil is what is required in revisiting the Holocaust. I am not saying that the slaughter of six million Jews is not an evil act. Nor that Hitler does not incarnate evil. What I am saying is that linking that evil to his insanity and then, by implication, that insanity to aberration, to anomaly, to a break in the natural continuity of order and sanity in which good and evil are equal combatants, puts a veneer on things. It's a classic realist simplification, one that enabled George Bush to hook up Hussein with Hitler. Is the relationship between good and evil there in the Arab world, the Arab world and us, what it was in Hitler's Germany? Once Saddam, and the Ayatollah and Kadaffi and Arafat before him, are demonized— through the Hitler story, through a sort of Disneyland depiction of good and evil—then we can take sides. We can enveil ourselves in good guy regalia.

What in the flux of everyday Third Reich life enabled the Germans to see some good in this very great evil? In what way does the story of Final Solution dominate all the other stories at play in the culture? What enables reason, our much applauded cognitive faculties, to engage a problem-solving task, solve it and implement it efficiently *without thinking about everything we have thought about regarding the Holocaust for the past fifty years?* Unless the evil perpetrated already existed as a trace within not only the order of the German culture before Hitler but in the order of human nature, that order could not identify evil nor without the contrast could it itself have an identity.

There is doubtlessly then an imbrication of good and evil, a constant play of difference, that is itself brought into play within a culture. Since no culture is single-voiced nor does it concoct one reality and one truth, there is nothing but contesting of narratives, of realities, of voices here. It is this culture in motion that for a time and place connects with an identity of not only good but evil. That the Third Reich settled on a good that the rest of the world settled on as an evil, is perhaps an unfathomable signification of that culture. To extrapolate a universal pattern of good and evil out of this flux is to rob the Holocaust of its fateful uniqueness and set up an easy stereotype by which to becloud the nature of our lives, the societies we build, and our moral valuations.

At some point above—I don't know exactly where—I am writing out of a re-awakened exchange between myself and the Holocaust, out of a renewed consciousness that seeing the film created. I am seeing this matter differently than I have seen it before, and seeing the film has jarred me into this. Not *what* I have said but the fact that I have been led to bringing the Holocaust into the foreground of my present attentiveness to the world, my present way of attending to the world.

But from this emerges my dilemma. I want to praise the film for renewing a dialogue with the past but I see it as having been done in such a way as to gloss over and conceal what Zygmunt Baumann calls the tropes of the "other of order": undefinability, incoherence, incongruity, incompatibility, illogicality, irrationality, ambiguity, confusion, undecidability, ambivalence.[2] All the tensions wracking firm moral categories are concealed. Constructions of "good" and "evil" are distanced not only from themselves but from us in the present. We are seduced into believing that we are not only distant viewers of this horror but that distance, our viewing, asserts our control of that horror. We *know* it, in other words. And this is precisely what we cannot say, that we have either the naive realist's domination over all or the modernist's way of knowing it, a way of knowing that also leads to domination.

So the film raises the issue, you might say, and brings me to a new engagement but at the same time the film is trying to close down that engagement—to not only give us a determinate mapping of good and evil, a mapping that we can apply in the present, but also a means of vanquishing that evil in the future. What I call the politics of concealment are in play in regard to the unreliability of our moral discernment at the time, the imbrication of our after-the-event moral discernment with the present's moral priorities, and our capacity to justify any choice as moral. I would argue that to hide from ourselves these discernments is the present's need, a strongly felt need to regain a clear sense of good and evil, truth and falsehood, to bring undecidables to an open and impartial court of decision. To restore the dream. The naive realist formula is always trying to shape a template that can be superimposed on the present as well as the past and the future. It's an all-purpose device.

If De Niro's Max Cady in Scorcese's *Cape Fear* crosses over from the bad guy side to the good guy side by getting us to root for him and not for Nick Nolte, then the knee-jerk reaction is to dig the dividing trenches deeper, put up firmer demarcations so there won't be any crisscrossing.[3] Since the world without us is obviously not good or evil but these valuations are our own constructions, our own observations, there is no way that those constructions, our various linkages, can be separated from the culture or the individuals who do the observing. And the framing of reality from which these observations emerge will change. They have changed.

This means that neither "good" nor "evil" will stay in their respective places. As signifiers linked variously to the world, they may crisscross—share the same linkages but be given different signifiers. They may link up with the same chunk of the real on different occasions but be signified differently. Or, they may link up with different chunks of the real and be signified the same. So "good" and "evil" are floating signifiers waiting to be attached to the world. Unless we impose a universal template upon them.

I am suggesting that because any such template invariably leaves something out, diminishes the complexity of intersections and interpenetrations going on, that it is useful up to a point. In fact we live on a planet that has numerous such universal templates, all establishing fixed categories of everything. They do not mark their own intersections nor do they focus on what they leave unmarked. It is from this unmarked realm that the Holocaust comes. And Spielberg's film tries to mark it from the marked side. We are presently doing the same thing, on an individual scale, with Jeffrey Dahmer. And film critics are trying to put Hannibal Lecter back into his marked space, that cell emphatically separated from us.

Spielberg responds to the present cultural need to make good and evil stereotypic once again—as in the good old days when we could make decisions, like Harry Truman's to drop a bomb on civilians—by coming up with a present success formula. It's not my purpose to dwell on this, it's too disappointing. We get a market player—Oscar Gordon Gecko Schindler (you remember Gordon from *Wall Street*, the quintessential market player)—as savior. By doing what Reagan said every American should be doing—trying to get rich—Schindler naturally winds up saving over a thousand Jews. You might call it trickle down morality. The Third Reich stands abashed as Schindler tells them they are not to interfere with the flow of business. [The Third Reich, like the Feds, are trying as usual to intrude into the one thing that really counts—the maximization of profits.] They submit. Even the certified Nazi commandant who shoots prisoners before breakfast instead of going for an early round of golf submits to the logic here.

You know if there *really* had been some good market players like Garfield and Gecko back then and if the world had discovered that market logic displaced any Führer, why then Jews, gypsies, homosexuals and anarchists wouldn't have been exterminated but just given Mc Jobs. Or vouchers. The Jewish Holocaust remains a "nightmare of depravity", uncodified, irreducible—its reality overloading the circuits of conceivability, overspilling the clarities of its newest representation on film. We haven't plummeted to the depths of our own depravity, it's not a nightmare resolved or covered. It's not over. We have to return again and again. Every reality frame we drift into has to struggle against the deftness of its own re-presentation capacities and toward the imponderable conceivability of this nightmare.

But we now replace that nightmare with those identified by Bob Dole. Our culture it seems continues to have nightmares despite the fact that we are in the midst of "restoring the dream." Perhaps the fault lies in our politics of concealment that repress our own "nightmares of depravity," our "scenes from the abyss"? Perhaps what is dream restoration to some automatically becomes nightmare to others? What may be even more perfidious— perhaps the restoration of an American Dream for some can only be accomplished by plunging everyone else into nightmare.

Notes

1. See Zygmunt Bauman, *Modernity and the Holocaust.* Ithaca, N.Y.: Cornell University Press, 1989.

2. Zygmunt Bauman, *Modernity and Ambivalence.* Ithaca, N.Y.: Cornell University Press, 1991.

3. See "Moving Laterally Across the Capes of Fear," in J. Natoli, *Hauntings.* Albany: State University of New York Press, 1994, pp. 33–46.

Nightmares of Depravity

Summer 1995

"We have reached the point where our popular culture threatens to undermine our character as a nation."
Senator Bob Dole, in a speech in Los Angeles, May 31, 1995
"It's always easier for a Senator to blame fictional characters than to blame themselves for their inability to take guns off the streets and provide jobs for people."
Lara Berghold, quoted in the *New York Times*, "Dole Lashes Out at Hollywood," June 1, 1995, A10
"Hollywood in its presentation of violence and sex has no more to answer for than the Congress of the United States. The name of the game in the entertainment business is short-term profit. This is exactly what Congress is all about—how can we get re-elected in the short term and every other value be damned."
Norman Lear, quoted in *The New York Times*, June 1, 1995
"I'd like some objective opinion as to whether guns or lyrics are causing the kind of turmoil among America's youth that's tearing at the fabric of this country."
Michael Fuchs, ibid.

What Nightmare and Whose Is It?

In this summer of 1995, the 1996 presidential campaign is in its prepping stages: the family values agenda vs. . . . exactly what? In the last election, Dan Quayle had gone after *Murphy Brown,* a TV comedy whose morality, or lack there of, Quayle denounced. Presidential hopeful Bob Dole, in his bid to re-etch the family values agenda, moved to the fore front of conservative critics by lambasting Hollywood for producing "nightmares of depravity." He named names: *Natural Born Killers* and *True Romance.* Full of family values are *The Lion King, The Santa Clause, The Flintstones, Forrest Gump,* and Republican Arnold Schwarzenegger's *True Lies.*

"Nightmares of depravity" promote, in Dole's view, "casual violence and even more casual sex." Gangsta rap, as performed by groups like Cannibal Corpse, Geto Boys and 2 Live Crew, also give families with values nightmares, via "mindless violence and loveless sex." What's going on here in Dole's view is "an undermining of social values." On the other hand, what might be going on here is what Michael Lind has called the enactment of "allegorical conflicts" which hold out of sight the opposing agendas of those who have and those who don't. Behind the allegorical conflict of family values and nightmares of depravity lies the American dream: "every American who is not a maid or gardener might be able to afford one."[1] Family values, whose and whatever they might be, do not determine who will have a maid and who will be a maid. The "realities of business" do that—realities that Michael Fuchs, chairman of the Warner Music Group, claims Bob Dole is not paying attention to in his attack on gangsta rap.[2] But both Fuchs and Dole know their allegorical parts—Dole to pursue some other values beside the reigning "All for ourselves and nothing for other people," and Fuchs to wait out the headlines and the election.

In actuality, "other people," meaning those without maids and gardeners, *are* dreaming of having maids and gardeners. The whole country is complicit here in this allegorical conflict over family values and nightmares of depravity. It's not just the oligarchic elite who need a fronting alibi like family values. The salaried non-elite want to win it all for themselves and let the chips fall for others as they may. But they, too, need a protective shield, need to be involved in an allegorical conflict, a moral drama played out in public, in the headlines, in which they are cast as morally indignant. Their moral fabric is being torn apart while the whole nation's character is being undermined. And so on. All of it the work of popular culture.[3]

Can you be moral and still socially mobile? Dole holds out the wiser choice in regard to morality—you can be morally indignant, which will suffice. But can you go from being the maid to having a maid? Or, is that possibility already preempted by the fact that in this country our real morality is "all for me and nothing for anyone else" and the "all" has already been allocated to those, like us, who have "all" simply because they share nothing with anyone else?[4] Put bluntly, in order *not* to be the gardener, you have to buck the person already paying you *to be* the gardener. The "quality of life" and "well-being" of those already living well would be diminished if their gardeners quit, if real work could not be bought by nominal work. By nominal work I mean the work of money itself, its buying, selling, exchange, investment, floating, lending, laundering, brokering and so on. Our post-Fordist or post-classical climate combining investment capital, electronic financing, and transnational goals adds up to a very high–stakes poker game where only a few can afford to sit in. Now this is a nightmare some eighty percent of the country is having.[5]

The idea that "income inequalities arise from the independent actions of individuals with different skills and assets who are rewarded according to what consumers and producers are prepared to pay" is itself an entrepreneurially packaged idea.[6] It focuses attention on "justly earned rewards" and defensible determinations of winners and losers. And not on chance. Academic discourse, in the form of Charles Murray and Richard Herrnstein's *The Bell Curve,* comes along to give a "rational explanation" as to why the lines drawn between rich and poor are also racial lines.[7] There exists, in the authors' opinion, racial differences in intelligence. Besides this "enlightened" view of intelligence and race as an arbiter of success and therefore class, we also have a lot of talk at the moment about assuming personal responsibility, the implication being that the well-off are responsible folks while everyone else is seeking—from off-handedly to desperately—someone to blame for their lot in life.

Enter contingency. Chance. Accident. Fortuity. The goddess Fortuna. The nemesis of Enlightenment thinking; the one presence in life that has put the angst in twentieth century modernism. "Bad luck does exist" Michael Kingsley admits.[8] And so too does good luck. But first contingency has to be admitted. Whether it's good or bad depends on the p.o.v., itself wrapped up in a life at a particular time in a culture at a particular time. This contingency is not to be confused with anomaly, the odd bit in the otherwise orderly course of things. Rather, it is *in* the courseway, the very reason we are endlessly mapping the world. And we do so as if we could map out the play of disorder. That disorder not only affects our lives, but it provides the only "logic"—the non-logic of contingency—to the global market's present determination of winners and losers. Everywhere else but in market matters do we set up some defensive structure between ourselves and the pure play of contingency. And since we construct reality through the play of order and disorder, through what we can represent and what remains inconceivable to us, our play at the market roulette wheel is, in effect, an abrogation of our role in the creation of our lives and our world.

In speaking of a "paradigm shift" in the organization of our present economic life, Nigel Dodd describes the way in which a sort of financial play strictly on the level of the signifier generates wealth and has replaced both investment and production:

> This alleged paradigm shift has also been associated with a massive expansion of international monetary and financial networks . . . This has arguably led to a more volatile international economic environment, with the volume of cross-border monetary transactions increasing at a faster rate than the transfer of raw materials and manufactured goods . . . Advances in telecomunication have meant that the sheer speed of the transmission of information between financial centres acts to closely (and instantly) co-ordinate price and purchasing fluctuations between them. Both the sheer quantity of money caught up in international financial networks and the synchronicity of transactions within them have enhanced opportunities to make money not through investment as such but on the basis of continuously shifting prices. This has led to postmodern commentators such as Harvey to suggest that 'the financial system has acquired a degree of autonomy from real production unprecedented in capitalism's history, carrying capitalism into an equally unprecedented era of financial dangers.'[9]

The manner in which our arbiters of values are made has precious little to do with talent, intelligence, skills, a superior moral sensibility, a honed sense of personal responsibility and all the rest. We live in an economic climate in which access to wealth is being increasingly denied those who do not already have it, regardless of how much intelligence and energy they possess. A globalized computerized networking of finances—"a three-layered sandwich of digital information systems that form a net over the globe "—has set the wealthy up to skim the cream from the top of any efforts of invention, production, and, indeed, investment.[10] At this level of what MacKenzie Wark calls "virtual geography"—where the economy appears to us only through computer imaging—real wealth is nonetheless accrued. And that wealth cannot trickle down to any noticeable degree because wealth itself is one's only access to this economic virtual geography. What *is* a "nightmare of depravity" and who's really having it, and what is *the* American Dream and who's really defining it are questions a different sort of paradigm shift—a postmodern cultural paradigm shift—are raising.

All of this renders any efforts to define family values or nightmares of depravity beside the point—they're distracting and meant to be. They substitute a narrative frame in sway—call it the oligarchic frame—with one that isn't—call it the nightmares of depravity frame. How questions are answered, dilemmas defined and resolved, nightmares shaped, and family values construed depends on what reality frame you adopt. Look at the question of casual violence and even more casual sex, or, in regard to gangsta rap, "mindless violence and loveless sex."[11] If a film or a song were concocting these and they did not already exist in the society, would that society have the means or interest in connecting with them? Could they respond to what did not already exist in the world? And, if they already do exist in our world, shouldn't our attention be directed both to their reflection in film and rap *and* to their existence in the society? Our cultural battles, especially the deep, dark, haunting ones, are grist for our films and popular music. Undistracted by one nightmare, we may yet be having another. We might direct our gaze elsewhere, perhaps to a correlation between increasing poverty in a society and violence in that society. Is our violence "mindless" and "casual" or is it the by-product of the unrelenting efforts of the global rich to have and to hold by taking more and more from everyone else?

It is hardly surprising that, in a culture working hard to link personal identity with consumption, people will enact this connection by any means, fair or foul. Denied the "fair," or legal means, they remain supersaturated with desires of possession. Frustrated, with violence looming, an anger sets in that is itself without mind. The culture provides only a comparatively weak resistance to the "all for ourselves and nothing for other people" narrative—a narrative that, as I say, has ironically been adopted by the "other people." That undiagnosed anger—unobserved, as Henry James would say, in its broadest context—is there to be directed, to be given a "mind." In point of fact, there is much danger, globally, if mindless anger and violence wander toward the "realities of business." Under this light, we are all distracted to the staging of nightmares of depravity.

That staging has not totally mesmerized the paramilitary nationalists—a matter I consider in "Looking into the Abyss: Madmen
and Fanatics." Their attention is wandering. It is quite clear after
the Oklahoma bombing that the hoped for connection between
family values and violence, between a dominating Christian
morality as defined by those who can market morality in a
market-safe way, is breaking down in the heartland.[12] After all,
political control has been won through appeals to racism, sexism, homophobia, xenophobia, chauvinism, religious intolerance, ethnic rivalry, welfare bashing and the like. A heartland
constituency which sold such products for the last twenty-five
years in a postmodern media, advertising, and campaigning blitz
can hardly be expected to instantly "gumpify." That film-long
clash between the mindless Gump and the angry, explosive Gary
Sinese parallels a battle going on in the culture. And off-screen
the angry and explosive haven't been defused by whatever amor-
phous, unexpressed values Gump is supposed to represent.
What we're throwing at the raging heartland now is everything
we can market: Pat Robertson and his Christian Coalition on his
TV show, *The 700 Club;* Forest Gump and a whole range of movie
tie-ins; all manner of police in action TV shows in which we are
repeatedly being protected from Rodney King; and now Bob Dole
in a campaign speech against Hollywood's nightmares of depravity. Let's call this a discourse of distraction. It's important
because without it, other efforts, direct and immediate such as
more prison building, determinate sentencing (no paroles), capital punishment *and* for more and more crimes, extended FBI
powers etc., would be vulnerable to counter–discourses.

I have no doubt that there are many who do not see this discourse of distraction as distracting, nor do they see themselves
engaged in an allegorical conflict. If we could get back to family
values, the mindless violence and casual sex would end on the
screen and in our music. We wouldn't be tempted to be mind-
lessly violent or casually sexual. The whole family values thing,
which promises to be very big in the upcoming 1996 Presidential
election, is the elite's sop to their own conscience. Intertwined
with this is their concern for the conscience and behavior of the
new and expanding underclass, (thanks to recruits drafted from
the middle class.) Without a moral conscience, these people are
a potential threat. They can hurt you and your property. They
can be a drain on corporate profits, if those in Washington attempt to retain some semblance of egalitarianism through a va-

riety of taxations which reverse the trend of regressive taxation. The "Contract with America" is not designed to reverse this trend: "In the version of the "Contract with America" legislation first passed by the House, two thirds of the spending cuts would come from programs for low-income families, while roughly half the money from the cuts would go to the wealthiest ten percent of American households. Fully one fifth of the savings go to the wealthiest one percent of families."[13]

At the heart of the "Contract with America" is sex and violence—sex and violence propel that "Contract" forward. We have a national debt because for too long we have given handouts to people unwilling to work, unwilling to get out of the wagon and help the rest of us push. And those people live lives lost in mindless violence and casual sex. They endanger the rest of us through their violence and through their overpopulation of the planet. Deficit reduction is just another front for another program of reduction. We want to reduce the underclass to invisibility—push them from *our* state to someone else's, push them across the border, into extinction. Only those willing to be brainwashed on the likes of *Forrest Gump, The Flintstones,* and *The Santa Clause* will be hired as gardeners and maids. The discourse of distraction is also a discourse of recuperation, of "restoring the dream." And, not surprisingly, we turn to film to see how it works, this passage from nightmare to morality.

Searching for Nightmares

I search the new releases section of my local video stores for signs of gumpified films, films exuding family values. More precisely, those designed to capitalize on family values but in the ways of our current postmodern culture, not of the culture that produced *Boys' Town,* (Newt Gingrich's favorite film because it serves an ideological purpose he has at this moment.) To grasp the America that the *Contract with America* wants to return us to, one has to ferret out the cultural lode the old Spenser Tracy and Mickey Rooney film bears. It involves a different kind of recuperation than what we see, for instance, in a contemporary bid at family values like *Milk Money.* Father Flannagan's world was built on faith, hope and charity. Who administers this investment portfolio today? Boys' Town would have been built today if the good Father found a lender who saw a short-term profit in the deal. Or, Fr. Flanagan could send some grant proposals to private philanthropic foundations. And not hold his breath. Mickey Rooney in this film is a street kid, but he can be redeemed. There was little fear in the culture that one might not be better off, be better educated, and have more leisure time than one's parents. Mobility and progress were not reserved for transnational corporations.[14] They could be experienced by individuals. Where is the Detroit Boys' Town? The East L.A. and South Central Boys' Towns? We're all white in Newt's Boys' Town—kids may have gotten on the wrong road but all the roads are in the same reality garden. There's no nightmare here. It was out there but it didn't reach the screen. Its presence was inconceivable.

So I continue to search for the representation of this Conservative discourse of recuperation, of nightmares of depravity obliterated by family values. I wind up with three hopefuls. Besides *Milk Money*, directed by the talented Richard Benjamin, I take *Dolores Claiborne*, (written by Stephen King), and *Safe Passage*, (with Sam Shepard once again a Dad and Susan Sarandon the Mom.)

Safe Passage is most obviously a family values film. But Mom smokes pot (once) and knocks back Tequila (once). And Susan Sarandon is back playing her *Thelma and Louise* wife but this time she has seven boys and she's thrown her husband, Sam Shepard, out of the house. Now it's her turn to have a life. Her turn to have a life? Don't women find fulfillment through being wives and mothers, and, of course, entrepreneurs as long as they manage to fulfill the other obligations? Our safe passage to redeemed family values is threatened here. It seems as if she wants the kind of life Murphy Brown has and *that* life incited Dan Quayle's wrath. She wants to be a single parent, pass her civil service exam, sell the family house, move and get a full–time job as a social worker. As much as she yearns to begin her own life with an identity not synonomous with "wife" or "mother" ("I didn't stop cutting somebody's meat at dinner until I was thirty-five"), she can't stop identifying herself as the mother of seven boys. What she wants to be over—her mothering instinct—lingers. Why? According to the film, because it is innate. What about Sam? Can't he mother? Can't he do "housewife" chores? In response to his wife's criticism that for twenty years he has thrown his tea bags in the sink and left them there for her to put in the garbage, he says "Where *is* the garbage?" Later in the film, Sam flings another tea bag nonchalently into the sink. His role is obviously equally innate. No one here is guilty of constructing the reality they live in. That reality—including the nature of wives and husbands—is outside and beyond human constructedness. This seems foundational. You can't have family values unless you accept the fact that values are outside your control, non-volitional. They're in the nature of things, root causes, objective determinants, natural, biological, substratum, in the blood and gene actualities. They are therefore absolute and universal.

Rather than make an attempt at resolving the dilemma—of exactly how do women get a life in this culture beyond that of a life that satisfies a societal function and a biological imperative—the film sets up a plot distraction. When that is accomplished—was one of her boys killed in an explosion in the middle east?—the family bonds, Mom and family embracing in the final scene. Family crises require Mom's attention—from an angry dog on a child's paper route to a son missing in action—drawing her into ministering to their lives and forgetting about her own. Therein lies the message, the family value to be emulated. Mothers should be selfless; family first, personal life last. She remains a functionary, a second class human being in her own home.

Because Susan Sarandon takes her Mom motivation here from her *Thelma and Louise* role, she exudes an anger for which the film ultimately denies her any justification. What we wind up with is a middle–aged mom and wife who is angry, abrupt, impatient and just not fun. Her discontent is denied any credibility. She is innately bitchy, a sort of menopausal bitch. Because it is not Sam the father who is in revolt, he is far more content with this reality that has not made a revolutionary of him. In a scene at the table when father and boys are having fun, Mom casts a cold and censorious eye. We get the sense that regardless of what reason she gives for interrupting their levity, here is a woman angry at her exclusion. She can't join in. Not only because she is thinking of the plight of her missing son, but because she's driven to turning away from all this in order to start living her own life. Is her discontent the result of her wanting more than her nature allows her, or is she merely showing the signs of having bent too long to an unaccommodating construction of her nature? And because the film opts for a safe passage rather than tackling the dark, turbulent waters of constructing a non-elitist identity for women in our culture, it is also menopausal. It dries up the juices that are flowing out there. Astoundingly, this film's *bete noire* is a vicious dog and in their second tryst, Mother wrestles the dog to the ground and is about to kill him when her son calls her off. What are these carefully set and mounted scenes supposed to mean? My guess is that in a film in which Mother/Sarandon/Thelma anger can go nowhere—not even off a cliff—some totem of anger, struggle, victory and release is yet required. She *has* to bite someone but in effect this becomes a film in search of a dog to bite.

Not so with *Dolores Claiborne,* a film playing in a recent re-run theatre out on Route 69 on a night so hot you can't sit without sweating. I go for the air-conditioned, cool darkness. The film too is cool darkness. You might say that everybody in this film has already been bitten by a rabid dog but all you see are the effects, everything else is a mystery. The thing is to go back and see how it happened. It's a film about family life: a wife who doesn't divorce, a daughter who knows how to repress, a father at the center. This is the traditional family of heterosexual union; both the male and the female representation of the social order of things is to be passed on to their offspring. Murphy Brown by herself is an unreliable and inefficient societal surrogate. Why? Perhaps she lacks authority. Perhaps she knows more about living under someone else's authority than she knows about acting with authority.

The bedrock premise of Ralph Reed's "Contract With the American Family" is that family values do not emerge from the single parent family. Or from homosexual, lesbian and bisexual families. What they need to grow is a proper patriarchal family—mother in the kitchen, father at work and kids in school. This family goes to church on Sunday, preferably a Church that believes in the birth, death and resurrection of Jesus Christ. This family watches the Family Channel where a firm sense of good and evil, just and unjust, sane and insane, proper and improper, orderly and disorderly is transmitted through such vehicles as *I Dream of Jeannie, The Partridge Family, Eight is Enough, The Brady Bunch, The Donna Reed Show, Leave It To Beaver, The Dick Van Dyke Show, The Mary Tyler Moore Show.* It seems as if for young minds to be kept pure and safe in the last decade of the twentieth century they have to be fed a steady diet of mid-century TV fare. Now my intention is to take a look at the dark side of all this in the film *Dolores Claiborne,* which makes no pretense, as does *Milk Money,* to turn dark edges into light comedy. But first I want to follow an intersecting path here: if we construct the reality that constructs us, why can't we re-contruct the old '50s values by following something like Ralph Reed's "Contract With the American Family?"

Launching a Balloon

I myself was brought up in the '50s and regularly watched *Ozzie and Harriet, Lassie, I Love Lucy, Phil Silvers, Our Miss Brooks, The Life of Riley, My Little Margie, I Remember Mama, Father Knows Best*, and a host of westerns from *Maverick* and *Cheyenne* to *Gunsmoke*. I've had this foundation of '50s TV fare and have now a postmodern attitude, what is frequently called an anti-foundationalist attitude. But how am I to know if my having been brought up on '50s TV fare is not a *sine qua non* for the development of a postmodern attitude? Really, I have no way of knowing. It may be that one journeys to postmodernity through the sort of foundation that '50s TV fare provides, one full of clear-cut, determinate family values. The larger question frequently asked is does postmodernity rely on modernity? Is postmodernity a realization that only comes through a full confrontation with and realization of Habermas's modernist project? What would a postmodern attitude that knew nothing about modernity, in both its Enlightenment and twentieth century modernist modes, be like?

I suspect that even though we are force feeding young '90s minds '50s fare and values, they automatically convert the '50s program into a '90s program—rather like the way Wordperfect 6.1 will automatically convert Wordperfect 5.1. This could only happen if the contesting attitudes of the postmodern '90s were already in the air we breathe, the voices we hear, the language we use. Even children kept in a very strict notion of what family values are will have the whole culture around them signifiying and vibrating with different meanings and values. Whether that carnival of meanings and values can be cut back, cut short, wrapped up and put out of sight is a question that only a perusal of history can answer. What is suppressed at one point, pops up at another; what is repressed at one time, haunts a future time.

The answer then to my own question regarding Reed's contract is this: we construct amid other, challenging constructions that make up our cultural morass. Our cultural reality and realizing is growing more and more labyrinthine, truly Borgesian; and our social order, as if in response, is intent on repaving the

Golden Road to the Truth. Reality is neither constructed on one side of the path nor on any one path but in the daily crisscrossing flux of all the narrative balloons we are currently launching.

"Sometimes the Only Thing Left for a Woman Is to Be a Bitch"

Back to *Dolores Claiborne*. We begin with a death. Is it an accident or a murder? Later, we are with Dolores' daughter, Selena, who desperately needs to be given an important magazine assignment in Arizona. There's a book in it. You don't understand she tells her editor: "I need this." Dark shadows under her eyes, face too pale, running forward to the next assignment, running from something. There is no love between mother and daughter—it's been fifteen years since Selena has been to this Maine island to see her mother. She comes with a purse full of pills and drinks Scotch until it fails her. And then she takes her pills. She'll be an entirely new person in ten minutes. Give her ten goddamn minutes.

There is no key to Selena in the present. She has little to say; her hard, witty edge seems a holdover from Jennifer Jason Leigh's portrayal of Dororthy Parker. It's clear she's learned to smoke and drink in a dark mood from that film. But it serves—both are haunted. It's not just a matter of flashback device—the matter of time crisscrossing here is ontological. This is the way we have our being in the world: moving in and out of present, past and future significations, hooking up with what we see in the present in the light of what it was and meant before or what it propels us toward in the future. But there is no future in this film, not for Selena or for Dolores. And why that is so serves to break the back of our contract with the American family. Simply put, this film shows us you can not only *not* proceduralize and legislate any kind of values, but you can't locate a master framework that can reliably sponsor a universal set of values, family, individual or societal.

The reason why Selena is not inhabiting a four dimensionsal universe is because the past has been blocked off for her, the present is therefore groundless and the future is something she can't get on her own. She needs to get the assignment: "You can be in the future." She doesn't get it. Right at the moment she is prepared to leave her mother to face the charges of murder that are sure to come, she is told by her editor that someone else has been given the story. The future, therefore, is now also blocked. So she remains on the island and drinks and does her pills. But her mother must bring up the past for her sake; because she knows Selena is stalled somewhere out of time, out of her own life. The past that is replayed in a variety of scenes has never past, not even for Selena who cannot see it but nevertheless has never really left it. And when she does see herself in the past, she sees what she ran from seeing: her father molesting her. The film has no mercy on the father: drunk, wife beater, child molester, thief, tormentor. What if the patriarchal center is rotten? Then there must be some distribution of power in the family so that that tyranny can de displaced. Is there any sign of this in this family?

Yes, there is, but as every woman in this film attests "Sometimes the only thing left for a woman to be is a bitch." In the very first reunion scene between mother and daughter, Dolores tells Selena this. But later on as past intersects present, we find out where Dolores has learned this bit of wisdom. Vera, her patrician employer, has appraised the power situation between men and women and adopted a surviving attitude. To be a bitch is to accept the assessment of empowered males. There can be no conversations between those with power and those without, as Foucault reminds us. To act and speak *as if* you expected to be treated equally is to earn the epithet "bitch." When Dolores tells Vera that her husband has been molesting Selena, Vera advises her to retaliate, to arrange an accident for her husband. Men have all the power, Vera tells Dolores, and we must be ruthless and clever to survive. She herself has arranged for her own husband's "accidental" death.

So there is a displacing power but it is that of the oppressed and suppressed in the face of a power that in every way diminishes them. Rush Limbaugh's "femi-nazis" then are, in the view of this film, not the destroyers of family values but the proponents of equality in all unions, heterosexual, lesbian, homosexual, bisexual. If family values are linked with hierarchy, as are all formulations from the Enlightenment onward, then they may benefit a society seeking to impose a strict hierarchy of values and meanings. However, that hierarchical society, like the individuals brought up within it, has in essence given up the struggle for values and meanings which is growth for both individual and society. Fortunately, cultures are most active when social orders are most insistently constraining.

Milk Money

Disney films, TV family sit-coms, and *Saturday Evening Post* and cereal box illustrations by Norman Rockwell have for the most part constructed our present reality linkage with the word "family." Out of that construction comes our sense of "family values." Juvenile delinquents, (as in *Blackboard Jungle,*) and teenage rebels, (as in *Rebel Without A Cause,*) didn't upset the image, they simply confirmed it. This was what happens when family values deteriorate. Afterall, '50s rebellion was contained within a white middle-class reality frame. Once African-American filmmakers and rap artists began to tell their story, now followed by Chicano filmmakers, Asian-American and women filmmakers who all began to unravel their Disney assignments, and gays began to openly express the difference they could make in family life, it became clear that it is not just the rules of the game that are being challenged but the nature of the game itself. Can a society maintain a stability necessary to do business if its values and meanings emerge from incommensurable reality frames? I don't believe any social order of things wants to engage in this experiment.

The answer lies in offering a bridge from one reality frame to another. Money is the answer, entrepreneurship is the way to riches. We can bring the outsiders back into the Disney frame of family values—the foundation for future social values—if we get them back into the white middle–class. Since of course we are now severely divided between rich and poor and that middle–class is diminishing, and the entire country is "browning," this bridging of realities seems impossible. The point, however, is to make it appear possible. The idea of mobility is as much a fabrication as is the idea of the American traditional family. Mobility is to be represented as real, and in a postmodern world in which our lives are lived within representations of reality and not reality itself, within a symbolically mediated buffer zone, we must necessarily attend to our signifying, mediating ways.

Thus, while *Dolores Claiborne* is a film marking the fallibility of our faith in family life, *Milk Money* is a film trying to build a bridge between those who for one reason or another have strayed out of the family where fathers knows best, Lassie followed us to school, and Mrs. Cleaver (with a fresh smock), greeted us—the Brady Bunch—with a peck on the cheek and dinner on the table. How do we make the family whole again, bring everyone back to their proper roles? The *Milk Money* family is not whole. We have a father and a son but no mother. There was a mother but she didn't run away or divorce: she died giving birth to the son. Having only a Dad has taught the son a lot of responsibility: he puts the coffee on in the morning, nukes the TV dinners, and does the wash. Dad is distracted with a wetlands project: he wants to save it. No one seems to be experiencing the ill effects of single parenting. But the son wonders what it would like to have a mother. Enter Melanie Griffith—who is a prostitute on the run from murder and mayhem, running in fact from the margins to the center, from life on the streets to the Brady Bunch household. "Nothing bad ever happens to the Brady Bunch" she says, deciding to hide from her underworld pursuers here in the yuppie suburbs. And yuppie it is: just like on TV, Melanie says but this is not Roseanne's working class neighborhood or Riley's. It's the American Dream neighborhood: large houses with ample lawns set well back from the street, jogging neighbors, kids off to ballet school, dogs being walked, hired clowns at birthday parties. But this is not just the suburbs. This is actually a small town because Melanie wanders into it and it might very well be Main Street Disneyland, small town America resurrected. She walks this street looking to make some travelling money but is immediately detoured by the son. He thinks she looks like Grace Kelly, a woman who married a prince and became a princess. Now Melanie has a photo of Grace Kelly in her apartment because she's already into the princess story. And Dad, Ed Harris, has raised his son on a story about his Mom having looked like Grace Kelly. "I don't look like Grace Kelly and she doesn't look like her either," Melanie says when she finally sees a photo of the dead Mom. It doesn't matter. The Grace Kelly story and world exists for them, specially tailored. The fact that Princess Grace died under very suspicious circumstances—an ending that threatens to deconstruct the entire fairy tale of her life—is not part of the hyperreal Grace being worked up here.

Dad is dazzled by both the Grace Kelly story and by Melanie Griffith. Melanie is dazzled by the fairytale life here outside the dark, sinful city. Once the pure and sweet life is seen, it makes those on the margins want to be part of it. The desire to leave one

world and enter another is there. One of the paths to instant social mobility has always been marriage. If a hooker marries a rich
man, say, as in *Pretty Woman*, she immediately jumps into a
world where all the family values the religious right wants to in-
culcate become "reality fostering." These sorts of values enable
one to hold on to what one has; they are the values you want others to have so that they will respect your right to have what you
do have. Thus, those living comfortable lives in yuppie havens
have to export their family values or there will be no constraints
placed on those living worse off to improve their own lot by any
means necessary. Put blankly, those living well cannot afford to
stay out of the private and family lives of those not living well.

But marriage as the road to success is not something a
culture on the boil with feminism and deep interrogations of
sexuality can adopt as a policy of social mobility. And yet
the marriage of Robert Reich-ian "symbolic analyst" to another
"symbolic analyst" has created a meritocracy elite whose well-
to-do status connects them to an entrepreneurial mindset.
Christopher Lasch, in his last book, *The Revolt of the Elites*,
points to "assortative mating" as the most frequently used access
to elite status: one professional marries another.[15] There is something foundationally undemocratic in this plan to create symbolic analysts who will then intermarry so they can be wealthy
enough to have an identity in an entrepreneurially–run society
that disenfranchises everyone who isn't wealthy. This sounds
like a social experiment conducted by Dr. Victor Frankenstein.
What goes down better than social engineering in regard to social mobility is the crap shoot of the market. Thus, the road to
mobility lies in entrepreneurship, which is of course a story we
were prepared for. Melanie literally gets her hands on a whole bag
full of money, buys the wetlands for Ed, a new car for herself and
a business . . . right on Main Street U.S.A. And will she marry Ed
and become the kid's mom? That's a choice she may or may not
make, now that she has earned her new social station in life herself. Now that she has *more* than milk money, she doesn't have
to marry. She doesn't have to have a family. Maybe she'll forget
the money is supposed to be just for milk and nothing else. That's
the problem with money and values, including democratic, egalitarian values; there's no real tie. Indeed, as post-Fordist, post-
classical America is discovering, one obviates the need for having
the other. And that's the very reason our society is mobilized to
conceal that disconnection.

Notes

1. Michael Lind, "To Have and Have Not," *Harper's* June 1995, p. 43.

2. Mark Landler, "Coalition is Taking on Time Warner Over Gangsta Rap," *New York Times* June 1, 1995, A10.

3. See Bernard Weinraub, "Senator Moves to Front of Conservative Critics," *New York Times,* June 1, 1995, A1.

4. Lind, "To Have and Have Not," traces this "all for me" attitude, an attitude Christopher Lasch described in his final book, *The Revolt of the Elites and the Betrayal of Democracy* W.W. Norton, 1995; see also Peter F. Drucker, "The Age of Social Transformation," *Atlantic Monthly,* Nov. 1994.

5. See John McDermott, "And the Poor Get Poorer," *The Nation* November 14, 1994, pp. 576–580; "Slicing the Cake," *The Economist* November 5, 1994, and especially Michael Lind's *The Next American Nation,* New York: Free Press, 1995.

6. "Inequality," *The Economist* Nov. 5, 1994, p. 19.

7. Charles Murray and Richard J. Herrnstein, *The Bell Curve* New York: The Free Press, 1994,

8. Michael Kingsley, "The Ultimate Block Grant," *The New Yorker* May 29, 1995, p. 38.

9. Nigel Dodd, "Whither Mammon? Postmodern Economics and Passive Enrichment," *Theory, Culture & Society* v. 12 (1995), 1–2. The David Harvey quotation is from *The Condition of Postmodernity* Oxford: Basil Blackwell, 1989, p. 194.

10. McKenzie Wark, *Virtual Geography: Living With Global Media Events* Bloomington: Indiana University Press, p. 205.

11. Bernard Weinraub, "Dole Lashes Out at Hollywood for Undermining Social Values," *New York Times* June 1, 1995, A1.

12. For a good look at the "politics of sin," see C. Carr, "The Politics of Sin: Christian and Secular Conservatives Unite to Wage a Virtue Crusade," *Village Voice* May 16, 1995, pp. 26–30.

13. Lind, "To Have and Have Not," p. 38.

14. For a succinct view of the power of transnationals, see Richard J. Barnet, "Lords of the Global Economy," *The Nation* December 19, 1994, 754–756.

15. Christopher Lasch, *The Revolt of the Elites and the Betrayal of Democracy* New York: W. W. Norton, 1995.

Now, That's an Alien!': Expanding the Repertoire of Alternative Descriptions

October 1994

"The first ethical principle to which poststructuralism is committed is that practices of representing others to themselves—either in who they are or in what they want—ought, as much as possible, to be avoided."

"The poststructuralists' commitment to a principle of anti-representation is bound to their commitment to another ethical principle: that alternative practices, all things being equal, ought to be allowed to flourish and even to be promoted."

Todd May, *The Political Philosophy of Poststructuralist Anarchism*

"*Ed Wood* has a certain outré allure, but, like its hero, it's all dressed up with no place to go."

Terrence Rafferty, *New Yorker*

As Bill Murray settles into his role as Bunny Breckenridge playing the role of the alien brain behind a plot to resurrect the Earth's dead and turn them against the world, Johnny Depp, playing the film's writer and director, Ed Wood, in the film *Ed Wood*, written and directed by Tim Burton, remarks: "Now, that's an alien!" The film that Johnny Depp as Ed Wood is shooting is a film released in 1958 titled *Plan 9 From Outer Space,* referred to up until now only as the worst film ever made. I say up until now because after the big rush to put all Ed Wood's films into video-cassette format, the entire Ed Wood repertoire will have gone postmodern—no one will be able to see *Plan 9* on a simple walk-in level. The film has gone duplex. Tim Burton's film focus on a certain period in Ed's life and on Ed's film and filming shadows our present viewing of an Ed Wood film. His films go holographic in a way with their own ineptness reappearing under the focus of

Burton's laser beam as only part of a multi-dimensionality that we now see. *Plan 9,* for instance, can no longer be the worst film ever made because now Ed Wood's attempt to put visuals together is no longer alien. The alien, so to speak, has become conceivable to us. What was a disjointed, inept mess before is now assisted by a narrative of representative connectiveness that we can provide. We can provide it because we have been at play with Burton's film; we ourselves have connected Wood's signifiers of "worstness" into emerging, palpable signifieds. We're beginning to put a face to a witness's description. Here we have two witnesses: Ed Wood and Tim Burton. And two descriptions: all of Ed Wood's films and all of Tim Burton's. What was alien to us before is coming into focus, coming to form in the mind as something.

Indictments of "worstness" testify to a total absence of connection. Here, we are saying, is where I fail utterly to connect. At the same time, we can say: "I have extensive textual evidence to prove why no one can hook up with this film." From where I am, it is an easy matter to see what connects with where I am, with what therefore makes sense. "Eptitude" can only come out of a fulfillment of an order of aptness. When we can achieve what Richard Rorty calls "The One Right Description" we also know how and when that Right Description is not being achieved. We also are under no obligation to develop "an expanding repertoire of alternative descriptions." What I mean then by "emerging, palpable signifieds" is that Burton's film cracks the One Right Description mindset and brings us back into the drama of conceivability and representation.

Here in a capsule is the One Right Description mindset: we are only interested in representing what is already conceivable to us. The "alien" is what is denied conceivability; its representations have no existence for us, or at best, connect with the obverse of our own notions of connectedness and meaning. The play or drama of conceivability and representation that we reenter is an open-ended process. We are no longer totally in the closed confines of the One Right Description.

Plan 9 From Outer Space doesn't become the "best" film or even a good film, nor does it ever totally escape the verdict of being the worst film ever made. However, caught now within the parody and pastiche of Burton's film, *Ed Wood,* all of Ed Wood's films can be viewed in a way in which those verdicts seem beside the point. In fact, we begin to see that Ed Wood's films are all about rendering verdicts, making distinctions, capturing the essence of anything, including human identity, the cruelties of winnowing out the *dreck* from the sublime, the pain and suffering of the victims from the possessors of the One Right Description.

Burton's film, in other words, brings Ed Woods's films into the play of our own present in which "cultural miscegenation" can only see those films as struggling to "expand the repertoire of alternative descriptions." Of what? Of us, our hybridized multi-cultures, and the multiple realities they engender.

Edward D. Wood, Jr. was a man of vision after all: he had a vision in which he and all his cockamamie friends were doing "good work." All he wanted to do was tell the stories that were in him to tell, stories that he knew would entertain. That he was so confident that the cockamamie stories he brought to the screen would entertain and bring him acclaim is the very heart of his vision. He literally sees what we do not see. He believes when we do not believe. He conceives what we do not conceive. And, finally, he represents in his films the sum total of this alien vision.

A character in *Plan 9 From Outer Space* says: "There comes a time in every man's life when he just can't believe his eyes!" John Walker in the latest *Halliwell Film Guide* quotes this line as one justifying the "worst film ever made" tag. It just may be. A sort of cliché made cockeyed in the inimitable Ed Wood's way. And yet Ed Wood can point to Bunny Breckenridge and affirm that Bunny has captured "alienness." And he can write a line affirming the existence of a moment in a man's life when he can't believe his eyes. When does that moment come? Or, is it a part of the alien vision, the alien faith that is Ed Wood's?

Clearly, the vision and the faith have been inherited by Tim Burton. In our postmodern world no claim to foundationally secured descriptions of anything pass muster. In this postmodern world we are not morally engaged within any narrative of moral absolutes. Rather we are morally engaged in expanding the repertoire of alternative realities. And our focus is here, with Ed Wood's vision for it is a quintessential vision of pain, suffering, cruelty, rejection, and oppression. What is alien stands forth as unrecognized, voiceless. "Pain," Rorty writes, "is non-linguistic." Those who suffer and who are "victims of cruelty" are languageless. "That is why there is no such thing 'as the voice of the oppressed' or the 'language of victims.' The language the victims once used is not working anymore, and they are suffering too much to put new words together."

Where does the pain and cruelty come from? Both our reality and our human nature are grounded in conceptions of a commonly shared human nature and a commonly shared reality. The oppressions and suppressions ensuing from this now untenable mythos are precisely what Ed Wood's vision is trying to break through. He does twenty-five takes in one night, putting his alternative stories on film. He is a wild eyed dreamer, dreaming that his viewers will no longer believe the reality their eyes have grown to believe. Once they see outside the frame of "One Right Description Seeing," the pain and suffering, the oppression and rejection of other ways of seeing ends. The evil spell that has held the world captive since the Enlightenment is broken. I see that in Ed Wood's films now through the filter of Tim Burton's film *Ed Wood*. In both cases, it is a matter of commonly shared connections of image and world being unadopted, or in Deleuze's terms, deterritorialized and reterritorialized. Culturally imposed mainstream ways of attending to the world fall apart and alien ways take their place.

We see the price to be paid for this in the lives that fill Tim Burton's film. Despite all the pain and suffering we see, Rorty is wrong about the suffering of the "non-linguistic" preventing them from putting new words together. The "non-linguistic" have merely broken off from the commonly forged chain of cultural signification. The world and they, themselves do not come to meaning and value within a Natural, Unalien Frame of Reality and Truth. Rather than being without any word/world, representation/reality, signifier/signified connections, they have forged other connections.

In this postmodern age, we are, in the words of Rorty, becoming more and more sensitized "to the pain of those who do not speak our language."[1] But Burton's interest is from the other side of things: alongside the pain that our claims to a foundational conception of human nature and of reality have caused others comes the alien. We are scouring both past and present for the alien efforts, the signs untransmitted that lie amid the signs that were transmitted. All Ed Wood's stories on film, all the dialogue, all the events of his life, have to be received now on a different channel, a channel we do not get, a channel that does not come in or only comes in as the worst channel, a bad channel. Tim Burton boosts the transmission and the reception; he crosses wires. And positioned now (as we were not in the '50s), in the cultural miscegenation of postmodernity, we begin to pick up outside "normal" channels—channels whose "normalcy and normativeness" are not foundational but only "hot-wired." The film, after all, is not about Ed Wood but about us now. Why make so much of a film that is clearly what used to be called camp? A pastiche, a kitsch film, a black and white cult film about film for film buffs? A metafilmic film, an avant-garde pouf, a baroque send-up that can't escape its own commodification? A private nightmare of Tim Burton's exorcised on the screen, only partially accessible as anything to a patient audience? A demi-monde film of sordid perversity that passes as art in a decadent postmodern age? Did I give the impression that our postmodern positioning held some sort of hegemonic sway in the present? We are, rather, in the present loaded with odd marriages. Our cultural miscegenation marries African-Americans with the "color of money;" Clarence Thomas *and* Anita Hill as successes *without* having to expand the repertoires of alternative realities; young women who are Conservative *and* pro-choice, as if the Conservative mindset could expand the moral repertoire to include "alternative moralities." Has heterosexuality been displaced by alternative sexualities? Has the free market metanarrative been displaced by steady state economics? Has identity been displaced by difference? Have Truth and Reality been displaced by multiple truths and multiple realities? There is then no hegemony of the postmodern "description" but there is doubtless a rising tide of the postmodern in our contentious culture—by virtue of a contentiousness that resists being "put down."

Ed Wood is only "clearly anything" through the lens of viewing one adopts. I have adopted this one: to be able to say along with Ed Wood "Now that is an alien!" is to put off one lens and put on another. In that act we clearly say that the world is as we construct it and our lives are lived in those constructions. We are therefore compelled to expand our repertoire of representations and thus expand our realities and our lives. The film then rises in significance—a foray into the margins but not a marginal film. A film about films and filmmakers but not a film therefore distanced from reality. A film with neither a universal message nor a deep symbolic level of meaning, but a film holding off both, feverishly.

Confronted with the insistence of his Baptist financial supporters to turn the film onto a Christian path, Ed Wood flies into a tantrum: "These goddamn Baptists are killing me!" He rushes into a dressing room, enraged, not knowing what to do next. And then in minutes he emerges dressed as a woman. He slides into an Angora sweater that makes him feel better, makes him feel good. He slides into an alien part of himself—a part of his sexuality that he, unlike the Baptist ministers, can accept and slide into. Because this film slides into, crosses onto, opens itself onto a repertoire of otherness that the One Right Description has elided, denied, suppressed and so on, it becomes for me a film fulfilling the most provocative gesture of postmodernity—articulating other realities and truths. Is it surprising that this provocation receives both defensive and offensive responses? I point out that William Bennett's *The Book of Virtues: A Treasure of Great Moral Stories* is contemporaneous with *Ed Wood*. Efforts then to expand the repertoire of alternative descriptions go on at the same time that efforts to close down that repertoire and reconfirm the old verities, the One Right Description, are going on.

So what do I see in *Ed Wood?* Ed Wood is fascinated by outer space. Something is coming from outer space. Something alien. Something outside, if you will, the norm. And he's into the ghoulish. Grave robbers from outer space. Or there's something inside us—a man's yearning to dress up like a woman. And then there's something about us and our world that is outside "normalization," something that cannot be held to the norms that have been created in regard to what people are and do and what world they are in and do these things in. Not within the norms of the viewer are Ed Wood and his friends "doing good work." Within those norms they are doing the worst possible work. So here is the effort on Ed Wood's part to do "good work" in "other ways," within alternative ways of doing anything. And that effort—or, again, vision, because it is a "vision thing"—to engage in alternative practices, is literally an engagement and not a representation. Ed Wood is not re-presenting the "alternative repertoire" to others. He is not measuring the distance from the norm, calibrating therefore both identity and difference, the norm and deviation from the norm. Difference, you might say, is here flourishing, or attempting to flourish, not being represented—not being represented in the sense of re-presenting what the norm has already implicitly described. Representation here is in the sense of bringing into conceivability what previously did not exist for us.[2] Our repertoire of conceivability expands. We are prepped, in other words, to see. We are now capable of hooking up. How we see will depend upon our life-world, how we bring what is now conceivable to some sort of representation, to a sayable level even. But neither Ed Wood nor Tim Burton *says.* They enact; they bring to performance; they practice, promote, flourish. They film. Burton films Johnny Depp playing Ed Wood, who is filming scenes from an Ed Wood film, but they are scenes filmed by Burton in Burton's film *Ed Wood.* It is as if the final representation is being resisted, being deferred. They won't fix or freeze difference for a clear view by the norm. They won't represent difference to itself—a representation intent on identifying—a representation therefore already ensnared in the repertoire of conceivability we are already in. Representation of others to themselves is then not an expansion of the repertoire but a repetition/imposition of the identity already described. Both Burton and Wood would be filming for the norm.

Along this line of thinking, Ed Wood is really mentor to Orson Welles, and not vice versa as the film shows. He isn't trying to follow in Welles' footsteps. Or, he is but only in regard to holding fast to a vision and not bending to the "norm." But Welles' vision, you might say, was to eventually get where Ed Wood began. *Citizen Kane,* which was the only film to come out of Welles' vision without outside corruption—and Vincent d'Onofrio who plays Welles in *Ed Wood* tells Ed Wood this—yearns to break the dark tragedy of late modernism and romp in a postmodern expanded repertoire. While Welles' vision never got beyond the late modernist compulsion to track down every different reality frame around and never got beyond or away from the angst of never being able to quite bring them into one reality revealing one truth, Ed Wood's vision begins with a totally undisturbed—meaning untroubled, unquestioned—acknowledgement of multiple realities and therefore multiple truths. Ed Wood sees difference as box office—everyone is ready and able to identify with "alternative practices," ready to expand the repertoire, if you will, beyond their own frame of real-izing. And they do this because they are free of the modernist, early and late, compulsion to establish Reality and Truth by winnowing out false, deviant, immoral, irrational, insane, primitive descriptions. Everyone in Ed Wood's audience—in Ed Wood's mind—is anxious only about one thing—expanding the repertoire of alternative descriptions. Herein lies the crux of his radical difference, his "descent" into what we can only deem as "worst." Nevertheless, he displays a postmodern ethic.

Everyone in Ed Wood's entourage understands this ethic. They live in constructed realities and because of this they refrain from representing others to themselves while also flourishing their own realities and allowing others to flourish. Criswell the Great, Seer Extraordinaire, floats future realities like so many balloons. "If you predict something with absolute confidence," he tells Ed Wood, "people believe you. I make it all up." And so, too, does Eddie. And so too do we all, the only difference being between the language-players who are aware of the constructed nature of reality and who construct with aplomb and the language-users who live within those constructions that are shaped for them as "normative." Ultimately, Ed Wood's films mediated through Tim Burton's film does what Criswell does. It predicts a future in which making the alien conceivable in the hope of representing difference within an expanded repertoire of identity comes true. It becomes the very present we are in, the world from which the film *Ed Wood* emerges.

The film, however, is not up-beat, not confident that the repertoire is really changing. We are drawn back to facing the pain and suffering that results from fixing a limited, constructed repertoire of the real as The Real, defining what is normal within that construct, and holding people to it. Bunny Breckenridge, for instance, doesn't want to be held to the norm regarding sexuality. He lives outside the norm while at the same time displaying all the pain of not being able to pull off that miracle. No one lives outside the norm. They are caught within in it like a spider's web. In the film *Dracula,* Bela Lugosi easily walks through a spider's web without disturbing it. Normal, earthbound types, like Renfield at the film's beginning, get caught up in the web and have to break free. The Bela Lugosi who appears in Ed Wood's films and in *Ed Wood* is earthbound, exhausted, defeated by the daylight, if you will. He has been a junkie for twenty years, finding in drugs an escape from a reality that oppresses him. His arm pocked with needle marks comes before our eyes more than once. It becomes a sign of repeated attempts at flight from the Hollywood that no longer "gives two fucks for Bela." Scene after scene that Bela appears in reveals to us his artistry, the gift he has to *create over* the world he is in, to expand the repertoire of our reality and his reality at the very moment he is constrained within a far less liberating reality. On a streetcorner, in broad daylight, he transforms himself and that artistic transformation receives a round of applause from passersby, whose afternoon lives are suddenly transformed. The norm is stretched. That normalization appears in *Ed Wood* as the lifeless rubber octopus whose operating motor has been lost. It is up to Bela to bring those tentacles of rubber to life, to make them seem alive, to make it seem as if he is fighting off a cold, dead chunk of reality. He does it masterfully. And Ed Wood captures the scene. For Bela. He captures Bela's victory over what has no life and is intent on taking the life from him. And Tim Burton captures Ed Wood filming that scene. For Ed Wood. For the repertoire. For us.

Notes

1. Richard Rorty, *Contingency, Irony, and Solidarity* Cambridge: Cambridge University Press, 1989, 94.

2. See Wolfgang Iser, *Prospecting* Baltimore: Johns Hopkins, 1989.

"Klaatu Barada Nikto"

December 3rd
Town Global Propane

"What's your name?"

"I'm R. C."

"I'll be right over, R. C."

By half four Woad was pulled up in front of Town Global Propane. He crouched down and peered under the van at the tank he had welded in place. Question was, would it meet federal standards of safety?

Inside the hangar–like structure, the office was vintage. Propellers of paper on a couple of army issue desks, farm calendars on the walls, black phone, a woman with a craggy face, heavy bags under her eyes and ropes of grey hair hanging down, cigarette at the corner of her mouth.

"R. C. around?"

"Out back. The big one with a beard. Got a bark on'm."

R. C. had a way about him.

"What the fuck is this?" he said, sprawled out on the ground, shiny blue work pants shoved into one boot, down on the other.

"I think it should hold about forty pounds," Woad said.

R. C. pulled out from under.

"Can't do it without the right coupling. Won't be safe."

"Okay. What's it gonna cost?"

R. C. scratched his head.

"Gotta check the prices with Margaret."

Back in the office, Margaret's eyes were half closed.

121

Later when Woad wrote a check for the part and then pulled out his wallet to show his driver's license, R. C. waved it aside.

"Hey, wait a minute. Let me see that photo."

"That's something else. Look at mine."

R. C.'s photo on his licence looked like him with a flattened head but otherwise it looked like him. Margaret squinted at them from her desk as R. C. showed an earlier photo, one in which he looked a bit leaner and beard more scraggly. Woad took out an earlier photo of himself.

"You look like an alien, man," R. C. said, laughing.

"Got time for a cup of java. I bet you don't drink java?"

In the back, R. C. poured out two cups from Mr. Coffee and they sat down at a picnic table that had been dragged inside.

"I been up in one of them you know," R. C. told Woad.

"One what?"

"Alien spacecraft. They tend to hang around propane tanks like we got here."

"You can't use combustion for space travel," Woad said.

"Whata you use then?" R. C. said, slamming his cup down. Got a bark on him Margaret had said.

"Where they take you?" Woad asked.

"Outer space," R. C. replied. "Took Margaret too one time. That's why she is the way she is now. Wasn't like that before. Before they took Margaret for a trip she could keep an office cleaner than a spit polished pair'em boots. And she could talk some too. Didn't smoke neither. Now she watches things fall apart."

"But it didn't change you any?"

"No, I'm the same. I was a smoking slob before they grabbed me and I'm a smoking slob now."

"I don't suppose you saw how that alien spacecraft operated," Woad asked just before driving off.

R. C. laughed.

"Between Margaret and me we could fly one of them things to Mars and back."

Woad cut his engine.

"What keeps it from dipping below hundred feet?"

"You gotta ask Margaret that one. You know Margaret was a blonde before they whipped her up there? Had a face as smooth as a baby's butt."

Woad restarted the engine, reminded R. C. to call him when the part came in and then drove off.

Pancakes used Patti's hand to ring the bell. She had to have Patti ring it several times before a tall man with a very pale face came to the door. He looked like Commander Data from *Star Trek: The Next Generation.* Pancakes immediately liked him because she liked Data.

"Patti wants to say hello," Pancakes told Data.

"Hello, Pancakes," Data said, focusing his attention on Patti.

"Are you Patti's new neighbor?"

"Is Patti transmitting her questions telepathically to you?"

Pancakes laughed.

"What?"

Kenny was washing dishes and looking out the window where he saw Pancakes talking to their new neighbor.

The phone rang. It was John Swingle.

"What's up?"

"We got a gig."

"I'm gonna blow a note nobody's ever heard before," Kenny Kirk Douglased.

"It was pure contingency," John replied. "I had lunch with my sister today at Abe Fata's and there was this guy come in and post this notice for a group to play at the next meeting of the Virtual Reality Conversation and Support Group. They want standards from the '60s and '70s. And get this. Motown and R & B only need apply."

"That's pure contingency?" Kenny said, stretching the phone back to the window where now all he could see was Pancakes and not the new neighbor.

"I think we need this," John said.

"If that's pure contingency then I have pure contingency happen to me on a regular basis."

The back door opened and Pancakes came in holding Patti in two pieces. She held up her head.

"He put a tiny positron brain into Patti's head," she told Kenny.

"Put Patti's head back on, Knuckle," Kenny told her.

"Seize the contingency," John told him emphatically. "If you don't, life passes you by."

After Kenny hung up he went into the living room to straighten things out before Bess came home. It was while he was dusting that he heard Pancakes talking to someone upstairs.

He went to the foot of the staircase and called up.

"Who you talking to up there, Knuckle?"

"Just Patti," Pancakes called down. "She has verbal eyesation skills now."

Kenny was waiting by the driveway when Bess pulled up. Out of the corner of his eye he saw someone standing on the top floor of the house with the new neighbor.

"Did you know Pancakes can really do voices now," Kenny said, when Bess got out of the van.

Bess stared at him for a long while.

"There's a gig you want to do."

Kenny nodded.

"It was pure contingency," he said, trailing her into the house.

From the upstairs window Data began to check the readings he was getting from the probe he had put in Patty's head.

Virtual Jack led Lucy Powell in one of the best tangos she had ever done. She caught the eye of Kenny on bass guitar as she and Jack swept past. In turn, Kenny wondered how she could make that sweeping turn without falling. It was almost as if she were dancing with someone. There were of course some people dancing in twos but most were dancing alone. Everbody seemed to be enjoying themselves. Kenny knew it had something to do with the computer packs they were all wearing, plugged into their chosen hyperspace programs. The tango request had come from a thin young woman who said she was dancing with Arnold Schwarzenegger whom she said liked to tango. Kerry, who could play anything, had led them into it and they were sort of holding their own. Now the girl with Arnold jiggled by, arms outstretched high over her head, clutching empty air, a smile of thorough delight and enchantment covered her face.

Kenny next got up to the mic to sing I've got two lovers who love me just the same.

"If you unplug me," Jack told Lucy later, "I'll kill you. I can reach you wherever you are."

Lucy unplugged anyway. Everything went grey and dull, smoky and dribbled with the smell of perspiration. The music was all sour notes; the players looked like caffeinated marionettes. Voices cracked, feet pounded the floor, mouths hung slack, eyes were full of pearl jam.

When she stopped running she was at the far end of the Whipple Shopping Center parking lot. She wound up vomiting alonside Kenny's vintage 1977 Olds Cutlas. When she stood up she looked into the marble eyes of a small doll that she recognized as Pancake's doll. At that moment she chose to plug herself back into her program and Virtual Jack stood beside her. Jack looked good to her but she didn't like the way he was moving toward her. Jack felt a scan on his program and before he could react, his program was overwritten.

"Self-destructive program erased," a voice said.

"I don't think so," Lucy yelled. "Who the hell are you? I am in love here. I am in love with Virtual Jack. I want him back. Hey!"

Woad drove past in his pickup truck with R. C. and Margaret squeezed in alongside him. The cigarette smoke was killing him in spite of both windows being open. R. C. and Margaret had been doing duelling Camels since they got into the truck.

"Ever since Reagan, the youth in this country got it too easy," R. C. said, scowling at Lucy who had climbed on to the roof of Kenny's car.

"You didn't have your own kid," Margaret said. "That'd take the bark off ya."

"I was around fifteen when Reagan took over," Woad said. "There's no need for a fifteen year old kid in entrepreneurship. Except to buy things with money I didn't have."

"That's why aliens are way ahead of us," R. C. said, lighting up another Camel. "They let their kids buy Camels right off."

R. C. paused and blew out some refreshing smoke rings.

"Outer space is pollution free on account of there's no oxygen to pollute in the first place."

"I suppose aliens don't have lungs?" Margaret snapped.

"Did you see any?" R. C. said.

"Don't have to see 'em to hav 'em," Margaret re-snapped.

"They have a filtering system," R. C. said. "I seen that. Every month or so they put new filters in all round. Lungs, kidneys, liver. Bunch of filters anyway."

"This is interesting," Margaret said sarcastically.

"And they ain't got any hearts or time," R. C. concluded.

"Time?" Woad said, turning down past Neelye's Target Range where he had the alien spacecraft hidden.

"In space, you move so fast time stands still because you outdistance the speed of light. On the lightwave is the images of what's going on. It's only when what's going on changes that you have time. But if you're faster than that, then just when the images start moving ahead you pass them and they sort of float back to where they were."

"You've experienced this phenomenon?" Woad asked.

"You're a witness to my experiencing it," R. C. exclaimed.

"Me?"

"Sure. I'm eighty-three years old but I look like I'm your age. And Margaret here. Shit, Margaret looks like she's in her sixties but she ain't no more than twenty–two, twenty–three."

Woad craned forward and looked at Margaret who looked back at him.

"Don't believe him about hearts," she said. "They got hearts. If R. C. didn't have so much bark on 'em he'd know they had big hearts. I miss those folks. I miss them everyday. Everyday I think they'll be a fire in the sky right above my head and they've come to take me back. And this time I won't return. They'll have to keep me. And their hearts are so big that they will keep me."

Kenny, Kerry, Scraps, John Swingle, and CeeCee Cooper hauled their instruments out the back door.

"Pancakes thinks our new neighbor is an extra-terrestrial," Kenny said.

"You know why the government doesn't want to say that people have been abducted by UFO's since the '50s?" Scraps said. "Because they'd have to admit that aliens been observing us when we can't even be sure they're here. You know what that means? It means we're just alien case studies. They're controlling their experiments and we're like rats in a cage who don't know what's being done to us. Soon as they government admits that, it admits it can't protect us and then what you get is a mad rush to the doors. Order has to be maintained at any cost."

"That is an unusual amount of bullshit coming out of your mouth, Scraps," CeeCee said. "Who told you all that? Your main man Rick–the–kid–killer Monte?"

"Wanna go over to Sweeney's new place?" Kenny said, slamming the car trunk closed.

"What in God's name is that?" Kerry said, pointing up at a star-filled sky.

"Yeah," CeeCee said, looking up. "Like sutton's on fire. A long, long, long way off."

"I bet it's one of those Discoverers or Voyagers out there," Kenny said. "Afterjets burning."

"More like one of those cable satellites," John Swingle said. "Or maybe they decided to launch trash out into space and torch it."

"It's getting closer whatever it is," Scraps said.

"Hot meteorite like the one that hit Jupiter," Kenny said.

"The Universe is subject to pure contingency," Swingle told them.

"Oh, shit," Kenny said. "Who's coming to Sweeney's?"

Sweeney had modeled his place after the diner in the movie *Diner:* five booths on either side of the door, a two and a half foot aisle between the booths and the counter which ran the length of the diner—forty-four feet. There was a juke box at one end of the diner and every inch of wall space was covered with photos of film stars and movie posters dating back to the '30s. For his part, Sweeney assumed the role of Rick in *Casablanca,* a presence, smoking, drinking, quipping. Insead of a tux he wore the square shouldered, wide lapeled suit that George Raft had worn in *Johnny Allegro.* He was tieless and his greying hair was drawn back into a sort of bun that Marlon Brando had worn in *Mutiny on the Bounty.*

Sweeney was sipping coffee at the counter, which was occupied only by a couple of truckers on the far end. Half of the booths were taken but Sweeney figured the place would fill up once the Virtual Reality Support Group Rocker was over. Lucy Powell came in just then with a guy Sweeney had only seen on TV because for some reason the guy looked an awful lot like Commander Data on *Star Trek: the Next Generation.* They took a booth next to the juke box. Sweeney wondered whether Lucy would play the box and do one of those kootchie dances that Juliette Lewis always did in the movies.

"Hey, Lucy," Sweeney said, going over to the booth. "How was the blast?"

Lucy looked up at Sweeney.

"We were in high school together," she told Data who nodded.

"Sweeney," Sweeney said, putting out his hand which Data grasped.

"I'm pleased to meet you, Sweeney. I am David."

Sweeney nodded, noting that the guy didn't have eyebrows nor pupils in his eyes. Why would a guy wear contacts that hid his pupils? Sweeney chewed the invisible gum that was always there when he needed it.

"You're in the support group, right?"

David shook his head, puzzled.

"I am new in this town, Sweeney," he said."But I would like to be in a support group."

"English ain't your mother tongue, right?"

"I speak six hundred and fifty languages, Sweeney," David said.

"My Virtual Jack program glitched and then I met David," Lucy explained.

Mike Woad came in followed by R. C. and Margaret.

"Guy over there says he speaks six hundred and fifty languages," Sweeney said, sitting down next to Woad at the counter. Woad looked over at David and then back at his menu. He wasn't in the mood for this because neither R. C. nor Margaret had ever seen anything like his spaceship before. Margaret didn't think it was a spaceship. Fakery she had said. And after inspecting it thoroughly R. C. had declared it looked Japanese or Korean. Woad had even taken them for a little spin. A short spin. People were reporting sightings and he was afraid that one of these nights he was going to get intercepted by the Air Force as a UFO. Or, his inability to fully control the ship would take him into a fatal nosedrive to Mother Earth.

"I bet I can speak one he don't know," R. C. said, getting up and going over to Lucy and David.

They both stared up at him as he stood there, Camel cigarette blowing smoke into his left eye which was half shut.

"Klaatu barada nikto," R. C. said very slowly.

"Please sit down and join us," David said, obviously delighted by R. C.'s greeting.

R. C. hesitated and then sat down. David handed him a menu.

"BLT," Margaret said to Betty Lip who did a midnight to six a.m. shift behind the counter. "Coffee. Black."

"Cappuccino?"

"Coffee. Black."

Faye Fata came in alone and Woad got up and went over to her. The two of them took a booth.

"Who's that?" Faye said, nodding toward Margaret who was blowing Camel smoke into Sweeney's face but Sweeney kept on talking and didn't seem to care.

"Know' em?" Margaret said. "I lived 'em. Each and every one of them."

"Okay," Sweeney said, "What about that one?"

He pointed to a black and white framed photo over the grill. Margaret stared at it.

"*Not Of This Earth*," Margaret said. "1957."

"Wow!" Sweeney said.

"An alien comes to Earth looking like a human being so he can get blood to save his planet."

"What about that one?" Sweeney said, pointing to the photo next to it.

"*Day Of Wrath*," Margaret said as Betty put a cup of coffee in front of her. "An old woman is burned as a witch. 1943."

"If we ever had to get away from here," Woad was saying to Faye, "I've got a way. I've got a . . . a vehicle." Faye nodded.

"You mean the starship you found out behind the Town Mental Facility this summer? I was with you, remember? You've gotten that thing to go?"

"Sort of."

"Sweeney!" Scraps the Loudmouth yelled, coming in the door. "You should have been there. We were like Pavarotti hittin' high C's."

"Pavarotti my ass," CeeCee mumbled as he and the other band members came in.

Kenny saw his new neighbor at a booth with Lucy and R. C.

"We saw some kind of red fire ball in the sky and then it was gone," John Swingle told Sweeney.

"I'll tell you what happens if you report it," R. C. said, legs stretched out into the aisle. "They put you down as a looney in their computer banks so when you get stopped for pissing in the grove or pressing the metal the computer spits out "looney" next to your name."

"Did anybody see something land out behind the Town Mental Facility 'bout an hour ago?" former Sheriff Jake Wilcox shouted from the doorway.

John Swingle saw the smile on R. C.'s face.

"We seen a big fire in the sky about half hour ago," Scraps yelled back.

A very pale, highly caffeinated Frank Coletti cowered behind the bulk of Jake. He hadn't shaved in days and his hair looked like a rat's nest. He peered out from behind Jake at David.

"That's one of them," he croaked. "That son of a bitch killed my dog Fatima twenty-five years ago and abducted my old man."

Jake went for his pistol and then remembered that he didn't carry a pistol any longer since he wasn't the sheriff anymore.

"Who's this fella, R. C.?" Jake said to R. C.

"This here is an American citizen," R. C. replied. "With all the rights and privileges thereof."

"I think we got an alien problem in this town," Scraps put in. "Come in, go on welfare and there you go."

"Look, Jake," Kenny said, trying to cool things down. "This is all pure contingency."

Jake returned this with a frown.

"He says his name is David," Sweeney said, not wanting to get Jake Wilcox angry in his new place. "And he can speak about a thousand languages."

"Sixty hundred and fifty to be exact," David said. "I can only speak one human language however. German."

David's smile was infectious.

"I do the Data bit as a promotional gimmic," he explained. "I sell for Michelangelo Anti-Virus and Computer Surveillance Software. We're a subsidiary of IBM. But I do know a lot about computers it's just that having people think I'm Data makes them think I know an awful lot more."

Jake Wilcox stood there frozen for several seconds and then he turned and looked at Frank who was shakily drinking a cup of coffee Betty had handed him.

"I'm all right now, Jake," Frank said.

"What about that fireball we seen?" Scraps asked as Jake and Frank were going out the door.

"Get me a couple of photos of it next time," Jake said, waving.

"That was probably you, right?" Faye said to Woad who shrugged.

"Just a spin around the block."

"The face at the window," Margaret said.

"Right," Sweeney said, glancing at the photo way over in the far corner of a scene from the 1939 film *The Face At The Window*.

"No, I mean that face at that window," Margaret said, pointing.

When Sweeney looked to where Margaret was pointing he saw nothing.

"He had a face shaped like a Vick's lozenge," Margaret said, laying her lit Camel in her saucer and biting into her BLT. "Red eyes almost vertical in his head."

Some of the tomato fell out of the sandwich and she fingered it.

"Long neck like a goose. No clothes. The whole body was shining."

"It was Tod Slaughter's juiciest role," Sweeney said, recalling the movie.

Looking into the Abyss: Madmen and Fanatics

August 1995

> "I am but mad north-north-west. When the wind is
> southerly, I know a hawk from a handsaw."
>
> *Hamlet*

"Being Don Juan"

The film *Don Juan de Marco* will be our starter, a fable's intoning of madness. And then for the main course—Koresh at Waco and its reverberation here in the spring of 1995 at the Alfred P. Murrah Federal Building in Oklahoma City. Delusion, madness, and fanaticism are poisoning the American dream. Or, are the dreams of escape of a large percentage of the population turning from "allegorical conflict" and fragmented bickering to real threats to "the ruling and possessing class," a class that almost all Americans seem to agree does not exist?[1] Are present signs of madness, signs of revolt? Are delusions attempts to escape the hegemony of the overclass? Is fanaticism an alternate route to political expression in a country in which both political parties are working to sacrifice the many for the sake of the few?

There is madness and then there is mental illness. Foucault in *Madness and Civilization* argues that we should be free to be mad. Mental illness in Foucault's view is no more than a fluctuating social determination and the medical science that tackles it has been less scientifically progressive than socially responsive and expedient.[2] Psychiatry has tackled mental illness in order to "cure" it, although the practical agenda has always been to "manacle" it. William Blake provides the crossover: we really fall into madness when our imaginations are manacled. And we do that to ourselves, individual efforts coagulating into a societal order of things, a repressive regime of Urizen ("Your reason"). Like

133

Foucault, Blake imagined that we cure ourselves of this form of madness by dreaming something else.

We are free to dream of something else because our science is not worthy of our madness: "Psychology can never tell the truth about madness because it is madness that holds the truth of psychology."[3] Madness is a ranging from an imposed order of things, an order of things that the psychiatrist serves and responds to. Foucault's point is that every age shapes its own view of madness. Such arbitrariness cannot in the end be allowed to constrain humankind's capacity to create and live in narratives that a particular society at a particular time has no eyes for. Blake is more of a psychologist here: if indeed we adopt the priorities of our own age in regard to how our energies should be circumscribed, then our ability to imagine and dream something else diminishes. Redundancy leads to entropy, Blake's fallen state, a state of single-vision, meaning limited perception.

Don Juan de Marco (played by Johnny Depp, our Ed Wood here portraying someone who would fit nicely into Ed Wood's repertoire of difference) tells his shrink, Dr. Jack Mickler (Marlon Brando) that the good doctor has dust flowing through his veins, yet he sees his salvation in Don Juan's message of love and passion. And indeed Dr. Jack is drawn to the spirit of Don Juan—he is retiring but he feels he hasn't lived for a long, long time. The sap has run out of him, although the sheer bulk of Brando here leads us to think that he does love greatly but his love is food. This is not a trivial intersection: if I went to a psychiatrist so grossly overweight, so obviously needing to spend a good part of his day eating to support that three hundred or so pounds, I would wonder whether the mad story I was in was any madder than the story my psychiatrist was in. Without mentioning Dr. Jack's weight, Don Juan does tell him that if he, Don Juan, is mad so too is Dr. Jack. They both should take the "med" that the head of psychiatry urges Dr. Jack to prescribe for Don Juan. The chemicals will wipe out the delusion. But Dr. Jack resists. What remains he asks when the chemicals wear off? And why wipe out Don Juan's charisma, his gift of turning others on to love and passion? Don Juan becomes Dr. Jack's cure for what ails him: death-in-life. Juan may be delusional but he is alive. Dr. Jack has no delusions that offend societal norms, but he also knows he is dead before his own physical death.

I know I am in a mental hospital, Don Juan tells Dr. Jack, but I do not allow this to limit what I see and therefore what I am.

In other words, he knows he puts a spin on things, a Don Juan spin. As does Dr. Jack, but not a Don Juan spin. Dr. Jack's spin, in Juan's view, has worn out—it's a spin which has led him to believe that both he and the world are limited to what his medical science says they are. He is then like a man who lives on a beautiful tropical beach but believes he occupies a barren cell. His imagination has been devoured by his reason. Juan hooks up with the world in a far richer way and says why not? Where is the harm in doing this? And what is the authority and justification for forcing him to give up his perception of the world for another's—in this case a society that is spinning itself away from love toward a cold, cybernetic, greed-filled, class-divided future?

This film doesn't rise above fable in our minds because it fails to set up the world that Juan is toppling by the power of dreaming differently. But neither reality nor dream are easy to represent in the present. What is "really" going on in this country is an overdetermined matter—we have a dissensus of interpretation and meaning. When people say they are sick of politics today, they are responding to their inability to represent what is going on in the country in any clear, stable way to themselves. And in the case of dreaming differently, we seem not to be able to dream beyond our interest in the bottom line. Our dreaming, in effect, is always already commodified. Thusly frustrated, we get signs of that frustration all around us. In our traditional Enlightenment way of talking I could put the matter this way: violence, fanaticism, madness and delusion are as much by-products of our times as of individual "merit" or "demerit." Occasion and individual intersect.

I want to put this in a postmodern way that elides the distance and dualism here—world and individual interpenetrate as signs within a flux of clash, coincidence, and contingencies. What we signify to ourselves and what others signify to us must always go on within one or more stories of what things, events and people mean and how they are to be valued. And these stories are of human creation and both already exist in the world *and* are in the process of coming into existence. While it is undeniably true that we exist as physical entities, so much carbon and so much water, or black or white, yellow or brown, we are both to ourselves and society brought to meaning and value within a cultural semiotics. That this semiotics is an increasingly contentious one is one of the significations of our postmodern climate, rued by some, celebrated by others. The black race, for instance, has been involved in a painful struggle to decouple it-self from a resident signification in this country and shape a new one. Ditto women, Native Americans, Latinos, gypsies, homosex-uals, and every marginalized group. The desire here is to dream and imagine a new linkage of self and world, to wipe out the old linkage and replace it with a new one. New construction is what is needed here but since that new construction must take place in a world in which we are already being constructed within and by existing constructions, we already exist within stories that are defining our search and constraining our dreams. Those born well-off are born into a well-off cultural chain of signification, as difficult to break as is a completely different cultural chain al-ready forged for the poor. It is not a matter of outside determi-nants locking us into one lifestyle or another, but rather of residing within certain stories and having those stories reside within us. The world then is brought to a certain meaning and value for us because we know it means and is to be valued in a certain way. We produce the world steadily from within stories that only persist because we keep up that sort of production.

The rich know the world in a rich way, within a rich story. There is a linkage between being rich and being conservative be-cause they are mutually reinforcing stories. They coincide and do not collide, producing a single, unitary reality. In the same fashion, that reality is non-violent and non-radical because it cannot produce these and at the same time maintain that real-ity. That reality is already being produced by a way of knowing the world, a narrative of reality and truth, that finds meaning and value in the status quo, in non-deviation, stability, non-dis-ruption. The rich story they are in cannot produce Don Juan de Marco's delusion. To be delusional is to know the world within an entirely different narrative frame, and while there is impetus to do this among the poor, there is little among the rich. The poor and disenchanted live within a poor narrative that just as naturally finds meaning and value in violence as the rich narra-tive finds meaning and value in the status quo. Neither delusion nor violence, therefore, are perverted individual choices that have nothing to do with cultural narratives. If our society is ex-periencing more of both, it is not a matter of the loss of individ-ual moral values and family values but rather because more and more people can only connect to the world from within a narrative of increasing poverty. There is now an unbridgeable gap between knowing the world in a stable, contented way (and thus producing that world by knowing it in that way), *and* knowing the world in a discordant, discontented way. Unfortunately, the reality of contentment is grounded in self-interest and therefore can only continue to produce itself by at the same time producing a reality that daily augments the reality of discontentment.

Violence today represents a desire on the part of the "fragmented many" of this country to escape the ravages of the American class war, specifically the ravages caused by what Michael Lind calls "the new American oligarchy."[4] If our society now displays a "growing concentration of power and wealth in the hands of a privileged minority," then concomitantly there must also be a growing domination of a reality frame which continues that privileging.[5] Those connecting to the world within different and marginalized frames must increasingly bend to the reality imposed by the privileged minority. This is a sort of ontological tyranny, and I suggest that it alone can produce the sort of violence and madness that our society is presently experiencing.[6] In the end then, *Don Juan de Marco* does not go nearly far enough in tapping into both the rising tide of privilege and suppression in this country and the blind, desperate, fantastical, fanatic attempts at escaping it, of dreaming differently.

"Koresh at Waco"

> "The Oklahoma bombing is a reminder that the wounds of Waco have never healed."
>
> Peter J. Boyer, "Children of Waco," *New Yorker* May 15, 1995, 38

The nightmare of David Koresh's Branch Davidians at Waco takes us into the heart of the territory: madness, delusion, fanaticism, violence, dreams of escape. And while the narrative of the new American oligarchy had no way of connecting with this debacle, the connections elsewhere proliferate. The connection between the Oklahoma bombing and Waco materialized when the FBI apprehended Tim McVeigh and the Nichols brothers. These three were then linked with the militia movement and "patriot" groups, all of which have developed narrative frames from which they derive meanings and values that not only baffle the oligarchy but crisscross Democratic and Republican party lines. In short, there has been a good deal of dreaming differently going on in this country, but it took a totally unanticipated event—the Oklahoma bombing—to bring this within the ken of the oligarchy. And that event took us back once again to another event—Koresh at Waco—that also totally disconcerted that oligarchy. There was nothing in the favored way of attending to the world that could connect with Waco, could make sense of it. It was never fathomed or made "realizable." The Davidians and their leader remain inconceivable. If it weren't for the Oklahoma bombing it would remain filed away in American oligarchy memory as a meaningless, powerless drama enacted by a few lunatics. It was an event, after all, which had little meaning for the market although it had market value. It could be played up until the next commodifiable event came along. O.J. Simpson obliged.

While the whole country was in a state of shock over the sudden conflagration of the Branch Davidian compound, television seized the moment with *In the Line of Duty: Ambush at Waco*, starring Koresh look-alike, Tim Daly. The title revealed all: the agents of the Bureau of Alcohol, Tobacco, and Firearms were ambushed while doing their duty. What propelled the ATF toward this sense of duty? Was it the weaponry? And was that weaponry illegal? Or, was it a certain image they developed of David Koresh taking advantage of others, abusing women and children, brainwashing the innocent, that propelled the ATF toward their duty? "Is he mad?" one ATF agent asks another. "Not all the time," is the response. Maybe, like Hamlet, Koresh is only mad north-northwest and when the wind is in the south, he's okay. Strain as the ATF does toward convicting Koresh of something—rather like Christ at the hands of the Pharisees—the film merely shows him as a biblical exegete. He seems to be abusing only the "unfaithfuls'" notion of realism and rationality, freedom and choice. Koresh does no more than prophesy what will happen in the present in line with his own interpretation of *Revelations*. And he gets others to buy his biblical view, the goal of each and every Southern holiness preacher. Koresh's venue is, of course, drastically different than, say Louis Rukeyser, but the drama is identical. An individual espouses views that others see the well being of their own lives directly linked to. They sit at his feet and listen dutifully and when they can, they enact his teachings. America may once have been a land first settled by those following the directions of their own dissenting interpretations of the Bible. It now, however, has no way of connecting with such mindsets—it all becomes so much drivel, a word used again and again in response to the question as to what Koresh is saying to his followers.

Koresh is condemned in the film as a "false prophet," the line the Fundamental Right has taken. Unable to attack Koresh and his followers for their devotion to the Bible, the Christian Coalition has to condemn Koresh as false, as really the Devil in a minister's garb. Perhaps Koresh was led to madness by sex, violence, and rock and roll—a connection queried by two moles of the ATF in the film: "Guns, preaching, and rock music? What's going on here?"

But the blame comes to rest on the Bible and Koresh's fanatical belief in it. "Are we ready to die for me?" he asks his followers. Why would anyone be willing to die for someone else? What profits a man if he loses his life and thus his profits? This is the point of slippage between Koresh and the Feds. A year before the Waco tragedy, Rosebud Abigail Denovo was shot dead by an officer. She had broken into the mansion of the University of California chancellor, armed with a machete. In her pack the police found a note that read, "We are willing to die for this land. Are you?"[7]

"Bomb-o-gram"

> "How do we construe the American idea of freedom, and what do we mean by democracy if we must communicate with one another by bomb-o-gram?"
>
> Lewis Lapham, "Seen But Not Heard"
>
> "Even a gruesome event like the Oklahoma City bombing becomes an economic uptick by the strange reckonings of the GDP. 'Analysts expect the share prices [of firms making anti-crime equipment] to gain during the next several months,' *The Wall Street Journal* reported a short time after the bombing, 'as safety concerns translate into more contracts.'"
>
> Clifford Cobb **et al.**, "If the GDP Is Up, Why Is America Down?"

Now, after the Oklahoma bombing it is clear that those willing to die for this land are also willing to kill for it. Those in the compounds, if you will, are not waiting to be besieged. And that sea change has come about in the aftermath of Koresh at Waco. "We'll get you!" Idahoans shouted at federal marshals besieging Randy Weaver, a man accused of selling shotguns to an undercover agent.[8]

In the spring of 1995 we were unwillingly following the traces of Waco, Oklahoma and the militant right. The oligarchy is willing to trace it only to commodify it. Since increasing audience share drives the pursuit, the American audience will be and have been led down each and every path that augments their interest in the story. How these events connect to the rifts and discord of our culture wars proves to be a less sensationalistic pursuit than reducing them to oligarchic protocols of perceiving and realizing. I mean that those who are in charge of representing what has gone on to us invariably cannot represent it outside an oligarchic frame of realizing. There are, to be sure, other and dissenting ways of grasping the significance of these events, but they are fewer than one would think, given the notoriety of our present cultural dissensus. The liberal view is increasingly quite like the conservative view. They coincide within a greater, subsuming frame of representation: the minority of wealth and privilege. Those trying to escape the narrow framing of reality we have, as a country, gotten ourselves into, are expressing themselves at posse meetings and weekend militia gathers. They've expressed themselves at the Federal Building in Oklahoma, at a standoff in Ruby Ridge, Idaho with white separatist Randy Weaver, and out at the Branch Davidian Compound in Waco with David Koresh. They're not in the political conversation so they're having their own. Such as it is.

What has and continues to be swept aside is our public rendering of not only liberalism, which Liberals have given up trying to define, but conservatism defined as either a market conservatism—unfettered global capitalism—or a social conservatism—family values predominating.[9] The real players have been referred to as the violent Right, which as Michael Kelly points out in "*The Road to Paranoia*" is an alliance of radical fringes on both left and right, and the guild Oligarchy.[10] They are not at war, at least not in an old fashioned cold war duality. But they are connected: the violent Right is the Frankenstein creation of the guild Oligarchy. It therefore only deserves the appellation "Right" because of this association. "Right," "left" and "center" are otherwise irrelevant categories. And because this is so, it is extremely difficult for a public discourse caught in a Right-Left narrative to get a finger on either the violent Right or the guild Oligarchy.

Here is Marc Cooper in *The Nation* attempting to identify the cross-boundary affiliations of what he calls a "nationwide militia movement," the "gun-toting citizen soldiers of the hard right," and whom Christopher Hitchens in the *London Review of Books* simply calls neo-Nazis:[11]

> More than religious or racial fundamentalists, they claim to be constitutional literalists. And in an age of globalization, in which ordinary people rightfully suspect they may be mere slaves on a worldwide plantation, the militia's message has exercised a heady attraction. With no contending voices able or willing to make themselves heard in explaining the plight of scared white Americans, the militias and the 'patriot' groups have come up with their own mythology: The cold war enemy, Global Communism, has been supplanted by the specter of Globalism itself. America is on the verge of tyranny; the federal siege at Waco was merely a dry run for nationwise martial law; the United Nations, aided and abetted by the federal government, is about to take over the United States; the Feds will furnish the occupying Chinese Army troops with Russian military equipment; soon the government will confiscate all private firearms; some forty-three concentration camps are ready to house resistant libertarians; the government has put secret markings on road signs to facilitate the coming takeover by One World forces; clandestine squadrons of black helicopters are mapping all of America; Hong Kong police and Gurkha troops are training in the Montana wilds 'to take guns away from Americans' by order of Bill Clinton; and so on. All this is to usher in a New World Order, itself a vast conspiracy of elite, international bankers, including David Rockefeller, in cahoots with Mikhail Gorbachev and even Newt Gingrich. And of course the twenty percent decline in your real wages in as many years is somehow linked to all of the above.[12]

Now let's see how far we've gotten in identifying the "guild Oligarchy," Michael Lind's term in his *Harper's* essay *"To Have and Have Not."* The problem here of representation differs from that of the violent Right where representation has been confounded by a Republican desire to hide its dark side and a Democratic desire to see the increasingly angry and disenfranchised "salaried majority" as its constituency. The "guild Oligarchy" seems to be a signifier without a signified, a word that represents nothing in the world. "The American oligarchy," Lind writes, "spares no pain in promoting the belief that it does not exist." Nevertheless, it is controlling the discourse on the left, right and center—different discourses but the same ends. "The American elites that subsidize and staff both the Republican and

Democratic parties have steadfastly waged a generation-long class war against the middle and working classes." And here is who Lind says they are:

> Amounting, with their dependents, to about twenty percent of the population, this relatively new and still evolving political and social oligarchy is not identified with any particular region of the country. Homogeneous and nomadic, the overclass is the first truly national upper class in American history. In a managerial capitalist society like our own, the essential distinction is not between the 'bourgeoisie' (the factory owners) and the 'proletariat' (the factory workers) but between the credentialed minority (making a living from fees or wages supplemented by stock options) and the salaried majority. The salaried class— at-will employees, lacking a four-year college education, paid by the hour, who can be fired at any time—constitute the real 'middle class,' accounting, as it does, for three-quarters of the population.
>
> The white overclass, then, properly perceived, is neither a middle class nor a high bourgeoisie but a sort of guild oligarchy, like those that ran early modern Italian and Dutch city-states.[13]

A member of the violent Right may hate Gingrich and the "Contract with America" as much as he or she hates Clinton and his friends. A member of the guild Oligarchy may be as anti-Government, anti-environmentalist, and anti-United Nations as the violent Right and at the same time look to scrunch all American wage earners within the machinery of global economics. Family and community may be ploys of both the Republican and the Democratic parties these days but they are not "costed in" by the guild Oligarchy, which crosses party lines. Well-being and progress are tied to our GDP accounting which counts only transactions involving money. "This left out two large realms: the functions of family and community on the one hand, and the natural habitat on the other."[14] National health care may be Clinton's liberal objective for all those who have no health insurance but it brings none of the "disaffected" anti-governmentalists, who may all benefit from such legislation, to his side. That sort of socialist hand-out to the underclass has no hold on libertarians, who assume that the guild oligarchy has made an underclass of ghetto minorities but not of them. Indeed, the militant disaffected have little idea of the existence of the guild oligarchy, except to define it as some global conspiracy which the U.S. federal government is part of. The New World Order is an order of enslavement. The target, nevertheless, has been federal bureaucracy and not the Fortune 500. It was the Alfred P. Murrah Federal Building that was bombed and not the world headquarters of R. J. Reynolds or I.B.M. That target may change however and the violent fringes—which may actually lie not too far from the fringes of what Kevin Phillips calls a "populist, anti-elitist" constituency—may enact a fear of the guild Oligarchy: a fear that the disaffected may just throw this country into the sort of tribalist mess the former Yugoslavia is now facing. And from another perspective, the guild Oligarchy is itself rushing us toward the same sort of turbulence. It is eroding our egalitarian democracy, one that grew to share the spirit of communitarian fraternity inspiring the French Revolution. The guild Oligarchy has extended measurements of well-being and progress that mask "the breakdown of the social structure and the natural habitat upon which the economy—and life itself—ultimately depend; worse, it actually portrays such breakdown as economic gain."[15] Thus, our political arena is noisy with the spins from Democrats and Republicans, each trying to spin the nightmare into the ideology of the other, each defining the new abyss as the creation of the "other."

Despite the hectic "culture wars" we are led to believe that Democrats and Republicans, a.k.a Liberals and Conservatives, are engaged in, when it comes to hooking up with Don Juan de Marco, David Koresh, Tim McVeigh or Randy Weaver, Richard Wayne Snell and the like, both parties can only deal with them insofar as they relate to the interests of growth and investment. We are indeed in a "culture war"—what Pat Buchanan calls a struggle for the soul of America—but only one of the warring factions has a niche in the government that is. The other has had its populist/anti-elitist/ libertarian impulses blocked by the elite of both Democratic and Republican parties. The press' "culture wars"—stereotyped in the image of a liberal "feminazi" with a pro-choice banner and a Pat Robertson Christian Coalition fanatical fundamentalist with a pro-life banner—have little to do with the sort of madness the country is heading toward, judging both by the Feds response to the Branch Davidians and the violent disaffected's response—in Oklahoma City—to that response and then, once again, the government's response to that response. Lewis Lapham describes how estranged our legislators are becoming from grasping the difference between corporate "wealth" and democratic "illth":

> [A]s I watched the C-SPAN broadcast of the testimony [redrafted legislation meant to protect the country from outbreaks of terrorism], I was struck by the willingness of almost everybody in the room—the senators as eagerly as the witnesses—to exchange their civil liberties for an illusory state of perfect security. They seemed to think that democracy was just a fancy word for corporate capitalism, and that the society would be a lot better off if it stopped its futile and unremunerative dithering about constitutional rights.[16]

Both with *NAFTA* and *GAT,* Clinton has proven that conservative economic values mean more than the well-being of the blue collar anti-elite. His and Hilary's national health care proposals sabotaged populist need for the sake of private sector conciliation, a sector that proved unreconcilable on the topic of anti-elite or liberal economic entitlements. Rather than take the Democratic Party toward something "new," Clinton has totally confounded anyone's understanding of that party's position in the "culture war". It may be that Pat Robertson's Christian Coalition is made up not of "economics first" elites but cultural elites, those with a sense of cultural "correctness" grounded in religious Truth. Pat Buchanan's followers are neither economic nor cultural elites but rather wildcat, independent "anti-elites" of the Michigan Militia and Tim McVeigh stripe.

If this is indeed for a vast number of Americans not just a secular "culture war", the kind George Will and Michael Kingsley can verbally crossfire, but a struggle for the soul of America, then it is indeed, as C. Carr writes in *The Politics of Sin,* "a cosmic struggle between good and evil." The Christian right sees itself "fighting satanic forces and all's fair in that kind of fight," which means that in the final analysis the Republican elite are just as unlikely to find a place for these cultural elites as are the Democrats.[17] Moral imperatives can be just as intrusive in the play of the global free market as ideological ones. The response of public record by both parties to the violence of the anti-elites remains a purely economic one, the sort of response that fuels the desire of the anti-elites to escape the domination of the elite oligarchy by any means necessary.

There is very little difference between our resident ideologies' inability to grasp what the fuss is all about in the former

Yugoslavia or Rwanda or Somalia or Chiapas or Chechnya and its inability to grasp what's going on inside McVeigh's or Weaver's heads. We may want to bring our cultural dissensus in line with our societal bowing to the market, but that doesn't prevent human actions from arising from a roll call of human desires, compulsions and propensities. We are on our public level of discourse, both social and political, losing touch with the "foul rag and bone shop of the human heart."

At the very moment when Newt Gingrich's *Contract with America* seems to more directly and expeditiously serve the guild oligarchy than Clinton's roundabout obeisances to it and therefore may lead to Clinton's defeat in '96, another player comes on the scene, in as unlikely a place as Oklahoma City. And that *other* unlikely place, Waco, Texas, which we already thought we had gotten out of the headlines, once again looms as not an anomaly but as part of something, part of something going on in this country that may do more than sweep one party out of office.

In the end, delusion is a form of escape; fanaticism, a devotion to what a societal order cannot conceive; and madness, a discourse unrepresented by lobbyists. When really only one discourse is being lobbied in Washington—what's good for American corporations and foreign investors—it is not surprising that our country is now producing more and more madness. The deeper we get into the narrow "all for ourselves, nothing for other people" vision of the Oligarchic guild, the more other people and their visions will be discarded on the inconceivability pile. The closer the salaried majority are driven to dehumanizing/impoverishing global salary levels, the more they will seek to escape by any means necessary. Driven to the wall by British taxation, American colonists fought for their independence. They were being used and scrunched, bled to death, denied identity. Sabotage, outbreaks of violence and rebellion, fiery speeches, arson, terrorism, murder, and bombings—tea parties gone mad. Our roots lie in such madness.

Notes

1. Signs are everywhere that we are waking up. See the notes to Michael Lind's chapter "The Revolution of the Rich," in *The Next American Nation* New York: Free Press, 1995, pp. 403–406. For opposing

arguments—that America is not class divided—see William Buckley, "Not So! Our Meritocracy is Alive and Well," *Detroit Free Press* August 7, 1995, 7E; Theodore Caplow, *American Social Trends* San Diego: Harcourt, Brace & Jovanovich, 1991; David Frum, "Welcome, Nouveau Riches," *New York Times* August 14, 1995.

2. Michel Foucault, *The Birth of the Clinic* New York: Pantheon Books, 1973.

3. Michel Foucault, *Mental Illness and Psychology*, trans. A. Sheridan. Berkeley: University of California Press, 1987, p. 74.

4. Michael Lind, "To Have and Have Not," *Harper's Magazine* June 1995, pp. 35–47.

5. Lind, p. 47.

6. Lewis Lapham suggests that we demonize those whose dreams we no longer share because of the "marvel of postmodern communications" which has us all "receding from one another literally at the speed of light." "Seen But Not Heard," *Harper's Magazine* July 1995, p. 31. I, on the other hand, feel that we don't share dreams and realities because our dream making and reality constructing is blocked off by the hegemony of the global economic metanarrative. Rationality and realism, sanity and wisdom are calibrated within the single vision of market values. Those made invisible by this form of national accounting are either simply delusionist, like Don Juan de Marco, or simply paranoic, like the militant libertarians.

7. "Outlaws on the Left and Right," *Time* September 7, 1992, p. 23.

8. Ibid.; for a look at the anti-government, militant faction see Michael Kelly, "The Road to Paranoia," *The New Yorker* June 19, 1995, pp. 60–75.

9. Michael Lind, "Why Intellectual Conservatism Died," *Dissent* winter 1995, pp. 42–47.

10. Distinctions are blurring more and more. Kevin Phillips blurs the market distinction between left and right, referring to the Democratic Party as anti-elite in economic policy and supporting "rapid economic growth." There are, however, elitists on social issues, which Phillips defines as "secular and nonchurchgoing." The Republicans have an elite economic policy and are socially conservative. Populism vs. elitism is Phillips' preferred dualism. "The People vs. the Parties," *The American Prospect* Fall 1994, pp. 69–73. Jacob Weisberg in "The Rad Right" connects liberal social elitism not with a mandated elitist "cultural literacy" but with a "hands off on private conduct" style, which is very much "true libertarian." And Republican social conservatives, like Bill Weld is a "rock-and-roll-loving Republican governor of Massachusetts who professes himself a libertarian and who does support gay rights and choice on abortion as well as smaller government." Libertarians and Republicans go arm and arm in their attack on government but split up

over something like Republican Phil Gramm's Christian Coalition social conservatism. And if libertarians can be deemed our new populists *and* those populists are both anti-government and anti-New World Order, anti-GATT and anti-NAFTA, they are not global free-market conservatives but old-time nationalists, the group that Pat Buchanan speaks to and for. In restricting the free play of the global market to suit their own nationalist agenda, these populist/libertarians move toward the economic interventionist style of liberals. "Global" becomes synonymous with "elitist" and not "populist." See James Ridgeway and Jeffrey St. Clair, "Where the Buffalo Roam," *Village Voice* July 11, 1995, pp. 14–16. Those whom Michael Kelly refers to as the "disaffected" and Kevin Phillips identifies as populist and disenfranchised are what Lewis Lapham calls "seen but not heard." Unsignified as well. "Seen But Not Heard," *Harper's Magazine* July 1995, pp. 29–36.

11. Christopher Hitchens, "Look Over Your Shoulder," *London Review of Books* May 25, 1995, p. 12.

12. "Montana's Mother of All Militias," *The Nation* May 22, 1995, p. 716.

13. Michael Lind, "To Have and Have Not," p. 37.

14. Clifford Cobb, Ted Halstead, and Jonathan Rowe, "If the GDP Is Up, Why Is America Down?" *The Atlantic Monthly,* October 1995, p. 62.

15. Cobb, "If The GDP . . . ," p. 60.

16. Lapham, "Seen But Not Heard," pp. 35–36.

17. *The Village Voice* May 16, 1995, p. 27.

"The Romance of Truly Natural Born Killers"

The Climate of Violence

There's a suspicion that lies behind my interest in the films *True Romance* and *Natural Born Killers* and it plays throughout all my observations of these films and how they hook up with what's going on in our "culture wars": we get tougher on crime and violence as it becomes clearer and clearer to us that it's a natural by-product of our globally designated way of attending to the world. This is how I see it working: an uncontested free market "logic" is a casino "logic," the kind of logic you get in Vegas. And out of this logic you get a casino reality: winners and losers. Now, we are presently seeing state after state turning to state run casinos as the answer to their economic woes. This isn't just because gambling appears to be a good market venture. We're legalizing the practice of gambling more and more because the whole country has already pushed aside liberal, social democratic, and socialist "logics" in order to make room for the "market" meta-logic. Casino logic, in other words, is Casino Meta-discourse, the transnational discourse that enables us to practice and institute within a certain framing of the real, within a certain sense of realism, of efficacy, of wise practice, of ultimate benefit to large numbers of people who share in the winnings of the "high rollers."

Let's bring the camera in close for a look at casino logic and its attendant sense of realism. First of all, self-interest propels competitiveness in the only arena that really counts: the market arena. Everyone is competing on every level—at home and globally—for the consumer's dollars. Everyone is envisioned as being both a consumer of products and services and a pusher of products and services. This means that it is the mind of the consumer that is being competed for. A desire to consume *something* has to be enkindled and then that desire must be transformed into a need. What is being constructed then out of a varied "cultural imaginary" is a special imaginary space that girds an order of things, a social imaginary, that frames the consumer and generates a "sense of realism" for the consumer so that maintenance and defense of this space rests in the hands of the consumer. New desires are fomented in this imaginary space.

I don't know why there is such objection to Baudrillard's notion of hyperreality—as if by describing the extent to which we have turned our planet into a shopping mall right out of Alice's Wonderland, he is responsible for having built it. You recall that in Wonderland nothing seemed to quite hook up the way it should, unbirthdays with Mad Hatters and all that. We never knew what to expect, what would happen. The market arena in our post-Fordist, post–industrial stage has enveloped itself within hyperreality and on this plane things matter as they do at the Hatter's tea party and the rules are the same as in the Queen's croquet game. Since needs are only false needs, and the desires behind them are only trumped up, there is nothing outside the play of desire and consumption to govern it. Or, we might say, free market play is a groundless, floating game.

So desire creation isn't where it's at, so to speak. It's not where the real action is because given the right staging, any desire can be marketed. "Right staging" then is the crux and it is here that the "right" staging is "any" staging that winds up floating. What is presently floating and what is going to float? The wheel spins. Louis Rukeyser speaks; we overhear E. F. Hutton; we learn how to trump with Trump; we become willing to see Milken as an American hero; we know that only players count and that only money talks; the Dow signifies—but what? The nightly business report reports. Economic trends, market forecasts. Fortune 500 reveals the winners. *The Wall Street Journal* chronicles the play after the event. Analysts and investment advisers, brokers and players, barbers as tipsters, cycles and flows. The market suddenly turns bullish and everyone scrambles to figure out why. It turns bearish and the same reasons can be summoned. We hit recessions whose existence can be denied by Presidential administrations and in this hyperreality no kid can come forward and say "Look, the President doesn't have any clothes on so there must be a recession!" Anything can be made to float in the hyperreality but since we are in the hyperreal there are only hyper indicators and no real indicators. Enlightenment logic serves you as well as it does the fellow who goes to Vegas with a fool-proof method for winning at roulette.

Of course we are constructing the hyperreality that constructs us; we are using the computer twenty-four hours a day to catch sudden shifts in the wind in currency exchange, in when to buy and when to sell. We are trying to navigate the waters of the hyperreal but we are without charts, compasses, quadrants, sextants. It is not in postmodernity that "anything goes," but here at the heart of our beloved new Grand Narrative of global market free play. Postmodernity has no stable investment in market hyperreality but rather cannot fail to narrate dissenting ways of attending to the world—ways inspired by the actual existence of a real world and real people. Within the market hyperreal, however, anything may happen. Whether your occupation will be an occupation, whether your community will be a community, whether your values will get "costed in," whether your individual life will get "costed in," whether a Civil War battlefield becomes a shopping mall, whether what is a quilted America becomes Disney's America, whether you will get the health care you need and so on—all this waits for a throw of the dice. Don't hold your breath expecting equality, social justice, wealth redistribution, ecological sanity, sisterhood and brotherhood, representative government and the survival of the planet to come out of this. We can send up more balloons in this hyperreality, desperately trying to send up another one just before the one we're drifting on pops. How the "dream restorers" get away with building stable family values, decisive verdicts, firm moral categories and all the rest on top of this "grounding" market contingency, this casino logic, is of course the great mystification of the last quarter of the twentieth century.

How and where does violence fit into this casino reality we are constructing for ourselves? First, let's trace the framing of a casino reality. Winners and losers. The house—now the state is legalizing itself as the "house"—is the steady winner, over the long run the odds are in its favor. There is no attempt in casino logic to distribute the winning and the losing, the joys and the sufferings, equally. Nor, quite to the contrary of what is often stated, does contingency reward talent and industry with success.The goddess Fortuna spins the wheel. The turn of the card, the roll of the dice. The old battle between faith and reason is preempted; whether the imagination is in its primary or secondary mode and revealing a unity beyond all diversity is a yawn; whether the body has its wisdom or consciousness is all; whether the heart wants in spite of what the mind knows; whether a dream is more real than real life—all of this is emptied, blows in the wind, is nothing more than wind. Contingency is all. Contingency constructs the way things will be.

One wonders whether any variety of political utopia, including our own "life, liberty and the pursuit of happiness" vision, ever anticipated that we would be putting all our eggs in the Chance basket. After all, some argument can be made for the view that casino logic is the abyss we've been trying to climb out of. Any order of things is order precisely because it pretends to have some control over contingencies. Note I say "pretends to" because the unmarked space of the world always succeeds in overspilling any order of things we impose upon it. What we leave unmarked visits us—like Scrooge's three ghosts—and plays the very devil with our concocted order of things.

And yet the play of order and disorder has been maintained; it appears to be abiding; it appears to be that very play of differance, of identity and difference, that Derrida makes much of. It is a play that moves us both to ravelling and unravelling, both to marking what is other and inconceivable, to opening our redundant ordering to the "unthought", namely, the will to power as the irrational fount of our "rationalism", the desires of the unconscious, the disturbing mania of ludic art, and the frightening looming on the horizon of contingency.

Casino reality is a bypass reality: if the play of order and disorder is at the heart of things, casino reality constructs a bypass route: it makes contingency an elevated highway. To what? Here our framing goes baroque: the big table winners want to uphold casino reality because a fall into, say, liberal democracy or worse, would erode their winnings by seeking some more just and humane, rational and equitable, order of things. On the other hand, accumulated winnings want to preserve themselves against the continuing play of casino logic. No winner is willing to leave the ultimate disposition of what Walter Huston in *Treasure of Sierra Madre* calls their "goods," in the hands of the goddess Fortuna. Allowable contingencies in the market order of things are not therefore allowable in the overall cultural order of things. Others must be constrained by . . . by "-isms." Who are these others? Well, let's go back to Vegas: the losers outnumber the winners on any night by a notable majority. Over a week of gambling, the losers grow more numerous. In Atlantic City, New Jersey the losers and the losing is more visible, the atmosphere more "tacky" and soiled because here the casino reality is not isolated

in the desert but it is in the midst of a megalopolis already rav-
aged by casino logic.

There must be again some defense against contingency; a
world in which anything is liable to happen, in which we always
fully expect not to know what to expect—this world is clearly no
longer permissible if you already have your "goods." A constraining order of things is needed but not one that replaces casino logic
as foundational cultural logic. The struggle to achieve this has
been going on since large profits were reaped at the end of the
Vietnam war. You might say the Reagan-Bush administrations
initiated the "culture wars" that would pull off this neat trick of
grounding society in one cultural representation of meaning and
value while making sure no system of meaning or value impeded
the extra-value/extra-meaning "play of the free market."

Back to violence finally: the very minute it becomes clear that
this trick—imposing an order of cultural meaning and value on
top of a foundational free-market play—cannot be performed,
our whole culture is mobilized against violence. We urgently need
a crime bill. Three strikes and you're out fever seizes the country. More prisons. Prison escapes can make or break a political
campaign: in the present Michigan gubernatorial race, the
Democratic challenger is criticized by the pundits for not seizing
the opportunity afforded by a prison break in Detroit to scrunch
the Republican incumbent who allowed the break to happen. If
government were doing its job properly, that prison break would
have been anticipated and therefore prevented. Government's
proper functioning after twenty years of politics in which candidates won on "get government off our backs" platforms is now in-
disputably disciplinary. Capital punishment is now the rage; to
be weak on crime, to be accused by your political opponent for
being weak on crime becomes an indefensible accusation. The
accusation elides whatever the reality may be. Both liberals and
conservatives rush to express their "tough love."

We are saturating ourselves presently in a discourse of violence, a discourse that urges us to put into practice all sorts of
crime deterrents, none of which pay more than lip service to notions of criminal recuperation, of redemption, of salvaging, of
bringing minds propelled by contingencies back to some "re-
spectable, godfearing, lawabiding, humane order of things."
Why? Because our casino culture can only give lip service to any
-ism of redemption for fear of that -ism taking off like a disease
and infecting a sufficient number of people who will show up at

the polls and vote down casino logic candidates, casino logic proposals, casino logic obstructions, and, most tellingly, replace casino logic omissions and absences with the intentions of their -isms. Remarkably, Christianity proves to be an -ism that—in the hands of Pat Robertson's Christian Coalition—helps demonize and hereticize the "losers," the pool of candidates from which the violent are "elected."

Clinton's election in 1992 is a break in casino logic. Whether or not what it threatens can be realized, this Democratic administration's concern with intervening an -ism into the play of casino logic has already mobilized a threat-dissolving force. What -ism the Clinton administration may be pushing is at once neither clear nor sufficient in the eyes of those who want to replace a foundational contingency with some vision of justice, equality, democracy, and ecological recuperation. However feeble, then, the Clinton administration may be in countering casino logic, that feebleness is already too much for that logic to bear. This situation reveals the degree of cynicism at work in the consideration of violence and the violent.

The violent were not "costed in" *before* they became violent. Now that we face the aftermath of a couple of decades of casino reality as the transcendent reality, we are forced to cost in the violent. And who they are will expand, just as within Hitler's logic how a Jew could be identified stretched widely, interrogated deeply, or within ante-bellum south, how a Negro could be identified stretched widely, interrogated deeply. All the South Central L.A. violent were "rioters." All the Boston Tea Party violent were "revolters." Are the "homeless" violent, or potentially so? Are gunowners, hunters and militia members violent? Are the young who violate town curfews violent? Are the incorrigibles in schools and companies, in families and in neighborhoods violent? Does the U.S. Post Office breed violent incorrigibles? Is there a violent art that should not be federally subsidized? Are there violent ethnic groups, sisterhoods, neighborhoods, rockers, dreamers, slackers, panhandlers, sex workers, unemployed, gangs, socialists, anarchists, patients, children, pensioners, strikers, addicts, blue collar workers and on and on?

The category of the violent has to expand because casino logic will be strewing more and more bodies in its wake and these bodies must be controlled. Their disenchantment, if you will, cannot be abated or forestalled; it is an inevitable result of a casino logic that will not obstruct its own dispensations. We are in the gruesome stages of preparation, rather like the way Hitler's extermination camps had to prepare themselves for the increasing number of people to be exterminated each day. Our society is being called upon to physically incapacitate a growing number of people it has already incapacitated economically and therefore, within a system in which money is identity and power, politically. A potential remedy for this is too dangerous to apply because it would risk the inviolable, unimpedable sacred order of economic contingency we choose to stand by regardless of the cost. "We can't go on, we go on"—Beckett's words take on a new cast. We are at the same time aware that all remedies float in a postmodern aura of undecidability and indeterminacy.

In this fashion, in this climate, does violence come to the screen in the present.

Natural Born Killers: The Order of Masterless Men and Women

"It's all about death in this country, it's all about fear, it's all about crime. It's all about terror. The media have sold the American people this enveloping sense of impending doom. I've got Justice Department figures that say the level of violence has been flat for 30 years."

Oliver Stone, quoted in the *San Francisco Chronicle*

"The United States has a higher rate of incarceration than any other country in the world except Russia, according to a case study done by a private group . . . Only 16 percent of the 155 percent increase in new court commitments to state prisons from 1980 to 1992 came from violent offenders, while drug, property and public-order offenders accounted for 84 percent.

The current emphasis on tough crime continues policies which were adopted over the past 20 years, 'that we now see have failed to reduce violent crime,' said Marc Mauer, assistant director of the Sentencing Project."

The Associated Press, September 13, 1994

"Nearly $10 billion of the $30 billion bill [Crime Bill] goes for state grants to build new prisons. The final compromise provides that half the money will be reserved for states that follow the federal government's lead and abolish parole."

"Crime Dog," *The New Republic* September 19 & 26, 1994

"Whatever else one thinks of his movie [Stone's *Natural Born Killers*], it's visually compelling, an acid trip through modern America's killing fields."
                    Frank Bruni, "A Killer Trip," *Detroit Free Press*
                                                    August 26, 1994

I have crisscrossed economics and politics with violence in order to contextualize what I have to say about *Natural Born Killers* in this chapter and *Reservoir Dogs* and *True Romance* in the next chapter. Violence is not new to the screen. I recall the chatter about Sam Peckinpah in the '60s and his fascination with it. Our great simulacrum of frontier courage was the Duke—John Wayne—who connected that frontier spirit with violence. A couple of years ago when Duncan Rinaldo, the TV Cisco Kid, died, it was mentioned that, although he wore a gun, he never fired it. He didn't want to show violence as an answer to anything. Of course, Cisco had a lot of fistfights as I recall. But he didn't fire his gun. I never noticed. Closer to the present we get films like *Dances With Wolves*, in which the white violence against Indians is shown to be savage. Our violence is now no longer part and parcel of our frontier spirit but a cancer on it. Stallone tries to free himself of his Rambo rampaging image, but the audience won't let him succeed as a comedian. Der Ahnald Schwarzenegger parodies his own Terminator image in *Last Action Hero* but the box office won't allow it. Violence continues to sell tickets no matter how repentant the culture seems to have become. Within the casino reality that I have described violence and the violent cannot be recuperated but rather must be contained. America better start remodeling its attitudes here so as to accommodate the expected swelling of the "violent class." So the repentant attitude we find in Costner's *Dances* just a few years ago, a film that ran away with numerous Oscars, is now defunct, out of the play, not to be "costed in." Costner was repentant; he wanted to make amends. The film "argues for" a rehabilitation of the white man, of Western civilization, of his audience. The Indian wasn't violent but simply violent in defense of his way of life. We are violent because violence is at the heart of our notions of competing, winning, progressing. Any belief in or gesture toward the rehabilitation of the violent criminal holds partially to this view that it is the reigning hegemony that must be rehabilitated. Clinton's original crime bill—unpassed—would fund certain social programs geared toward preventing/preempting violence by detouring the potentially violent onto a less violent path. But the country doesn't want rehabilitation; it wants containment, efficient, cost-effective, clearly enunciated and enforced arrest, prosecution and punishment of the criminally violent—a group that is blossoming.

Given this "hegemonic consensus" of a transparently inhumane casino logic and reality, (namely, that the violent are an inevitable offshoot of a "let the chips fall where they may" social philosophy) I am not surprised to see violence and the violent assume double-coded stature in popular film. On the one hand, every popular film in order to be "popular" with the mainstream populace must confirm the consensus beliefs of that populace—in this case, our recent drive to "end violence and put the violators away for good." On the other hand, a popular film must do more than show to that consensus populace film they have already been rolling in their own minds. The trick here is to plug into fears and anxieties that propel our retooled relationship with violence and the violent. Fear of violence, of running into the violent, is a perennial fear. Hollywood has never failed to tap into this fear but in every case the "perennial" is brought within a very specific social imaginary. Or, at least, the attempt is made. I have called the social imaginary of the present a "casino realism." What haunts this realism is the violent as an "anti-realism" force, violence that dispels the cast of the prevailing social imaginary. Here the violent become revolutionaries; psychopaths and sociopaths become agents of change, of the last, desperate instruments of market interruption, of a not to be denied intervention in the flow of market reality. People who have "screws loose" or are labeled as such, who prove incorrigible in school, on the job, in the military, in prisons, who don't respond, who are too busy working out "personal demons" to attend to the supremacy of market values in everyone's life, who leave off doing their jobs, of living in families, and take to the streets, roaming, affiliating with kindred souls, who hang at malls but don't consume, who are always eying everyone else's routines from somewhere outside, on the fringe, who tear at the holes of the way things are supposed to go, who live most healthfully when things are falling apart, who pull at the wires to reap their rewards—these are all the new provocateurs of an "anti-realism," an anti-market, *another kind* of social imaginary, that reaches out to its audience.

Hollywood has always sought to bring these miscreants back into the fold, as if the social order is doubly-redeemed and confirmed when these "masterless men" as Falstaff calls them are made to serve the order of things. The New Historicism builds its narrative of historical retrieval on a connected notion of hegemony in collusion with its own dissenters. Robin Hood's outcast crew stand behind Richard the Lionhearted; Francois Villon's gutter rats route the English; Jean Lafitte's pirates come to Andy Jackson's rescue; the Dirty Dozen route the Nazis; time and time again the worst are enlisted to redeem the social order. What chance of this now in 1994? Can casino reality even hope to have itself approved and strengthened by the lives it has not "costed in," by those it has beggared and continues to beggar in growing numbers each day, by those whose revolting can for just so long be signified as "rioting"?

It is because these masterless men and women cannot be brought into the fold without the fold opening itself to meet them, without the gratuitous dispensations of the global market being constrained, governed, deflated, dethroned, that the violent and the violence become demonized into an abstracted entity that denies them and their crimes any particularity, any individuality. Just as "Charley" in 'Nam could never be one individual Vietcong with his or her own name, so too must the violent now signify beyond any human life-world within the preferred social imaginary of casino reality. And the whole cultural imaginary seethes outside.

Let's sort through the quotations that begin this section. First, Oliver Stone tells us that violence is a media creation, that it has been flat for thirty years. The findings of the Gross Sentencing Project, however, indicate that despite tough crime policies over the past twenty years we haven't reduced violent crime. Blacks are in jail at six times the rate of whites and eighty-four percent of those in jail are nonviolent: drug, property and public-order offenders. The new Crime Bill rewards those states that abolish parole. Finally, we ask, does Oliver Stone's *Natural Born Killers* take us through modern America's killing fields or just through a *picture* of them, an acid induced trip through Stone's representation of violence in America? Stone himself claims that the media has "sold" the American people on violence and doom, that all we have is a distorted representation of it. Is he then mirroring that distortion in his film? Or, is he mirroring it and distancing himself from it so that we can see through the media distortion to the reality of violence underneath? But that reality he says is non-existent; there isn't much or more violence out there. It's about the same as it has been for a long time. Now, that representation doesn't slip into the film, although if we buy the notion that the film is parodying a media-constructed violence, then we would be led to wonder what the undistorted view of violence might be. That's if the film does distance itself from its own trip through the America's killing fields. In other words, Stone is taking the same trip as he accused the media of taking. If they can make a buck on enveloping us in a sense of terror and doom so can he. But he inflates the media in the film to intrusive proportions, mainly through the Robert Downey, Jr. character, an Aussie host of a TV showed called "American Maniacs." So the media is implicated but neither the implication that violence is a media creation nor the trip through the killing fields which is the trip the film takes reveals to us that violence has been "flat" in this country for thirty years.

Stone, then, misses the boat here. Media's love affair with violence in this country is old hat, but the way in which the social imaginary of violence is now being shaped is not old hat. It is very much a product of fundamental changes in our notions of liberal and social democracy. Violence is the answer to the question: Can there be such a thing as a market-run democracy? a democracy whose assertions as to equality, social justice, *human* individual freedom depend upon casino logic? Violence and the violent *are* increasing but we have not only altered who classifies here legally as violent and what classifies as violence but we have altered the moral frame within which the violent can be distinguished from the heroic, violence from disorder. Since the social imaginary within which violence and the violent are being gauged is no longer commensurable with earlier social imaginaries we cannot calculate real changes. But our interest should not be comparing the violent of one reality with the violent of another— even if we saw that such a postmodern condition were the case. Rather, our interest should be in describing the full extent of the whole cultural imaginary out of which our new privileged, social imaginary connections are being made with violence and the violent. We cannot stay within this preferred social imaginary—a "spin" imaginary"—and yet understand what it has already by its own rules dismissed, demeaned or demonized that makes up the infinitely wider and deeper cultural imaginary.

Popular film plays into this turbulent cultural imaginary despite the fact that such films must always, for purely market reasons, reflect the rising social imaginary of the day. For instance, although Stone's thesis would have been old in 1955—namely, that violence is a media/market hype—and although the thesis works him away from our new "opening" into violence—namely, that more and more of our nonviolent underclass are making the grade as violent and are being incarcerated—he astonishingly reveals something of the violent as revolutionary, the sociopath as our "last action hero," the incorrigible as the "great equalizer." He touches a cultural nerve. Let me go into this.

Mickey (Woody Harrelson) makes eerie contact with us. In line with what Stone thinks he's up to in this film, Mickey is supposed to be a whacko whom the media makes a hero out of and turns the American public into his fans. "Kill me too, Mickey," one sign reads. But Mickey is overdetermined; he overspills the role, he becomes more than his function in the film. I mean that what he *is* and what the media *makes* of him blur. Stone wants us to see that Mickey's charisma as a killer is imposed by the media. It's not really there. What's there is a psychotic, sociopath tortured by childhood trauma. A nut. Now the media wants to sell Mickey's charisma which is part and parcel of his terribleness, his unthinkableness, his monstrosity. They have an investment, so to speak, in packaging him this way. But Stone, who is ostensibly critical of this, wants to expose this nonsense. Why then does he give us a Mickey who seems morally superior to everyone else in the film except Mallory, who, like him, is also a killer?

Of course, Stone wants it both ways: he wants to get the pay off from enveloping Americans further in a sense of impending doom *and* he wants to be critically appreciated for exposing the media's complicity and our mindless fascinations. But because Stone, like us, is in the new social imaginary he must also respond to it. Mickey and Mallory then appear as rebels who within an earlier social imaginary would be represented as just that. But now in our own '90s, rebels and incorrigibles, dissidents and disagreeables, wanderers and drop-outs, the homeless and confused, the sodden and luckless—have been re-packaged as the violent, their transgressions become violence.

I am not, of course, ignoring the fact that they kill nor do I in any way condone killing. But it is not the number of violent criminals, including killers, that has significance in the new social imaginary. It is simply the most effective guise within which to package all those who are now signified with the words "violent" and "violence." They most clearly make the point for those whose point is that we must be tougher on crime, deny parole, not waste money on "pork" crime programs (meaning rehabilitation programs), get the violent off our streets once and for all. The thought of Mickey and Mallory propels us all to vote for harsher and harsher measures against the violent. And while we are thus occupied we do not think of questioning the expansion of the categories here; the very fact that it is not the violent we are putting away but those growing numbers of unemployed, homeless, extinct blue collar workers, grifters, drifters, bankrupt, angry veterans, druggies, truants, rabble and rebels, "masterless men and women all," and public offenders of all stripes.

And so we have two extremes: on one hand Mickey is a mass murderer and on the other hand he is a rebel in a road movie. Maybe like The Dean. Or Brando the Wild One. Violence and the violent cannot now be totally submerged within the niche our new social imaginary has created for them. We glimpse signs of the dissident spirit, the disruptive voice, the untamed vehemence against a social order that is disenfranchising and diminishing more and more each day and which concocts a social imaginary that will maintain this growing injustice. More and more have to be defended against, more and more lives have to be encompassed within the scope of the "violent," more and more actions within the compass of "violence." And thus, Mickey slips through as one of Gilles Deleuze's "deterritorializers," a "desiring machine" whose road is a "line of flight" from the social imaginary, a schizorevolutionary seeking a "reterritorialization" of that imaginary and the order of things in sway. And what is in sway? Have we any other order of things presuming to territorialize the entire globe but one—the casino logic of the market? In the end, Mickey and Mallory are escapees from that order, from MacJobs, from no benefits, no security, no work, no future, no life in the present, no economic equality and therefore no political equality, no dreams, no justice, no fraternity. No desires but the desire to make their desire part of the social imaginary. And they will kill to get this.

"The Abyss as Reservoir: True Romance and Hard Love"

> There is something desperately wrong with a society
> incapable of generating opposition to class privilege . . .
>
> Gary Gerstle, *Tikkun*

Desire is too often itself wrapped up in old stories of true romance. It's caught in dream. In the film *True Romance*, written by Quentin Tarantino, Clarence Whirley, played by Christian Slater, hangs out, reads comic books, listens to music, goes to see triple showings of Sonny Chiba martial arts movies, and converses with an imaginary friend, Elvis. He's young, futureless, as they say, and doing all this sort of hanging out in Detroit, a futureless city. But time doesn't really matter to Clarence because he's got a head full of colorful spectacle: comic book panels of true romance, TV's Partridge family good vibes, a curled-lip Elvis, a Sonny Chiba who isn't being a bad guy or a good guy. He's just a mean mother-fucker as Clarence explains to Alabama, played by Patricia Arquette. She's three dates into being a call girl and she runs into Clarence before she can go further down those Detroit mean streets. He rekindles her own dreams—that she can be true in a true romance forever. "I'm not poor, white trash," she tells him; "I'm one hundred per cent monogamous and I swear to you I'll never lie again." It's only the second panel of this "True Romance" but they've found each other and from that moment on "the dream was real."

It's a true romance plot their love has to journey through. Everything they desire—from Clarence wanting to be like Elvis to Alabama wanting her whole life to be just background for a true romance—are fables, comic book stories, pulp fiction, constructed and then enacted. Violence is in their dreams because it is what Elvis advises, what Sonny Chiba does, what comic book heroes face in life. But who dreamed up Elvis? Or, what was in the culture at that time that brought Elvis to the Sun Studio in

163

Memphis and thereafter made a myth of him? Does Clarence want to live in an Elvis-style true romance, be the hard, sneering Elvis of "Jailhouse Rock" hyped by Colonel Tom Parker? Or, did the "young and the restless" at that time select and shape the Elvis of their dreams? Violence and the violent are not simply media induced, blown into hype proportions as Oliver Stone suggests in *Natural Born Killers,* but entwined within the way we dream. We dream within the myths and fabulae of our culture—the culture dreams us. But we also dream the culture into existence. The media and popular culture plug into the hot wiring of our dreams and fears, what we desire and what we are haunted by. They play back what we've already constructed.

We are in the present more mesmerized by popular culture than by the classics of Western culture listed by E. D. Hirsch or the moral treasury anthologized by William Bennett. There is more of Homer Simpson in our dreaming than the blind bard; we desire in the shadow of Elvis and not Epicurus. In Tarantino's world of true romance, there are no bad guys imposing bloated spectacles upon us, filling us with hype for their own profit, forcing us to drop reality and feed on simulacra. Rather, we create the bad guys and the good guys and have been doing so since the "dawn of man"—which explains why women have to do so much storytelling in the present to catch up, to create first a "dawn of women" and then go on. We're all living out our stories. The media is the messenger but the message is ours to ourselves. As it is a message that dreams of capturing a reality and truth outside its own representation, its own words and images, but fails to do so in any determinate, steadfast way, we fall back on the messenger, on the media, on our transmitters. But we give them life.

True Romance has a different slant on this than *Pulp Fiction.* In *Pulp Fiction* the way we fabricate and dream our reality is the substance of the film. The postmodern ontology and epistemology takes us for a ride down new corridors of time and space, emplotment and narration. Unity, coherence and continuity meet their postmodern fractal equivalents. It's an introduction to postmodern real-izing; a tour of a postmodern being-in-the-world. And it's a giddy ride, an exuberant tracing of the *real* new world order. The canvas is therefore big, as big as the world because the film is ultimately making "worldmaking" its subject. *True Romance,* on the other hand, makes the world a true romance and gives us a panel by panel narrative true romance sequence. The world is reduced to one story; the focus has narrowed to the proportions of a true romance comic. And this comic book treatment has no challengers, which means that rather than being in a postmodern world of contesting narratives and realities, as in *Pulp Fiction,* we are really in one fantasy world that plays out within the protocols of naive realism. I mean that Clarence and Alabama take their true romance to a Cancun beach at the film's end. And in between, their concoction of true romance swallows all other realities, except Brad Pitt's Floyd, who remains on the couch watching TV and smoking dope. Even though *his* world is not shown in a clash with Clarence and Alabama's, it remains unabsorbed by them, resistant, oblivious. True romance here is going on in a radically different way. But we are not directed to this vulnerability of Clarence and Alabama's reality to other realities because the director, (not Tarantino, but Tony Scott), is following through on true romance as camp, as a sort of cross between a Mel Brooks movie, a true romance tabloid, and a Hollywood road movie. The problem then is that their dream does become real when *Pulp Fiction* shows us that multiple dreams create multiple realities and multiple realities create multiple dreams—dreams of truth, romance, desire, ambition, violence and so on, none of which agree to wind up in the same place, say, Cancun. The imposition of one dream on a world of colliding dreams can indeed only go on in a true romance tabloid.

Because no one dream can shape an uncontested reality, there is no hint in *Pulp Fiction* that the stories we create and live in will override and overwrite the total unmarked space of the world, the reality that is there but we can only selectively, variously and not incrementally mark with our storymaking. The ghostly remnants of a Detroit that once was cannot be erased by a true romance reality. Violence is neither to be reduced to a Sonny Chiba movie or an Elvis macho charisma. It can rise out of pure chance or any number of cultural constructions, including those we shape by our political and economic agendas, as well as by our moral agendas. Therefore, if we want to argue that the darkest part of the postmodern abyss is our relapse into true romance simulacra, our living out comic book fantasies, our being fed on a diet of spectacle and not reality, we can only do so if we accept a disconnect between reality and our representations and accept the existence of unrivaled constructions of the world. I mean that our reality is in our constructions, our dreams, (which do show up in comic book fantasies and elsewhere), but our constructing is always in motion and never unchallenged. While *True Romance* fantasizes dream and desire as universal and unrivaled and allows the same to construct and deploy violence within its own framing, *Pulp Fiction* shows us that reality is pulp in many hands and with many different and divergent results. No one in *Pulp Fiction* controls violence nor is free of being a victim of someone else's expression of violence.

But there is a scene in *True Romance* in which Tarantino's multi-focused writing is not directed down one path.

"That Means You're Part Eggplant."

The scene is between the two resident neo-baroque personalities of the screen: Dennis Hopper and Christopher Walken. Walken is Vincent Cacardia, the Sicilian *consigliere* to the mobster Blue Lou Boyle, whose cocaine has accidentally wound up in the hands of Clarence, Hopper's son. Walken wants to know where Clarence has gone and he makes it clear to Hopper that he will torture him until he reveals his son's whereabouts. Surrounded by Sicilian-speaking goons, Hopper sits there and signals to us with his eyes the course of his own narrating of the scene. Walken stands in front of him at first, only later when Hopper begins to tell his tale of Sicilian "black blood" does he sit down, cross his legs and listen. At first Hopper refuses the cigarette that Walken offers. He doesn't want to sit and smoke with these intruders. After Walken smashes his fist into the bridge of Hopper's nose and then offers him his handkerchief to wipe the blood and then orders Hopper's hand slashed which is now wrapped in the same handkerchief, Hopper is no longer interrogating with his eyes. He now knows the cycle: reasoning, violence, relief—until there can be no relief. He doesn't know Vincent Cacardia but he's an ex-cop and he knows how the violent can sometime play out their hand—like Christopher Walken playing cruelty with a sick smile in a Christopher Walken movie. But Walken isn't in Hopper's dream; he's real in a way that has nothing to do with Hopper's dream. He's not Gary Oldham's Drexel, the white guy pretending to be black, who Clarence confronts and kills as if he were Elvis vanquishing the bad guys with a curled lip. While Alabama and Clarence are at that very moment heading cross country with the cocaine that will buy them their Cancun dream—living out their true romance—Hopper is in tabloid time and slow time. A retired cop, he's now working as a nightwatchman. He's got a dog, no beer in the frig because he doesn't drink anymore, and when Clarence rushes in at tabloid true romance speed, Hopper tells him to slow down. It's not that for Hopper reality isn't a patchwork of all kinds of fabrications. He is in that flux but also not being swept away down any one course. The world goes at a faster pace for Clarence and Alabama because they've both been swept away down a true romance, white water rapids as if this dream, this fabrication could become real in an unconflicted, unchallenged way. And maybe, just maybe, it's only "true romance," unconditional love that can do this.

Now at this moment as Hopper accepts a cigarette from Walken, lights it up and begins to talk about his love of history and relate a bit of history he had read regarding the origin of the Sicilians, he has a clear sense that escape is a dream that will not be realized. But he also decides to construct his own end so he tells the one story that will antagonize his Sicilian torturer. His tale of Sicilian "black blood" perforates Walken's resolve to slowly torture Hopper until he finds out where Clarence has gone. The "black blood" story is a tabloid tale that haunts Sicilians—not a story of "true romance" but of suppressed romance. The Moors, who were niggers Hopper tells Walken, overran Sicily and fucked the Sicilian women. And because of that, today Sicilians are part eggplant—they're part black. That means you're an eggplant he tells Walken. Faced then with a Sicilian *consigliere* out of a tabloid Godfather reality, Hopper counters with another tabloid tale.

Reality is neither coerced by nor lost in such tabloid renditions. Spectacle seduces us into accepting it as reality but since reality is for us nowhere but in spectacle, we are always caught within a play of contestatory seductions. And although violence is tabloid and spectacle bound, no story of true romance, or of "black blood," or of Sicilian torturers, or of Elvis and Sonny Chiba dimensions, or definitively brought to the screen in a film like *Coming Home in a Body Bag* either can reliably stand in for or encompass violence and the violent. We do, however, live at a moment when more and more lives are spun in stories of violence while tales of social mediation of violence proliferate. It's not surprising then that a tale of true romance wending its way through violence and out into the sunlight gets to be told. It tells us that violence succumbs to romance. But Tony Scott directs that succumbing. To see how Tarantino will direct his own words we have to turn to *Reservoir Dogs*. But first a look at who and what breeds such dogs . . .

**"Markets are not about justice. They are about profits."
Joel Nelson, Post-Industrial Capitalism**

Our present "global imaginary" is not really set on showing how violence succumbs to romance, not even true romance. Violence and the violent must be curtailed and contained. We must all succumb to the notion that violence emerges not from people like us but from underclass mutants, sociopaths and psychopaths, whackos and sickos. They either have something wrong with them genetically or they were nurtured in a welfare world with a single parent or no parents at all. These comic book panels run like this: because of a damaging liberalizing of family values these people are incapable of assuming personal responsibility. They all travel the same road to violence: welfare dependency which breeds a "society owes me a living" attitude which enervates a sense of personal moral responsibility which in turn has no trouble in accepting a "take it where you can get it" approach to life which leads to violence and crime in order to get all they think they deserve. In order to help these people we have to cut them off from every form of social assistance, hold them consistently to the laws and norms of society, and then for their own sake lock them up when they don't comply. Thus, we are presently deeply into a romance of "tough love."

"Liberals and conservatives alike share a new consensus that the most pressing social problem of the 1990's is not poverty but the behavior of poor people. The solution is coercion and punishment."[1] We may lose a generation or two but eventually underclass young will be reared within the expectations of society and not within a destructive climate in which individuals are victims and society is at fault. It is vitally important within our present inequality for a society which is giving a generous living to those now in charge of "restoring the dream" that this golden goose of a society not be altered. Not be altered except, of course, in regard to those who might through violence threaten the resident order.

We cannot now be talking of sociopaths and psychopaths, those societal anomalies whose proportions to the overall population probably haven't changed since Cain and Abel. We are making a greater effort to label more people as such but that represents a need of our present society. And we have a much greater facility now in publicizing a Jeff Dahmer or a Son of Sam or a Unabomber than we did a hundred or three hundred years ago. We have more of these whackos because we have a much larger breeding pool. What is increasing is the number of people who are neither ill-natured nor ill-nurtured but simply economically scrunched. They turn to dealing in drugs or to breaking and entering to support drug habits. Or they pass bad checks, work credit card and insurance scams, shoplift, rob from the register, work door to door scams, drive while drunk, get picked up for public indecency, resist arrest, run out on child support, turn tricks, receive welfare, live on the streets, have children outside of marriage, drop out of high school, do drive bys, join gangs, abuse wives and children—in short, lead an "underclass life."

"'Underclass' is a protean word, widely adopted because it is so vague," Thomas Sugrue writes in his review of Herbert Gans' *The War Against the Poor*.[2] It is now a signifier attached to the poor in such a way that their lapse into uncivilized, violent behavior is due to a lack of a proper work ethic, to the inculcation of family values, to any sense of a "moral imperative." And much more:

> In the demonology of the New Right, poverty is a symptom of immorality. Like born-again Calvinists, conservatives view poverty as the outward manifestation of inner depravity. The poor, in their view, are lazy, violent, sex-crazed, and addicted to drugs. Bad mothers and absent fathers breed a generation of criminal boys and promiscuous girls. Barely beneath the surface are assumptions about racial inferiority. Although the majority of poor people in the United States are white, the popular image of poverty has a Black face.[3]

Everything is summoned in order to focus blame on the underclass and not on their economic and political disenfranchisement which has resulted as a by-product of the unimpeded workings of the global market. While our own national market logic tells us that everyone has an equal opportunity to compete and failure to do so is a matter of personal resolve and commitment, assumption of personal responsibility and self-determination and so on, we yet live in climate in which "over the past twenty-five years, the gap between rich and poor has widened. Wages have stagnated or declined. In 1992, the average income for the poorest fifth of families in the country was a mere $9,708. Hit hardest are residents of inner cities, where joblessness rates often exceed forty percent."[4]

And what is this market climate like and who is lives in it—besides the underclass?

> Owing to increased use of strategic management, to the grow-
> ing knowledge base of business, and to greater organizational
> flexibility, business has been more able than in the past to in-
> crease its political domination and to intensify and widen eco-
> nomically competitive fields. Inequality in the absence of
> conflict is the result—suggesting little political opposition in the
> near future to increased inequality or to the growing importance
> and influence of the business community . . . Professionals
> and managers schooled in business administration are the ap-
> plied arm of free-market economics, providing expertise, advice,
> and direction in the spread of the marketplace.[5]

Unfortunately for this professional class, whom Michael Lind
calls a "white overclass," they yet have to live in the world they
have made, a world in which inequality and social injustice
touches the lives of the many. Overclass lives, therefore, have to
be distanced and protected from underclass lives—a process
which Lind calls "Brazilianization" in honor of the endemic status of rich and poor in Latin American countries. What we are
presently seeing, then, is a withdrawal of the overclass "into
its own barricaded nation-within-a-nation, a world of private
neighborhoods, private schools, private police, private health
care, and even private roads, walled off from the spreading
squalor beyond."[6] And as the overclass withdraws into a se-
cluded privacy in which its behavior is not visible, it leaves behind in full view the underclass, whose behavior makes tabloid
TV the success that it is. In a country in which now only thirteen
cities publish rival newspapers—newspapers with different owners—and these newspapers are owned by transnational con-
glomerates, there is little hope that attention and the camera will
turn to the values of the insulated.

The camera is turned on the very visible underclass because
the powerful, in Gans' view, are obsessed with their idea of a
dangerous and potentially more dangerous underclass. Rather
than trace the deteriorating social conditions to the "market tri-
umphant," the powerful have engaged in a campaign of demonizing the underclass in order "to justify punitive social
policies."[7] Lind turns the camera on the white overclass: "a husband and wife, each with a lucrative professional job, plus a
maid." And this three parent ideal family distances itself in every
way, from geographical to psychological, from the underclass.
The white overclass is obsessed with losing weight because of a
"fear of lower-middle-class vulgarity, of the animal grossness,

the unself-conscious corporeality associated with 'rednecks' and 'hardhats' and 'Bubbas' and 'ethnics' and 'white trash.'" We see these people daily on *Jenny Jones, Danny!, Carny, Maury*. Messy lives, no self-consciousness or critical awareness. Welfare reform is presently being advocated because we must cease to reward "bad behavior" on the part of the underclass. "Tough love" will get them back on the right track. What's wrong in their lives always fits into "the demonology of the New Right"—they are innately depraved or just lazy, sex-crazed, drug addicted, racially inferior and so on. There's never a reservoir dog in the bunch.

Reservoir Dogs

"Nobody tells me what to do."

Mr. Orange

So what's a reservoir dog? "A title I don't understand," Stanley Kauffman writes in *The New Republic*. "The title itself is probably a nod to *Straw Dogs*" Terrence Rafferty writes in *The New Yorker*.[8] In the context of Tarantino's film these "reservoir dogs" seem to fulfill the demonology bill, the Hollywood classic realist formula in regard to bad guys, the small independent movie's "difference" from that formula, and Tarantino's own "mean streets"/"tough guys"/"street lingo" fascination. The film has all of these threads but the total weave removes them from the criminal underclass we see on TV's *Cops* or the "white trash" we see on the TV talk shows. You will find a poster still of the black-suited reservoir dogs plastered in the rooms of undergrads. Could there be a cultural fascination for these reservoir dogs that has nothing to do with fear, "tough love," "bad behavior," and "punitive social policies"? That sort of fascination is one mesmerized by fear: will those who have been economically written off blindly riot and will riot turn to revolt? Tarantino taps into a charisma of violence and the violent, a dark reservoir of restlessness and resentment, of discontent and rebelliousness. These dogs are recalcitrant, ungovernable, nonconforming, defiant, unwilling to follow the rules, incorrigibles who behave as they like, oblivious to both liberal attempts to rehabilitate or conservative attempts to punish "bad behavior." "Bad" here takes on the street sense of transcending good and evil, of acting so outside social norms as to startle and impress. These dogs can bite.

They'd be too risky to book on a tabloid talk show, regardless of how engrossing they might be. And they won't appear on *Cops* because they don't follow type—shirtless, addicted, whining, lazy, depraved and as cowed and pliant as the bad, poor and abject should be in the face of righteous authority. Tarantino's dogs aren't lining up for obedience class.

I am drawn to the fact that at a moment when there is a strenuous effort being made to link the underclass with all forms of depravity and inferiority (and thus to all forms of violent behavior), there is an opposing linkage of violence to free expression and radical will, to a spirit indeed of revolutionary iconoclasm. Tim McVeigh, Randy Weaver, and Claude Dallas before them play out a sort of American outlaw motif while the whole militia conclave can be viewed as nothing more than an outcropping of underclass rebellion. I am not suggesting that there is any trace of solidarity between reservoir dogs and gangsta rappers and the Heartland's militants. They do, however, have a similar impact upon the present effort to restore the dream, a terrorizing terrorist impact. A "nobody tells me what to do" response is the response Mr. Orange, a psychopathic stone-cold killer, makes to his hostage cop when the unfortunate cop refers to Nice Guy Eddie as Mr. Orange's boss. Mr. Orange doesn't recognize any legitimate *de jure* authority out there. The difference between his declaration of being a "bad subject" and that of the Heartland militants is that Mr. Orange is a thorough-going, fully aware bad subject of state, society and private sector. The rebellion of Heartland militants is focused on the federal government which has created all our problems both at home and abroad. Thus, our global market problem is federal government caused; our societal problems can be traced to affirmative actions and multiculturalism—all engineered by the federal government. One wonders how long the Fortune 500 will remain on the militant's "good guy" list. One wonders if the target may change from a federal building in Oklahoma to a multicorporate headquarters.

Reservoir dogs don't bomb federal buildings; they rob jewelry stores. They go after the money. But their drive to break in and steal is tied to their sociopathy: they mock what "society says" and to them, "cops aren't real people." There is here an animosity toward authority that does not spend itself attacking that authority. Instead it takes a short cut to what gives anyone in our society authority—money. Money creates identity, choice and freedom, dignity, opportunity, comfort, health, respect, power and so on. To have money and the things money can buy is to be enfranchised not only economically but politically. The South Central L.A. rioters looted their own neighborhoods, but we ill-prepare ourselves for the future if we think that their rioting and looting was not itself fuelled by an animosity toward the authorized and authorizing "winners" that is at the core of political rebellion. Political disquietude is here fuelled by an economic disquietude that soon finds itself looting the economic status quo. The "Wild West Backlash" against the federal government, which itself has close ties to the militia movement, right now expresses the same kind of hatred for authority that our reservoir dogs display: "Threats against federal employees working in the rural West have become almost commonplace with workers having to travel in pairs, maintaining constant radio contact with home offices. Their families routinely receive threats aimed not just at the workers but also at their children."[9] This political animosity has an economic connection: federal public lands, the rebellious Westerners argue, rightly belong to the states and the counties. The land is the loot and it's theirs to take. Of course, if the ownership of this federal domain "devolved" to state and local ownership, it would easily "devolve" still further to privatization, or ownership by multinational corporations. Western local governments would find it difficult to resist both the money and jobs—universally alleged—that sale to the highest bidder would bring. It is hard to believe that the Westerners themselves will be "players" in this privatized world divided on the global market block and that anything but political unrest would follow. The economic repercussions might not then be against a disconnected federal government.

If the reservoir, then, is our economic coffers, our wellspring, our gold mines and bonanzas, the dogs that threaten to both pilfer it and despoil it are not just Tarantino's reservoir dogs. There are varied packs throughout the country at this moment who may bite the hand of authority as well as bite into our horde of loot, amassing in fewer and fewer publicly accessible reservoirs.

Notes

1. Thomas J. Sugrue, "Poor Vision," *Tikkun* September/October 1995, p. 87.

2. Thomas J. Sugrue, "Poor Vision," *Tikkun*, 10, #5(September/October 1995), p. 88.

3. Sugrue, p. 87.

4. Sugrue, p. 87.

5. Joel I. Nelson, *Post-Industrial Capitalism: Exploring Economic Inequality in America* Thousand Oaks: Sage, 1995, 159.

6. Michael Lind, *The Next American Nation: The New Nationalism and the Fourth American Revolution.* New York: Free Press, 1995.

7. Sugrue, p. 88.

8. Stanley Kauffman, "Blood Lines," *The New Republic* November 23, 1992, p. 30; Terrence Rafferty, "Men Overboard," *The New Yorker* October 29, 1992, p. 106.

9. James Ridgeway and Jeffrey St. Clair, "This Land Is Our Land," *Village Voice* June 20, 1995, p. 16.

What Shoes Can Tell You

"Same-old, same-old," Scraps said, passing a hot water sprayed plate onto Rick Monte who took it and towelled it. "I go home. My old man is down in the basement trying to fix something he had in his youth that broke before I was born. My mother is in the kitchen frying dinner. I go watch a little bit of OJ in the white Bronco. I got it on tape."

"That's pathetic, man," Rick replied, accepting another hot plate from Scraps. "Any chance your Mom could put out another plate tonight?"

Scraps leaned toward Rick and whispered:

"Betty Lip's got the afternoon special stashed away for me."

"You mean the 'Hannibal Lecter' kidneys and chianti special?" Rick whispered back. "I pass on that."

"No, that was yesterday," Scraps whispered.

"You remember 'The Shoes of the Fisherman' cod Sweeney served up last Good Friday?"

"You know you get the 'Pat O'Brien' lamb stew," Scraps told him.

Rick made a face. He didn't like the green coloring Sweeney put in the stew and the red dyed potatoes that were supposed to look like Pat O'Brien's nose after he had a few.

"Tomorrow it's extra special," Scraps said. "I'm talking about the 'Babette's Feast' dinner special Saturday's only."

"Enough for two?"

Scraps nodded.

"Betty's got the hots for me."

"Yeah, I know how that is. I get free prozac from Lucy Powell."

"Prozac? That give you a buzz?"

"It's an aphrodisiac," Rick told him.

"What about those two guys?" Bowman Spin, sitting at the counter alongside Mayor Beth Swingle asked. Gladys had just pushed through a swinging door into the kitchen and for a brief moment Bowman and Beth had a glimpse of Scraps and Rick potwalloping.

"What about them?" Beth replied.

"Nothing, only it would be interesting to find out just where they broke down on the yellow brick road."

"Maybe they didn't break down," Beth said, trying to rip through the cellophane to get at the crackers. "Maybe when they're not washing dishes they're composing symphonies. Or painting masterpieces."

The crackers splintered out on the counter. Beth pushed them under the soup bowl.

"Maybe they have more of a life than we do, Mr . . . ah . . . I'm sorry I forgot your name."

"John Devereaux. Everybody calls me Jack," Bowman replied, smiling.

"Well, why don't you get down to it, Jack," Beth said. "Why is *People* magazine interested in me?"

"It's a piece on small town mayors," Bowman told her. "The focus is what are you doing to get your people working, back into the economic flow? Is small town government on the people's backs? is the lead for my piece."

"How does small town government get on the people's backs?"

"You know," Bowman said. "Regulations. Taxes. Welfare programs. Free lunch programs. Free everything for those who don't want to work. General business impediments. You know obstacles to entrepreneurial creativity."

"Well, we wouldn't want to impede entrepreneurial creativity," Beth replied. "So I'll tell you what we've done. We've cut property taxes. Suspended town regulations on businesses, increased police protection in the wealthier neighborhoods, and have privatized the public schools."

"Really?," Bowman said, obviously caught by surprise.

"Sure," Beth said. "Why not? I'm not going to win elections doing things for poor people who don't vote anyway and don't have enough political sense to know when they're taking a hit and when they're not. So get all this down. I mean for your article."

She began to spiel at a rapid rate. Bowman now was jotting all this down in a leather encased notepad set down next to his coffee cup.

Beth watched him write.

"We've also graduated facilities all over town . . . "

"Graduated facilities?"

"Like a graduated income tax but in reverse," Beth explained. "For instance, at all our major shopping locations the closest parking is for Ferrari, Mercedes, Jaguar, Rolls, Cadillac, Lexus, BMW. Chevy and Ford pickup trucks in the back lot."

Bowman's eyes went wide. Beth sipped her soup. An *Eating Raoul* soup du jour.

"You see that young man's shoes?" Harry Powell said to his daughter Lucy as they sat in a rear booth at Sweeney's. Lucy turned to look at Bowman Spin's wingtips.

"They're real shiny," Lucy said, looking back at her Dad.

"Well, I had a pair of shoes like that when I got my first job. Not my first first job but my first job with a law firm. Barfield Simmons's dad, may they both rest in peace."

"They're millions of pieces now," Lucy said, staring at the neatly cut club sandwich in front of her. It was Sweeney's new 'Mildred Pierce' special because of the way the toothpicks pierced the club lozenges.

"Then the rain waters them and the roots of trees and roses suck them in."

"The shoes I wore on my first job weren't even shoes," Harry said, stirring his W.C. Fields mocha java. "They were U.S. Keds sneakers. Hightops they call them now but in those days there were only tennies, which were always white, and black and white sneakers. This is way before the Michael Jordan Air Jordan craze."

Lucy was busy unlayering a tiny portion of her club with a toothpick.

"I had to unload tar buckets from the back of a lorry onto the loading dock at Bullard's Hardware. May he rest in peace. I remember getting some tar on those sneakers and tracking it into the kitchen and your grandmother raised Cain. May she rest in peace."

"If a piece of Grandma," Lucy said, holding up a piece of swiss cheese on the end of a toothpick, "mingles with a piece of John Fitzgerald Kennedy," holding up a piece of ham on another toothpick, "and they get sucked up by the roots of an apple tree and then I eat an apple from that apple tree."

She looked up from the toothpicks at her Dad.

"Do I get to be like them?"

"I still remember the first pair of shoes my Dad bought for me," Harry replied. "I've got them up in the attic. I've got every pair of shoes that I ever wore. They're sort of my memorabilia. You know what memorabilia is, Lucy?"

"We've issued Gold ID's for our wealthiest citizens so they need never wait on a queue," Beth said. "Flash and go on through to the head of the line. Supermarkets, cinema, basketball, plays."

"Remarkable."

"We're also bringing the wealthy into the poorer neighborhoods by guaranteeing them Manor House privileges in that neighborhood, including *le droite de signeur.* If you recall your feudal history, that's the right granted a patron to sleep with any of the women in his domain."

"Bloody remarkable," Bowman said, no longer writing.

"You are surprised?" Beth said, smiling. "You expected us to be a backwater casualty of social Darwinism?"

"Not at all," Bowman spun. "I'm just surprised at the extent of your . . . your policies. And none of this . . . of these policies have generated a hostile reaction. From the citizenry?"

"Why should it? When the benefits are trickling down each and every moment of every day."

"Astounding. You have programs to aid those in difficult circumstances?"

"We have a thirteen week Cold Turkey program," Beth said, smiling her widest smile.

"How does that work?"

"An unemployed person is given absolutely no assistance of any kind for a period of thirteen weeks."

"Not even a twelve point redemption program?" Bowman said archly.

"Not a hint of compassion or commiseration," Beth said. "The purpose of the program is to re-enkindle the passion to survive, to make it and be a winner."

"Astounding," Bowman said, thinking he was feigning his feigned surprise. "What if there is no passion to win? Let's say just enough passion to lose. Which they've already done."

"At the end of our thirteen week Cold Turkey program he or she is either dead, living, or moved on elsewhere."

"Astounding," Bowman said. "The dead and the moved on are no longer problems for you."

"And those that are still living have either found work, have become adept hunters and gatherers. Or they have been imprisoned."

"Astounding," Bowman repeated. "You don't initiate training programs?"

"We have no city bureaucracy," Beth replied. "We allocate no public funds for training that will occur in the private sector. If a person succeeds in being hired."

"When I was wearing those grey bucks," Harry told Lucy, "I had one thing in my mind and one thing only: get out of this town and be somebody."

Lucy saw Ginch passing by and she went out to pet him.

"I married your mother in a pair of suede and moroccan leather shoes," Harry went on, not noticing Lucy's departure. "By that time I wasn't thinking about leaving town."

Mark Wonder left Ginch with Lucy and came into Sweeney's to see what was going on. Outside, Lucy walked Ginch over to Mike Woad dressed as Santa Claus in front of a Salvation Army bucket.

"I'm taking the saucer out tonight," Woad said to Lucy. "If you want to come. It'll be me, Faye and Peaches. We're gonna look for RC and Margaret."

"Can Ginch come?" Lucy said, pointing down at Ginch who had assumed a sitting position and was looking up at Lucy.

"Sure," Woad said, ringing his bell at a couple of passersby. "But the experience will be wasted on him. He won't be able to appreciate the alien vibe."

Commander Data, who had been monitoring Ginch's positronic brain, parked his Lexus and walked over to Woad and Lucy. Woad rang his bell at him. Data took out a hand full of coins and dropped five of them slowly, one at a time into the bucket.

"How many, Ginch?" Data said and to Lucy and Woad's surprise Ginch barked five times.

"Five coins, five barks," Data told them smiling.

"Great," Woad said flatly.

"You're not impressed?" Data said.

"Sure, I'm impressed," Woad replied. "But just think how impressed Ginch here is with me. I talk."

"Well, let's see," Data said. "Give us a few words, Ginch."

"Everything is alien to me but my own feces," Ginch said in a thin metallic voice.

"What about work for welfare?" Bowman asked Mayor Beth Swingle. "Surely the town can put people to work on the roads and so on to earn their keep?"

"Road repair, public park maintenance and the like are all privatized. There is a profit to be made in all these endeavors. This town does not socialize what can be capitalized."

"Can I quote you on that?"

"Of course," Beth replied. "The town only picks up the tab on the private security used to protect the homes and property of our wealthier citizens. We bury all our non-recyclables and toxic waste in the poorer sections of town."

"So those young men washing dishes in there . . . "

"They went right up to the thirteenth week before they found jobs here," Beth said.

"What if they would have turned to violent activities?" Bowman asked, doodling on his pad.

"We have a one strike and you're out policy," Beth told him. "Touch-tone sentencing and no parole. A man is innocent until proven guilty but guilt is implicit in arrest."

"Astounding. Well, I've got to take this all back with me. I'm sure your town will be a prominent part of our piece."

"We have laws against lawyers accepting personal liability suits on a contingency basis. We have only family values TV programming from the hours of eight in the morning till midnight. We have a White Trash law which forbids certain dress or language on the streets. We have an above the ear haircut regulation, life imprisonment for destruction of property values, the death penalty for four hundred and eighty-four offenses . . . "

"Well, thank you," Bowman said, getting up and backing toward the door.

"We've reinstituted slavery . . . "Beth called out as Bowman made his escape.

"Okay," Sweeney said to Harry Powell, "your whole life story thus far is revealed to you in your collection of shoes."

"I look at a pair of shoes, I remember every day I wore them," Harry snapped back. "Bingo! Just like that. I see the shoes, I remember."

"You think that's something?" Sweeney said, standing by Harry's booth. "That's just personal. Your life. That's not history."

"That's my history," Harry said. "My shoes are my artifacts. Shards of my past life."

"Your past life is like a fart passing through the mind of human history," Sweeney said angrily. "It's a trickle of piss in the oceans of time. It's a bee buzz in the ear of the infinite. And your shoes . . . "

"Don't say anything about my shoes," Harry warned.

"I've got a positronic brain chip in that mutt's head," Data told an amazed Lucy and Woad. "It's sort of an experiment."

"Let me ask you something," Woad said as an idea began to form in his brain. "If I gave Ginch here something of RC's so he could pick up the scent, say one of RC's boots, could I hook up Ginch to a computer in a spacecraft, fly over an area and have Ginch, through the computer, put us on the trail of RC?"

"You'd have to have a pretty sophisticated computer," Data said. "One that could feed off the positronic chip. You have to understand that chip is purely experimental. I mean I got the idea from *Star Trek The Next Generation* and I just went with it."

"I know human history," Sweeney told Harry. "I know it through movie history. I see a movie, I know the way the world was when that movie was made. I know the world that that movie is capturing."

Harry thought about that.

"You mean you recognize the shoes that are being worn in the film?" he asked Sweeney, suddenly aware that Sweeney had escaped the walls of a personal history.

"I know what shoes every leading man wore in every movie since *Intolerance*. Elmo Lincoln had on a pair of maroon cordovans for most of the film."

"I was wearing a pair of penny loafers when I went to see Gene Kelly and Rita Hayworth in a film called *Cover Girl*," Harry mused.

"Kelly was wearing brown penny loafers in that movie," Sweeney told him. "Too thrilling for words, so they set it to music."

"I was on a date with a girl named Eve," Harry said. "I bought her two bags of popcorn."

"Two bags of popcorn is just personal history," Sweeney retorted. "Rita Hayworth's big smile of American optimism captured the period. And then boom! Thirty years later, Rita Hayworth and the whole country has Alzheimers. You still see big smiles, but now nobody knows what they mean."

"She married Frank Overton in 1953, the year I was wearing blue suede shoes."

"Frank Overton was in *The Dark at the Top of the Stairs*," Sweeney said. "He was wearing hobnail boots but Robert Preston was the male lead. He wore loungers throughout."

Meanwhile, Mark Wonder was in the kitchen trying to talk Rick Monte into running for mayor. Both Rick and Scraps were enjoying a fifteen minute break with cigarettes and coffee.

"You'll be the Ross Perot of this election," Mark told Rick.

"Lay it out for me," Rick said, sniffling and dragging hard on his Camel at the same time.

"Okay," Mark said, his head bobbing nervously. "Beth Swingle is New Deal Liberal which is old, over and adios. I know through Deepthroat that Whine Berg is going to run one of his boys. That will be strictly a Get Government Off Our Backs ticket."

"Sounds okay to me," Rick replied. "What do you think, Scraps?"

"Who's Deepthroat?" Scraps said, busy trying to chew a wad of old gum, smoke a Marlboro and sip his java.

"No, but you don't see the beauty of it," Mark Wonder said, now jumping from one foot to another. "You come in as a Get the CEO's Off Our Back kind of thing."

"Get the CEO's Off Our Back?" Rick repeated. "What kind of thing is that?"

"Get the advertising industry out of our lives," Mark said, ticking off his platform with his fingers in front of Rick's face.

"Get the market out of our lives. Get the corporations out of our lives. Get the credit card companies out of our lives. Get the brokers out of our lives. Get technology out of our lives. Get big business off the planet."

Rick thought about that.

"So what do we have left?" he asks.

"No jobs," Scraps responds.

"Get Bill Gates and John Malone and Ted Turner and Donald Trump and Gordon Gecko out of our lives," Mark said, eyes wide with enthusiasm now.

Rick glanced at Scraps who just shrugged his shoulders.

"Let's get the Dow out of our lives," Mark shouted. "Dow Chemical. Dow Jones. Let's put the T'ao into our lives."

"Oh, yeah," Rick said. "The T'ao."

You turn on your TV," Mark said. "No more commercials. You get your mail. No more advertisements. You dig in your garden, no more toxic waste dumps. You take a ride in the country, all you see are family farms."

"That's nice," Rick said."

"We don't make anything any more," Mark said. "We get production out of our lives. You take a ride in the country, all you see is cottage industry. People spinning wool and things like that."

"People spinning wool, eh?" Rick replied.

"We don't import or export anything anymore," Mark said. "We get the global market out of our lives. You take a ride in the country, all you see is local growth, local consumption."

"Local, eh?" Rick said.

"We get out of financing and banking services," Mark said. "We get the brokers and financiers out of our lives. You take a ride in the country, all you see is people bartering shit back and forth."

Bartering shit, eh?" Rick said.

"I got a question," Scraps said. "How does everybody take all these rides in the country?"

"Say, that's right," Rick said. "Where's the gas and the cars coming from?"

"Trains," Mark said. "Passenger trains crisscross the whole country. Solar energized. Windmills in your back yard. Solar converters."

"And you think people in this town will go for this kind of thing?" Rick asked.

"People want change," Mark said. "It's the way to go. It's a marketable idea. Its time has come. All I need is a front man. A guy who can sell anybody anything."

"Yeah, that's me," Rick replied, blushing. "I'm in between products right now."

"Think you can push this platform?" Mark said. "Get the message out?"

"Yeah, I think so," Rick said. "How do I get paid?"

"You'll see when the contributions start rolling in," Mark told him, winking. "Remember the message: Save the planet from Global market greed! Get Big Business Off Nature's Back!"

"How about: 'Let's Find Out What's Going on in the Corporate Boardroom!" Scraps shouted.

"That's the idea," Mark said.

"How about: 'I'm Being Harassed by TV Commercials!" Scraps shouted.

"Even better," Mark said.

"How about . . . " Scraps began but Rick cut him off.

"Take a ride in the country, Scraps," he said.

On her way out of Sweeney's, Beth Swingle ran into Mark Wonder, who held the door open for her and then followed her out into the street. About a half block away, Mark could see Lucy with Ginch. It looked like Data was with them and another man whom Mark didn't recognize.

"I've been meaning to stop by your office, Mayor," Mark said to Beth. "I'm thinking I might be of some use to you in the coming election."

"What did you have in mind?" Beth asked, not knowing much about this new citizen except that he was some sort of deal maker.

"I've got a good idea what your opponents will be saying."

"I can get political opinions by the truckload," Beth said curtly.

"I'm an analyst," Mark told her. "No opinions. Flat results of computer generated statistical surveys. You're a New Democrat. You've got something brand, spanking new to offer. What will Whine Berg's toadies offer? Old, over and adios. Get government out of our lives. That's like having a problem and trying to solve it by saying let's get rid of the problem. Sure. But how? That's the question. And you're dealing with the problem. You're not just snapping your fingers and saying it's gone."

"I'm heading back to my office," Beth said, starting to walk.

"I'll walk with you if you don't mind," Mark said. "The Founding Fathers didn't create a federal government just to be a problem. It had a purpose. What's the purpose? If it's overstepped its authority, then maybe it has to back up. But what if the federal government is facing challenges now that the Founding Fathers never dreamed of?"

"Okay, what if?"

"What if the political intentions of this country—everything in the Constitution and the Bill of Rights and so on—need protection now? Who's going to protect them I ask you? The new global forces that are doing the threatening? No. Absolutely not. Now we take a look at the other side."

"By all means."

"Get global market capitalism out of our lives," Mark said. "That's old, over and adios. What do we replace free enterprise with? Castro's economics? The former Soviet Union's? No. Absolutely not. So, it's clear what we need is mediation, modulation, moderation, modification. Observe the mean. That's your platform. Whatya think?"

"I've already got a campaign manager," Beth said. "Harry Powell."

"Harry Powell?" Mark exclaimed. "You mean that old guy that was just back there at Sweeney's carrying on about how he remembers all the shoes he's owned? Let me tell you, dementia has controlling interest in that guy. His brain's passing ideas like stones through a kidney."

Beth looked at her watch.

"Sixteen minutes," she said. "Send me a bill."

"No, no, nothing like that," Mark protested as they stopped in front of City Hall. "Gratis. But let me tell you. You're gonna need me. There be lunatics yelling things like 'End Entrepreneurship in Our Time!' and 'Let's Shoot the Brokers!' And on the other end there, be lunatics yelling things like 'Let's Privatize the Government!'"

"How do you do that?" Beth asked, looking back at Mark. "I mean how do you have a privatized democracy?"

"Hey, it can happen, Mayor," Mark said, smiling. "I'm just saying I'm here for you. Think about it."

Beth hesitated.

"You could do me a favor," she said. "A sort of trial run."

"I'm your man," Mark said eagerly.

"Find out what you can about a man named Jack Devereaux. He claims to be a reporter for *People* magazine. He's staying over at the New Old Lompaw Hotel."

"You got it, Mayor," Mark said, saluting her snappily and rushing back toward Sweeney's. He didn't find Lucy and Ginch and went in search.

Stranger Murders in Strange Worlds

Summer 1995

"Our greatest fear is of violence from a nameless, faceless stranger . . . Citizens of all races who are fearful of random violence have good reason for their concern. Storekeepers, utility workers, police officers, and ordinary citizens out for a carton of milk for a family dinner are all increasingly at risk."

> Adam Walinsky, "The Crisis of Public Order,"
> *Atlantic Monthly*

"[A]s life became more dangerous, more subject to hazardous fate, so it became progressively difficult to raise children in the settled peace they require. And more and more the most conspicuous models of success were the racketeer, the pimp, and the insidious drug dealer. So more and more children, deprived of reasonable nurture, were sucked into the vortex, to become in their turn the abusers and the destroyers of the children who came after them."

> From a speech by Congressman John Lewis, Democrat
> of Georgia

"I would be relieved to learn that the new restlessness with the burden of strangers' children is not simply a form of the alarming new unwillingness to take responsibility for one's own. I suppose no one had thought to graph accelerating rates of moral evasion among the prosperous and influential."

> Marilynne Robinson, "Modern Victorians," *Harper's*
> *Magazine* July 1995

"Bev Russell, a man who attempts to live by the stiff moralistic code called "family values" would have construed his behavior as sin; legal or psychological words like *statutory rape* and *incest* might fall quickly out of his mind. In the

world of sin, where guilt is a powerful defense, remorse
can feel like full atonement."

Blanch McCrary Boyd, "The Enormous Mother:
Reflections on Susan Smith," *Village Voice* July 4, 1995

"It is the evident policy of the entertainment industry to
seek profit by exploiting the most degraded aspects of human and social character."

Walinsky, ibid.

"If We Were Murdered in 1958 . . . "

Follow the way my mind, as in its own nightmare, inter-
weaves the above quotations: *other* minds, not my own, are increasingly being sucked into a moral vacuum where *my* life
registers as meat and not as sacred. A vortex in which sense and
senselessness swirl and I can make no rational appeal. An abyss
of dark, blind selfishness, greed and hate that displaces empathy, understanding, regret. Both a sense of prosperity (as fostered by our market capitalism), and a sense of guilt (fostered by
our Christian moral notions), are not defenses or remedies here,
but causes. And if murder is aleatory today, it is not due to "the
entertainment industry," to popular culture, but to our "you are
if you can pay" ontology and our belief that the adoption of certain moral proscriptions has an intrinsic, universally justifiable
authenticity and legitimacy. What happens when we violate
these proscriptions is by no means a universally prevalent sense
of "sin." That sense must be culturally inculcated in each and
every generation.

Why have we failed to do that now, at this moment in
American life? We now live in a postmodern climate in which all
cultural impositions are questioned and fail invariably to with-
stand that questioning. Our youth are not failing to develop family values and we are not failing to preach them. Rather, those
values are now afloat in a world that has lost all sorts of bedrock
foundations, including moral ones. There is less congruence
than slippage between our moral proscriptions and our present
notions of being-in-the-world, our sense of who we are individually and collectively, our sense of an essential human nature and
the so-called Natural Law that applies to all of this. This ontological slippage—between what we wish to legislate ourselves as

and what our being may be in itself—is itself framed within an order of things that reduces ontology to market forces and both individual and cultural construction to those same forces. This postmodern generation of Americans is aware that it buys the moral proscriptions that it wishes to consume. That is a fatal knowledge, for moral proscriptions are supposed to be outside a market/economic valuation. Though the adult generation of Americans already finds itself rooted in other framings of reality, ones in which "humaneness" resonates within in other than market corridors, our youth have had those foundations placed on moveable shelves in the marketplace. It is patently ridiculous, then, to attribute this ontological reorientation to the entertainment industry or to liberal policies nurturing a loss of a sense of personal responsibility, indeed a sense of personal failure, a loss of conscience, a failure to assume personal responsibility.

Rather than digging the abyss our youth now seem to dwell within, popular culture plays out all the movements here. At its best it shows us the new orientations, the new connections and interweavings, the new time/space discontinuum in a floating world. If this sounds like something you've seen in the movies, say, in *Batman Forever*, it's only because that film is filled with our new adventitious recklessness, our world of flamboyant, competitive, assertive self-constructions, a world in which no two people are assumed to be on the same path. Commonality and community give way to idiosyncratic marketing devices that we buy, not share. While we are busy arguing over whether ideology pulls the cart of culture or vice versa, all our popular culture, from TV and talk radio, from video to film shows us that the market follows cultural mindsets and that cultural mindsets are fed by the market.

Which of the very many cultural mindsets or attitudes are most profitably played by the market and thus fed by the market? This is strictly a bottom line determination: tapping into one reality construction as opposed to another is a net profit determination. Can the market then tap into and feed contesting cultural attitudes? Doubtlessly. The evidence is all around us. The plurality and heterogeneity of our market/mind commitments have proliferated in the last thirty years as Blakean "single vision," grounded in Enlightenment notions of self, truth, objectivity, reality, representation, reason, progress, language, meaning and value, has been attacked from many directions. Indeed, the tottering of an encompassing mindset with universal and absolute pretensions and the consequent release of a dissensus of heterogeneity *is* in essence our introduction to the postmodern abyss. We have moved away from a familiar mythos/mindset where unrivaled notions of unity, coherence and continuity, of truth and falsehood, of meaning and value, should not only be identifiable but should establish a reproducible, shareable identity. We have moved toward a strange world where reality is a self-designed affair and thus the realities of others have become the realities of strangers. By turning these realities into marketable values, the market thus brings them to a representational level. More and more we communicate with each other and come to understand who and where the "stranger" is through the conduit of the marketing media. Products help define us and identify ourselves. And although, as I have said, the market moves relentlessly to control and manipulate our shelve choices, to reduce our identity simply to one who consumes, it is at the same time running after strange mindsets, strangers to its prior marketing strategies. For surely the ontology of self-constructedness is neither elided by the market's own profit directives nor totally encompassed by it. In this postmodern abyss, we threaten market analysis with our proliferating strangeness. The very challenge of the market is to bridge a gap between product and strangeness. And in the process, in the attempt, the market creates a representational correlative for the variety of strangeness the postmodern abyss is itself creating. Computer technology, in its seemingly limitless capacity to configure and extenuate reality in new and strange ways, becomes a means, a model and a metaphor of our new found capacity to construct the reality that constructs us.

The reality of others has become the reality of strangers, a strangeness only mediated in market ways, in our postmodern abyss. We are therefore murdered by strangers only because we have first lost common links and threads of identity. A nuclear family, a mother *and* a father, does not guarantee the resurrection of a stable foundation upon which a common identity of self and world can be created. It merely represents a familial order of things that can be sustained and legitimated within a mindset that imagines the possibility and attainability of a bedrock, foundational order of things. Such a familial construction does not nurture the means of discovering this indelible, underlying rationality and realism. Rather, it simply reproduces a privileged order of things; it promises redundancy of a chosen rationality and realism. It promises identity that will lead to the capacity to identify others in the world and in turn be identified by them. It promises not to make us strangers. And, therefore, if we were murdered in 1955, when Ozzie and Harriet were the model American family, there was a nine out of ten chance, that the murderer was no stranger to us. There wasn't much of a chance that our murderer would be living in an alien construction of reality, would be a total stranger in a world of commonly shared identity.

The abyss of strangeness is shunned by a societal order of things. And while the market needs a stable social order, a realm of enforceable security and redundancy that bedrocks investments and goals, it is at the same time locked into making a profit in any way possible, even to bringing to a representational level ways of attending to the world that undermine the present status quo. From the side of a social order wishing to preserve itself and hold off both strangeness and strangers, popular culture must be censored and brought to heel when it exploits "the most degraded aspects of human and social character" in order to make a profit. But, inevitably, when popular culture reaches toward strangeness and does so under market imperatives—purely to make a buck—it is in effect bringing to conceivability what our present social order wishes to retain as "strange." At the same time, by bridging that strangeness only with products communication, with product and services correlative of that strangeness, the market reduces, as I have said, ontology to consumption. However, when the market works through popular culture, there is a concomitant representation of the mindsets of strangeness, of challenging attitudes toward the "reality-making" that introduces us to the flux of differing ways in which we are indeed "reality-making." The degradation, then, is of the unity and universality of reality, and of a single identity and mode of identifying. What is extended and enriched is our capacity to range into other realities, hook up with strangeness.

A Screen for Battyness

I want to explore *Batman Forever* for what it reveals about an alien but growing way we attend to the contemporary world. It is trying to represent a type of worldly interaction that is already here and thus appeal to those who "reality-make" in this way.

The film is making a great deal of money this summer of 1995, in spite of the fact that it has been critically attacked. I suppose if the critics who were writing and speaking in the national media found that the film was trying to transmit on their own attitudinal frequency, their own out of the ordinary way of configuring space and marking time, they would treat it like a beacon in the storm. Regardless of the delineated aesthetic inadequacies of, say, film by Latinos or African-Americans or gays and lesbians, or films about Native Americans, women, drug addicts, fat people, small people, homeless people, bi-racials, bisexuals, renegades and misfits, gang members and so on, these films are always hailed by those they seek to represent. They become benchmarks of an effort to bring to identity what we presently hold as strange. The question then—Is a "bad" film, then, worth the ink?—receives another question as an answer—"Bad in whose view and within what order of things?" It seems to me that if we accept the notion that any representation of reality is "good" if it reproduces in its own inimitable way the eternal verities concocted by a prevailing order of things, then both the representation and our critical representation of it are dedicated to confirming the redundant nature of reality and truth. We are really into a reiteration of the ways in which we mark identity and strangeness. Aesthetic order emerges from our identifying order. It follows, then, that we only break out of that redundancy when we attend to what is not re-presentable, what is strange and bad, bad because it is strange. I believe that it is more important to attend to what irks us than what supports us if our desire is to break down implacable categories of identity and strangeness.

"Badness" here, then, lies in either a weak or pale or confused attempt to broach the strange, or in a weak or pale or confused attempt to mirror a commonly shared state of identity. But while we can turn away from a pale or confused reiteration of what is already conceivable to us—old hat—we cannot dismiss any attempt to represent what previously did not exist for us. I attend to *Batman Forever,* as I have throughout this book attended to other films easily dismissed as not worthy of critical attention, because somehow it is crossing into the headlines and making something there conceivable to me. At the moment I was puzzling over the strangeness of Susan Smith, (the mother who buckled her two infant sons into their car seats and sent them and the car into a lake to drown to death, doubtlessly screaming all the while), I saw the film *Batman Forever* and found in it the very same gaps and disjointure that existed between my mind and Susan Smith's. So I attend to the film in connection with a cultural event, not a stranger murder but a strange murder, and I suggest that the ambience and attitude of *Batman Forever* explicates, if you will, the strangeness that for me, as well as many others I'm sure, surrounds Susan Smith.

The film does not elevate her action to aesthetic significance, and certainly not moral significance. But in a way her action does elevate the film to cultural significance. And this is not an insignificant or accidental matter. Popular culture intends on entangling itself into the fever zones of our culture and when it does so it brings before us what we respond to but cannot bring to either meaning or value. Unlike, say, *Forrest Gump,* which deliberately entangles itself within a conservative revision of the '60s, *Batman Forever* is not about Susan Smith. But it is about strangeness, and even makes an attempt at describing the roots of that strangeness: psychological roots, the trauma of murdered parents. On the Susan Smith side, her defense is also psychological: she did what she did because of what was done to her. But it is not these psychological defenses that I am interested in but rather the way the temporal/spatial domain of *Batman* reveals something of the world Susan Smith and I and the reader share— a world of Judaeo-Christian notions of sin and remorse, of good and evil, a world tinged by the flux of the postmodern abyss.

It's a strange thing when a man pretends to be a bat, Nicole Kidman, playing the part of a psychologist asks when she first meets the Batman. "Should I call you Batty?". The villains are equally strange. Jim Carrey is a scientist gone mad who transforms himself into the Batman's tormentor, The Riddler. Tommy Lee Jones' Two Face was once a successful prosecutor with just one face, one personality, but now he wreaks havoc on Gotham like a man driven to reveal to all the double nature of all things— the hypocrisy and duplicity of the Gotham order of things, of a moral order that thinks it has isolated itself from evil, made a sharp line, like down a face, between good and evil.

So we have some very conventional caricatures, indeed they are the heroes and villains of comic book worlds: the traumatized Batman, the megalomaniacal mad scientist, the schizophrenic unable to hold self and world within a single vision. And the youth, Robin, who comes into this world of good versus evil that is itself caricatured, a world in which anything of substance, any-thing of firm outline, including moral categories, dissolves into kinetic, disassociated hyperactivity. Robin is to find a niche in a world that is in motion, quantum motion, along fractal paths. All the licenses granted to a comic book world are seized upon here in order to create a reality frame that will not unsettle the viewer's own "really real" reality frame but at the same time enkindle an on going unsettling of that frame in our postmodern world. The comic book connection is therefore a screen upon which to play out the battyness of our contemporary world—to emulate a strangeness that can only avoid the negative vibes that strange-ness emits if it is offered as the strangeness of the strange worlds of comic book superheroes.

And what is this veiled comic book climate of strangeness? First of all, there is no inner life; existence is a montage of pre-sent actions; the self is in a vortex and no one seems to be able to get to the catbird seat, the place of calm, objective observation. Even though Batman seems to be sporadically caught within a dark introspection, he is not the pilot but the target. Batman does not provide us with a controlling focus. From whose per-spective do we see this world? We are even beyond the multiple perspectives of late modernism, exemplified for instance in film with Welles's *Citizen Kane* and in fiction with Faulkner's *Sound and the Fury*. There is to be here no probing of the surface for subtextual meaning. After all, this is a comic book world of comic book caricatures! Let spectacle exhaust meaning; let centrifugal forces pull us away from a still point, a center to which every-thing radiates. Here in this Batman world everything is in swirling, crisscrossing motion. Life is reduced to colorful, kinetic panels that engage us without raising any red flags to incite the rational and moral sense we came in with.

Swollen on a barrage of hyperactive images and given no time to impose an order of continuity, of connectedness, of meaning, in short, we lose facility and patience with the unstimulating cir-cumscribing efforts of all ordering efforts. We are, in effect, mov-ing at digital speed in this Batman world in which response time is so accelerated and so directly engaging that we do not think of applying any standards of judgment and critique. There is an in-commensurability between a mindset shaped by linear continu-ity, by analysis and distinctions, by a sense of logical, aesthetic, psychological and moral appropriateness, by a sense of under-lying depth and subtextual meaning, and a mindset shaped by a fractal discontinuity which offers no outside perspective from which to formulate and enact any brand of second-order narrating. There is no accompanying narrative of meaning-making or value-conferring in this Batman world. It comes as it is, as if the need to make sense of it, the need to stand back and see what is at stake, has already itself been packaged. Meaning and value are no more than images, played out from panel to panel. To attempt to isolate them would be to slow the whole works down. It would be like allowing a digital stimulus and response to be governed by a hand at an abacus.

You can see the digital biorhythms at work in the performance of Jim Carey as The Riddler—a performance in which he attempts to perform other voices, other gestures, other words, other lives, other contexts, other responses contemporaneously at digital speed. He's a one-man Ed Wood ensemble of players. It's a fractal performance; by which I mean he breaks the line he is pursuing, disconnects, diverts himself, contorts and twists himself in other directions, leaving a trail of lacunae, of gaps and fissures. There is neither time nor inclination to fill those gaps in; to do a psychological profile, to apply normative standards of social behavior, to hold up a moral rod. His is a face on tilt, askew, tilting in all directions so that only can he not gaze upon the world steadily and earnestly but neither can we who are watching his antics. And we are encouraged by an always-tilted camera to take up The Riddler's way of seeing; you can't find a spot to root yourself into and from which to gaze upon it all, capture it all, make sense of it all. We are drawn into the swirl, and the name of the game here with popular film is to keep us hooked, plugged in, digitalized. The information is in the image, the image is in motion, the motion encompasses us.

Susan Smith

It is a strange thing when a mother deliberately drowns her two infant sons. Is Susan Smith, age 23, of Union, South Carolina, "a placid town without a movie theater or a decent restaurant," in a hypereal Batman world? I am asking whether this is a strange murder, a murder we can't quite comprehend, because it was done in one world and we are trying to comprehend it from another? I am not talking about Union, South Carolina as an alien world but of the realities we shape for ourselves and live within. And it is not a matter of Susan Smith or ourselves being totally in a digitalized world in which conscience is a screen we over-write each day or in a world in which good and evil, sin, guilt, remorse, forgiveness are the ready-to-hand measures of our lives. But nevertheless, we are all fluctuating somewhere at or between these antipodes and so too, then, does this murder committed by Susan Smith. Susan's confession of the murder, and her stepfather, Beverly's confession of having sexually abused her, are told within fundamental Christian sin and revival narratives. Bev is a member of Pat Robertson's Christian Coalition but Susan remains only the victim of a sexual abuser who is a member of Pat Robertson's Christian Coalition. It is hard then to judge the hold sin and revival have on Susan. Her promiscuity may be that of a renegade from any doctrinaire sense of good and evil rather than the promiscuity of a sinner who has lapsed and will in turn be revived in the spirit and seek forgiveness. Whether renegade or lapsed Christian, Susan's life seems not to have subsumed a sense of good and evil, but only been subjected to them.

That life is also subjected to what the Christian Coalition, for instance, is subjected to: the fractalizing of firm, indelible moral notions, the postmodern positioning of good and evil within cultural context and, more broadly, reality frames. The moral absolute is dissolving into the moral relative. The Coalition is formed to defend against that turn away from the absolute. Every member, in other words, knows who the enemy is, what the fight is all about, and what the stakes are. That Susan is not only aware of this postmodern relativizing but is herself a relativist is something that she shows us when for nine days she held to a story of a black man hijacking her car before confessing that she made the story up, that she drowned her children. She told the hijacking story because it best fit her need at the moment: to escape arrest and punishment, to escape the consequences of her action. She attempts to construct a suitable reality for herself. Is she constructing because we now live with an awareness that everything is constructed, including our sense of good and evil, true and false? Or, is she just lying and knows that in that lying she is sinning and that unless she goes through the stages of revival, remorse, and forgiveness she will face absolute judgment by God?

We can extend this same ambiguity to the murders themselves. Does she roll that car with the imprisoned children in it into the lake to drown because it is part of a new fabrication of her life that she is making within a world made up only of self-fabrications? Or, does she do it because Satan has momentarily entered her life and she knows that on the other side of this sin is a forgiveness that she will in time seek? This is an unresolvable ambiguity which itself, however, resonates within our whole culture's struggle over values and meanings—a struggle between foundational and anti-foundational mindsets, between a coalition of traditional values and the postmodern abyss. The murders become strange to both sides because they each point to the other as providing the reality frame which can identify this horrific, inhuman crime. It is only because the postmodern abyss has yawned and consumed Susan Smith, torn her from her Christian conscience that she could have committed such an act. On the other side, the view is that it is only because an absolutist notion of right and wrong has replaced her own involvement in her own actions, that Susan Smith could have drowned her children. She did so because the act could escape the morality of the present and ascend to a metanarrative level of Sin, Remorse and Forgiveness. In other words, just as Conservatives accuse Liberals of having eroded a sense of self-responsibility among the poor through welfare programs, postmodernists accuse fundamental Christians of having eroded a sense of moral responsibility by projecting an absolute sense of good and evil, by bureaucratizing morality, replacing individual constructions of right and wrong and assumptions of moral responsibility with unswerving protocols.

The strangeness, then, of the crime is really only graspable in terms of its cultural impact. We cannot answer the question "how can we explicate this strange act in terms of our understanding of Susan Smith?" but we can explicate the act in terms of how our present culture will respond to its strangeness, will, in fact, make it strange. For example, fifty years ago, such an act would itself be culturally received in nearly the same way Bev and his step-daughter have framed it, namely, within a frame of sin, remorse and redemption. The sense of strangeness then would be abrogated precisely because we would have a story within which to place it: Susan Smith, in the utter depths of Satan's power, in the full service of Mammon, would have drowned her sons. The actions of others truly become strange when the story frames within which we seek to make sense of them prove inadequate. They have already been shaken.

Strangeness today unsettles us because we fear it does not register in the old ways—that we intend to feel the full impact of this strangeness only because we feel that we are losing our capacity to react to strangeness in the old ways. We fear our own insensitivity, our own capacity to devour image after image, sensation after sensation—digital spectacles that harden us to the impact of any spectacle.

Aloof from emotional and moral impact, we are aloof from the motives of others. The case of Susan Smith and our reaction to it shows us that we greatly fear this callousness, this distancing of ourselves from the human life-world. She is a wake-up call to us before we enter, in the name of progress, into the virtual reality of our own moral conscience. Within this virtual reality, no action takes us by surprise. No action is strange. All interaction has become nominalized, has no real import, no connectedness, and therefore all events float free of us, have nothing to do with us or we with them. Since we have not fully stepped into this mindset but are yet, so to speak, on the threshold, we can paradoxically have no problem with "grasping" Susan Smith's action and also be totally incapable of grasping it. In the former case, we display a sort of awareness of the digital possibility of everything. We are stunned not *by* the event but *before* the event. Our ways of responding have been feted and jaded on digital synapses and not life-world probabilities. This is the very essence of a sense of the abyss—the world has now become a place where everything is possible and all actions rush through cyberspace toward virtual actuality. In the latter case, when her action does not fit into our sense of human possibility, we are locked into a round of knowing the world and reproducing it only in that way. But we do not perceive the self-constructedness of this; rather we interpret our reality-creating as reality-responding. Susan Smith's action is not one we can reproduce from within our own frame. Therefore, it has no reality connection and becomes inconceivable, ungraspable. But since all attempts at remaining ontologically safe-harbored are under attack in our postmodern world, there is a certain interchange between those who are prepped to consume anything and those who are trying to preserve firm boundaries of conceivability and inconceivability.

If we are shocked by Susan Smith's action, it is doubtlessly the postmodernizing of our world that spawns that reaction. Is she indeed a forerunner of a moral conscience that is not lapsed within Christianity but lapsed because of postmodernity? Is she like the very first case of Ebola virus, the first sign of an epidemic that will sweep the country? Are we more liable to be murdered by strangers now because that conscience-devouring virus has destroyed what has both held off and linked us to others? In this view, postmodernity is a virus that invades reality and truth and devours their foundational pillars. On the other hand, are we more liable to be murdered by strangers now because our thorough-going market mentality has destroyed all connections between us except what Thomas Carlyle called the "cash nexus"? In this view, postmodernity is no more than an attitude toward ourselves and the world which denies the privileging of any master narrative and consequently unleashes a proliferation of world-attending ways. Postmodernity, in short, becomes the remedy for our self-constructed distancing of ourselves from each other. It engenders conceivability and representation at the sites of strangeness. The postmodern world becomes more entangled, more heterogeneous, more labyrinthine, more teeming and diffuse. And here strangeness is ultimately intersected.

Disorder/Order

April 1st
Door to Counter

Rick Monte put one hand to the top button of his white silk shirt to make sure it hadn't come undone and with the other hand rang the doorbell.

Dodger started barking his head off and then Mrs. Dodger came to the door.

"Yes?" she said through the screen door.

She had seen Rick around town and he had seen her. Rick knew her reputation. It would be a hard sell.

"Show dog you got there?" Rick said, pointing down to the still barking Dodger.

"Hardly," Mrs. Dodger said. "Unless you call dropping a dried turd in the living room a show dog."

"How would you like a free six month subscription to Doctors Smedlee and Brown Canine Newsletter?"

"I wouldn't," Mrs. Dodger said, closing the door.

"Wait," Rick said. "You see this?"

"What's that?"

"It's a tracking device. Stick it on your dog's collar and with this here monitor you can easily locate him."

Mrs. Dodger opened the screen door and took the device and monitor from Rick.

"What's it cost?"

"Forty-nine ninety-five for both."

She shook her head.

"I always find him," she said, handing the stuff back to Rick.

"Think of the time you'd save. Not to mention the embarass-ment of running all over the neighborhood . . .

"Who says I run all over the neighborhood?"

Rick took out a pack of cigarettes.

"This is a smoke-free doorway," Mrs. Dodger said.

"Twenty-nine ninety-five," Rick said, lighting up.

"Twenty," she said. "If it works."

"It'll work," Rick said.

Bending down to fasten the tracker onto Dodger's collar Rick heard a motorcyle turning onto the street. It was a guy in a business suit without a helmet. He looked strangely familiar. As soon the door was opened, Dodger ran like an escapee out of Leavenworth.

Mark Pinsky who was on the motorcycle and who at this moment didn't know he was Mark Pinsky or where he had gotten the motorcycle almost ran Dodger down.

Mrs. Dodger came out of the house screaming at the top of her lungs. but Mark had already roared off down the street and Dodger had disappeared in the Saito hedges.

"See what you've done!" she screamed at Rick.

"Use the goddamn monitor," Rick said. "If you don't find him in ten minutes, I'll give you twenty bucks."

Mrs. Dodger angrily brought the small monitor close to her face and Rick went on to the next house, Morio Saito to sell him a handy helper.

"I just saw Mark Pinsky drive passed on a Harley," Cleo Cooper told Dr. Joy Hearder on the phone. "Ain't you looking for him?"

"You're at the Simmons's?" Joy replied.

"Here at the kitchen sink. Look up and there he is. Doing eighty. Almost run over that Dodger dog."

Joy hung up and called the Sheriff's office.

"He's got fugue syndrome disorder," Joy told Fat Gus Wentes.

"How you spell that?" Gus said.

"What is dark hole insurance?" Mrs. Saito politely asked Rick.

"Black hole, Mrs. Saito," Rick corrected her.

"What is black hole insurance?"

"What is anything, Mrs. Saito?" Rick replied taking the high ground. "If you ask me what automobile insurance or health insurance or life insurance is, what do I say? It's protection for the whole family. That's what it is. It's peace of mind."

"Do you think PAC money is behind American government?" Mrs. Saito asked.

"Sure, but do you think the universe is as safe today as it was fifty years ago?" Rick said, seeing room to press. "Or even twenty-five years ago? Dark holes from other galaxies are threatening to suck us in, like a whirlpool. Do you know how dense these black holes are? Do you know how time and space get scrunched inside a black hole?"

"It is because light bends at infinitesmal incremental intervals," Mrs. Saito replied.

"Let's say you suddenly got sucked in," Rick said and then paused. "Say what?"

Mark Pinsky came racing around the corner again on his Harley. Rick waited until the roar had died down. But when it had Mrs. Saito had gone back inside. In the distance he saw Mrs. Dodger heading back. Without Dodger. Rick beat feet.

"You didn't have black hole insurance and you got sucked in," Rick was saying, awhile later, to Pancakes. "Right off you wouldn't know what the right time was. It might be the year 1800 for all you know. Or 1500. Or 1600. Or anytime. Bingo! the past would be on you like a black cat on an itsy bitsy mouse."

Rick did one of his werewolf lurches toward Pancakes who held Patti up to defend her.

"Time waves don't hardly move at all in a black hole it's so dense. You'd be hearing voices from the past. And seeing faces . . . "

"See Commander Data's face in the window?" Pancakes pointed. When Rick turned he saw a pale face with dark eyes and greased back hair looking out of the second floor window.

"That your new neighbor?" Rick asked as Mark Pinsky came roaring down the block. This time Fat Gus Wentes was behind him in his Deputy Sheriff's car, red lights flashing.

"You've heard of Star Wars?" Rick said to Data who stood in his doorway in his stocking feet.

"Lucas's or Reagans's?" Data answered.

"I'll bet you got a helluva memory," Rick said, switching his products and his pitch right off.

"Relative to what?" Data said.

"I don't know. Who else has memory besides people?"

Data gave Rick a head to toe scrutiny and then said:

"Let's just say my memory was shot to shit. Are you going to sell me a new memory?"

Rick laughed. This guy was going to be a hard sell.

"I got a method," he told Data. "To improve memory. Yeah. You get six lessons for fifty bucks. If you're not satisfied after the six lessons you get your money back."

"Okay," Data said. "But first show me how good your memory is."

"Listen," Rick said, whispering and drawing closer to Data. "I'm in kindergarten. I'm all of five years old. There's this little blonde sitting next to me. She says "Can I bowwro your purple crayon?" And I says "I ain't got a purple crayon.""

"Is the purple crayon a penis symbol?" Data said.

"Wha?" Rick said, wondering what was par for the hole in this guy's head.

"Listen to this," Data said, copying Rick's complicitous, whispering style. "I'm coming out of my mother's belly. The doctor, Doctor Smirk says, "See you have a bouncy baby boy.""

Rick takes a deck of cards out of his pocket.

"Okay," he says, squatting down on the ground and laying out card on top of card in a neat pile until he has about ten cards left in his hand.

"I seen all them cards once but I remember what I saw. And because I remember what I saw I know the cards I got left in my hand. How much you want to bet I can tell you all of them?"

"Nothing," Data said. "I bet nothing. You should have let me cut those cards then I would have known that you memorized the cards you turned over and not the few you've got left in your hand."

"You seen this trick, huh?" Rick said, picking up the cards.

"If I did, I don't remember," Data said, closing the door on Rick.

Mrs. Dodger appeared out of nowhere. Her face was red and her hair was sticking straight up as if she had raked it over and over again with her fingers.

She flung the monitor at Rick.

"This thing doesn't work! And I can't find Dodger."

"I'll get him for you," Rick said, not moving.

"And that maniac on a motorcycle almost ran me over," Mrs. Dodger said.

It took Rick over an hour to track down Dodger and bring him back to Mrs. Dodger. Dodger had knocked over one of the Simmons's garbage pails and was feasting on some T-bone remnant. With Dodger in his arms, Rick tried to sell Sally Simmons some black hole insurance, and then some memory and then some catalogue service. The catalogue service interested her. Rick could see that right off. He had her hooked. It was all a matter of setting the right bait.

"I bet you get about twenty, thirty entrepreneurial catalogues a month," Rick said.

"More like twenty a week," Sally said.

"And you got that burden of going through all of them, right?"

"I'm going through a Classic Gold Swimwear catalogue now," Sally said. "Gold foil, one and two piece, florals and solids. Custom, junior and contemporary line. I catalog really heavily."

"It makes you wonder what poor people do to pass the time of day, right?" Rick said. "If you didn't put the time in, you'd be missing out on a purchase that could possibly transform your whole life."

Dodger was making a good effort to get out of Rick's arms.

"There's a lot of stuff you can't possibly live without," Sally said. "I like unusual catalogs with novelties and spiritual products for the soul and cruise directories and antique furniture and all kinds of historic replicas."

"With the catalog service I'm offering you, catalogues come to you already looked at. Anything you yourself would desire is already marked in red so you don't have to waste time going through the whole catalogue looking at stuff you would normally just pass by."

"I bet it's done by computer."

"Right," Rick said. "It's all done by computer. You just fill out a questionnaire which is a sort of personality profile and then the computer makes a match between you and the catalogue. I'm talking about a mere $29.95 a month."

Dr. Joy Hearder noticed that Mark Pinsky had not touched any of the food he had ordered. She looked over to the counter where Fat Gus Wentes was having his lunch and chatting with Abe Fata. She knew where Mark was. Trouble was he didn't know. He was on his way back to being Mark Pinsky. The fugue syndrome was wearing off. For now.

"I've got one of the worst disorders, don't I Doc?" Mark finally said, poking at his tuna on rye sandwich neatly cut on a diagonal in his dish.

"Anything that happens to us we take personally," Joy replied. She saw Mayor Beth Swingle come in. She saw Joy and came over.

"The city attorney thinks he has a battered persons sydrome case," she said to Joy.

"I have dissociative fugue disorder," Mark told the Mayor. "I haven't lived in this town in years but today I showed up on a motorcycle, almost killed several people and didn't know who or where I was until about ten mintues ago."

Beth cleared her throat, looked at her watch.

"You know what I have? Chronic lateness syndrome. I was supposed to meet John at my office at one. I'll call you Joy."

"Anything that happens to me I take personally," Mark said. "But if I don't remember who I am and where I'm going or why I'm going anywhere or where I'm from when I get to someplace else . . . Then what's personal about that? I mean the thing that frightens the hell out of me is that I'm losing my person. I can't remember my personal life. And that means Lorraine, whom I loved all my life. And my daughters, Clara and May. When I can't remember them I'm adrift. I'm no place. I can't take anything personally because I don't remember who I am."

Mark let out a sigh so mournful, so profoundly sad that for a click, air didn't go out of Joy's lungs.

Rick Monte who was sitting at the far end of the counter with Lucy Powell and Peaches on either side of him, glanced over at Mark and Joy and shook his head.

"That guy comes into town, almost kills the dog I'm busting my ass to find and now he's with Dr. Joy who will get him off scot free. Did she ever do that for me?"

"He's got some kind of disorder," Peaches said.

"We all got disorders," Rick snapped. "We got disorders and we do things. Or we don't do things. When I do things with my disorder then I get arrested. When Mr. Pinsky over there does things with his disorder he gets lunch. I think you should give a person two years with a disorder and then put them to work."

"What kind of disorder do you have, Rick?" Lucy asked.

"I got what's called Antisocial Personality Disorder but that's only because I come out of a parental abuse syndrome."

"I've got two," Lucy said, stretching a bit of gum out of her mouth so they could all view it. "Histrionic Personality Disorder and Schizotypal Personality Disorder."

"Oh, yeah? Rick said, picking up one of Abe's menus. "This ain't a menu."

"What is it then?" Peaches said, sniffing. She had a feeling she was getting a cold.

"It's an *attempt* at a menu," Rick said. "What it needs is my eight classic hot sandwiches. You know what kind of business Abe would be doing if he had my eight classic hot sandwiches?"

"A hot sandwich business?" Lucy said as Gladys pushed three glasses of water in front of them.

"My lawyer said I had meek-mate syndrome," Peaches said.

"A hot meatball is one of my classic sandwiches," Rick said. "But I ain't telling Abe. Fuck Abe. Why give him the business? With that sandwich alone I could make five yards a week easy."

"There was a girl on *Ricki Lake* who had urban survival syndrome," Lucy said. "It made her think everybody was trying to do what she was trying to do before she could do it. Or before she could even get there. Or see it. Or get any. Or be anything at all."

"Do you have a hot meatball sandwich?" Peaches asked Gladys who shook her head.

"Tea with an English," Peaches said.

Fat Gus Wentes walked Mark out to the Deputy Sheriff's car and they both got in. Joy watched as they drove off.

"I got a problem," Abe said, coming up behind Joy.

"I'm batting zero today Abe. Can it wait?"

"It's not me," Abe said, gesturing toward a booth in the corner.

When they were seated he started telling Joy about Gladys the waitress.

"All of a sudden she's robbing me blind but I can't got proof. And if I fire her she collects unemployment and it comes out of my hide."

"Gladys? She's been waitressing here for years."

"And she's the best. The only thing I can think of is that she's got one of these menopause problems, like she's got to steal."

"Wait a minute, Abe. You're way off the track here. There's no connection between the two. What she might have is kleptomania. But kleptomaniacs are easy to catch. They're not professionals. They're just compulsives. Instead of having to wash their hands every ten minutes, they have to steal something. What's Glady's stealing. Money?"

"She does two checks," Abe said. "And pockets the difference."

"What?"

"Let's say you had a tuna on rye and a cup of tea. She gives you the check, you pay. But for me, she puts a muffin and tea receipt in the register and pockets the difference."

Joy looked over to the counter where Gladys was now serving Rick Monte and friends.

"Hey, how many disorders do you have?" Rick said, picking up the BLT Gladys had put in front of him and examining it.

"Who me?" Gladys said, putting a catsup bottle in front of Lucy. "Three, I think. My feet, my head, and my hands."

She ripped off three checks from her pad and laid them down in front of Rick, Peaches, and Lucy, then picked up a Silex coffee pot and took it from around the counter into the dining area.

"What if I connected one of my eight classic hot sandwiches with a mental disorder?" Rick said. "I mean I'm talking about a concept that could sweep the country. Franchises from Maine to Miami."

"Yeah," Peaches said, thumbing through the most recent *Desperate Enterprises* catalogue.

But Rick's concept landed on fertile ground in Lucy's mind.

"Dissociative trance disorder," she said, eyes bright, pointing an index finger at Rick.

"Okay, describe it."

"You're suddenly under the influence of a spirit, power, deity or other person which causes impairment in social, occupational or other important areas of functioning."

Rick's eyes went wide.

"Whata got that memorized?"

Lucy nodded.

"So what's the hot sandwich?" she asked.

"Under the influence," Rick mused then bit into this sandwich. "Trance. Spiritual power. I got it. A hot chicken françese hero."

Lucy grimaced.

"They connect?"

"Yeah," Rick replied. "It's like a subconscious connection. You see it on the menu. You got the disorder. You order. Disorder. Order. Give me another one."

"Avoidant Personality Disorder," Lucy said. "I had it before I got histrionic personality disorder. You could do both. Dr. Joy said I was trying to avoid life. And then when I went histrionic I wanted the whole wide world to pay attention to me."

"I gotcha," Rick said, wiping mayonnaise from the corner of his mouth.

"A hot frittata sub for the 'I want to avoid things' mood," Rick said, after awhile. "And a hot roulade of beef on bun for the 'pay attention to me' mood."

"Why not the reverse?" Peaches, asked looking up from her magazine. "There are a lot of people avoiding beef but they really want beef so they'll order it when they're thinking about avoiding it. But when they want people to pay attention to them they'll order a hot friggata sub in a loud voice so everybody'll hear them."

"Frittata," Rick corrected. "Not friggata. You don't even know what it is so how can you hook up with the right disorder?"

"Borderline personality disorder," Lucy said.

"Hot smelts and horseradish gyro," Rick shot out.

"Dependent Personality," Lucy said.

"Fried egg sandwich."

"Pathological gambling."

"Hot greens and fatback hoagie."

"Intermittent explosive disorder."

"Hot venison and garlic mustard hero."

"Dissociative amnesia."

"Sloppy Joe on a kaiser roll."

"I can't believe Gladys is this inventive, Abe," Joy said, shaking her head, after hearing several of Gladys's thieving strategms. "I mean even Willie Sutton wasn't this ingenious."

"What don't you understand?" Abe said, sucking at his own teeth.

"Well, for instance, you say that she tells customers she's collecting for Jerry's kids or Greenpeace or something like that. And she's not?"

Abe shook his head.

"It all goes into her own pocket."

"She hands out her own menus with her own prices on them? Really, Abe. Have you ever seen one of these menus?"

Abe shook his head.

"But I know they're around here someplace. Every item is fifty cents or a dollar more than on my menu."

"And you can't catch her?"

"I can't catch her."

"You have no proof."

"Nothing I can use as evidence."

"But you're sure she's cheating you."

"I'm sure."

"Why are you so sure?"

"Because she'd be a fool not to be doing it. The whole country is doing it."

"Abe, Abe," Dr. Joy said, putting her hand on his, "listen to yourself. There's a menu floating around with inflated prices on it. Sort of an alternative universe menu. And Glady's who has been working for you for years is suddenly swept up in a nationwide mania to steal? You know what it sounds like to me, Abe? It sounds to me like you're feeling guilty for not having paid Gladys better all these years. She's getting older. She's got no benefits. No retirement. She's beginning to disturb your conscience. So you want her out. Is that what you're up to, Abe? Because if it is, it stinks."

Abe stood up, his face flushed with anger.

"Everybody wants to be an entrepreneur but they don't have a pot to piss in. It's all as clear as the nose on your face."

Joy watched him walk away, exhaled slowly, shook her head, looked at her check. It was alright. She left the money and a tip on the table. Then she went back and picked up the menu to collate its prices with the prices on the check. They corresponded. She was out the door and turning left when she went back and peered into the window. Gladys was at her table, picking up the money. When she saw Joy's face at the window she waved.

Just then Lucy, Rick and Peaches came out.

"Post-traumatic street disorder," Lucy said to which Rick immediately responded: "Hot corned beef hash with chili sauce gyro."

Court & Culture: The Days of Our Life with O.J.

June 1995

"Soaps are the absolute bottom of the television hierarchy, lumped with game shows and professional wrestling in terms of their perceived moral worth. Being a soap viewer, let alone a soap fan, is about as low as one can sink on cultural taste hierarchies."

Soap Fans

"The world is teeming with narratives, a veritable planet of ragged noise. The global media vector picks up the thread of whatever narrative line seems necessary to stitch the event into the seam of things."

Virtual Geography

One Hundred Days of the O.J. Trial

Soap operas fascinate us because they're daily, like life and the verisimilitude is all in that. There is no rush to symbolize, synthesize, thematize, universalize, absolutize, abstract or extract; no rush to conflict, climax, denouement; no pressure to resolve and bring to closure. Soap operas mark time quite close to our own inner biological/psychological clocks. Plots go nowhere so writers are free to concentrate on the rush and fade of the present moment, like advanced Alzheimer's patients whose minds tie them only to this visual moment, this visual moment, this visual moment . . .

These are indeed the days of *our* lives—how could we afford not to tune in each and every day? We watch our lives unfold—talking about what characters do and why they do it is our way of being in the world. We share worlds, the soap characters and ourselves, although we know the difference. But we know the difference in a way that does not exactly separate us from our

215

identifying. Were our thoughts and feelings, our own inner lives, to go public and get a part on a soap opera, they would make their mark in these soap opera worlds—differences in degree but not in kind. We would know what our dramatic moments were, who we would confront, befriend, love, expose, guide, correct and so on. We are each day stepping into a world in which we have already daily been playing a part—we are positioned; we hear, respond, judge, despise, admire, curse, escape. After time it is not so much that these soap opera worlds enact fictitious worlds we can escape into but rather they enact our lives and supplement, with their own synchronized time, the time that makes up our own life. We are not viewing but living those moments. They, too, are a part of our lives.

On the soap opera end there is only the need to synchronize. Plots are already open-ended like the days of our lives; what remains is the need to place characters and events within the same nexus, the same drone, the same endless round, on the same schedule train our culture is on, which is the same flux we are in and spinning within each and every day. Yesterday's soaps contribute their share to today's reality or are straining in one or another plot streams to synchronize with today's reality as it unfolds. Plot directions and characters rise and fade with great rapidity, or, on the other hand, linger forever, simply because they resonate or fail to resonate with our cultural vibes. Here they find an opening into what is currently mesmerizing us; there they foretell a future fascination; here they lose the beat; there they begin to tell a story nobody is listening to anymore. Once a soap finds its share of the viewing audience, a symbiotic sort of relationship ensues. Viewer and viewed feed on each other. Wrong turns are not artistic failures but ontological breakdowns. Such breakdowns mean we can't realize the world together anymore— our realities are breaking apart. Maybe we, as individuals, have to be let go because for some reason unique to our own lives, we no longer project our own lives in this or that soap's daily round.

All this is a preface to saying that the O.J. Simpson murder trial has been like a soap opera: it goes on like the flux of daily time itself; it insinuates itself into our daily lives. A great share of the American public has found speaking parts for themselves in this drama, or, at very least, found seats in the courtroom and are listening *interactively.* Why this fascination, this absorption in a trial that has, at the moment I am writing this, gone on for one hundred days and shows no sign of losing its market share? For many, our culture shows no great enlightenment in such a fixation. The American Survey column of the British journal *The Economist* calls this trial "Lance Ito's circus." Lewis Grossberger in *Mediaweek* reserves a room in *Animal House* for the trial. Frank Rich in *The New York Times* refers to it as "Judge Ito's all-star vaudeville" and M.L. Stein in *Editor & Publisher* refers to it as a "media circus."[1] "A total media hype not worth serious attention" one colleague tells me. It's like a soap opera and not worth serious comment or attention. Rupert Murdoch's *Star* and other tabloids will keep up the sensationalism for as long as it will sell papers, but for the serious minded, the enlightened, the sensational is the opium of the people. Geraldo has found a focus for his show. Talk show hosts like Geraldo can play into every nuance of the trial, milking it for higher ratings. From its very beginning, for the enlightened, this trial can mean nothing, except perhaps that too many unenlightened people can be seduced by glitz. Now, after one hundred days, the same enlightened observers note that there must be deep problems in our justice system. It has obviously failed to contain, in a lofty and expeditious fashion, a trial for double murder.

From a post-enlightened view, I am interested in this trial because we have culturally invested ourselves into it and it into us.[2] And, like a soap opera we get addicted to, this trial could not have drawn us in if it had not already in some way worked its way into our lives in this American culture at this moment. We've been running and it's come up alongside us and kept our pace. A real exchange is ensuing; almost the whole country has found speaking parts. And this sort of symbiosis means that the trial will unfold in tune with the daily unfolding of our culture as a whole. I mean that what chunks of the unmarked space of the world become facts in this trial and what facts become evidence, who testifies and who doesn't, whether the defense puts O.J. on the stand or not, what stories of prosecution and defense will be concocted for the jury, how Judge Ito will temper his rulings and his daily courtroom approach, what rationalities, realties, imaginings, emotions and fears will be played upon—all this will be modulated by the daily changes in cultural disposition. And in turn the culture is constructing its daily reality in line not only with the Dow, Newt and friends, Bill (Clinton) and friends, Bill (Gates) and friends, Rush and friends, headline contingencies, opinion polls, the weather, the soaps, blockbuster videos, the 1996 presidential campaign, the deaths of Jerry Garcia and

Mickey Mantle, tabloid talk replacing Phil Donohue in New York City, Madonna on Letterman, who's on the cover of *Time*—and on and on—but also with this O.J. Simpson murder trial. We can sever ourselves from the web of interconnectedness here by merely choosing to be inattentive to this trial. We can say that we want no part of it. We can choose another channel, another column, another conversation. Then we're no longer interconnected. We've employed our interstellar Warp Drive and we're now somewhere else.

Good luck out there! Maybe you'll run into Archimedes' fulcrum from which you can alter and move things down here.

It is precisely because we want to turn away from this trial that it becomes for us a scene from the abyss. After all, if we had our Enlightenment way fulfilled we should have already been able to handle this trial in a rational and realistic manner. We would have been able to put a stop to the bread and circus inclination, negate the racism, tone down the emotions, and most importantly cut the hyperreal down to the bone of bedrock truth and reality. This trial would not have been a performance caught within the flux of our postmodern culture. No, it would have been distanced from that flux, objectified, and made subject to our strictly analytical probings. The law should succumb to both deductive and inductive approaches—claptrap can be sorted out if one adheres to the rules of evidence, of defense and prosecution. On the other side of this clash of arguments lies the truth. All it takes is disinterest on the jury's part, a disinterest that unfortunately must extend to their own lives and the culture those lives have been enmeshed within since birth. And there must not only be a distance between the subjectivities of the jury and the evidence as presented but that same distance between the trial and the culture. Nobody should have come from anywhere or be any place during the trial and at the moment of verdict.

If we can't have that, if that can't be created for us by some authoritarian order of things, if we can't go back to a time when our culture wasn't permeated with the haunting belief that we construct the reality that constructs us, then our course seems clear enough. We're going to have to explore what all our cultural constructions mean and how they are valued. We're going to have to accept the fact that regardless of our attitudes and ideologies, our party affiliations and religious commitments, our lives come to meaning and value within our own cultural constructions.

As my intent here is to meditate in a postmodern fashion on what in the headlines, in film and on TV and radio, became staged for our culture as a scene from the abyss, I certainly cannot ignore the center stage treatment we have given this trial. Every aspect of what many want to reduce to merely a simulated media event, a profiteering venture, connects with the fears and anxieties, haunting nightmares of our own culture.

Field of Dreams

Accused is a sports hero, the last hero left in a shattered American conscience. Duke Wayne's frontier heroism tarnished during the Vietnam years as he attempted to convert *that* indeterminate moral event into an old fashioned good guy/bad guy moral drama. The Vietnamese just didn't "gook" as easily as African-Americans had "niggered" and Native-Americans had "redskinned." Sports has always remained inviolate on the cultural stage, in spite of the 1919 Chicago White Sox fix, (which the films *Field of Dreams* and *Eight Men Out* redeemed). What shocked Americans more than anything else regarding Tonya Harding's connection to the knee-capping of Nancy Kerrigan was its "unsportsmanlike" quality. Things like that just aren't done in sports. Elsewhere, the entire society is engaged in a ruthless economic competitiveness—a no holds barred brawl over money and power where the desire to be rich vindicates and an avoidance of prosecution is just another hurdle on the course. All that is supposed to end when it comes to sports. Tonya tore into the cloth of that dream. And right in the midst of the O.J. trial, the 1994 baseball World Series was canceled due to "greed and sloth." Baseball players put aside their unsullied image and became "labor" fighting it out with management. What was so pernicious about that was their timing. With less than twelve percent of the American work force unionized, with strikes almost rendered extinct in an American market that needs fewer and fewer American workers, here were our major league baseball players uniting against the teams' owners. And most unforgivable was their transgression of the sports code. Americans talk sports because it's a talk unaffected by economics and politics. No matter how greedy an entrepreneur is in the market arena, Americans don't want to see it in the sports arena. And for the working class, what's left if they can't escape the assembly line and a diminishing standard of living by going to a ballgame?

I am suggesting that the tarnishing of the sports hero image in our culture during this time reaches out to O.J. When the gods became mortal they lost the respect of us mere mortals. But specifically what is going on here is our cultural disenchantment with a previously enchanted world. We are being weaned of such an attachment, we are going through yet another demystification. And it is hard. Is O.J. too heroic, too noble, too filled with the moral integrity earned through "true sportsmanship" to have committed these horrific murders? If we are now presently questioning that heretofore mostly unquestioned moral fiber then O.J., too, becomes subject to our questioning. Has his Southern California life-style filled him with the same "greed and sloth" that the striking baseball players exhibited in the popular imagination? It's not the "game" that compels O.J. any longer, just as the "game" doesn't mean as much as money does to the players or the owners involved in the present strike.

"I Can't Get No Satisfaction"

Money and what it can buy is the biggest player in contemporary American culture. And it shows up in this trial, from talk of "all the justice money can buy" to an enactment of American class conflict. The defense battery of attorneys is the "Dream Team," like the Dream Team the U.S. sent to the Olympics to play basketball. How could any of those "foreign" teams match up against our Dream Team, a team that had Magic Johnson on it? O.J.'s Dream Team can likewise perform magic. They can rework the ordinary laws of the universe to suit their purposes. Opposing them are a bunch of public attorneys—governmental workers, like post office workers. Anybody in a "public" office, even the City District Attorney's Office, is somehow too frightened or too incapable to get into the "private" sector. If Marcia Clark and associates were any good at what they did, they'd be in private practice where the money is. No public prosecutor can stand in the same arena with a private sector "Dream Team" and hope to win. Have I captured our cultural valuing at this moment?

At the same time, governments, whether city, state, or federal uphold the law. Arrest, prosecution, incarceration and the death penalty are public, not private matters. Keeping the violent locked up is as important a part of the Republican effort to "restore the dream" as national "defense." Who are the violent and what, besides bad genes, might make them violent? What *was* the "dream" in the first place and are there contesting "dreams" for America? Who are we now defending ourselves against, or is it a matter of being able to defend our markets wherever "our" transnationals decide to do business?

I believe the O.J. Simpson trial reveals something about the law and the market that riddles the American Dream. And it's revealed in the response to the trial one often hears: "all the justice money can buy." Is justice a market function? Will O.J.'s ability to buy the Dream Team inevitably buy him *more* justice than, say, Willie Horton? But Willie Horton himself got *too* much justice in the eyes of the many who understood that a vote for Bush would mean an end to putting people like Horton on the street again to commit yet another crime—against them.

Let's follow the money. If O.J. has enough money to buy a Dream Team defense, a top-of-the-line legal defense version of Bruno Magli dress casuals, then he's not the same sort of threat as Horton was. Horton was a threat because he had no money. At the same time, if the market were working its spell on him, he still had a desire to consume. In a society that says "to be is to consume," a black man seeking identity, seeks money. Even a man who only has a desire to pay for a visit to the doctor or for college for his kid and cannot fulfill that desire can become frustrated and angry. We may be engaged in disconnecting anger from violence—talk it through in counselling sessions with support groups and so on—but will this be part of the welfare reform that currently obsesses us? I mean are we presently talking about increasing our interactive network of social concern or "freeing" people to be personally responsible? And although we want to say that the anger-violence nexus is not biological but cultural and we can disconnect and reconnect it through cultural means, our culture is presently riven by wars that themselves are producing anger *and* violence.

In discriminating who has being-in-the-world identity and who does not, the market produces at a steady rate the fertile ground in which anger grows. Anger is not solely the possession of those who wind up with it; it must also be traced to the creating source. And the way those who wind up angry put that anger into action has everthing to do with the privileged values of the culture. Release comes within the path of desire, and desire is a market construction. The desire for more of everything: money, clothes, cars, jewelry, leisure, fun, sex. It all adds up to identity, an empowered identity. To be a winner is to possess the winnings, whose very possession nullifies the means of possessing. The art is in not being caught—an art that Nixon was criticized for not having. Ditto Milken and Bob Packwood. But then again, Nixon escaped a jail term and Packwood escaped with his golden parachute.

Violent means are the only means left to an increasing number of people in our society. And because they are caught within a cultural path of desire that propels them each day anew—not just commercials on TV but in the lives of those flashy winners who appear on magazine covers, on talk shows, in the soaps, in films, in our dreams—they come to see violence as a method of access. In the view of the violent, who do not see themselves as the "violent" but rather as "players," violence is a form of address. They too are playing to win. Their violence is only perceived as violence by their victims, actual or potential. They are "the violent" to those threatened. The workings of desire, frustration, anger and violence are mutually shared in a world of poor among poor, disenfranchised among disenfranchised. Violence has a home here. Within the reality frame of the well-off and enfranchised, violence and the web of desire that spins it are inconceivable. I am not saying that the wealthy do not know violence, but that they have no means of knowing it in the way the poor do. And the lines of communication are getting worse.

"How do we construe the American idea of freedom," Lewis Lapham asks after the Oklahoma City bombing, "and what do we mean by democracy if we must communicate with one another by bomb-o-gram?"[3] In short, what does violence mean within our American Dream now as we are living it? Our society is currently backing away from the abyss it has dug for a vast number of people. The further away it gets, the more personal histories of individual lives will fade and a nightmarish monolith called "The Violent" will appear. Amazingly, on the other side, "The Violent" continue to be absorbed in their own individual paths of desire, full of stories, reasons, goals and objectives, hopes and anticipations, actions taken. To themselves, I am suggesting, the violent may be no more than decisive, unafraid to take the necessary steps to fulfill their goals. In a society that immensely values the entrepreneur, why is it so unfathomable to imagine that "The Violent" see themselves as venture capitalists and entrepreneurs or as bold adventurers trying to escape anonymity? Even when they are beating their wives or their children, raping, barroom brawling, snatching purses, stealing for drug money, robbing cars, breaking into houses and so on, is it really possible for them to do any of this outside the culturally constructed path of desire, of ontology and consumption, of identity and spectacle that now stands in for the American Dream, if the American Dream can be seen as something different and now displaced?

"Pay-As-You-Go" Justice

If our market dissemination of identity is breeding the violent and violence, then our defending system of justice is two-tracked. Those who are already well-off are no threat to the well-off while those who are not well-off are a threat.[4] After all, it is not an invasion by the well-off seeking a place at the table of the poor. Neither do Conservative Republicans seek to restore the dream of a public morality for those whose morality is not a threat to them. The need is to constrain in every way possible—conscience or prisons—those who are subjected to the daily barrage of the consumption-ontology nexus but cannot fulfill it except through violence. Thus, while Willie Horton would be a threat to our social order of things, O.J. would not. The trial itself, however, has become so public that our system of justice is on trial rather than any individual.

On the one hand, we clearly now have a system of justice that is being propelled by judgments our market master narrative has already made. Justice will have to defend an increasingly lopsided disbursal of privileges in this country. And it will have to do it as if were still blind to such inequities. A winner in our casino logic system should be able to summon a good defense. Or, hire the right tax attorneys to hold off the IRA. Or, summon enough clout to get a minimum sentencing. Or, crush a parking ticket. Or, defy Anti-Trust, the Security Exchange Commission, or the National Labor Relations Board, or the Constitutional Bill of Rights. Or, launder drug money through legitimate businesses. Or, grant favors for lobbyists. And so on.

The problem with the O.J. trial is that it itself has been caught up within our casino logic: its notoriety has become a profit making business. Justice is all going on in front of the camera, on Court TV for the whole American audience to watch. If it becomes too clear that O.J. will buy his freedom, then our Enlightenment pretenses of objective, unbiased determinations of guilt or innocence will suffer yet another blow. The money-identity equation will go prime-time. It will be harder, as they say, to keep them down on the farm, in this case, keep them working for McDonald's at minimum wage and going to sing "What A Friend I Have In Jesus" on Sundays. We are a step closer to the abyss not because of "outbreaks of terrorism" in the heartland but because our society has been carrying on as if "democracy was just a fancy word for corporate capitalism."[5] "[O]ur political system hasn't faced up squarely to the issues brought on by globalization and technology because the portion of the electorate that pays for politics likes the economy the way it is. . . . "[6] Violence is the price they pay for their selfishness and they hope to pay less by putting the economic losers away before they can become violent. We are all equal under the law but because we now live within a corporate notion of social justice some people are more equal than others. Now, because of the televised play-by-play of the O.J. trial, following on the heels of two other money trials—William Kennedy Smith and the Menendez brothers—we have right before our eyes a view of what happens to justice within a society that has abandoned any sense of social justice (concern for others is socialism which died with the Soviet Union) and yet presumes to still dispense justice to individuals.

White Bronco Watching

Geraldo did a special anniversary show one hundred days into the trial, but he had reason to celebrate. The O.J. trial had boosted his failing TV ratings. For the rest of the country, the trial was getting to be a pain in the neck. It should go away, fade like a fad that has seen its day. Unfortunately, the dispensation of justice in a democracy does not follow the ups and downs of fad and fashion. It would go on until both the prosecution and the defense would rest their cases, the jury would deliberate and reach a verdict and the judge would pass sentence. The attention span of the "mass market" audience had been reached. Or, had it? Here we are this week wondering whether the gloves really fit O.J. and whether he really did have a pair of Bruno Magli dress casuals, (the kind that left those unusual footprints at the murder scene). The soap opera still draws us. But like all soap opera connections we connect at a safe distance, through a protective screen. Our lives are different, our actions more rational and focused. We are less driven by desires, less exposed to chance and the vagaries of others, to the darkness that engulfs the lives of others. This safe distancing is orchestrated by the soaps. They never take us beyond what is already conceivable to us nor into ways of representing the world that undermine our own. If you have an eye out for it, you can see how the waters of mass market reaction are always being tested on soaps. For instance, blacks in love, either with other blacks or whites, sporadically show up but then are withdrawn. The polls detect an uneasiness with these plot lines. They can't be handled in an absolutely sterile, disconnected-totally-with-your-reality way.

Our attentiveness or inattentiveness to the O.J. trial comes out of the reality frames within which we live. Extreme examples of this mediation of the world bring it into clear focus. David Koresh and the Branch Davidians for instance: "What the authorities apparently never recognized is that Koresh's preaching was to him and his followers the *only* matter of substance, and that a 'surrender' could be worked out only through dialogue within the biblical framework in which the Branch Davidians lived."[7] What are the framework-reality connections being made at this moment regarding the O.J. trial? What does it mean to those for whom democracy is "a summer vacation . . . a suburban idea"?[8] What about to those heartland thousands and maybe millions represented by Timothy J. McVeigh, whom Robert Wright in *The New Republic* called "a right-wing libertarian paramilitary drifter who already suspects the federal authorities have planted a microchip in his buttocks"?[9] And what does it mean to the rest of the "salaried majority" whose quality of life is deteriorating? Surely, for them it means that puzzlement rather than paranoia rules. What does it mean to the "underclass," the poor in and out of ghettos, who float in and out of being salaried and being destitute?

I return to what I have suggested previously but dismissed: maybe it all means what the media wants it to mean. Maybe if the media hadn't taken it up, we wouldn't have taken it up, and therefore it wouldn't have meant anything. Surely there wouldn't have been a Rodney King media event or a South Central L.A. riot if the beating hadn't been accidentally taped. Maybe if all the media handled it the way *The New York Times* did from the very beginning, we wouldn't now be making these culture-trial explorations. What has cultural value arises from our own attentiveness, and, likewise, our attentiveness focuses on what our culture values. In our market driven culture, attentiveness and marketability are joined. If we lose interest in the O.J. Simpson trial, then the Simpson stock goes down, which translates into a loss of cultural interest. The media, then, is not unilaterally creating the situation; the cultural reality of the trial is a composite of the day to day enactment of the trial, our attentiveness, and the media's response to both.

What comes first? Logically, it would seem the trial, which is a result of the actual murders. Those actualities seem to be the external reference points which control both our attentiveness and the media's reportage. But what if I said that neither the murders nor the trial could in any way exist for us if we were not already living in a culture at a particular time that had an eye out for such events? Now are we so predisposed because the media has set us up for sensational events, has gotten us used to a diet of tabloid events? Or, is it the other way round—our culture has become unmoored from any solid anchors of meaning and value and therefore is prone to drift in a sea of tabloid events?

There are countless events occurring each day—some finally make Sunday night movies, some bestselling documentaries, some get pitched to Hollywood producers every hour of the day, and the rest get forgotten, if noticed at all. From the very beginning—a black man in a white Bronco possibly fleeing from the murder of his white ex-wife being filmed from a copter overhead as the Bronco made its way down a Southern California highway—we saw in this event a crossing over from reel to real, from image to reality, from soap to our living room, from star to man pursued, another tale of the highway patrol. TV is filled with real life drama, from medical emergencies, cop patrolling, rescue 911, nationwide criminal searches, and so on. The money has been in watching ourselves. But why? If our culture was one in the way it identified, the way it concocted meanings and values, then there would be little interest in seeing our media reflections. But if a social order of things yearns for such homogeneity but is faced only with cultural heterogeneity, then this dilemma and conflict seethes with interest. We stare at what was not conceivable to us within our own reality framing—we cannot look away. I say then that we are a culture prone to seeing how difference breaks out and where it breaks out. We measure ourselves on such occasions, by means of such events. The O.J. trial is such an event. I want to say more about the media because they are taking the hit, not only here with this trial but steadily and with regard to everything. The media both capitalizes on where our gaze comes to rest and also in turn works to keep that gaze fixed on its mediating of whatever it was that was being attended to in the first place. However, just as there is no *one* American culture but many, there is no *one* representation of what goes on in our culture. *The Nation* has a different take than does *The American Spectator;* Mark Shields has a different take than Paul Gigot. George Will than Michael Kingsley. Rush Limbaugh than Mario Cuomo. The substance of the views tend to match the diversity of the culture itself. It comes to a wash here. But what doesn't come to a wash is the driving force that compels the different takes. O.J. plays because it pays; reporters report because they are assigned; TV covers it because it brings in cable subscribers or advertisers. Economics precedes ideology; in fact it supersedes it. The market may be exploiting the event but it has no interest in manipulating it. In other words, unlike the soaps, there is no orchestration here. Nor, on the other hand, any real attempt to do more than show all the signifiers involved. There is no attempt to connect word and world, image and reality, what is being televised and how it connects to our culture. On the contrary, when a mesmerizing event is connected to our social and political discourse, that connection is at once denounced. When Clinton made a connection between Republican anti-government discourse and the similar phobia of Timothy McVeigh, George Will in the *Washington Post* wrote that any "attempt to locate in society's political discourse the cause of a lunatic's action. . . . is contemptible."[10]

Ultimately, because our coverage of the O.J. trial is simply that—a "coverage" and not a crisscrossing into the culture—what that event means and how it is to be valued blows with the same winds that sweep the country. Those enjoying a suburban reality frame, a perpetual summer whose only hardship comes in the shape of crab grass (and that is handled by one's "lawn service"), have little inclination to see the links between the O.J. trial and themselves or American society. In a summer frame, what our culture may be is not subject to our daily constructions; rather it is grounded on real values and beliefs, real initiative, integrity, industry, competence, perseverance, competitiveness, aggressiveness and so. In other words, life is a garden party some have earned because they've demonstrated and relied upon winning values. The present system of social justice has bestowed their just desserts upon them, so it is obviously a system that works. If the Dream Team manages to get O.J. off, they will have reaffirmed our adversarial system of criminal law: justice goes to those who win in a competitive arena, just as success in life goes to those who win in the market arena.

The summer reality frame picks out the same irksome matters in the trial as they do in their own world. Our justice system is run too much like a liberal governmental agency of endless accommodation and not enough like a business. If every public official connected with the O.J. case had been held to corporate standards of competence and not governmental, bureaucratic ones, this trial would not be taking so long. It is not by accident that the Dream Team has focused on bureaucratic incompetence at the murder scene and in the gathering and testing of evidence. Theirs is an "anti-government" defense which currently plays very well throughout the country. And it plays well because it suits the reality frame, the valuing and meaning disbursements, of those who are living their American Dream.

Some will argue that when our system of justice turns into a media event, a tabloid and talk show carnival, then this becomes symptomatic of the wrong turn America took in the '60s. Now this is a cultural connection, the kind that Newt Gingrich has been willing to make. It plays well even among those people who were in one way or another enfranchised by a broad cultural revolution begun in the '60s and terminated in 1980 with the ascent of Ronald Reagan. Any act of murder and mayhem is linked to liberalism's soft posture on crime and criminals. Any outbreak of social unrest is attributed to liberalism's ready welfare program that brought up a generation of potential hard-working Americans as social parasites, as irresponsible threats to the rest of us.

Incapable of making any connections other than those that suit the most well-off in this country, the salaried majority and the expanding underclass drift in and out of those hand-me-down views, inattentiveness, media disgust, and a nihilism born of frustration. Reaction to the Simpson trial has been no exception, yet, as I have parsed, the culture/court imbrications are many and premonitory.

Notes

1. *The Economist* April 22, 1995, p.a32; *Mediaweek* April 10, 1995, p.38; *The New York Times* October 2, 1994, p.e17; *Editor & Publisher* October 22, 1994, p.8.

2. The American culture *after* the trial and the rendering of the verdict is proving to be even more interesting than the trial. Because I expect it will be a card played in the 1996 presidential election, I will eventually write about it from within the mêlée of that super spectacle.

3. Lewis Lapham, "Seen But Not Heard," *Harper's Magazine* July 1995, p. 30.

4. John Cassidy in a *New Yorker* piece entitled "Who Killed the Middle Class?" quotes the fear of William J. McDonough, president of the Federal Reserve Bank of New York: "These dramatic wage developments [increasing gap between rich and poor] raise profound issues for the United States . . . We are forced to face the question of whether we will be able to go forward together as a unified society with a confident outlook or as a society of diverse economic groups suspicious of both the future and each other." October 16, 1995, p. 113

5. Lewis H. Lapham, "Seen But Not Heard," *Harper's Magazine* July 1995, 36.

6. Roger Wilkins, "Powell's Race," *The Nation* October 9, 1995, p. 372.

7. James D. Tabor and Eugene V. Gallagher, *Why Waco? Cults and the Battle for Religious Freedom in America,* University of California Press, 1995.

8. Lapham, p. 36.

9. Robert Wright, "Did Newt Do It?" *The New Republic* May 15, 1995, p. 4.

10. George Will, *Washington Post.*

The Last Seduction: Commitment Is Murder?

"In other words, this was a genre case, and the genre, L.A. *noir,* was familiar. There is a *noir* case every year or two in Los Angeles."

Joan Didion, "L.A. *Noir*"

In the midst of the O.J. Simpson trial, just weeks before the Prosecution will rest its case, I watch John Dahl's film, *The Last Seduction.* At the very beginning of the film, Linda Fiorentino takes a hard, vicious, unexpected slap from a suddenly angry Bill Pullman, her husband.

In this film, she comes back to murder him, shoving a mace can down his throat while he is handcuffed and spraying until he suffocates. She's a cold piece of work is Linda. But so too is the murderer or murderers of Nicole Brown Simpson and Ronald Goldman. I cannot free myself of the crossover here: this is a playback where Nicole is in a power struggle with a man who wants to end her life but this time she doesn't wind up the victim. She wins. She plays it tough, mean and breaks all the rules. She doesn't bend to power; she becomes Linda Fiorentino.

One of the cracks in the naive realist portrayal of life has to do with power. It seemed to be always contained at the end of the film, only to reappear in the next. But our naivete persists: the power of evil, the Devil's work, is subdued by the power of the moral good, exercised by the morally strong; the law is linked with the punishment of evildoers; the rules are here for everyone's good. Even the power of Nature has been subdued for humankind's own good. In an egalitarian-based democracy, political power is never totally cornered, never monopolized for long—economic power benefits all; media power upholds democracy; individual power is foundational; social power is minimized in an American class-less society; familial power is ruled by Christian virtues; the power of men over women, husbands over wives, is illusionary, a spin by "Feminazis" to suit their own agenda.

231

At the heart of this *film blanc,* the film constructed within a naive realist notion of good and evil, is the belief that either reason or morality, or both, govern power. Power does not jump the traces here and take the driver's seat; it does not manipulate reason nor does it employ morality to work on its behalf. Or does it? The classic *film noir* is riddled with the suspicion that the individual is born into a world in which the power arrangements have all been made and like magnetic forces pull and repel the individual in the course of his or her own life. The "way things are" is designed and maintained to suit some but not others. The sense here is that power is beyond the individual to fathom or control. Or, only erratically. The good man goes down to unseen forces. The innocent woman can't quite summon a telling defense. The hard-working soul can't quite figure out what's sapping that soul. Happiness is unable to empower its own creation or its own continuance. Power, like desire, the hidden propulsions of the unconscious, and chance, wrack the enlightened soul and drives it into the corridors of *film noir.*

But that is not where Linda Fiorentino is. She has crossed over to the postmodern side. Power is neither dark Fate nor satanic forces at work nor an oligarchic cabal: it is the fluid running through society's whole system; it's the waters we alternately swim and drown in. If you focus on the weave in the curtain that both rational and moral as well as irrational and amoral concoctions of power drop in front of your eyes, you have a better chance to navigate and chart your course. Living in stories of how power works and doesn't work, how both mind and morals can personally empower you, does little more than encumber you. You've lost your flexibility; you're playing with the rules of your game but power is not subject to the rules of your game. So Fiorentino is a sort of Nietzschean superwoman who is wary of the fictitiousness of truth and morality in our own time. But has she deified herself? Is she free through choice? When you think about it, freedom of choice is as much a fabulation that muddles our interaction with the world as any other fabulation. The Fiorentino character would be wary of being a liberated woman, a free spirit, for therein lies a story frame that leaves her vulnerable. Hers is more clearly a Deleuzian, nomadic path, a schizorevolutionary who has an eye out for the way a place, person or event is territorialized.

She resists seduction. The same cannot be said for Nicole Brown Simpson. Once seduced by O.J., she lives under the power of that seduction until her death. Whether or not he killed her, his is the seduction that held her. Fiorentino's character, Bridget/Wendy, seduces Mike, whose own life has already been seduced by what Fiorentino calls a "brainless, countrified morality." Why is this then the *last* seduction? If Mike winds up being executed for the murder of Fiorentino's husband—and it is clear in the end that she's successfully set him up for this—it will be the last time in his life he will have been seduced. But perhaps it is the last seduction because this is the last time anyone in the last decade of the twentieth century will be seduced by a "brainless countrified morality." This is a narrative frame that will not be hauled out of the closet without alterations ever again. In short, no one in the audience wants to wind up like Mike or be like Mike. And everybody wants to be like Fiorentino. But upon reflection—by which I mean when we get back into the moral /rational frame that we came in with—we decide that Mike wasn't wrong with his "countrified morality" but she was just a "total fucking bitch" who seduced him off the right track. In other words, we fall back into storytelling, the way Mike did all the time. And Fiorentino never did. Mike wanted them to fall into a love story, maybe one that he had seen in the movies or read about in a book. Maybe he had seen *True Romance* and wanted his love for Bridget to be like Clarence's love for Alabama. He wanted sex to be an overture to a romance in which they were totally absorbed in each other's lives. Fiorentino, on the other hand, tells him "Fucking doesn't have to be anything more than fucking." And she puts up barriers between herself and him at every turn—asking him to knock before he enters her office, to go out of the room when she is making a "personal" call, to stay away from her when she's at work. While he wants their relationship to overwhelm the world around them, she refuses the mediation and heeds the power politics of every situation.

Not to be seduced is not identical with being liberated. Being liberated, as one could argue the wealthy and independent Nicole was liberated, does not forestall seduction. It is, as I have said, a form of seduction. Power works through the narratives that seduce us. Indeed, the narratives are always to various degrees products of power, power disseminations into our very being. If we imagine something like a continuum of seduction, Mike Swale with his knee-jerk respect for the rules ("You're always looking for the rules, Mike" Fiorentino tells him) is caught in a naive realist seduction, Nicole Brown Simpson is in a "freedom of choice" seduction, and Linda Fiorentino is in a "meta-seductive frame," a frame of self-reflexive, parodic dimensions. Mike meets the world through a filter of previously existing laws, commandments, rules, protocols, procedures. Sex, love and romance fit into a fixed order of things. He is seduced by a culture privileging such ways of interacting with the world and is also self-seduced insofar as he gives these myths ontological status. Fiorentino observes the patterns of observations she falls into. She is aware that she, like others, is always aware of things *in some way*. And she tries to find that way. She is very deft at doing so with others. When Mike first presses her about being more revealing she drops into the story he is trying to house their affair within. She plays the part. "Is that what you want to hear?" she asks him. She parodies his notion of what is going to be the "reality" of their relationship. And, later, when he presses her again to talk about herself, she starts to tell him the truth but he stops her and doesn't want to hear another story. It is clear that she does this for her own amusement, enjoying the power she has over him. He cannot distinguish the tight relationship between stories and power, cannot probe into a logistics that floats all stories. This story that she begins to tell him—that she ran off with a million bucks and was being pursued and had to lie low— is not conceivable to him within his small town Beston frame. It doesn't fit that Beston order of things that prescribes his own "realizing." Like a mentor with a student, she leads him in and out of lessons; a zen master of the art of living expressing unfathomable koans to Mike. After several times holding up to him the misleading seductive nature of his romance mythologies, she still reels him in with the line "We can have a relationship of equals." Mike, astoundingly, won't postmodernize. He can't jump paradigms. Of course, he has a long way to go. In fact, he has to first get to where I think Nicole was before he can reach Fiorentino.

Is this the "real" Nicole Brown-Simpson I am going to talk about? Or, is this the Nicole that is being represented during the trial? Is there one image we are getting of Nicole, or, are we, like the jury, in the process of representing Nicole to ourselves? For that matter, are we doing the same with O.J.? The fact that he is alive and his image is televised to us each day does not make it easier for us to concoct a reliable representation of his reality than of Nicole's. Of course, if she had somehow miraculously survived the attack, she could tell us what happened. And if she *did* point a finger at O.J., we would still be hearing his representation of the attack. We would still have to construct an image in our minds of Nicole and O.J. and what happened. We would still have to decide what she was "really" like: was she like Fiorentino says *she* is, a "total fucking bitch" who provoked O.J.'s wrath?

The "total fucking bitch" line is Fiorentino's parodying of the "total fucking bitch" narrative that is out there. It's one of the big stories about women that seduce both men and women. "Sometimes the only thing left for a woman is to be a bitch," every woman in the film *Dolores Claiborne* tells us. They can't escape the narrative that will inevitably greet their actions. Mike is drawn to this narrative as he tries to figure out who Fiorentino really is and what she's really like. Maybe, he says to himself, she's just a "total fucking bitch." And maybe that seductive story transfers to Nicole. Maybe O.J. had a hard time with her because she was a "TFB." Of course, this is no defense for murder and the Dream Team well knows this, but if the jury can be brought out of any sympathy for her as a totally innocent victim, then the sympathy saved can transfer to O.J..

Part of the "TFB" story has to do with women who have too much freedom—maybe they get a divorce, take half or all of everything, and go out and have a good time. Financial independence gives them power to pursue their own pleasure. A "TFB" will go into a man's bar, enjoy a drink and the newspaper and then pick out a guy who can give them pleasure. She's just doing what men do, but they're culturally licensed to do it. Even if they're still married. Fiorentino reverses the action when Mike tries to pick her up in a bar. He's hung like a horse he tells her, playing out a role from the "dirty" segment of the love, sex and romance narrative through which he reaches out for love, sex and romance. Okay, Fiorentino tells him, show me. He balks—this isn't *her* proper line in the script. And while he hesitates, she reaches over, unzips him and searches around. Biologically you're okay, she tells him, and then she questions him to make sure he's not going to be an AIDS risk to her. We're coming very close to touching reality without a lens here, without a mediating filter. But Mike looks at the world through enough lenses to make up for it. She's scriptless, out of order, and ultimately a real threat to the male/female hierarchical order of things. It's just the kind of behavior that intimidates men into seeking refuge in the "TFB" narrative.

The tabloids have been full of pictures and stories of Nicole as a woman freely choosing a life of sensation and pleasure for herself. She would go out on the town in her undergarments and a fur coat. She was, every image seems to suggest, sexually promiscuous. Divorced, wealthy, beautiful, young and living in Southern California. And, one more thing we know for sure, not careful enough. And *if* O.J. was her murderer, then she wasn't half as good as Fiorentino is in reading the people around her. Like Mike, then, Nicole is seduced by certain ways of looking at things. Unlike Mike, these ways aren't pages out of William Bennett's *Book of Moral Virtues.* They are in fact empty of moral substance. Being is fulfilled by the freedom to choose, a page out of Milton Friedman. So Nicole has her being-in-the-world within a free to choose narrative. This is a life-world pursued most energetically in Southern California and everything we get to know about Nicole indicates that she adopted it. As long as she is not constrained or restrained here, she is in control, both of world and self. The subjects of choice part of this narrative have to do with abortion—free to choose to abort or not—and products—free to choose among products on a shelf, or in a cat-alog, or off a menu, or channels on a remote, or hot vacation spots. Beyond this, our culture has little to say. And yet this way of mediating the world, this pair of reality filters, is touted as the be all and end all for women. If they can just be free to choose, they'll be someplace—someplace where they're equal, empowered and. . . free to choose.

Let's summarize how Fiorentino would judge this narrative. Nicole is no place but in a culture that wraps her up within ready to wear stories, including the "TFB". And she has chosen to adopt a script and a part for herself that says she is somehow outside this web making choices as to what she is, what reality really is, who other people are, what is going on with them in their inter-action with her and so on. She has the money and the freedom to make shelf selections. And if she had the need for an abortion she has the freedom to go ahead and have one. Meanwhile, she is in a situation that will lead to her own brutal murder, which means her freedom to choose has nothing to do with her control or grasp of anything. The labyrinth of events and motives, of ap-prehensions and fears, of desires and repressions, of accidents and best laid plans are the very substance of a world she thinks she has power over because she lives in a free to choose fable. For Fiorentino, there is only a rush to see and react seconds before the other guy. Out of the whirlwind of lives and world interacting, she observes the way others observe, including the fools who think the task is done when a free to choose I.D. is assumed. At the very end of *The Last Seduction*, Mike is behind bars and is pressed by his attorney to think of something that would reveal Fiorentino's machinations, something that would substantiate his story. And he does. But he's seconds too late as we see Fiorentino retrieve the bit of evidence, get back in her stretch limo and then burn it.

Someone was in a totally grieved fable regarding Nicole and what that someone was going to do had absolutely nothing to do with Nicole's sense of being free to choose. What Fiorentino displays, namely, an expectation that people interface reality in mostly scripted ways and that her life cannot avoid entanglement in these ways, is really a displacement of agency, of volitional self, from *here* to *there,* from self to world. Our present culture is geared to individual satisfaction, ever increasing desires fulfilled. It is the individual who follows a driving self-interest that maximizes pleasure and reduces pain. We are therefore culturally driven to look to ourselves as what the whole economy is geared to satisfy. The individual free to choose is the *summum bonum* of our society, the American Dream is tilted in this direction. Deceived by a notion that we can achieve a free to choose status that is itself not a story that binds and blinds us, that is not already a story transmuted within the dominating narratives of our culture, we think we are choosing when we have already been chosen. We are working our way through a world that is already working upon us. We can never shape a being-in-the-world in ways not already in the world. We select images of ourselves off the shelves of our cultural department store. To focus, then, on the act of reaching for something on a shelf and ignore *what* there is for us to choose as well as *where* the motivation for our choice comes from is, in effect, to display a culturally created focus. Nicole is as seduced by the story of free choice as Mike is by the story of "rules" while Fiorentino focuses on the inevitability of focusing itself, hers as well as others, and plays it all to her own advantage.

Fiorentino doesn't escape being traditionally *noir* in this film simply because she takes a good man down. "I don't want to be with you long enough to be like you" Mike tells her but he is fatally caught in her seductive web. Love, sex and romance are darkened by a beloved that doesn't know how to love or be loved.

At least not in the ways Mike has learned about love and what love is in the town of Beston. What happens when amorality and sociopathology wend their way into love? Fiorentino is postmodernly *noir* in this film because her abuse of traditional commitments exposes the seductive and concocted nature of those commitments. In order to break the laws of both God and Man, Fiorentino has to immediately become the "total fucking bitch" she herself parodies. And this bitch is an amoral sociopath. "Murder is commitment?" Mike asks her, astounded by her logic, shocked by her total absence of the moral conscience that enfolds his life. The postmodern slant reverses the question: "Commitment is murder?" Incapable of seeing past his own commitment to Beston "reality, rationality and morality," Mike has that commitment lead him all the way to jail for murder, a murder he didn't commit.

When we first meet Mike, he tells his friends that he tried to leave Beston for a big city, Buffalo, just to prove that he was too big for Beston, that he wasn't just really a small town guy. He tells Fiorentino more than once that he had to prove that he was bigger than Beston. The desire to break the commitments forged by his Beston life propel him toward Fiorentino, the New York City girl who lives way beyond Beston's sense of what living is. He chooses to break the bonds of Beston, but Fiorentino shows him, through her own words and actions, that he can't choose with a Beston mindset to go from where he is to where she is. A paradigm jump is needed here, and Mike can't do it. He falls back into a Beston order of things that the film shows us is actually constructed within stereotypes of the meanest sort. The appearance of a black man in the town of Beston is unnerving. When Fiorentino tries to explain to the sheriff what this black man did to her, she uses stereotyping language to which the sheriff responds, "Like in the movies." She has produced for him a reality that communicates, except for him it is reality and for her it is a representation of reality that he will connect with. Her sociopathy then becomes just another stereotyping concocted within a reality that is concocted of stereotypes. The *noir* factor here stretches from her to the town and beyond that to the culture that sustains the town. Countering this postmodern *noir* view is the view of the culture that sustains both the film and our viewing. Mike's innocence speaks loudly against Fiorentino's amorality; her cold seduction of a poor, innocent fool.

The film itself becomes the latest urge toward amorality emerging from the postmodern abyss. There is the figure of Ralph Reed standing behind Mike as he now stands behind the whole culture, urging us to see how far we have fallen into the postmodern abyss when we begin to conceive commitment as murder.

Asking For and Getting Chaos: The Abyss of Human Sexuality

> "Now I am not sure what human sexuality is."
>
> Marilyn French

Neither am I, although indeterminacy and undecidability here neither diminish nor sour my appreciation for the same. The same? Is human sexuality the same for everyone? Perhaps Marilyn French is not sure what it is because it means different things to different people. Gay sexuality is also human sexuality, although it continues its struggle for social recognition as an *acceptable* form of human sexuality. But what about pedophilia, S&M, fetishisms and sexual "aberrations" of all kinds? What about rape? Is it about violence and power or is it about human sexuality? Indeed, is all human sexuality as we presently know it a manifestation of patriarchal power and the subjection of women? Is pornography a cancer on human sexuality or a natural flowering? Obviously, one of our problems with determining what human sexuality is has to do with the variety of ways humans enact their sexuality, a great many of which are socially taboo, and, more than ever in the present, discourse variously about human sexuality. If we try, then, to know what human sexuality is, we must first position ourselves in one or the other of these already existing worlds of human sexuality.

French's admitted uncertainty points to our present postmodern awareness that what human sexuality is defined to be is not first an epistemological problem but an ontological one. As soon as reality itself—not only the reality of the world "out there" but of our own being, including our sexual nature—becomes a need-to-be-defined affair and not the universal locus for all our defining quests, then how we *know* any reality, including human sexuality, will automatically *produce* and define that reality for us. This has to follow because firstly, what we say we know reality is can never correspond to what reality is. It's a matter of not only not having an external point of reference by which to measure that correspondence, but not being able to "say" or to "mark" without marking something *out*. And secondly, once we adopt what we say about reality as reality then we will eat, sleep, drink, talk and have sex within our reality. We will live rationally and realistically, but here this can only be interpreted as meaning we will live within the frame of reality we have adopted. By continuing to produce human sexuality in our adopted way, we continue to underwrite that way of knowing it.

No one, therefore, lives within some foundational essence of human sexuality, the reality in itself of human sexuality, but rather within some inevitable mediation of that reality. It cannot be different for humans. Our sexuality is indeed ours—it is caught in the total way we bring the world to meaning. The way we package the world and ourselves into representational schemes or life-world narratives that never leave us capable of defining an unnarrated reality parallels our always already existing interpenetration with the world out there. Put blankly, whether there is or there isn't an essential, universal human sexuality does not affect our postmodern awareness that it can only be narratively and not objectively grasped. And by "narratively" I mean we can only come to know human sexuality within the narrative frame we are already in, our site of reality mediation, the narrative frame that produces our way of knowing, our pattern of knowing that continues to produce our narrating frame.

Maybe we once surely knew what human sexuality was. Maybe it was what a particular moral and social order said it was, no more and no less. But moral and social orders determine only to the degree that their determinations are adopted, either willingly or by fear or force. Even that biological determinism that Camille Paglia cites when she says, for instance, that "there are sexual differences that are based in biology" is a sort of floating determinism.[1] Even gender at birth is more often indeterminate than is commonly thought. Rather than allow such gender ambiguity at birth steps are taken to affix a determinate gender. Exactly what we are being determined by and how we are being determined has been up for grabs for centuries. Paglia goes on to indict academic feminists as being "lost in a fog of social constructionism." What human sexuality may be is not as hot an issue as where does our human sexuality come from. In order to demonstrate the difficulty of defining human sexuality I have gone back and multiplied realities out of which definitions of human sexuality might emerge. I have, in short, also entered the fog of constructionism. And now I want to pretend to step out of it.

The issue as to whether our sexuality is fixed and determined according to a biologism unaffected by cultural constructions, or whether our sexuality is first and foremost a cultural construction is an issue that plays out—not surprisingly—within our present culture wars. The biologism part, the determined part, never appears naked; it's always interpreted. It is caught in a web of what is "natural" or in a web of what "God meant it to be" or in a web of conservative family values, or in an ingenious narrative web like Paglia's: that homosexual men have produced the art and culture of western civilization and that women are guided by the natural cycles of the moon which, according to Paglia, do not lead to the cultural highpoints of western civilization. So to argue that there exists an irrefutable biological determination of human sexuality does not set up a counter to cultural constructivism. We are, in fact, merely arguing for a particular view of human sexuality—one that we say is not a view or an argument for a view but a reflection of a truth, a biological truth. Some constructions will admit that they are constructions—arguing at the same time that they are the most humane and rational amid a field of lesser constructions—and some constructions will make no such admission but rather seek to ground themselves in foundational religious texts, objective empirical discoveries and all brands of scientism, reproducible and quantifiable, or plain "common sense." The postmodernist charge that numbers and statistics are also narrated is a particularly disturbing one to the anti-constructivists.

Have we thereby hopelessly distanced ourselves from the reality of our own human sexuality? Do we only dwell in a hyper-reality of human sexuality and therefore we are all engaged in a struggle to empower our own favorite simulations of everything, including our own sexuality? Perhaps those who believe human sexuality is affixed for all times in the Bible see the postmodern abyss growing deeper and wider as gays, lesbians, bisexuals and transvestites fight for an extension of our sexual normatives. And if the social parameters of human sexuality are extended to accommodate the sexually marginalized who are finding voices in our culture, where will a limit be marked? Where will the new boundary line be established? Will sadomasochists, pedophiles, fetishists, necrophiliacs, voyeurs, coprophiliacs, scotophiliacs

and a whole host of others now classified as sexual deviants add
their voices to our cultural havoc and seek admittance into the
social order? Will incest, satyriasis, nymphomania and sadomasochism become just alternative forms of expressing human
sexuality? Will "snuff" films become part of "popular culture"?

In a postmodern world deprived of a universal rule of judgment, how do we justly and legitimately choose which constructions of our human sexuality should be socially acceptable and
which should not? How do we continue to privilege heterosexuality? How do we keep our sons and daughters from growing up
in an atmosphere in which any expression of sexuality is equally
permissible, equally true to their human nature? How do we do
any of this short of an exercise of power, short of an imposition
of a sexual order of things that best maintains a desired social
order of things? How do we do any of this short of imposing a universal moral order upon all, a tarring of certain sexual energies
as evil and a concomitant commendation for sexual restraint?
Here a moral order of things supports that stable infrastructure
which a society that seeks profits rather than an expansion of,
say, human sexuality, needs. It makes no difference what the
moral hierarchy is; what counts is that definite lines be drawn
and maintained. Order is not in its substance but in its preservation, production and consumption. And yet all these possible
solutions to our problem, all these detours around the postmodern abyss, rush head on into the words of William Blake in *The
Marriage of Heaven and Hell:* "One law for the ox and the lion is
oppression."

How then do we oppress least, at least in regard to human
sexuality? This seems a reasonable question. Until we realize
that reason emerges from reality frames: Catherine MacKinnon
and Andrea Dworkin argue that it is entirely reasonable to connect pornography with rape; the Antioch administration finds it
reasonable to believe that their rules will eliminate the ambiguity of "Did she acquiesce or didn't she?" Is it reasonable or not
reasonable to privilege heterosexuality above other forms of sexual relationship? Is it reasonable to see human sexuality as not
solely directed to procreation? Or is this a blindness to a "law of
nature," a law of species preservation? Are Freud's Oedipal the-
ories reasonable? Or, are Deleuze and Guattari's more reasonable? Or, is the Christian Coalition most reasonable?

I believe what is reasonable is a statement such as this: regardless of the many different ways human sexuality has been

represented, its existence precedes our representations and has not yet been encompassed by our efforts. The totality of human sexuality is an unmarked domain that we mark variously. Our observations and delineations are positioned in time and space, and emerge within a certain cultural frame at a certain time. We cannot fail to heed our own sexuality, but that heeding is not equal to what it attends to. Our gaze is constrained, constrained by the culture, the culture varying its constraints to the degree that it is a heterogeneous, pluralistic culture, a culture of many dissident voices.

It is not a matter, then, of present inadequacy that prevents us from giving form to our own sexuality. We can only give form to anything, bring the reality we are in to a figural level by circumscription, by enfolding what is in itself unfolded. We distinguish this or that and in the process cast what lies beyond our distinguishing into darkness, into absence. It is this absence that not only provides the backdrop for our highlighting efforts but also haunts our predilections, our fabricated hierarchies of sex gender and sexual preference.

Have I stepped out of the fog of constructiveness? Fog is a good term because it captures the feel of a buffer zone, the zone of symbolic or narrative mediation that we abide in. Between what and what? The reality of ourselves, of Nature, of society certainly. And on the other side? The reality of ourselves, of Nature, of society certainly. We do not *have* sexuality; we *are* sexual. But are the ways we are sexual limited to the ways we can enact our sexuality and our enactment capability limited to what we think about sexuality? Are we then ultimately limited by the ways we possess and have our sexuality? We try to account for the gap between what we feel on the pulse and what we say we are feeling by talking about tacit understanding, or a prereflective grasp, or a prepredicative understanding. All this serves to say that there is more here in our response than what we say, than we bring to the level of representation. Our bodies conceive both literally and figuratively. And that conceivability may or may not find representation and never does find precise corresponding representation. Women conceive a possibly existing reality and give birth to that reality. They fulfill that conceivability. No signifying system, including language, reliably conceives and fulfills reality in this way. All it gives us is narration.

We narrate more about love, desire and sexuality than about anything else, except perhaps death and taxes, which more than fills the postmodern abyss in these years. And this narrative zone does not have word and wordless polarities, or real and simulated ones, or discovered and constructed ones. In this zone that we humans inhabit, the unsaid vibes commingle with the explicit actions and public declarations, what we mark as simulations cohabit with real things, what we mark as what we *say* we discover interpenetrates what we *say* we construct.

Of course this all goes on within a paradigm of self and worldly attendance that projects dualities everywhere. Academic feminists want to construct a more sex-equitable human sexuality. Camille Paglia, to stay with her, wants to face the intransigency of biological determinism. Neither desire here, however, can avoid being crisscrossed by other desires in the narrative flux. Every assumed discrete position is already interlaced with other struggles to discover/construct a reality that supports present intentions. Since our narrating about human sexuality already goes on within cultural narratives which discover/shape this topic within their own agenda, all we have to do is step back and note the other players on the field in order to see in what guise human sexuality will present itself. Today. Now. At this very moment.

Let's trace the moment:

Tracing the Moment: Sex & Money

In *Restoring the Dream,* "the bold new play by House Republicans," *all* turmoil of the non-dollars-and-cents variety has to do with a "breakdown of values, civility, and family structure."[2] (191) And here it is the fortified family unit that is the nucleus—just like in the days of old!—of the restoration of the American dream: "We think a new approach is in order, one that centers on the concept of encouraging stable and constructive families. The family is the mechanism through which we transmit moral values, discipline, knowledge, and civility to our children." (191) There is no hint here that the guiding principle that "WEALTH AND CAPITAL KNOW NO BOUNDARIES"—to employ one of the section headings of this "bold new plan"—may have had something to do with "FAMILIES IN CRISIS." In my mind, there is a link between a society in which "egalitarianism and income redistribution" are now "unaffordable and defunct," and a large proportion of our population being in an economic crisis. (57) Our former middle income families are sliding into poverty and those families already impoverished are being set up as the perpetrators of everyone else's decline. But it is not this critique that holds sway but rather one that looks for a remedy to this "breakdown of values, civility, and family structure" in the family unit itself. Families are in crisis because they have moved away from a traditional mother/father/kids structure. Social decay doesn't have roots in the "WEALTH AND CAPITAL KNOW NO BOUNDARIES" mindset we have created for ourselves. Chaos in the community doesn't come from a credo of self-interest. It comes from faulty child-rearing practices, which we were alerted to thirty years ago by Sen. Daniel Patrick Moynihan: "A community that allows a large number of young men to grow up in broken families, dominated by women, never acquiring any stable relationship to male authority, never acquiring rational expectations about the future—that community asks for and gets chaos." [192, quoted in *Restoring the Dream*] The entire logic here changes by simply placing the word "wealthy" before the words "broken families." We live now in a world in which the casino logic of the market has precluded any "rational" expectations of the future. We now just have people who grow up without economic woe and therefore are privileged to *have* expectations regarding the future and people who are drowning economically and have no expectations at all. The community doesn't get chaos then when a child grows up in a *wealthy* family nor does society experience decay. They get a future "stakeholder" in that society.

Where is our human sexuality in all this? It has, as you can see, a very minor part, although the sexual correctness debate seems to be raging at center stage. That debate, in fact, is trying to culturally center itself, heedless of the crosswinds it is being moved by. This effort parallels the effort made in *Restoring the Dream* as it attempts to center the family itself, heedless of the economic flux it is caught within. The sexuality debate and the family intersect, but not as discrete academic issues. Instead they are each already hotwired to a vast circuitry of narrative emplotments.

The Republicans are now piloting the American Dream, not simply because they have won a major victory in the 1994 Congressional elections but because the culture had already adopted a mindset that led to that victory. The connections made here to the sexuality debate will either impose the meaning and value of that debate or at very least constrain it. First of all, if "FAMILIES IN CRISIS" are in anyway connected to the philosophy of "WEALTH AND CAPITAL KNOW NO BOUNDARIES," then boundaries on wealth and capital are sure to follow. And that's a liberal path, not a conservative one. The conservative path is to disconnect crisis from economics and plug crisis into the Dream socket. When the Dream is rewired, crisis is resolved. Since, however, crisis remains economic—but not for all—those who are blessed and feel no crisis, can overlook it. There's no need to restore *their* dream.

Examine the two paths here: either not identify a crisis as a crisis (which George Bush did to his peril regarding the economic recession of his last two years in office) or adopt a solution to the crisis which is not only compatible with the philosophy of WEALTH AND CAPITAL . . . but secures it, holds off possible threats. By offering a return to the dream of a traditional nuclear family as an answer to the present "FAMILIES IN CRISIS," the Republicans lowball a lot of the sexual debate. Gay and lesbian marriages and child-rearing? Hardly. Non-sexist and sexually correct language codes? Only if all sexual relationships are equal to "a father in the home" sexual relationship. And they're not. The patriarchy/power/sex indictment? A lunatic fringe indictment when part of the restoration of the dream is to restore "stable relationships to male authority." (192)

Most of the sexual debate gets thrown on the irrelevant and "not costed in" trash pile. The Antioch College Sexual Offense Policy? George Will mocks the absurdity of reducing Eros to due process: "Imagine," he writes in *Newsweek,* "being charged with making a 'gesture' that was 'irrelevant' or 'perceived' as denigrating."[3] Gays in the military? Neither the military nor the family is about establishing sexual relationships *between* males but rather "stable relationships *to* male authority." Pornography and rape? Pornography in the "WEALTH AND CAPITAL . . . "dream is more guided by a phobia to regulation than by a prevalent feminist logic of pornography nurtures rape. And rape itself simply does not reach the crisis stage in a society out to preserve "stable relationships to male authority."

Those caught in other sexual dreams understandably find most of these connections hard to swallow. Nevertheless, they will shape, detour and block off such contesting sexual dreams. Human sexuality is first and foremost something to be capital-

ized on in a "WEALTH AND CAPITAL . . . "society. If the growth
and expansion of human potential were the guiding principle of
a restored American Dream, then every aspect of the contemporary sexual debate would become significant. Such is not the
case. The family, also, is not in itself significant in the restoration scenario. It serves, as I have said, as an alibi discourse—one
that conceals the ways in which wealth and capital are undermining a previously more egalitarian and socially just society.

It also serves as a means by which to fend off a proliferation
of modes of order at the pre-corporate organizational level. I
mean that a lesbian family is set up to transmit other than male
rational expectations of the future, to transmit other than "stable relationships to male authority." As is a gay or bi-sexual family. Or a family in which Dad is a transvestite, a situation brought
to our attention in *Priscilla Queen of the Desert* and *La Cage aux
Folles*. Or, a family in which a son is a transvestite, as in
Torchsong Trilogy. The heterosexual union and traditional nuclear family is not, therefore, valued in itself, but only for what it
preempts. Its order is the surveillancing, hegemonic order.

If all manner of dissenting relationships multiply in our culture and bear with them different ways of bringing the world to
order, grounded perhaps in alternative expressions of human
sexuality, then we become "a nation of dysfunctional families"
(192) in the eyes of our restoration Republicans only because
such micro-"disordering" threatens our macro-ordering, our
"WEALTH AND CAPITAL KNOWS NO BOUNDARIES" ordering. If
you follow the money here earnestly enough you reach a point
where the procreation of human sexuality in a vast array of different forms is not a moral threat to society but an economic one.

Thus, the most pressing concern revealed in the section entitled "FAMILIES IN CRISIS" has nothing to do with the moral
threat to a certain family structure that we have culturally privileged. Rather, it has all to do with a possible collapse of civility
shown toward an increasingly elite order of things. I refer to the
first paragraph of this section where the House Republicans
speak for the American people and in the last two sentences
move from smokescreen to haunting fear: "They [the American
people] see that teenage out-of-wedlock pregnancies have
reached an all-time high. In addition, they see a general lack of
civility and respect in the way we treat each other." (191). Now
we're at the heart of the matter and it's all fear. Civility to whom?
To those who are willing to let a civil order shape itself as best it

can within the order of unfettered market play. Respect for whom? For those who have profited and will therefore continue to profit within a "WEALTH AND CAPITAL . . . ",world which respects little else but a bottom line of net profit.

What indeed will keep the cast offs in this vicious game of some win and most lose from extending their incivility to revolt? One South Central LA riot can go down as a riot; two, three, four and more may earn the title of revolt. There is no urgency in restoring a dream; there is great urgency in restoring an order of things. And that urgency is not felt by "The American People," but by a small percentage of the population who are civil to each other because they share the bonds of wealth and power. Under various guises, however, that urgency has been instilled in the hearts of a great number of people whose own urgency may in time call them elsewhere.

Our sexual debate has been so sidetracked, running down a track detached from the engine that has this country in tow in the present. Even Bill Clinton in the first days of his administration found himself focussing on gays in the military as if it were an academic debate topic, pulled out of a hat, disconnected from the power lines. What do I think about gays in the military? Or about a woman's right to choose? Or about condoms distributed in schools? Same sex partners being entitled to family medical coverage? The Antioch rules? Ordinances against pornography? Political and sexual correctness? You name it. Here's my answer, in brief: I'm not sure what human sexuality is. I am sure, however, that our interest in it, our discourse about it, and our practice of it are the only handles we have on it and they are all caught in the web of the cultural moment. Even our so-called speculative theorizing does not go on in a vacuum. Nor is any of it merely silly or inconsequential and irrelevant to most, even, for instance the Antioch rules. Rather, they enter the fray full of resolution and find their end in line with means already in sway. Gays in the military was re-routed from a sexual debate forum to questions of national security, presidential decisiveness, liberal naivete, democratic priorities, and, of course, moral decay.

Pursuing human sexuality in a de-politicized way, mindful only of the expectations of changing the social order, of raising a dissenting cultural voice, will wind up, in the end, serving other agendas. On my campus, women are periodically engaged in "taking back the night." Others are still fervent about "saying no to drugs." Here, "No means No" and the hope is "To end rape in

our day." Others are "proud to be gay" or urging others "To Join
the Fight Against AIDS." I often think that these are addressed to
invisible counter-contingencies; namely those who don't want
you to take back the night, who don't want to end rape in our day,
who think No means Yes. And so on. Sort of cold war polarities.

As I have suggested in this piece, nothing about human sexuality can be polarized, neither sexuality itself nor our discourse
about it nor those who engage in it and discourse about it. The
interpenetrations change, although the continuum of thrusts,
from forceful to tepid, may persevere. Indeed, human sexuality
at this moment is moving beyond the boundaries of our traditional demarcations *and also* being strenuously drawn back into
those boundaries. Whether the American dream is of new sexual
dimensions ahead or of restoring a pre-1960s sexual order, a
movement into a postmodern abyss, or a return to a Golden Age
of '50s family sitcoms, is the struggle human sexuality is in at
this cultural moment.

Notes

1. Camille Paglia, "Rape and the Modern Sex War," in *Debating
Sexual Correctness* New York: Delta, 1995, pp. 21–25.

2. Republican National Committee, *Restoring the Dream*, New York:
Times Books, 1995, pp. 201, 191.

3. George Will, "Sex Amidst Semicolons," *Newsweek* October 4,
1993.

Is a Foot Massage Sexual—on the Internet?

> "I'm not sayin' he was right, but you're saying a foot massage don't mean nothin', and I'm saying it does. I've given a million ladies a million foot massages and they all meant somethin'. We act like they don't, but they do. That's what's so fuckin cool about 'em. This sensual thing's goin' on that nobody's talkin about . . . "
>
> Vincent Vega in *Pulp Fiction*

> "DigitaLiberty is not hopeful that widespread freedom will come to the physical world, at least not in our lifetime. Too many constituencies depend upon the largess and redistributive power of national governments and therefore oppose freedom and the individual responsibility it entails. But we do believe that liberty can and will prevail in the virtual domains we are building on the net and that national governments will be powerless to stop us. We believe that cyberspace will transcend national borders, national cultures and national economies. We believe that no one will hold sovereignty over this new realm because coercive force is impotent in cyberspace."
>
> DigitaLiberty, "a 'group' that exists only in cyberspace, quoted in *The New Republic*, July 31, 1995, p. 12

> "Cyberspace is a safe space in which to explore the forbidden and the taboo. It offers the possibility for genuine, unembarrassed conversations about *accurate* as well as fantasy images of sex."
>
> Carlin Myer, quoted in *Time* July 3, 1995

Hugh Grant and Divine Brown

Let's start with the "sex thing," and then in true cyberspace fashion "jack into" the "unassailable liberty of cyberspace."

Maybe we're a few years away from virtual reality access on the Internet where we can get a foot massage in cyberspace. Would it be a "sensual thing"?

Let's switch from virtual reality to old-fashioned movie reality. In the film *Sirens*, Hugh Grant who plays the part of Tony
Campion, a minister in the Church of England is asked by his
wife, Stella, whether he thinks it's wrong for the public to see the
erotic (for Tony, profane) paintings of Norman Lindsay. "I think
it's not very good in the long run to get a lot of negative images
like that in one's head," Grant replies. Later on, he accidentally
happens upon a scene in which his wife and two of the painter's
models are carressing the body of another model. The image
stays in his head. When his wife, who has gone through a sort of
sexual awakening during their stay at the painter's villa, wants
to speak of these changes that she has experienced, Grant
doesn't want to hear. Some things are best left unsaid, he tells
her. To which she responds: "That means we'll always be
strangers." They'll be some mystery in our relationship twenty
years hence he quips. So he wants to keep this disturbing image
of his wife among the sirens on an unspeakable level. It's a scene
not to be directly and openly engaged. The image of his wife with
the sirens doesn't do *him* any good. His desire here to keeps such
things "unsaid" is like his desire to keep Norman Lindsay's paintings "unseen." The problem is, as Tony has already indicated, the
damage is already done once the paintings are seen. The damage
to Tony is already done once he has seen his wife and the sirens.

From virtual to reel to real: on his visit to Los Angeles to promote his new film *Nine Months*, Grant was caught by the police
while getting a blow job from a prostitute named Divine Brown
off Sunset Boulevard. The scene entered, if you will, the public
mentality and became the sensational topic of the moment.
Grant then hit the late night talk show circuit—the tele reality—
to tout *Nine Months* (a movie that *New Yorker* critic Anthony Lake
says "the Right has been longing for: 'The Contractions with
America'"). If you saw him with Jay Leno or Larry King, what you
saw was a man negotiating several realities. I suppose the only
one he wasn't in was cyberspace. But in a way—his way of responding to the incommensurabilities of his life as a movie heart
throb, his longtime relationship with "supermodel" Liz Hurley,
his transmitted image then on American TV, his momentary adventure with Divine Brown off Sunset Boulevard and his own life-
long connection with "Hugh Grant"—he clearly showed us that
he wouldn't delve into the dark mysteries of his own sexual behavior. He stayed on a "virtual plane"—a cup of tea and some
good books sort things out. The way out lies not in a turn toward

moral or philosophical hermeneutics nor in "depth" psychiatry. Indeed, his responses show that he didn't fall into a black hole of human paradox and mystery but remained on the surface, rebooting and changing a cup of tea and a good book program for a Sunset Boulevard program. And he did it on a TV program.

So back to reel reality: we had all seen how Richard Gere in the film *Pretty Woman* had fallen for Julia Roberts. Who could blame Gere? Who could blame Grant? Divine Brown wound up appearing in the London *News of the World* dressed as *Pretty Woman* Julia Roberts. But there's another turn of the plot, another flipflop from reel to real: Hugh Grant was at that moment riding a crest of popularity following the phenomenal success of *Four Weddings and A Funeral.* He was as much a romantic film idol, a sex god, as Julia Roberts had been a goddess following *Pretty Woman.* The Hugh Grant on the screen who was setting hearts aflutter had been the Hugh Grant in his car paying for sex from a stranger.

Both the fans *and* the idol seem to be having sex in their heads. But actually the way in which they desire is shaped by the story of love, sex, and desire that they are already in. Is that story pure simulacra, as Baudrillard suggests? Only if we are prepared to believe that our stories don't come out of an already existing interpenetration between ourselves and the world. Can we so totally leave the world behind and dwell in the hyperreal, in cyberspace? Is a sexual urge virtual? Was Hugh Grant having sex off Sunset Boulevard or in the film *Pretty Woman?* If we are all videotaping lives being lived on a videotape, is there, then, no politics in the world, no economies, no sexuality? Is a cup of tea and a good book response signage to life signage?

We are already in a film, not one that is running before or independent of the world, but one that takes its cues from worldly interaction. And, in turn, that interaction is brought to focus by our mental screenplay, our continuously spinning sequence of signification. What will be our desire runs true to what we have already realized as desire. We can produce no other desire than what we at any moment realize as desire. But, of course, desire can be produced for us by others in differing ways. That production comes out of a variety of realities, the variety waxing and waning, from carnivalesque riot to fascist restraint. And yet this colossal human, cultural production never departs, transcends or replaces the resident urges of human sexuality itself. The total unmarked space of the world may not be sexual but *we* are and therefore we sexualize those parts of this space that we distinguish, and distinguish variously over time.

Hugh Grant's desire may have been following a *Pretty Woman* script but that script is only trying to signify the sort of startling urges that would, for instance, pose Grant and Divine Brown off Sunset Boulevard at that moment in time. If, in other words, there was no desire except on film, in hyperreality, in cyberspace, then there would not only be no Grant and Divine off Sunset Boulevard but there would be no viewers of the film, no sojourners in the hyperreal, and no travellers in cyberspace. We cannot see and cannot identify in a worldless way; nor can we have a world in a story-less way, dwelling in the "world-in-itself." We are true to our imbrication—for us the reel and the real interpenetrate. Dwelling in the simulacra of the hyperreal is our way of being-in-the-world. Reel desire is our way of reaching real desire. But both real world and real desire engender our never-ending, always contentious storymaking.

Is this story of desire I am telling the sort of story of desire that can shape our technological future? And what is so different about this story of desire that it becomes culturally significant in a different way than other stories of desire?

Let's take the story of desire that Rev. Hugh Grant tells in *Sirens* and that lies behind, or foundationally supports, the Communications Decency Act. It goes like this: Love is ineffable, at its best going beyond Rod Stewart's admission in *"You're in My Heart"*, ("the attraction was merely physical"), to some higher plane. Sexuality, unless detoured from its natural path, is a purely biologic, procreative force working through the human species. It is the instilled precipitator of species preservation. And it is sweetly pleasurable either because it's one of God's gifts to us, or because if it were painful, none of us would be here right now. In other words, the sexual urge has to work for a strictly preservation of the species reason. Such a biologic determinism almost guarantees the uniformity of sexuality working through the species, except for mutations, hormonal imbalances, brain dysfunctions and other accidents which engender anomalies. Cultural censorship and prohibitions do not alter that sexual sameness but rather change the ways in which it can be expressed. Without the overlay of such taboos, decency codes and commandments, human sexuality would purr along at a steady biologic rate. Which means that just as human sexuality can be uniformly constrained it can also be uniformly stimulated. We are all therefore, so this story goes, wrapped within the same story of sex and desire.

The story of sex and desire I am telling includes video taping. Sex and desire slowly come into focus in an act of videotaping— an act by which what sex and desire signify to us individually happens as we daily hook up with the world. The procreative urge can be strengthened or diminished by the videotape/narrative we are in. What is enveloped in desire and appears sensual follows no universal script. When it comes to human sexuality, morality has not supposed such a mutually adaptive, self/world scripting but rather an instinctual abyss circumscribed by moral imperatives. Morality's scripting holds that we are all one in the body's desires. And because we are unified and uniform in our desires, the counter of morality can and must be unified and uniform. There can be negative images that stir up the sexual instincts that morality hopes to constrain. In my videotape story of desire there is no way of predicting or judging how an image will come to focus within an individual mind, how a sound will resonate, a touch will feel, a smell will provoke. If morality were innate and if the world could be marked without, in the process, leaving something unmarked then we surely would have a way to know what sex and desire are for each of us. Such is not the case.

Vincent and Jules

We have to go back to the dialogue between Vincent and Jules at the very beginning of *Pulp Fiction* to see this deconstruction of a determinate human sexuality.

On their way to "strike down with great vengeance" some punks who have cheated their boss, Marsellus Wallace, Jules asks Vincent if he remembers Tony Rocky Horror. Vincent refers to him as a fat guy but Jules corrects him and says Tony has a weight problem. "What's the nigger gonna do, he's Samoan," Jules tells Vincent. Does Jules mean that obesity is in Samoan genes, or is he saying that Samoan culture just leads to obesity? Either way, in Jules's view, obesity responds to difference and difference shapes obesity. What Jules is hinting at is indeed the way in which obesity has a positive rather than negative connotation in Samoan culture. Tony Rocky Horror doesn't see his fatness in the way Vincent does; it means something different to him and he values it differently.

Jules goes on to tell Vincent that Tony was thrown out of a window by Marsellus for giving Mia, Marsellus' wife, a foot massage. While Vincent thinks that Tony should have anticipated some angry response from Marsellus because a foot massage is a sensual thing, Jules insists that a foot massage "is nothing." Instead of obesity we are now considering the sexual connotations of a foot massage. However, unlike the obesity exchange where Vincent's reply to whether he recalls Tony ("Yeah maybe, fat right?"), which we accept as a description not needing interpretation, the foot massage exchange has us considering rival views. We have advanced from simple description ("fat right?") to an arguable issue, an issue which produces differing interpretations ("Is a foot massage sexual?") What really happened, however, was that even the question of Tony's fatness was not simple; it, too, was up for interpretation. Tony was fat in whose eyes? What did they interpret that fatness to mean? What value was placed on it? The foot massage issue is much more complicated. Not only must we connect with the act of giving a foot massage in terms of what we may or may not find sexual, but we must also consider, as do Jules and Vincent, what that foot massage meant to Marsellus. Jules thinks Marsellus overreacted but Vincent thinks Tony should have expected a reaction from Marsellus because Marsellus "ain't gonna have a sense of humor about that shit."

Now I know the backcover blurp on the published screenplay of *Pulp Fiction* refers to Vincent and Jules as "thick-witted hit men" but I suggest that not only do they debate the subject pointedly but we are left no space to configure ourselves in that debate as "sharp-witted" arbiters. We are afloat amid our own connections to the sensuality of a foot massage, siding with one or the other to the degree that what each says connects to our own sexuality reality. Now that indeterminacy is replaced with determinacy later on in the film when Vincent and Mia are at *Jack Rabbit Slim's*, the retrofitted '50s roadhouse. Vincent brings up the subject of foot massage, wanting to hear Mia's side of things. She takes the part we should have easily taken in the earlier discussion, especially since it was a discussion among the "thick-witted." She applies critical reason: "Marsellus throwing Tony out of a four-story window for giving me a foot massage seemed reasonable?" The very mention of reason puts Vincent on the run: "No, it seemed excessive. But that doesn't mean it didn't happen. I heard Marsellus is very protective of you." Here, Vincent doesn't play the same cards he played with Jules. He doesn't tell Mia his story about the undeniable sensuality of a foot massage and the sheer impossibility of Marsellus seeing that act as anything but a sexually aggressive one. All of a sudden, in a different setting, with a different interlocutor, the foot massage seems less sensual and less reasonable as a motivation for Marsellus throwing Tony out of the window. Mia is unhesitating in her grasp of the matter: "A husband being protective of his wife is one thing. A husband almost killing another man for touching his wife's feet is something else." (49)

What makes one voice resonate with reasonableness? How, where and when we are positioned. In the conversation between Jules and Vincent, a foot massage is discussed as whether or not it can be interpreted as sexual in the views of two men. A foot massage is a sexual or not a sexual thing to do to a woman: "It's laying hands on Marsellus's new wife in a familiar way. Is it as bad as eatin' her out—no, but you're in the same fuckin' ball-park." (13) And here Jules disagrees: the two acts are not even in the same ballpark. But Jules and Vincent are in the same reasoning ballpark, you might say. Such is not the case when Vincent is with Mia. He cannot present to her the comparisons he made with Jules because he realizes in this context, those are other or male contextual connections. The male reasoning doesn't travel. In fact, what a foot massage is to a woman, in this case, Mia, is unknown to Vincent—a possible reason why he has brought the subject up. He is curious and she thanks him for asking her side of things. Sexuality has a "side to it," as does reasoning. Not only can't Vincent summon the reasons of another context, but he is clearly sensitive to the rules of this new ball-park. This has been revealed in a previous scene when Marsellus's bartender has slyly hinted at the danger in Vincent taking Marsellus's wife out on a date. To which Vincent replies: "Look, I'm not an idiot. She's the big man's fuckin' wife. I'm gonna sit across the table, chew my food with my mouth closed, laugh at her jokes and that's all I'm gonna do." (29) So when we actually do have the scene with Vincent sitting across the table from Mia at *Jack Rabbit Slim's* we know that he is nervous about enkindling Marsellus's jealousy and possibly also getting thrown out of a window.

Mia's words, then, resonate with reasonableness because it is possibly what she will say to Marsellus that will count. And within this context, Vincent is entirely more willing to hear and accept Jule's view: that a foot massage could not possibly have led to Tony Rocky Horror's being thrown out a window. Yet

another element lurking in this scene is a certain sexual mag-
netism between the heroin laced Vincent and the coke laced Mia.
Maybe Vincent is thinking of Mia sexually. After all, he's giving a
million foot massages to a million women, and they've all, in his
words, been sensual. Thus, whether a foot massage is sexual and
also whether an act is reasonable has all to do with what you
might call differing political contexts: gender, power, and desire
generating differing universes of choices.

"Child Molestors Hanging Out in Electronic Chat Rooms"

"[S]ome people and groups are in far better positions—po-
litically, economically, and psychologically—to speak than
others . . . some discursive subjects and positions are
more authoritative than others."
Steven Best and Douglas Kellner, *Postmodern Theory:*
Critical Interrogations, 1991
"Children should not be subjected to these images."
Linda Mann-Urmacher, quoted in *Time* July 3, 1995

In *Pulp Fiction* fashion, let's jump back to an earlier narrative and entwine the Rev. Tony Campion, (as played by Hugh
Grant in the film *Sirens*,) into a discussion of sex on the internet.
Negative images don't, in the long run, do anyone any good, Rev.
Campion tells his wife. Fresh from the Jules and Vincent scene,
I want to ask the good Reverend two questions: "Is a so-called
negative image called negative in the same way a foot massage is
called sexual?" And "Is a negative image as shaky an instigator
of universal harm as a foot massage is shaky as a cause for
Marsellus throwing Tony Rocky Horror out a window?"
The July 3rd, 1995 cover of *Time* magazine ran the words
"On A Screen Near You: Cyberporn." There were clear images in
the minds of Senators Exon and Coats who introduced amend-
ments to the existing Communications Decency Act in order to
censor pornography on the net. "I knew it was bad," he [Exon]
says. "But then when I got on there, it made *Playboy* and *Hustler*
look like Sunday-school stuff." (42). There was a whole world of
criminal intent lying behind the images. At least in the minds of
the anti-cyberporn bill proponents. There was a dark side to Vice
President Gore's dream of an information superhighway: "This is
the flip side of Vice President Al Gore's vision of an information

superhighway linking every school and library in the land. When the kids are plugged in, will they be exposed to the seamiest sides of human sexuality? Will they fall prey to child molesters hanging out in electronic chat rooms?" (40) Will the sexual harassers stalk the victims on the net? Will potential rapists be incited to rape by downloading the sexual images on the net? To complement the Communications Decency Act there is The Electronic Anti-Stalking Act of 1995 and The Exclusionary Reform Act of 1995 which will sanction electronic search and seizure, even if it doesn't make it easy to do.

If we adhere to Vincent and Jules's deconstruction of determinate reckonings of sexuality—in other words, answer "yes" to the above two questions—then all censoring of sexual images is an imposition. It would be like Marsellus Wallace declaring once and for all that foot massage is sexual because he is the "kingpin" with the power. In a democracy, a negative determination regarding some manifestation of our human sexuality simply means that a majority of those who vote hook up negatively here. At the same time, the voting majority is positioned in a certain way at a certain time in order to know these images as negative. Is there any part of human sexuality that is negative in itself? The question as to whether this or that aspect of human sexuality is good or bad, or even indeed true or false, is not comparable to asking the same of the "world out there." In the latter case, these judgments are clearly not in Nature but in us. But human sexuality is already ours. There is no human-less human sexuality in the way that, absent of the human species, there still would be Nature. The total unmarked space of human sexuality is always human although the way in which we conceive and represent it varies from age to age, culture to culture. Therefore, although our representations of the world cannot fully correspond with the world and therefore are always either arbitrary—without a binding logic—or imposed, our representations of human sexuality are always culturally imposed but cannot be considered arbitrary. They emerge from the logic of our cultural positioning which has no outside reference, not only in the sense that we cannot point to a discrete outside point of reference by which to assess our representations but in the clear sense that in regard to human sexuality there is no "outside."

What I am getting to is this: although we each decide whether a foot massage is sexual, or an image on the net is pornographic, within relative reality and perceptual frames—and therefore we live in different sexual worlds—and although we are culturally at any time voicing only some of our connections and societally only legislating majority hook-ups, this is the inevitable lot of a totally human contextual matter. Since there is no total unmarked space of a larger, non-human sexuality with which human sexuality is intertwined, we are never guilty, in regard to human sexuality, of misrepresentation or arbitrary hookups of a reality with which we fail to signify in itself. Put blankly, if we take up a sexual style for ourselves, culturally speaking, that later on we want to unbutton and unravel, we aren't in the same position as when we decide that time and causality abide in Nature and not in us, or that progress results from our unlocking "Nature's secrets." In the former case, we are manifesting what only comes to existence through and in that manifesting. In the latter case, we are asserting a unilateral, discrete "truth" from within an imbricated, interrelated situation. We cannot fail here to misrepresent, to leave something out, to falsify. In regard to human sexuality, we are not falsifying a prior, independent reality. The ways in which we accept or censor our own sexuality, the ways in which we decide that a foot massage is sexual or not, have only the culture from which they emerge to answer to. Gay sexuality can be validated or invalidated not by an appeal to a universal court of Reason, Nature, or Justice. Negative images lose their negativeness not by a similar appeal. Nor does pornography cease to be pornography. Nor can pedophilia, hebephilia, and paraphilia attain legitimacy and acceptance through such an appeal. The only court of representation is the culture itself, the final determination made by the legislation of the society itself. Because human sexuality can only be manifested in an interrelationship of culture and individual—unlike the injustice of slavery which denies human status to a human—and has no human-context free existence, then the culture either nurtures or does not nurture the relationship. Cavemen and cavewomen did it within the culture of the cave; I don't know what the report is on feral folks. Were they polymorphously perverse? Or, did they just note the sex habits of some fellow creatures? In the film *Nell,* we observe that Nell has already been brought up in the home of a rape victim, her mother, and thus expresses a fear of the male organ.

Societies variously impose sexual standards within a culture that cannot give determinate accounts of what sexuality is or what is sexual or what isn't or how any image, act or word will reverberate on the moving sexuality scale. The culture cannot do any of this because it is not one and, theoretically, each of its component members may be intertwining himself or herself with the culture in different sexual ways. In actuality, there are "asymmetrical power relations" in play at any moment which shapes the sexual interaction, as displayed in the Vincent/Jules/Mia exchanges.[1] Human sexuality is being enacted and realized on an ongoing basis. And while there is no way of affirming the "negativity" or "positivity" of a sexual image in the light of any universal rule of determination, these determinations nonetheless have been made and are being made within our present cultural ambiance. And, as I say, since there is no outside appeal, nor outside determinants to which we must bow, the shaping of human sexuality by humans is a natural state of affairs. Although the process may be appropriate, the results—how sexuality is shaped at any time and legislated into being—must always produce dissent because there are more individual shapings of sexuality than a society, always caught within a hierarchical ordering of things, can authorize. Our culture, however, has never been more filled with dissenting narratives of human sexuality than at the present time.

I want to finally return to *Pulp Fiction* to get a look at the sexual arena represented there. Jules and Vincent differ in regard to their view of the sexuality of foot massage, but there is an already existing ambiance of sexuality in this *Pulp Fiction* world that everyone's take on sexuality resounds within. That arena is filled not only with societal legislation and cultural transmissions but contingencies as well. And it merits a close look.

The Sexual Arena

Asymmetrical power relationships within a culture skewer the debate regarding whether or not foot massage is sexual either one way or the other. Or, they disempower the debate. In other words, we already exist within a culture of previously sorted or suppressed images. What you get in the film *Sirens* is a clash between a Christian moral frame and an aesthetic hedonist one, so that what human sexuality is and how it is to be expressed is caught in struggle for mastery. What sexuality is to mean and what sexuality is to be valued and not valued are being contested. In *"Asking for and Getting Chaos"* I have already suggested that our present market ordering of reality has only a market interest in human sexuality and the struggle to identify it. What it comes down to is that a human sexuality bound by a

culturally pervasive Judeo-Christian code is more liable to produce and perpetuate an underlying cultural stability than would
a "shape your own" sexuality "disorder." Stability is produced by
manufacturing uniform connections in regard to, for example,
human sexuality. Those same connections, however, serve a
market reality in other, more potentially volatile ways. Consider
that our market reality has inevitably resulted in inequities and
injustices to which a culture not already bound by a "stabilizing
moral order" might lash out against. Our postmodern attitude
has already unsettled that moral order in a way that modernity
by a faith in reason was preempted from doing. And we obviously
live at a time when many are lashing out in many ways against
the mindless allocations of a casino market logic.

Therefore, constraints designed to maintain the stable order
of society, a society now almost totally shaped to fulfill a market
agenda, do not have human sexuality as a specific target. You
might say that human sexuality feels the after-shock. There is no
way to loosen the hold on the cultural mindset of human sexuality without loosening the whole frame of market reality and its
notions of "life, liberty and the pursuit of happiness;" its notions
of individual freedom, choice, self-interest, social justice, community, the environment, government, progress, reality and rationality. Human sexuality, however, provides daily front page
illustrations of what happens when moral constraints are either
loosened or absent. In turn, the more the society opts for its fundamentalist moral agenda, wrapped in family values, the more
we will find dissenting voices in the culture. Individuals and
groups are not only incited into the arena of identity politics but
the whole culture is keyed to represent that dissent, both as legitimate and as a further scene from the abyss.

We, as a culture, have an eye out for sexual deviation because the whole question of "deviation" has been problematized
in our postmodern climate *and* because our present market order and the culturally conservative politics it engenders has us
looking for tears in the fabric of moral and social order. And
the sexual tear cuts the deepest. The sexual outrage that is a
total disconnect with our sense of moral order may be the result
of the sort of constraint that Blake felt bred pestilence. Our sexual energies are breaking out in hostile and violent ways. Or,
it may be the result of our postmodern breakdown of all order. All this front page sexual deviance, as well as its presence
in pop culture, is pouring out of the postmodern abyss. It may

also be a display of individual sexuality that is always unrecognizable to a society, regardless of what the power schema of that society may be. In this case, societies have always been plagued by different displays of human sexuality, although our own society of the spectacle is more likely to make a spectacle of such anomalies than a society that fears spectacle itself. We are a society that now flourishes in and through spectacle; one hundred years ago we were a society that identified spectacle as the problem.

All of this makes up the present sexual arena out of which our sense of human sexuality is shaped. But the arena is not hereby conceptualized, systematized, comprehended nor anticipated. Not only does a pluralistic, heterogeneous culture raise more voices than we can conceptualize and so on, but there are more individual expressions of sexuality than a culture at any time gives voice to. In regard to sexuality, then, we may stay on the superhighway of societal legislation, but there is nothing to stop us from running into a cultural detour or intersection. And if we intend to travel down as many cultural paths as possible, we yet may run into an individual crossing that's not on our cultural map. In short, contingencies fill the sexuality terrain. Are we more likely to experience the accidental here than elsewhere? And if so, why? Perhaps it's because sexuality inhabits an unconscious terrain as well as a conscious one and therefore the fortuitous can pop up not only out of the culture around us but out of our own unconscious minds. When it comes to human sexuality, a lurking dark side can interrupt our sexual debates. Human sexuality is interwoven with desire which has so many faces and has been so long legislated against that it is itself a reservoir of contingencies, the site of what we can never allow ourselves to anticipate.

Thus, it is not only societal legislation that is shaping human sexuality, but the whole cultural debate. And it's not just both of these that are shaping human sexuality, but contingencies that perforate the societal and cultural landscape and veer us down unexpected paths. In our own time, AIDS has been the most consequential of such contingencies. Contingencies have always indicated the presence of an abyss that we prefer to leave alone. Regardless of the postmodern theoretical attentiveness to contingencies, we are, in our market reality, more fearful and more armoured against contingenies than at any previous time. We can neither cost them in nor cost them out.

Hillbilly Psychopaths

Butch, the fighter who has double-crossed Marsellus Wallace, has returned to his apartment to retrieve his father's watch. He has slipped in, gotten the watch and killed Vincent with Vincent's own weapon. Now on the way back to the motel where his girlfriend, Fabian, awaits him he revels in his good fortune. He has outwitted his enemies: "That's how you're gonna beat'em, Butch," he tells himself. "They keep underestimatin' ya." (98) At the peak of his self-confidence, he stops for a red light at the very moment Marsellus is crossing the street. Neither man believes what he is seeing—Marsellus has just bought some donuts and Butch has just made his escape. But now pure chance brings them into a collision. Butch runs Marsellus down and is sideswiped by another car. Both men are injured, but Marsellus stumbles after Butch, gun drawn. Butch finally dashes into the Mason-Dixon Pawnshop where he clashes with Marsellus when Marsellus comes running in. Butch is just about to shoot Marsellus when the proprietor, Maynard, aims a shotgun at both men and forces Butch to give up his gun. "Look mister," Butch says, "this ain't any of your business . . . " But Maynard makes it his business, knocks Butch out and then makes a phone call: "Zed? It's Maynard. The spider just caught a coupl'a flies." On the floor, Marsellus overhears this and then passes out.

When Butch and Marsellus are revived they are tied and gagged and in a basement remodeled as a dungeon. They look at each other communicating bewilderment, terror and a sudden helplessness. That exchange and all it implies regarding the unexpected turn of events—the total replacement of a reality we have been in and following to another reality that mystifies us—arouses a deep dread in us. We now have to switch mental tracks at a furious rate to keep up with a track switch that has come out of the blue. What is offended here? Perhaps it's first a break in the aesthetic order of things that we bear within us as if it somehow reflected a supernal order of Truth and Beauty. Popular film, like pulp fiction, is sensationalistic, superficial and full of disconnected plot turns. But then this film calls itself *Pulp Fiction;* it is deliberately taking on the qualities of pulp fiction and yet successfully reorienting notions of rationality and realism. I mean accidents are not aesthetic flaws here—they work, they seem to produce the postmodern reality we are in.

Before we know what Zed and Maynard are up to behind that closed door, we surmise that it is sexual. Perhaps it is the presence of Gimp—who is kept in box and on a chain and whose head is covered in leather bondage gear with only a zipper where his mouth should be—who alerts us to sadomasochism in the works. When Butch hears Zed and Maynard beating up on Marsellus, he panics and tries desperately to free himself. We are realizing what's what at the same speed Butch is and as he struggles to break free, we grow anxious—his fear is our fear. There is something perverted and sexual going on behind that closed door. Are we going to see it happen to Butch? This film has proceeded in such a way that we do not know what to expect, but we know that we should expect anything. When it comes to sexuality, what are our most dreaded, most frightening expectations? The scene plays on this. Out of the blue, we are snatched from one quantum universe and thrust into another. Zed, Maynard, and Gimp are our worst nightmares. In point of fact, they are our cultural nightmares, whether they are stalking you in real life or on the net, their sexuality is wrapped in incomprehensible, alien, distorted desires.

When Butch opens the door, samurai sword in hand, we see what we feared: Marsellus is being raped by Zed who is bent over him. Anal intercourse. Some more flies in the spider's web. How many have they caught? And what may have been now transmitted to Marsellus? It's an accident that Marsellus is snared by the spider, and if he does contract AIDS it will also be by accident. He had not planned on being raped by two hillbilly psychopaths. Contingency lies now at the heart of sexuality, and it is a fearsome thing. That fear fills this scene; we see it in Marsellus's eyes as he tells Zed: "I'm gonna git Medieval on your ass." (108) He wants revenge, not only for the rape but for the abduction. He was taken from a life he was in control of and plunged into a reality over which he had no control. In that reality, he became the sexual toy of other men, his own sexuality corrupted, obliterated, shamed.

We live, therefore, in a culture in which the sexual nature of, say, foot massage can be debated, and also one in which all our debates can be interrupted and replaced by a violent sexuality. Generally speaking, contingencies have a great deal to do with the way we wind up shaping our sexuality. Specifically, our culture is more than aware of the Zeds and Maynards out there who can at any moment break into our realities and corrupt them. The vengeance that Marsellus seeks, the anger that both he and Butch feel against Zed and Maynard as sexual violators, crosses into the audience, into the culture. But the film has only accepted what is already in the culture. The fear, the hate and desire for revenge, the sense of violation of our intimate, sexual selves in a totally fortuitous fashion, are all present in our sexual arena.

The audience is as anxious to escape this nightmare as is Butch, but when he stops and listens to Marsellus' cries, when he turns from one who is happy to get out of there, to one who decides to return and seek revenge, then I believe the audience shifts with him. It is not just the totally unforseen visitation of AIDS upon our sexual lives, but the spectacle that we have made of our own sexuality—in stories from Jeffrey Dahmer to the murder of Polly Klass and the incessant sexual imbroglios recounted each day on the talk shows—that feeds our own cultural desire to raise a samurai sword and strike down what offends us.

That attitude extends now to our pornography on the Internet debate. Cybersexuality is playing out the individual versus society thing. Here in cyberspace, there are no societal restraints on individual expression of anything, including sexuality. This virtual domain fits, in the view of its devotees, a pluralistic culture the best. But for those neither enamoured of sexuality plurality nor any other sort of pluralism, cyberspace becomes an extension of the postmodern abyss, an anarchy of representation that the market cannot commodify.

So, is a foot massage sexual on the internet? It depends on who is hooking up with it. Does the whole societal/cultural response to sexuality shape that sexuality. Yes. Are both power, desire and contingency wild cards in such a shaping; leaving human sexuality overdetermined, not subject to total demystification or conceptualization? Yes. Will human sexuality play out differently on the net than in real life? The response to that lies in the next meditation.

Notes

1. Steven Best and Douglas Kellner, *Postmodern Theory: Critical Interrogations* New York: Guilford Press, 1995, p. 288.

Retreating to Xanadu:
Technophobia.Technophilia@USA.1995

> "If you'd had any brains, you would have realized that there are a lot of people out there who resent bitterly the way techno-nerds like you are changing the world."
>
> Unabomber to the Yale University professor of computer science he had savagely disfigured.

> "We might yet find a promised land for the imagination inside our Pentiums, an Oz where body and soul can morph at will in an eternally marvelous journey down the yellow-brick road, destination home."
>
> Kathleen Murphy, "Rebooting the Bard," *Film Comment* July 1995

> "[A]t bottom, that cyberkiss is not the same thing as a real kiss. At bottom, that cyberhug is not going to do the same thing. There's a big difference."
>
> Mark Slouka, in the *Harper's* forum, *"What Are We Doing On-Line?"* August 1995

> "Growing up in the Fifties, I felt I was living in a very real place."
>
> Sven Birkerts, *"What Are We Doing On-Line?"*

"Dream-Time"

There is a dilemma lying at the heart of the cyberspace debate and the last quotation addresses it: if we are now aware that "growing up in the '50s" was "growing up in the hyperspace of the '50s"—from Cold War mythos to *Father Knows Best*—how can we seriously challenge cyberspace with the "face-to-face reality" of the '90s? We probably can because the '90s hyperspace is a *fin de millennia* hyperspace and *its* drama overwrites all others. Hillel Schwartz describes in *Century's End* how a *fin de siecle* spirit concocts pervading nightmares of damnation and

269

salvation, natural disaster, chaos, barbarism, and all manner of dystopic configurations.[1] In this mood, it is not hard to imagine that cyberspace is nothing more than a window to the abyss. With the advent of the modem we can now accelerate our inevitable journey to that abyss at warp speed.

Still, there are the technophiles who can't wait to be "modemed into richly interactive dream-time."[2] The question is clearly whether we are interacting more in dream-time in cyberspace than in "face-to-face reality"? We are talking about layers of mediation, or what Sven Birkerts calls "layers of scrim," because reality is always coming to us through one or more filtering screens. I stand looking in a mirror in a "face-to-face" reality moment and I am positive I see myself as I truly am. Moments later, however, I sit with others and view a video in which my face suddenly appears. I see that mirrored self now differently; I look strange to myself. Is it because I am seeing amid the seeing of others? Or, because video images alter me more than does my bathroom mirror? Or are both moments mediated by some "dream-time" narrative my mind is in? I don't see all the grey in my hair or in my beard in the mirror but I do in the video. If I had an out-of-the-body experience and had a "face-to-face" encounter with myself, would each of me see and come away with a different reality?

There is more to this "face-to-face reality" then than meets the eye. Indeed, what meets the eye has taken a detour through a narrative the mind is in. If our fear of cyberspace is our fear of entering virtual reality and leaving "face-to-face" reality behind, then it is a fear involving a different kind of mediation. The difference becomes clear when we think about the "face-to-face" kiss and the cyberkiss. The kiss of long ago, filtered through a James Dean narrative of self, nonetheless involved flesh and blood—two young bodies with two pairs of lips. It's really a Platonic thing: we are all, not just the poets, twice-removed from a Platonic really real Reality; but hackers are infinitely progressively removed, as responses in cyberspace multiply in an enclosed system of reference.

We live amid images of desire and sexuality because the reality of sexuality and desire inspires, compels and propels that imaging, that mediation. We can turn Puritan; we can censor and we can rely on repression but because our sexuality is of real-time, although subject to our dream-time, we are again and again, in a variety of ways, brought back to yet another narrative of desire and sexuality. And when it comes to desire, clearly the interaction between our bodies writes our mental scripts. We can write against the body and desire, or we can write of many different ways of acknowledging and expressing both. But we cannot fail to live within some interaction between ourselves and the reality of human sexuality. Our bodies and the sexuality that is embodied there is not virtual. Our experiences, from sexual to mystical, however, are something we have in the way of both sensing and knowing. Our knowing proceeds from some narrative frame of reality which entwines itself in and around what we sense and feel. Is there a nano second when what we feel is free of such an enframing? I think if we could "experience" that disconnect we could answer the question we always direct at the "lower orders:" what are they thinking? What is going on now in my dog Jenny's mind as she looks directly into my eyes? How is time passing for her? What is she experiencing when she growls or whimpers in her sleep?

There is no disconnect in human experiences between what comes to us in the way of senses and the way in which we receive them, our narrative reception of them. This means, of course, there is no way to backtrack from our representation of what we experience to some germinal, unnarrated reality. The search for such is guided—and therefore constrained—by the reality that we already know and are producing. And we know and produce that reality in line with our experiences, whether we say they are mystical or empirically verifiable or consensually validated and so on. A version of the hermeneutic vicious circle. Vicious only, however, if we are intent on establishing a "true meaning" to things. But the situation is ontological and not hermeneutic: humans "have at" reality through their experiences but these experiences can only "have" reality within their own limited experiential compass.

Reality, then, is not virtual; it is only necessarily virtualized by us. So I do not agree with Brenda Laurel, who asserts in *Aperture* that the term "virtual reality" is a contradiction.[3] It is not a contradiction for humans. What is, however, always necessarily duplicitous is for humans to assert the "reality" of this or that. That reality surely exists, and our experiences prove that existence, but they do not give it to us in an unexperienced way. Therefore, as long as we are humans who have experiences, we cannot encompass this reality we are always appealing to as an arbiter for the variety of "virtualities" we live within. In the absence of such binding arbitration, one person's virtualizing is as legitimate and as "authorized" as the next. It is up to the "lower orders" or the "ethereal orders" or the "alien orders" to see an un-virtualized reality, a reality free of human perception. Short of that, you sit there in your virtualized reality reading a virtual account of reality.

Where are you, then, when you enter cyberspace? Well, first of all we take the virtual realities we are already in with us into cyberspace. Here we are, as I have arcanely asserted, "infinitely progressively removed" from reality, from the "whatness" that in-augurates an experiencing that can never correspond to it nor ever be ratified by it. I mean that in cyberspace we can begin with reality initiated experiences—or virtualities—intersect others within a web of networks in which we give up the concreteness of the world as our interactive medium and interact with simu-lacra. What Baudrillard has said of all reality—a hyperreality, a reality of simulacra—is reified within cyberspace. While we ad-mittedly live within virtualized/mediated/narrated realities we cannot hold our experiences *while we remain in the world* within a simulacra to simulacra interaction. No matter how far out we may get in our concocted experiential frames, the reality of the world "out there," of other people, of ourselves remain as present as our simulations.

While simulations float upward and burst at various levels—some of course longlived and far wandering—what sets them afloat, the launching site, persists. Paradoxically, this fixed site is, from the point of view of every balloon, located differently. One person's bedrock reality is another person's hot air. And, to ex-tend this imagery within the narrative I am setting afloat here, there is for any human observer and within any human experi-ence no fixed launch site and no free floating balloon. There is only life in the passageway and we are always running back and forth somewhere along the cable. Some of us I suppose are closer to the launch site than to the balloons and some of us—I can't help thinking of Jeff Dahmer—*have* to be floating totally in a bal-loon. But except for such clear cases of "virtualization without comprehensible motive" who is really to say—in a *de jure* and not a *de facto* way—whose hook-up is closer to the "nature of things" than anyone else's?

I want to end this particular meditation indecisively, in the sort of too accommodating way that Clinton's critics accuse him of. When we stay off-line and out of cyberspace we continue to make ourselves available to reality; we remain connected to a raw reality that we are never permitted to experience as raw. You might say that "raw reality" is unexperienced reality, seen but not brought into our perceptual frame. When something enters that snare and meets our protocols of significance, we begin to observe. We're set up for a real experience. Not of raw reality but already what our narrative frame adopts as a "real experience." When we are not in cyberspace we continue to interact with the total unmarked space of the world. For all its megabytes, cyberspace remains a market universe. Digital technology is an ever-expanding matrix of ones and zeros, a continuous movement of presenting and absenting, a continuous either/or marking. The total unmarked space of the world doesn't communicate; it isn't a communications system. And if it did, its technology would be an "and also" series—one which forced us to distinguish, *at the moment we are in the act*, what any act of distinguishing leaves undistinguished. The total unmarked space as it is cannot be communicated within any system of communication, no matter how complex. It also follows that no system of reality-distinguishing and information communication can correspond to the total unmarked space of reality.

Nevertheless, cyberspace is showing all the signs and promise of being that nominal reality, that shadow reality, that Plato avowed we are already living within. There is no doubt that simply reading a book puts us into dream-time, but it's scope of interaction is limited to ourselves and the page whereas cyberspace involves networks interacting with networks, innumerable representations posted by innumerable minds. Film and TV are also interactive, but in an unimpressive way compared to cyberspace. It is when we not only post our input, but enter it via a computer generated virtual reality that we begin to enter the dream-time reckonings of other minds. When we slog away at the growing amount of e-mail we receive each day, or print out reams of information gathered on computerized database retrieval services, we are augmenting the designated ways in which we are presently "getting at" things. Is more information delivered faster and faster a blessing, and for whom? Or, speaking not in market terms but in human terms, if we are always inevitably opening a row in reality by covering up two potential rows on either side, does it make a difference if we are digging faster and deeper today than yesterday? From my crazy point of view, this sort of acceleration puts some things out of sight at the same rate that it uncovers other things. And since the driving force behind all our hoeing these days is bottom line net profit and short term windfalls, I know that the speed and brilliance of cyberspace will be a blessing to a few and a curse to the many.

But what about virtual reality? Do our encounters in virtual reality provide us with the sort of experiences that can be turned to coin in the real world—not only by the market, but by mere unmarketable humans? Does virtual reality provide a synthesis of mind possibilities and worldly actualities? Reality and imagination? As it is impossible to leave our worldly experiences behind and come into virtual reality within our own experiential frames of realizing, could we not extend those frames by interacting on a virtual level with the realizations of others? In turn, could we not extend the world to the dimensions of our imagination and interact with that within virtual reality? Is that an extension or is that a substitution? And since our imaginations do not make things conceivable to us outside our frames of conceivability, does a virtual reality programmed by our imaginations free us or continue to fool us? Let me bring the point home by once again bringing up sexuality: do we expand our human sexuality by being able to interact with what we sexually imagine? It is quite clear here that the digital revolution has not resolved the question lying at the heart of our pornography debate: do we as human beings benefit more from restraining or not restraining everything we can sexually imagine? Do we find our "truest and noblest" sexuality by taking a good look at the worst? Or, do we find that the "worst" has a cultural politics to it? Do we perhaps find that we only come to cherish and experience our own sexuality when it has a dream-time existence denied to it in the real world?

Who knows what will come of virtual reality. We are not yet in a cultural frame of conceivability. Surely, it has the promise of opening up the very rate at which we are capable of conceiving. We can virtually walk in the shoes of another. Clashing societies can play out in chess fashion all their adversarial moves. Individuals can run into their repressed, shadow selves. Men meet their anima; women their animus. Jeff Dahmer might have profitably confronted his own nightmare self, been repelled and thus redeemed. There is a genuine possibility of human values exceeding corporate values here, human promise rather than market promise. At the same time, the growth and implementation of such an expensive technology is a market matter. And it is not individual self-development and growth nor cultural enfranchisement and social justice that the market seeks, but rather an "economic bonanza." At this very moment, *Forbes* reports that neither the Internet nor World Wide Webb have been yet tied to "a concrete economic mission."[4] What businesses are reporting is a firm resistance to actual purchases of anything on the electronic network. I guess real people want to see real stuff on real shelves. And if cyberspace and virtual reality don't make market hook-ups soon, vast infusions of venture capital will cease and venture elsewhere. Are we facing a technological dystopia because this might happen, or because it won't happen and cyberspace will succeed as another "really big place for people to shop?"

We are now out of dream-time and into real and reel-time, where cyberspace is pictured as more abyss-like than transcendent.

On A Screen Near You: Cyberspace Wars

Real-time is presently absorbed with cyberporn; families filled with family values are wondering if children will "fall prey to child molesters hanging out in electronic chat room."[5] Of course they might just as easily fall prey to Zed, Maynard and the Gimp hanging out in the pawn shop. The question arises: should we be attending to real-time molesters or cyberspace molesters? In our current climate of "restoring the dream" of a *Father Knows Best* America, we clearly want to do both. And probably with the same rate of success, or, lack of success. "For technical reasons, it is extremely difficult to stamp out anything on the Internet—particularly images stored on the Usenet newsgroups. As Internet pioneer John Gilmore famously put it, 'The Net interprets censorship as damage and routes around it.'"[6] It seems that wandering on The Net is like wandering around New York City—you don't know what you'll run into. When you "hang out" in real-time, you are subject to life's contingencies. You're running away from Marsellus Wallace and you run into Maynard & Co. You fall prey. It is not at all clear that you can fall prey accidentally to virtual Maynards and Zeds on the Internet. You don't accidentally turn "binary files on the Usenet into high-resolution color pictures . . . The chances of coming across them are unbelievably slim."[7] We must all, children included, first fall prey to our own desires before we become prey to the pornographers. And I suppose as long as child molesters remain in "electronic chat rooms" they will remain virtual molesters. Is, however, desire a corruptible thing"? And is a child's desire unformed, unrealized—dangerously polymorphous—until it is shaped through cultural interaction? If indeed human sexuality does not itself display the distinctions we make, rather like Nature itself, but has those distinctions inculcated, then it is easy to see why a family values culture is so upset by pornography on The Net.

If the culture surrounding The Net is also polymorphous—marked by a heterogeneity of dissensus, filled with real-time chat rooms in which attendees of different and alternative realities are hanging out—then clearly the social order has a problem with this cultural dissensus that is logging on to The Net. We thus have a real-time culture war and a dream-time culture war, and they intersect. The cyberspace wars have their own *Star Wars* cast: the Empire of Venture Capital seeking to extend the credo of "To Be Is To Consume" into cyberspace, and the Adventurous Hackers filled with the daring intrepidity and rebellion of Hans Solo.[8] What do they seek? My guess is that they seek a space for alternative constructions of reality, a realm of cyberspace dialogic and not societal monologue. A space finally to play out ways of attending to the world that do not restore THE dream but dreams. Period.

So a lot of the venture capital can't venture too far unless hackers with cyberspace dreams concoct the needed technology. And while Bill Gates, Hacker Turned Richest Entrepreneur In The World, rules a Berkeley-like Microsoft campus of millionaire entrepreneurial hackers—led to the entrepreneurial "dark side" the way Darth Vader had been enlisted by The Empire—The Net is filled with flying-by-the-seat-of-their-pants Hans Solo type hackers who have been concocting adventuresome programs and festooning The Net with their own idiosyncracies. They have also blocked off The Empire with ever-new generations of computer viruses, the weapon of choice in cyberspace wars. The virus is not only the newest emissary from the abyss, it is also, ironically, very marketable. Sheer genius lies behind the Columbus Day virus or the Michelangelo virus. The virus itself is not marketable, but the cure is. Every new virus requires new scanning and cleaning programs. Could this indeed be the second most profitable venture in cyberspace, the first being the marketing of guides to a cyberspace *untroubled by viruses?*

Installing a virus—by amazingly clever and sly means—in cyberspace is an act of terrorism because our societal order has grown to depend upon the nominal representation of that order in computers. When I say "societal order" I mean everything from DMV records to police and FBI records, IRS records and so on. At the humming center of our present social order, however, is market order: indeed the 1987 Stock Market Crash—"Black Monday"—was not virus–created, but it was the result of an unbridgeable slippage between real-time and dream-time. McKenzie Wark in *Virtual Geography* describes what occurs here:

> [A]n 'automation of capital' may be occurring, not completely unlike the automation of labor. On the day after 'Black Monday,' Wall Street banned computerized program trading, on the grounds of restoring 'some human common sense.' That sensible, i.e. human, control needed to be restored, or at least that regulators thought it needed restoring, seems to indicate a fear that the technology may become a thing apart from its agents. As the allocation of liquid capital becomes a minute-by-minute decision, or even second-by-second, computerized systems execute more and more decisions according to preprogrammed instructions.[9]

Market reality has gotten itself inextricably attached to cyber-reality, our real-time taking its cue from dream-time, our citizenry more and more marching to the sound of a virtual drum. Virus terrorism haunts the corridors of entrepreneurship. But when a popular film like *The Net* shows up filled with both technophobia and technophilia and gives itself ultimately to a dystopic vision, this vision is *not* filled with the horrors of the market's gradual distancing itself not only from "some human common sense" but from the liberty, equality and fraternity of modern democracies. Rather, it is that conservative nightmare—an unbridled, intrusive centralized government, the bane of individual freedom (read corporate entrepreneurship)—that is at the heart of this dystopia.

The Net

> "Who am I if someone's stolen my pocketbook, and the records of my social security, credit cards, and driver's license no longer exist? Such is the riddle of identity in the postmodern information age."
>
> Amy Taubin "Bad Company," *Village Voice,*
> August 1, 1995

"I've talked to a lot of people who go on to the net and take on alternate personas. I mean, why the hell would you do that?"
Mark Slouka, "What Are We Doing On-Line?" *Harper's* August 1995, 43

Sandra Bullock is Angela Bennett, a free-lance virus buster. Systems struck down by viruses are diagnosed and then cured by Bullock. As a free-lance hacker, she lives like a round the clock jacked-in hacker. She's one of Robert Reich's new breed of "symbolic analysts." But she can't survive financially unless she works—albeit at home—for the private sector. She can't go off and do her own thing in cyberspace. She has to do something that will make her a living. I emphasize this connection because on the radical cyberspace fringe—wherever that might be within a matrix of networks—there is a sense that cyberspace can totally disconnect from governmental control and lead us all into a libertarian future of total individual freedom. Unfortunately, "freedom" has come to mean "choice" and the market is busy marketing what that has come to mean. Cyberspace may indeed be generating a whole new breed of what Falstaff called "masterless men" and what feminists now hope to be "masterless women." Nevertheless, it is hard to see how we are to be "masterless" in cyberspace when we misidentify how we are being "mastered" in real time and space.

The question is: are we being led to a new identity and way of identifying in cyberspace? Could it amount to not the libertarian version of Max Stirner's "the ego and its own," but the sort of communitarian, collective ethos that Marx envisioned? I see the downside to both. In one dystopic scenario, a total loss of face-to-face contact and communication strictly via electronics leading to a decrease rather than increase in our empathy powers (slim, I admit, when we consider the West's response to Bosnia). In the other, a totalizing electronic hook-up in *Star Trek The Next Generation* Borg fashion. I can hear myself saying "We Are Borg" when asked for my personal moniker.

Identity is a problem for Bullock in *The Net*, not one of the problems I hypothesize but a simple one: her "official" identity as encoded in all computer systems is deleted and she is given a cyberspace identity. Now with this new—and false—identity she has a criminal record and soon has the police after her, as well as the terrorist hackers who set her up. They set her up because she has discovered their plan *to take over the country by invading computer systems, including the governments!* So she's on the run—like *The Fugitive*—except in this case she doesn't assume different identities in order to elude. Rather, she has to run because she's been given a false identity. The hacker who has given up face-to-face contact with anyone but the mailman finds herself struggling to assert her "real time" identity against the computer designated identity—real time versus virtual time.

Bullock's "real world" job is in cyberspace. She spends most of her time on-line and therefore when she needs her neighbors to identify her as the "real" Angela Bennett, none of her neighbors know her or are really sure what she looks like. They've only seen her at a distance going in and out of her house. Her real-world identity is already shaky so she becomes an easy victim of the terrorist hackers who have failed to take her life and now try to take her identity. That provides another tear in our cyberspace enthusiasm big enough to look through. While we are a society focused on the freedom=choice equation—the greatest opportunities for choice envisioned in cyberspace—the "we" who do the choosing have become problematized in brand new ways within cyberspace. Always subjected to another equation—we are what we can represent ourselves to be—we now face the formidable representational powers of our computer systems. Our identities are strung out on The Net, interacting with other Net identities, not sure what physical presence lies behind the on-screen signifiers. Perhaps that interaction itself will become the cultural milieu in which identities are constructed and deconstructed, territorialized, deterritorialized and reterritorialized. We are not only invited to fill in the space as we wish, within our own comfort zones, but we may already be dealing with altered identities. We may be led toward misidentifying what is or toward identifying what isn't. We are, in the end, only what we are in cyberspace. We are, in the end, only what the vast network of computer systems identifies us as. In the same fashion that market players on "Black Monday" paid more attention to computer representation than to their own real-world situation, we may soon find ourselves attending more to cyberspace than to self, Nature and society—all of which, of course, will have a surrogate cyberspace presence.

When things get tough for Bullock, she looks for some help from her friends. On The Net. She belongs to a cyberspace support group, an electronic talk show constricted to the size of an old fashioned coffee klatch. So she goes on-line and tries to find the real people behind the signifiers she has been talking to for years. For the first time, she tracks down—by "working" The Net—her interlocutors and discovers that only one—CyberBob— is close enough to help her out. Of course the CyberBob she does hook up with is not the *real* CyberBob. He's been replaced by one of the terrorist hackers. I admit that face-to-face encounters with our fellow human beings may not do anything more for us than lead us astray. You can't judge by appearances, although we inevitably use the presence there in front of us in order to connect with what that presence signifies *to us at some particular time and place.*

Identification in the real world is a floating crapshoot but it floats from one real world site to another. Identification in cyberspace is a crapshoot floating in cyberspace. If you can break into cyberspace, that is, gain access to those computer systems that modulate our lives, then you can run the game. In *The Net* that's what the brains behind the Gatekeeper computer surveillance corporation want to do. Of course, for centuries we have believed that if you break into the real-world and gain access to its foundational protocols, you also can run the game. Perhaps, if you read a little bit of Plato you can do this. Or Aristotle. Or Kant. Or Donald Trump. Or Newt Gingrich. Or Shakespeare. Or the Bible. Or the Koran. Or the rules according to Hoyle.

It almost appears that in our frustration with gaining access to the world, we have created for ourselves an electronic parallel universe, cyberspace, which we have constructed and therefore can control. We are thus busily engaged in turning ourselves into cyborgs within an electronic universe, rather like Charles Foster Kane retreating to Xanadu. Defeated by our own mediations of the real world, we now turn to a totally artificial world that we can mediate anew. Unfortunately, unlike the real world which runs within a paradoxical presence *and* absence "logic," cyberspace is grounded in a presence *or* absence logic. The results of this cyberspace alteration lead to a very, very big problem, namely, representations in cyberspace do not screen the horizon out of which they emerge. There is no unmarked space of the world still present within which all representations resonate.

When Angela Bennett appears on The Net as someone else, there is no signified, no chunk of the real also present, which any signifier attempts to bring to full presence. No signifier can achieve this; nevertheless, it is the presence of what is being signified which incites and revises our representations—continuously. In cyberspace, the nominal is the real. We can therefore break into the system, find the correct password, and alter the signifiers without fear of a template reality hovering on the screen. Certainly such a template reality is never for us a verifying reality, an unmediated outside point of reference. But it is nevertheless the reality that we mediate and that remains "being there" regardless of what mediations of it we construct for ourselves. When Angela Bennett loses her identity in cyberspace and is given a false one, that false identity is only bytes interacting with other bytes. Only a multiplication of falsity can result.

So the fear that this film registers of computer terrorism is filmic but also real. As long as cyberspace is a real-world construction we face difficulties on both sides. Real-world terrorists with real-world agendas (not mentioned in *The Net* but we can round up the usual suspects: desire, accident and power), can invade a system and reprogram it—an act of reterritorialization. Cyberspace can inflict a view of things upon us that can lay waste our real-world—from personal identities to stock markets. While the real-world "Black Monday" stock market crash of 1987 reveals this latter event, the film *The Net*, in spite of a hackneyed plot structure and a mechanical rather than digital style, reveals the former.

The future actualization of both these fears, however, must now take place within an environment that has an eye out for them. The stock market is now wary of its computerized representations of what is going on as well as the slippage between responding to computer information and real-world response capability. I don't say this problem has been solved; I am speaking of an awareness that exists within which our market reality now shapes itself. Computer terrorism is a problem-solving matter: for every virus that turns up, we create a scanning and cleaning program. Bullock analyses virus-struck computer systems and cleans them but she winds up introducing a virus into the Gatekeeper system in order to destroy it. Computer viruses, then, can be used as anti-weaponry, like anti-ballistic missiles. Someone sends a virus in and another virus, a Patriot virus, is released to counter it. The chess game begins, but this time in cyberspace.

For every new venture to break into private sector or governmental computer systems, there is a new "gatekeeping" device. A society in which the "winners" feel safe only behind real-world gates and gatekeepers plus a mindboggling array of electronic property protection devices has now to expand its worries to cyberspace. Invested capital is "computer posted" capital. The cyberspace thief then has to break into the computer to get the gold, just as the old time Western stage robbers had to break into the strongbox. *Plus ça change, plus le même chose.*

Virtualizing the Imagination

> "The great secret of morals is love; or a going out of our own nature, and an identification of ourselves with the beautiful which exists in thought, action, or person, not our own. A man, to be greatly good, must imagine intensely and comprehensively; he must put himself in the place of another and of many others;. the pains and pleasures of his species must become his own. The great instrument of moral good is the imagination."
>
> Shelley, "A Defense of Poetry"

Does cyberspace change not the way the game is played but the game itself? Does it change not the way the narrative could go but our way of narrating? And if there is to be a fundamental change, a re-construction of ourselves within a fabricated electronic universe, will we be better off then than now? Let's adopt the market criteria for "good, better, best." Will this Third Revolution, the cyberspace revolution, increase net profits, expand and grow the economy, maintain an unfettered entrepreneurial environment and so on? Inquiring market minds want to know. Then we have the two dystopic scenarios I projected: we'll either become like the underground creatures in Jules Verne's *The Time Machine* or a roboticized Borg-like collective. We'll either be home alone jacked into cyberspace and only unjacking when Nature calls, or part of an electronic hive pursuing the paths of our e-mail. I want to, however, apply the Romantic poet Shelley's criteria of judgment because I think it addresses both what we are as individuals and our relationship with others.

Moral goodness, Shelley affirms, exists when we can expand beyond self to others, when we can pursue our own desires within a frame that includes desires not our own but of others. To be able to identify with the frame of reality of another depends in Shelley's view on imagination. What he calls "ethical science" cannot take us where we want to go: into the place where others perceive and make sense of the world. That "science" can rationalize and order but only within the limits of what has already been imagined. We must first be able to conceive what our own reason has not distinguished. And such conceivability is brought to us through the imagination. Shelley goes on to argue for poetry as a medium of imaginative exercise. Poetry enables us to exercise the imaginative faculty and thus, in the end, serves a moral purpose of the highest order.

Technophiles look to cyberspace as a place where our imaginations will be exercised and strengthened and therefore the pleasures and pains of the race will become more conceivable to us. Technophobes see cyberspace as a place where our capacity to empathize with others will diminish as we wander amid simulations of a hyperreality—a reality severed from the real world and the pleasures and pains of the real world. Cyberspace becomes a place to escape into, to shuffle off the human coil, to become denatured, dehumanized. For technophiles, cyberspace becomes an alternative reality in which we can work out what we cannot in the "real world." It therefore becomes a testing ground for what can be enacted in the real world. The virtual reality dimension of cyberspace can only increase our imaginative powers, bringing to conceivability what our own limited real world situation may block off. Here, cyberspace become more powerful than poetry as it becomes itself the realm out of which poetry is born. Kathleen Murphy, writing about *Reboot,* a TV show which Mark Dery in the *Village Voice* describes as "a Saturday morning cartoon for tweenage mutant neuromancers,"[10] envisions a new cyberspace storyteller:

> [I]n my optimistic moments, I wonder if there's a new breed of storyteller coming, the mutant offspring of a technonerd and a latterday D. W. Griffith—a visionary who might give the new medium its own aesthetic grammar and syntax. Such a Merlin might teach us how to become authors and artists of ourselves, modemned into richly interactive dream-time.[11]

Murphy's vision of "an eternally marvelous journey down the yellow-brick road, destination home" is thus a journey on the wings of imagination via a Pentium chip driving an interactive CD-ROM. "Could we rediscover magic?" she asks.

One wonders if the "radical" Shelley, radical in all things, would have jacked into virtual realities to extend that "moral goodness" he writes of in "A Defense of Poetry." One wonders whether the most visionary of all Romantic poets, William Blake, would have joined forces with "master storytellers Quentin Tarantino and Steven Spielberg . . . to create an interactive CD-ROM that empowers the player to shapechange a storyline through multiple moods, modes, and genres." (42). Or would Blake see all this as an imposed nightmare of Urizen—"your reason"—and not a forging of Los, the Imagination? Would Shelley refuse to give up the "real world," untransmogrified by the imagination and yet the only place from which a search for "the beautiful which exists in thought, action, or person, not our own" can begin?

There is an episode in *Star Trek: The Next Generation* in which Riker is given what looks like virtual reality spectacles by an alien intent on taking over the starship *Enterprise*. The interactive game that Riker is introduced to proves addictive and ultimately transforming. He shares it with everyone else on the *Enterprise* but Data, who is "shut down" at once by the "brainwashed" crew because he is not a human and hence cannot be seduced by the virtual reality device. In the end, Data saves the entire crew by shortcircuiting, I suppose, the devilish device. But such virtual escape is also represented in a positive way on this TV show. On the *Enterprise* people enter the Holodeck—a computer generated interactive hologram world—to relax, to escape the day's pressures, or to play out a fantasy or engage in their favorite sports and games. Virtualizing our world is something we can be entirely in control of, without fear of it becoming addictive or controlling us. In Wim Wender's *Until The End of Time,* another virtual reality device is created: one that literally films the unconscious mind. Characters in that film wander around with the device strapped to their heads, lost in solipsistic self-contemplation. Lovers fall out of love, the world goes to rack and ruin through neglect.

Neglect. The other side, the dark side that Shelley hoped the imagination would bring into the light. In the *Harper* forum "What Are We Doing On-Line?" John Perry Barlow, an advocate of the protection of civil liberties in cyberspace, twice cites Nietzsche as defining sin as that which separates.[12] The broadcast media separates, in his view, while The Net does not. When we are on The Net we are communicating, interrelating. When we watch TV or film, we are not interactive but passive, lulled into whatever escapist or manipulative fare we are watching. Virtual reality, then, becomes an extension of such interaction. But in order to have that virtual reality interaction, we have to turn off the physical world. If you are William Wordsworth, another devotee of the imagination, you would have to give up your walk in the Lake District and perhaps take a virtual reality walk in a simulated Lake District. Will the virtual walker go on to write "Tintern Abbey" or will the urge to create be expended, be played out—with perhaps great satisfaction to the virtual Wordsworth— in VR? Or, will the virtual walker walk daily into a more stimulating Nature than ever he experienced in the real Lake District, and thus be stimulated to even greater levels of creative output— poetry that we can all share, poetry that illuminates a world we all share and not a uniquely tailored Holodeck program?

Will our empathic imaginative powers be increased in cyberspace? And if they are, will we be less likely to neglect thoughts and actions not our own? Less likely to neglect other people? In other words, will we be like a virtual Wordsworth incited to write a great poem after we have had our virtual walk? Or, will that walk itself take us further and further from real world identifications, real world hook-ups, concerns, pleasures and pains? Destination home. In a society in which the top one percent possess forty-four percent of the wealth and in which, in the decade of the '80s alone, the number of two-earner couples increased twenty percent, there are clearly radically different homes people are heading for, or have the time to be in once they're home. And if our destination home is to be conducted through cyberspace, clearly there are those who will never be able to get on board, who will never be able to keep up with the newest generation of computers, the newest version of Windows. E-mail accounts, home pages on World Wide Web, CD-ROM capabilities, the latest software programs and so on will have a hard time finding their way to the majority of Americans at a time when public programs, including education, are threatened with privatization, with the rules of the market in place whereby "you pay as you go."

If you can't pay, you don't go. Destination left out. Neglected. [I don't know whether a trip in cyberspace transports us to a higher level of humanity when cyberspace is ultimately no more than a space constructed and shaped by, and, in the final analysis, responsive to market forces.] "We believe that cyberspace," the DigitaLiberty "group" writes," will transcend national borders, national governments and national economies." It sounds painfully like what our market metanarrative has already accomplished, plus transcending the individual lives—needs, expectations, and desires—of the majority of Americans.

Notes

1. Hillel Schwartz, *Century's End* New York: Doubleday, 1990.

2. Kathleen Murphy, "Rebooting the Bard," *Film Comment,* July 1995, p. 42.

3. Summer 1994, n136.

4. David C. Churbuck, "Where's the Money?" *Forbes,* January 30, 1995.

5. Philip Elmer-Dewitt, "On A Screen Near You: Cyberporn," *Time* July 3, 1995, p. 40.

6. Quoted in Elmer-Dewitt, p. 45.

7. Ibid, p. 40.

8. The film *Hackers* presents the eternal rebel youth as a hacker To the question posed to Marlon Brando in *The Wild One*—"What are you rebelling against?" to which Brando answered " "What've ya got?" the rebel hacker now has the tyranny of cyberspace encryption and password access to break through.

9. Indiana University Press, 1994, p. 211.

10. August 8, 1995, "*Reboot*'s Rules of Order," p. 39.

11. "Rebooting the Bard: Hi-Tech Storytelling," July 1995, *Film Comment,* p. 42.

12. John Perry Barlow, et al. "What Are We Doing On-Line?" *Harper's Magazine* August 1995, pp. 35–46.

Spray and Fire

Out on the Old Town Road

"This might be just what you've been looking for," Barfield Simmons said to Cleo as she poured him a second cup of coffee.

"Say what it is again, Mr. Barfield," Cleo replied, going back to the stove where two eggs sunnyside up were sizzling.

Barfield folded over the first page of the *Town Courier* and then picked up his coffee.

"Well, you know what Disney does, don't you? Elvis's Graceland? Universal Studios? Six Flags Over Texas? But did you know Mayberry is in China what all those are in this country?"

Cleo slid the eggs on a plate, waited two clicks and the toast popped up and brought all of it to the table where Barfield moved his paper aside so she could put his breakfast down in front of him.

"Mayberry?" she repeated.

"Mayberry. Plus Gilligan's Island. Gilligan's Island is watched by more people in India than in the whole world combined."

Cleo appreciated that but then a look of puzzlement covered her face.

"Look, sit down, Cleo," Barfield said.

"Yes, sir."

"Certain really big global players are behind this package," Barfield told her. "I'm buying into it heavily. And I'm offering you the chance to come in."

Cleo considered that.

"What exactly am I coming into?"

"The first year four Mayberry's, each the size of Disneyworld and the Epcot Center combined, get built in China. The next year,

four Gilligan's Islands are built in India. And that's only the beginning. You could double your investment in two years."

Barfield waited, but Cleo said nothing.

"Sally said you were saving for a rainy day."

"For some health insurance," Cleo said. "I was waiting for
them Democrats to bring it to me but that's the end of that I suppose."

Barfield pointed a slice of toast at her.

"That little venture would have cost this country plenty," he
said. "Entrepreneurship is the answer. You make the right investment, you can buy the best health insurance in the world. I'll
send my agent to talk to you."

"Thank you, Mr. Barfield."

"Well, think about it," Barfield said, wiping his mouth and
getting up. "Tell Sally I'll call her if lunch is on.

"Remember," Barfield said, as he went out the back door
leading into the garage where his Mercedes and Sally's Jag were
nestled on a tile covered floor. "Don't wait for the government to
provide for you. This country was built on entrepreneurship. And
now we're doing it globally."

Cleo nodded.

"You know you have to have applied for a job at least three
places, Mr. Coletti," Susy Lip, the youngest daughter of Mr. Lip,
said to Frank Coletti, who sat before her desk with former Sheriff
Jake Wilcox sitting beside him at the Town Unemployment
Office.

"I did," Frank said, almost at the end of his rope although it
was only eight-thirty A.M.

Susy had noted that both men were dressed in hunting out-
fits. Frank even had a bright orange vest on. And instead of the
Stetson Jake usually wore he now had on a black and red wool
cap with extra long brim. Frank had an L.L. Bean bomber cap
on his head.

Susy picked up the three scraps of dirty paper Frank had
handed her.

"Hudson Liquid Chemical Spraying?" she read. "What position did you apply for there, Mr. Coletti?"

"Sprayer."

"Sprayer?"

"General home lawn care."

"And was there an opening?"

"No, but they expect one any day. They said they'd call."

"I see. It's December, Mr. Coletti. They probably won't call until the Spring. What about a job this winter?"

She picked up another slip.

"Simulated Security, Incorporated? What position did you apply for there?"

"Hooking up fake surveillance cameras," Frank said, suddenly feeling hot in his bomber cap and taking it off.

"How far did you get?"

"I had some legal trouble with the divorce," Frank said.

"Legal trouble?"

"I had to arrest Frank for violating a court injunction," Jake said. "He wasn't to get a hundred yards of his wife but he did."

"And I take it they don't want someone with a criminal record hooking up fake surveillance cameras for them?"

"That's right," Jake said. "The whole idea is that the criminal mind thinks the place is got electronic security so they pass it by. Not to say that Frank here has a criminal mind which he doesn't. Frank is the gentlest man I know."

"MicroLab Opto-Mechanics?" Susy said, picking up the last slip.

"It's Morio Saito's business," Frank explained. "He needs someone to find, clean, position and mount objects."

"What sort of objects?" Susy asked.

"Anything he said that was very old and had an irregular surface."

They all thought about that.

"Did he give you an example?"

"Yeah, he said, like Jake's face."

"Like to blow me over," Jake exclaimed.

"He wanted you to clean, position and mount Jake's face?"

Frank shook his head.

"I don't know. It sounded too weird to me. I think he's like a taxidermist but he uses a computer? Sort of thing."

"I told Gus," Jake said. "He's got Saito under surveillance."

When Frank and Jake left, Gladys sat down.

"What are you doing here, Gladys?" Susy said in surprise.

"Abe fired me. After fifteen years waitressing in that place, he fired me."

"But why?"

"He said ever since Sweeney opened up his all-nite diner, business has been bad."

"What's Abe gonna do, wait on tables himself?"

"He's got Jill and Faye is gonna work weekends. Abe said he had to cut back. He says Sweeney will give me a job. He even gave me this letter to show Sweeney that says what a good waitress I am and Abe would've never let me go if it wasn't for the drop in business."

"Well, if you can get a job with Sweeney, you can't collect unemployment," Susy said.

"I don't wanna waitress anymore," Gladys said. "I'm tired of waitressing. Fifteen years is enough. I want a different kind of job."

"Like what?"

"I don't wanna stand on my feet all day."

"The question is, Gladys, what else are you trained to do?"

"I like jewelry," Gladys said, wiping at her nose with a crumpled tissue. "I like being around jewelry. Maybe I could be one of those stone polishers. The ones that sit on high stools and wear goggles."

"Have you ever done that kind of work before?"

"I always wanted to work for the post office. Sit in front of one of them pidgeon hole things throwing the mail into the right holes."

"I could read the news on TV behind one of them desks. I could be a lifeguard. I could have my own talk show like Ricky

Lake. I could become a rock star and go on tour like Madonna. I could be Hillary Clinton's personal assistant. I could pose for *Playboy*."

Susy held up her hand to stop her.

Susy sighed and then picked up her phone. She called Sweeney's. She had Gladys Farquarson here looking for a job. Yes, the Gladys who worked at Abe's. Was there an opening? There was? Thank you.

Susy looked at Gladys.

"Sweeney says you can start tomorrow. You can't collect unemployment if there is a job like your previous job available. I'm sorry, Gladys."

"You don't know what I can really do," Gladys said angrily as she stood up. "And I ain't telling you."

She walked about five feet from Susy's desk and then turned and said:

"There's two ways to serve, you know. You serve them. And you serve yourself."

You serve them and you serve yourself Susy repeated to herself later on when she was standing at the coffee machine. She finally decided it was some kind of waitressing credo and had to do with tips.

At that moment Clara and May Pinsky were being brought in to see their Dad, Mark Pinsky. Mark had not fully recovered from his motorcycle fugue and the girls just might accelerate his return to his true identity. He was about halfway back Dr. Joy told Mark's wife, Lorraine. He remembered his last name but not his first. He remembered his Mom's name but not his Dad's. He remembered four digits of his phone number, the first seventeen years of his life in detail, the first half of his favorite movie, John Wayne's *The Alamo,* the upper part of his wife's body, what his car looked like from the rear but not from the front, the first four digits of his social security number but not the last. And he hooked up with half the words that he used or heard. When Clara and May walked into Dr. Joy's office, he cried out:

"May!" and then looked blankly at Clara.

"Clara," Clara said, hugging him.

"You want to go back home with us, don't you Daddy?" May asked, tears in her eyes.

A look of fear came into Mark's eyes.

"I don't want to go all the way back home," he said, shaking his head. "Not all the way back."

"Why, Daddy?" May asked. "It's not that far. Mommy could drive."

"It's old and dusty back there," Mark said, breaking away from his daughters and sitting on the edge of a chair. "Everybody is long gone. You wake up in the early morning and go down to the kitchen and nobody's there. My mother and father are ashes blown away out back. In the fields."

May shuddered but Clara knew where he was and where to take him.

"Maybe they're ahead of you, Daddy," Clara said in a very low, calm voice. Mark looked at her.

"Clara," he said.

"Maybe you have to go ahead until you meet them again," Clara said. "Just like May and Mommy and I came here to meet you."

Mark studied her face carefully and then nodded.

"From now on we all go ahead together," Clara said.

"And you can tell us stories on the way home," May said trying to be upbeat but the comment flung a dark shadow across Mark's face.

"They'll be telling stories about me," he said. "Then those stories won't be told anymore. Or they'll be told wrong."

"Not by me," Clara said gently.

"I hear somebody telling a story about me," Mark said, standing up, listening, listening hard. "I'm a long way in the past. I have only a thin recollection of who I am. They only tell stories about the dead."

He jumped up and grabbed Clara by the shoulders.

"You have a daughter. Your daughter has a daughter. Your daughter's daughter has a daughter. And where am I? I mean, there's not even a day left of me. To tell anyone. I'm a long way back there. And no one's looking for me."

He was crying and shaking uncontrollably and May was crying silently. Clara gave her sister a "knock it off" look and then said to Mark:

"Cover your eyes, Daddy," she said. "Go ahead. Cover them. And don't peek. If you peek it's not fair."

Mark hesitated and then covered his eyes with both hands. Clara spun him around three times one way then two times the other way then one time back again.

"Okay, now with your eyes closed, Daddy, you have to find us. We're going to hide somewhere in this room."

Clara motioned for her sister to get under Dr. Joy's desk and then she herself stood by the window.

"I can't," Mark said, hands still over his hands. "How can I?"

Two hours later Barfield Simmons was waiting for a tow out on the Old Town Road. It was a favorite shortcut of his and he had been driving along nicely when all of a sudden the Mercedes lurched to one side, spun around and went off the shoulderless road and into the ditch. It turned out to be a rear tire flat but there was no way to jack the car up. Barfield made a call on his car phone for a AAA tow. After about thirty minutes, the tow truck arrived and a thin man with sandy hair whom Barfield had never seen around town got out. The name "Carl" was monogrammed over his shirt pocket. Carl was a man of few words, not responding to Barfield's own comments on his bad luck.

"How fast were you going?" Carl said, after thoroughly examining the situation.

"I don't know," Barfield said. "Forty-five, fifty."

"I bet you could go sixty on this old road and that car would handle it like a dream."

Barfield nodded.

"Top of the line," he told Carl.

"It's good luck to have a car like that," Carl said. "Not bad luck."

"Excuse me?" Barfield said, not quite following.

"You were telling me just before how bad your luck was," Carl said. "Your luck can't be too bad if you drive a fifty thousand dollar car."

"Which is now in a ditch," Barfield said. "Are you going to pull it out? I want to go on with my life."

"That's what the judge told my wife after the divorce. Now she can go on with her life."

Now here was a melancholic towtruck driver Barfield thought, hearing the profound sadness in the man's voice.

"And did she?"

"She's someplace, I guess," Carl said. "You know if you bury a body in only a couple of feet of good dirt there ain't nothing left but bones in about a month?"

Barfield didn't know if that meant she was dead. But all of a sudden he knew that Carl wasn't exactly right. He knew it the same way he knew when an investment wasn't sound.

"But we tie up a lot of good land with cemeteries," Carl went on. "When all we need to do is bury'em shallow, pick up the bones, grind them as a soil sweetener. I don't see any sense in revering the dead like they was property. Whata you think?"

"I think I'm in sort of a rush," Barfield said, looking at his watch and then pulling his coat collar up. "And my feet are beginning to freeze."

Carl's face was a blank but his eyelids fluttered ever so slightly like moth wings. They were pupil-less clay brown eyes.

"I'm sorry," Carl said. "I've been having a bad day. All day. A woman locked herself out of her car and I accidentally broke her window trying to get it unlocked."

Barfield sympathized.

"Will that come out of your pay?" he asked.

"I don't know," Carl said, walking back to the tow truck.

"I'll have to see your club card."

Barfield took out his AAA card, walked over and handed it to Carl who was back in the truck. He took the card and clamped it to his clipboard.

"Can you pull it out and change the tire?"

"Yup," Carl said. "Unless something is broken under there."

"What could be broken?"

Carl stopped writing and stared open mouthed at Barfield.

"Things get broken and have to be fixed," he told Barfield. "Somebody has to fix them. Not you. But somebody."

"Yes, and somebody pays to have it fixed," Barfield said. "That's why I have AAA insurance."

"You don't have to pay me," Carl said. "I'd rather help people out if I can and call on them to help me out when I need help."

"Where's your sense of independence, man?" Barfield said. "Liberals have turned this whole country into long lines of people looking for handouts. God helps those who help themselves."

"Okay," Carl said, pulling a tire iron off the seat next to him and jumping out of the truck. "Gimme your wallet."

Barfield stepped back, a nervous laugh caught half way up his throat.

"Within the law," he finally got out. "You help yourself within the law."

"I'm going to bury you shallow," Carl said, stepping toward Barfield, tire iron raised.

Carl was on his way back to the station when a man waving his hat in the middle of the road flagged him down. It was former Sheriff Jake Wilcox. He was out of breath.

"Me and Frank spotted something in there," he said, pointing to the woods which the Town Mental Facility abutted on the south. "Frank's watching it and I was on my way into town to report it. I need a lift."

"Sure," Carl said. "Jump in."

"Boy," Jake said, wiping his brow. "Frank and me was just strolling them woods looking like we always is looking and boy did we find something this time."

"What did you find?" Carl asked, shifting gears.

"Looks like one of them UFO's and it ain't any bigger than this here truck 'cept its lozenge–shaped. Somebody had it camouflaged real good."

"Like in a shallow grave?" Carl asked, his voice sharing none of Jake's excitement.

"Yeah, I guess so," Jake said, folding his handkerchief and then checking his wristwatch. "Spotted it exactly two oh eight."

"You think aliens will make a difference?" Carl said after awhile.

"In what?" Jake said, wishing Carl would drive faster.

"In the way some people have it good and some people don't."

"I don't follow you, son," Jake replied.

Carl didn't respond.

"Once you see it," Jake said, trying to regain his earlier enthusiasm, "see how small and compact it is and almost the color of air, like it ain't really an object more like a copy of an object, you know why it's been so hard to prove they're really there."

Carl didn't bite but after another few minutes he did say:

"I think those college kids bother me so much because I didn't get a chance to go to college."

"What college kids?"

Carl took his eyes off the road and looked at Jake.

"The other day I went out on a call," he said. "Two girls from the college. One of them had on a see through knit top and when she bent down to pick up her bag I could see she didn't have anything on underneath. She didn't care. She just laughed."

Jake checked his wristwatch.

"She didn't have no shame," Carl said. "She was gonna be as wild as she could be with her parents paying the ticket. They don't even look when they're crossing a street. And they drive like they're the only people on the face of the earth."

"I bet Frank's trying to drive that thing right now," Jake said.

When they were in sight of town, Carl said:

"I bet you think I'm some kind of pervert talking about that girl like that, like that's all I do on this job is look down girl's blouse's."

"Next corner will be fine," Jake said, pointing to the next corner.

When he got out he told Carl that someday he'd remember being there when the first UFO was found out behind the Town Mental Facility.

Carl didn't reply but just drove off.

Post-Apocalyptic Rust and Rubble: *Waterworld*

"Its storytelling, remarkably crude for such an elaborate production, takes a back seat to its enthusiasm for post-apocalyptic rust and rubble."

Janet Maslin, "An Aquatic Armageddon with Lots of Toys," *New York Times*, July 28, 1995

"It's after the end of the world. Don't you know that yet?"

Sun Ra Intergalactic Solar Arkestra

It took some two hundred million dollars to make yet another good guys versus bad guys movie, a movie in which no matter how alienated and alienating the hero, Kevin Costner (the Mariner), is, we know he's the good guy and Dennis Hopper, (the Deacon who is leader of the Smoker gang, an aquatic Hell's Angels), is the bad guy. Why are our films projecting scenes of the near and far future faltering so badly mid-decade as we head toward the third millennium? Witness *The Net*—an opportunity to envision ourselves living with and in cyberspace that dwindles to yet another version of total innocence framed and pursued by total evil. Witness *Hackers*—a film about a subculture with ties to a Third Economic Revolution that turns out to be not revolutionary, but a revolting *Revenge of the Nerds*. Witness *Virtuosity*—an opportunity to envision workaday and virtual reality intersecting that dwindles into a hard cop versus super-villain. Of course, you don't expect Jean-Claude van Damme's *Time Cop* to do anything more than stage some martial arts moves with a techno backdrop. Nor do you expect Stallone in *Judge Dredd* to give us anything more than Judge Rocky Rambo. But somehow I am disappointed in *The Net* and I guess it's because there is so much talk these days *about* The Net and the huge telecommunications deals that are being made as the global players jockey for good seats in the theatre house of the third millennium. And the whole concept of a virtual reality fills us with even greater wonder. Imagine all the fractious Balkan leaders

getting together in a virtual reality setting, playing out their ambitions and witnessing the consequences. Imagine presidential
platforms in virtual reality format so that voters could enter
promised worlds and see for themselves whether they work. But
Lawnmower Man takes us into yet another version of scientist
megalomania and madness and *Virtuosity* into yet another Dirty
Harry scenario.

Waterworld is the most disappointing because it is the most
ambitious. Rather than tackle a technological segment of the future, it tries to screen the landscape, now a waterscape, of the
next millennium. Whose mind isn't on that? Forget about dreams
of restoring the past and fears of hamstringing our children with
our national debt; the question that looms bigger and bigger as
we approach millennium's end is whether we are bequeathing to
our heirs a dying planet and a dystopic future. In *Waterworld*, the
future is dystopic because this waterscape is the result of a polar ice cap melt, the most haunting scene from the abyss that we
have imagined for ourselves in this last decade of the century and
of the millennium.

It is a very hot August day here in Michigan and the whole
country is going through a plus one hundred heat index. Even
southern California is caught in a very unusual period of high
humidity. Are we experiencing a global warming, the result of a
greenhouse effect that our own technology has produced? Are
the polar ice caps indeed melting, perhaps at this moment imperceptibly, the waters of Pacific Islands rising, jeopardizing that
Pacific Rim which the market has announced as the most happy
of economic regions? *Waterworld* appropriately opens in the
summer, amid record breaking heat waves. Those without air-
conditioning enter the cool theatres. In the summer it doesn't
matter too much what one is about to see; what matters is that
we escape the heat for awhile. And the summer bill of fare is for
escapist movies, the trick being to capture huge audiences and
entertain them the way they would be at *Disneyworld*. Or
Waterworld. There is a waterworld not far from everyone's home.

The way in which this summer commercialism wends its
way into *Waterworld* is clear; in fact the bold reach of this film
is sold out for these summertime market reasons. One tenth of
the amount of money would have produced the escapist action
film that *Waterworld* tries to become. And one tenth of that one
tenth would have produced the Dennis Hopper road movie that
it tries to become. And one tenth of that one tenth of one tenth

would have produced the paean to difference that it tries to become. And. . . . would have produced the hero and his horse romance (this time it's a boat). It's as if the whole dystopic future waiting for us round this decade's bend, the whole new (chances are riot-filled, terrorist-laden, class riven, politically retrogressing) millennium that faces us can't come to the screen, can't even make it into popular film. Now I call that a an overawing, paralyzing fear.

The "backstage melodrama of bringing *Waterworld* to the screen" has an ontological dimension then: we are too close to the new millennium timewise and too close to dystopia technologywise to look without fear and trembling, sickness unto death, at a picture of what we have done to our world and what we have become. The "cold-war wish-fulfillment fantasy" (according to *Halliwell's Film Guide*) of *The Day The Earth Stood Still* at century's midpoint is a warning from ourselves to ourselves. Even *Terminator II* could face a dystopic future because it could posit the possibility of a recuperation. Der Ahnald could go back in time and prevent that moment when cyborgs reach consciousness. The war between humans and the machines they had created could be overwritten. But now it is 1995 and it seems too late for warnings. *Waterworld* tells me that in its flight from any engagement with the new millennium to the mindless succor of a Mariner against the Smokers water movie. Someone with a vision was brought up short by a Nietzschean fear of becoming what we behold. This film is first overwhelmed by a loss of courage before it falls back into the drivel of "B" movie imagination.

II.

The Mariner is a preverbal a-hero (a- in the sense of a-moral and also in the sense of aporia, pathless) because unlike the eloquent Michael Rennie who comes to warn us in *The Day The Earth . . .* , the Mariner doesn't have any words of warning nor does he want to give us any words of warning. It's both because this post-apocalyptic world has passed the warning stage and because, in the world of the viewer, warnings are liberal messages and we're all sick and tired of liberals. Dystopic futures can get $200 million backing but no script can get approval. What we finally get is a script from the 1950s, without the warning. Indeed, without words that could in any way be tied to meaning. So the

Mariner is a before-telecommunications creature; he doesn't go on The Net nor would he if cyberspace somehow still loomed in Waterworld. He jumps from the sea into the nets spanning his trimaran. So much for nets and networking. That's all over with. Obviously, cyberspace did not foster that web of personal inter-connectedness, that communitarian elan, that the enthusiasts of the last decade promised. Everything has gone off-line again and we wind up with the Mariner, a mutant in the water, and not a hacker at a terminal.

One of the reasons the Mariner has no warning to give us is that he hates us. He's no longer a human being; he's mutating into a whole other species, perhaps an atavistic return to the sea. Meanwhile he's neither fish nor human. He's different. I suppose if this had been a Costner film from the beginning, we would have seen as much cultural diversity and difference as we did in *Robin Hood: Prince of Thieves* and *Dances With Wolves*. But this time it is not a rapprochement between cultural differences that could realistically play but rather the end of the species and a move-ment to a different—a non-human—ruler of the planet. Differences did our species in. The new millennium will stage our fall from power.

This is cold. It's not a fantasy but a nightmare and like all nightmares it has potency—what Jung called mana value, the power to fascinate us, draw us to it. One of the things we can see when we look toward the next millennium is our own end as a dominator of the Earth. And because this is a real imagining that arrests us all, it can, when brought to the screen, draw us in. Since, however, we live now in an atmosphere in which a new Conservative revolution promises to "restore the dream," no pop-ular film launched with the venture capital of this market dream can afford to underwrite—via script—the Mariner's disgust with us and confidence in his own superiority, the superiority of a dif-ferent species. Much of the criticism of this movie has been di-rected at Costner, the film being his own "hubris filled exercise." Since there is a certain Costner focus on Costner in his other films that plays out here as well, hubris may indeed be at work. But let's consider the rift between the Mariner/Costner and the critics from another point of view.

We are in *Waterworld* past the warning and possible re-write stage. The polar ice caps have melted; we've screwed up. It's all over. The film decides to run—or swim—away from shooting this straight on so it lashes the total project to floating cowboy hero and a pack of jet-skiing villains. So in the end when Mariner/Costner wins, we supposedly are winning something. Things turn out for the best, or better. Land is found. Maybe humankind can begin again. But the Mariner doesn't like the way the land "moves" so he heads back out to sea. Just like Shane leaving Brandon DeWilde behind in *Shane*. But at the same time, the Mariner is already disconnected from the never ending story of the human race. It has ended. We've got some dinosaurs left trying to live on a slag pile—the *Exxon Valdez*—which is giving them their last gallons of fossil fuel. And smokes too I guess. And then when they're gone, it's all over. So they're dead but they just don't know it.

The Mariner, however, is a disjuncture, a real break in the human story. He has gills and webbed feet, can swim like a fish and breathe underwater. He doesn't respond to the ties that bind humans, or at the very least, he's breaking way. He's heading in a new direction. Here's a hero, then, who scorns the human race and prefers his own company. Until I suppose Nature throws up more such mutants. Or doesn't. Early in the movie when a bunch of citizens of mixed race ask the Mariner to marry one of their kind so as to invigorate their line, the Mariner tells them that they're already dead. They're already extinct. He won't waste time on them. He finds them revolting, totally out of sync and sympathy with the new planet order. More fearsome than any revolutionary who, after all, only sets out to topple one human order of things and replace it with another. The Mariner is an evolutionary, his presence augurs the end of our own species. The film, of course, doesn't pursue this line. But it's a line in the water nevertheless.

Is it surprising that at a time when an upbeat Conservative "revolution" is trying to market itself throughout the land, that this hint of evolutionary replacement by the Mariner/Costner doesn't play well? After all, the Mariner is not only turning away from a political party, but from the entire human race. And although Conservative revolutionaries, filled with the evaluative criteria of the market, may ask: "Who gives a damn if a spotted owl becomes extinct?" they doubtlessly would consider human extinction as even worse than a steeply progressive income tax. But this sort of talk of human extinction is, at the moment, always caught in a Conservative spin: it's a Green Party scare tactic; once again, at base, it's a concept thrown out along with Liberalism. I mean that human extinction is here an extinct topic. Market values find no value in long term contemplation of the possible effects of short term profiteering, of our progressive production, our progressive exhaustion of the planet, our gradual surpassing our planet's capacity to bounce back, to recoup, to survive. The odds in Vegas are in favor of this: we will alter the planet and kill ourselves off. In *Waterworld* some scraps of humanity survive, and the Earth has indeed changed.

As we watch the Mariner turn a scrap of paper over and over again in his hands, we see our ambitious technoworld as only the latest and last Ozymandias empire of fatal presumption. All this talk of progress in the global market and a new world order is now nothing more than scraps of paper sold by oddball entrepreneurs drifting above our own watery graves. When the Mariner takes his slow dive into this dark, watery grave, bearing along with him the human Helen in an air filled balloon, the whole drama of extinction hits home. We see the Mariner slowly drifting down and across what looks like a Manhattan skyline, now a Manhattan waterline, silent, ruined, finished. This, finally, is the result of all our experiments, all our goals, all our global financial wizardry

Wizardry. The Mariner as *bricoleur.* For instance, that's a curious diving bell that the Mariner has put Helen into. As they descend it fills with water but by the time they reach the bottom, there is still enough air for Helen to breathe. You need to know some physics to get that archaic looking diving bell designed just right. And what about the Mariner's fishing style? He charges something with an old battery, hangs out at the end of a line as bait and then bang! he's swallowed by Moby Dick, whom he somehow implodes from inside the belly of the whale. And he's got his dinner. But it's the catamaran itself that displays the Mariner's *bricoleur* style. It's a floating gizmo contraption, wheels, gears and wheels within wheels—a servomechanism on the high seas. It's the result of a lifetime subscription to *Popular Mechanics.* And the Mariner works his catamaran with the aplomb of Errol Flynn swinging onto a quarter deck.

The Mariner has mechanized his boat by making use of what lies at hand, that is, what lies at the bottom of the ocean. He has foraged the sunken streets of, maybe, New York City, and come up with a clutter of stuff. A pair of ski boots get thrown into the catamaran's net and later on he wears them and is asked whether he wants to sell them. Former use is not an available context for present use. No one but the Mariner seems to know that they are not at the beginning of something but at its end. The real age of exploration already happened; it's over. Water covers all of it. Or, almost. Position is everything and where anyone is positioned in this movie, including ourselves, remains murky. Although the polar ice caps have melted and the world that we are now living in has ended, the human race is still at the ending stage. The final breath is yet to be taken; but the Mariner has gills as well as a nose so in this waterworld he may still be breathing when we have all stopped. He's not in this waterworld the way we would be. And if he were in the audience, he wouldn't be seeing this film the way we do. Position. The humans in this movie position themselves at the starting line not the ending line. They're in search of their beginning on land. They have heard stories of land and life on the land. They have seen the signs of such life: the lemon tree and tomato plant that the Mariner has on his catamaran. And I suppose for the Smokers, land is a place to grow tobacco.

Ignorant then of all the many products that line our shelves in our world—and the uses these products serve—these post-Armageddon survivors, including the Mariner, re-attach our world's flotsam to their own waterworld needs. And the Mariner is a Leonardo of *bricoleurs*. He scours the sea bottom like a present-day bottle return scavenger but one that does not know the value of what he finds until he creates that value. This could be used for this; that could be used for that. As well as guarding his "stuff" fiercely, he also trades shrewdly for what others have.

Is there a hint here then that a new species will take the old paths of entrepreneurship, from hunter-gatherer to inventive *bricoleur* to tradesman to property owner to one seeking protection for his property from others? Do gills and webbed feet not really mean a sea change in the market constructed joint "determinants" of all human behavior—the acquisitive spirit in the service of self-interest? The Mariner is no altruist; humans are not his peers or indeed his kind. Is he therefore the solitary entrepreneurial pioneer with a new vision heading out to sea once again, when everyone else thinks the future is "in land"? He's putting his money into seaspace, the new space of entrepreneurial ingenuity and individual freedom.

And then again—maybe he's not a retread of *homo sapien*. Maybe he will continue to be a *bricoleur* who wears ski boots on a boat, his ingenuity not taking him on an "ascent of mariner" trek but leaving him a drifter, a *flaneur* in a waterworld. The

Mariner's attachment to the flotsam relics of our civilization that he brings up from the bottom may not be the beginnings of a new entrepreneurial spirit. We might have to look not to our technological past to understand it but to all those ways of attending to the world that our technological advance coupled with our "Enlightened" mission scrunched. Think of the Mariner gazing at something like a computer that he has scrounged from the sea bottom: he's gazing at it totally without any cultural context but his own waterworld one. Rather like aborigines in the film *Black Robe* attending the chiming of Mr. Clock as the voice of deity. The big difference, however, would be that the Mariner knows the thing wasn't made by anyone who knew anything more about living and surviving than he did. In fact, the Mariner knows they knew a good deal less.

Eschatology

March 18th
Nouveau Noire Holiness Church

"There are three hundred and fifty-eight billionaires on this planet . . . ," Rev. Aldrich told the congregation at the Nouveau Noire Holiness Church, situated only two doors away from the First Nutritional Services Inc.

Rev. Aldrich let that fact sink into the collective mind of the congregation. Carl Firewoad who was sitting in the back with Gladys Farquarson, was paying particular attention.

"With a combined net worth of seven hundred and sixty billion dollars," Rev. Aldrich said and then paused. The only sound that could be heard was Frank Coletti praying in muffled tones for the soul of former Sheriff Jake Wilcox. Young Frankie nudged his father who opened his eyes, looked at his son without comprehension.

"You're praying too loud," Young Frankie told his Dad.

"The bottom forty-five percent of the world population," Rev. Aldrich boomed, "they have the same combined net worth as these three hundred and fifty-eight billionaires."

"What's their names?" Carl mumbled.

"Let us pray now for those who have gone before us," Rev. Aldrich said.

"Okay, now, Dad," Young Frankie said but Frank who slipped back into a speechless catatonia didn't respond so Young Frankie got up and said:

"For my father who disappeared twenty-three years ago."

"For Further Cooper," Antony said, standing up. "The Black Mountain King."

"For Dodger," Mrs. Dodger said, getting up, tears in her eyes. "My little . . . my little soldier . . . "

"For my dear friend Mrs. Hearder," Mrs. Woad said, getting to her feet with the help of her cane.

"I'm over here, dear!" Mrs. Hearder called out from the rear of the Church. "In the back."

"Oh, my!" Mrs. Woad exclaimed. "I take it back."

"Sha Na Na Na Na Ding Dong!" Lucy Powell cried out jubilantly from the first row. Rev. Aldrich frowned down at her but Lucy's mania did not abate.

"For my husband Barfield," cried out Sally Simmons, dressed this time like Jackie O at JFK's funeral. "He wasn't robbed. He was just murdered. Which makes no sense. No sense."

John Swingle took the opportunity to go into his newest guitar piece, a song he called "I Respect You Because I Respect the Lord."

"I respect you because I respect the Lord
Who made you who are the love of my life . . . "

"The Lord is of incidental importance in that song," Mr. Zowie whispered to Walt Pinsky, who ignored him.

"Let's thank the Lord for the good things he's given us this week," Rev. Aldrich said when the last notes of the guitar had faded away.

"I'd like to thank the lord for my family," Mark Pinsky said, jumping up. "Who have waited for me when I have strayed and who have welcomed me back from places I just wandered off to. Which I wouldn't have done had I known who I was and who they were, but I didn't know anything when I woke up in the morning except I was off to someplace. I was in the middle of a trip somewhere. Part of the way through a journey and I had to keep going."

"Amen, brother," Rev. Aldrich said, putting an end to what he knew might turn out to be a tortuous identity journey.

"Patti wants to thank the Lord for giving her a brain," Pancakes said, getting up and showing the congregation her doll Patti.

"The Lord gives souls, not brains," Rev. Alrich told her.

"Patti has both," Pancakes replied defiantly.

"She don't have either one, girl," Rev. Aldrich replied angrily.

"Allow me, Reverend," Mr. Zowie said, rising. "Brains are genetic, my dear. Only living things have genes. Your doll is not living. Therefore she doesn't have genes and can't have a brain. She can have a soul though. Souls are imaginary. You can imagine your doll has a soul."

"What you doing here anyway?" Rev. Aldrich said to Mr. Zowie.

"Belief interests me," Mr. Zowie said. "Belief is interesting. I come here because this is where the belief is."

You a man who don't believe in nothing," Rev. Aldrich snapped.

"Murder interests me but I don't murder," Mr. Zowie replied coolly and then sat down.

"Oh, there'll be peace in the valley some day," Lucy Powell sang out. "Some day. No more problems, no more sorrow, no more pain. La De Da De Da."

"I'd like to thank the Lord for bringing me to such a wonderful town," Mark Wonder yelled. "A town full of family values. I'm thinking of investing. If anyone here has a stock option pending or is finessing a leveraged buy-out . . . "

"Sit you down, brother," Rev. Aldrich boomed. "Buy yourself an ad in the bulletin next time. Now we ask the Lord for his help. Brothers and sisters, what all are you seeking?"

Mike Woad jumped up.

"I'm going to need some help trying to track down R.C. and Margaret," he told the congregation. "I need some people on the ground to set up checkpoints."

"And what you need the Lord for, brother?" Rev. Aldrich said, wiping the perspiration from his brow.

Woad was dumbfounded but Faye Fata stood up:

"He needs the Lord to give him hope," she said.

"Be ye not full of hope," Rev Alrich cried out, unappeased. "The Lord helps them who helps themselves."

"I'm relying a bit on technology," Woad said, clearing his throat.

"Just make sure you steer the technology and the technology don't steer you," Rev. Aldrich told him.

"That's the truth," Harry Powell testified to all. "I remember my father saying that when they got a phone in nobody took to it at all. Didn't fit into their way of life. And then gradually they found a place for it. Now we got kids plugged into the Internet twenty-four hours a day. No lives but in technology. It's a goddamn shame."

"Amen brother," Rev. Alrich affirmed, nodding.

"I'd like the Lord to help me find my husband's murderer," Sally Simmons said.

"The Lord ain't no detective," Rev. Aldrich told Sally. "What you mean is that you hope the Lord will put his finger on the murderer's soul and show him how Satan's got a hold on it."

Sally shook her head.

"I don't give two fucks about the murderer's soul," she told Rev. Aldrich. "I want him fried."

"The Lord don't like that kind of language," Rev. Aldrich warned her. "The Lord will slap you down you use that kind of language in his house."

"I think you should stop saying "His," Dr. Joy, standing in the back said. "The Lord may be a woman and if so, she wouldn't like being called a man. She'd object to *your* language, Reverend."

"You another one just interested in being here watching us believe?" Rev. Alrich shouted back.

"I'm interested in conscience," Dr. Joy called back. "It does a better job in getting the guilty to talk than hypnosis."

"I would like the Lord to help those poor aliens that the U.S. Government has under lock and key," Sweeney said.

"You talking about the Haitians or the Mexicans?" Rev. Aldrich asked, wiping.

"Aliens, Reverend," Sweeney replied. "Like in *War of the Worlds* or *Plan 9 From Outer Space*. Or *Starwars*. From another planet. Not human."

"What about them?" Rev. Alrich queried.

"We have to get the government to release them," Sweeney said.

"Why?"

"Why? Because they've come in peace. That's why. Didn't you ever see *The Day the Earth Stood Still?* I mean we shot Michael Rennie when all he wanted to do was be our friend."

"The Lord don't watch movies," Rev. Aldrich finally concluded. "The Lord may be up in the clouds but he . . . or she . . . ain't got his head up his ass. Like some folks in this congregation."

Sweeney tried to laugh this off but he was crushed and sat down in disgrace.

"Anymore requests from the Lord? Okay. Fears. Who's gonna express the fears?"

Carl raised his hand and Rev. Aldrich pointed to him.

"I wonder if the Lord could give me the names of them billionaires," Carl said.

"What you want with them names?"

"I just need them," Carl said, smiling down nervously at Gladys. "I just need to see them."

"Sit down, brother," Rev. Aldrich told Carl, who hesitated, frowned and then made a move toward the pulpit but Gladys reached up and pulled him back into his seat.

"I'm worried about the deficit," Scraps said, jumping up so suddenly that he woke up Rick Monte who was there to make his first campaign speech. "Seven generations from now who's gonna be walking in our moccasins? What's it gonna look like out west when the Japanese own all the dude ranches?"

"The Lord hears your fear honkey."

"Yeah? And so?"

"That's it. He hears your fear. Now sit down and shut up. You the kind of honkey who got the fear of a black man siding up to his white wife. Black man taking your job. Black man riding a Mercedes when you is riding a Ford. The Lord give you them fears so you can work through them to the other side."

"Wait a minute, Reverend," Rick Monte said, getting up from his seat slowly, adjusting the lapels of his jacket. "I think what Scraps here is saying is that what we need in this town is less government."

"That's it," Scraps agreed.

"What's your fear, brother?" Rev. Aldrich said.

"I fear Big Brother," Rick called back in stentorian tones. "I fear Big Government running our lives. A man can't ride in a car without the government telling him how to sit in it and what kind of gas to buy. And look at corporations. They gotta worry about some jerk suing them. And doctors. They can't perform their surgery because some jerk is gonna slap them with a malpractice. And do you know how many people in this town would have jobs if there weren't things like minimum wage and child labor bullshit and safety standards and unions and strikes and fair labor bullshit. Government don't know shit about self-interest so it's bound to get in a man's way. That's what I fear."

"It weren't no states that freed the slaves," Rev. Aldrich said. "It was the Federal Government. And it weren't no states that integrated the schools in this country. And it ain't no corporations right now respecting the Bill of Rights. I ain't seen no democratic, egalitarian, human rights corporation yet. So sit down and shut up."

"Hey, I'm running for mayor here," Rick yelled back.

"The Lord's the mayor here, brother," Rev. Aldrich shot back. "Now if there ain't any more fears . . . "

"This isn't a fear, Reverend Aldrich," Kenny said, standing up. "I know this as a fact. There's a one in twenty-nine thousand chance that the plane you're on will crash. But there's a one in two thousand chance that the Earth will be struck by a large meteor that will upset our revolving around the Sun."

"That ain't the way it goes in Revelations," Rev. Aldrich told Kenny.

"There's a better chance that we will collide with something from outer space than there is that an earthquake will send California out to sea."

"Then you better pray brother."

"We'd all go back in bits and pieces into the cosmos," Kenny said, all eyes on him now. "And maybe in a couple of billion years, all the pieces would sort of come together again and there'd be another Big Bang and another Earth would start up all over again, but this time we wouldn't evolve. Insects would evolve."

"Into what?" Rick called out, voice full of ridicule.

"No brains," Kenny said, shaking his head. "This time the big thing would be . . . would be music. Notes flying everywhere."

"Until somebody sprayed the whole planet with DDT," Rick responded.

"That's a sour note, brothers," Rev. Aldrich said, shaking his head. "Leave it to two white members of the congregation to turn this service sour. Um, um. A white man is flush out of fears they making for the rest of us so they got to concoct some cockamamie fear of some meteor crashing into the Earth for themselves. Lord, fool, what you worrying about something you can't do nothing about and you won't know what hit you for?"

Rev. Aldrich turned to Antony who stood in a red silk robe behind him.

"Take us out of here, Antony."

Antony nodded. John Swingle ran a guitar lead.

"Dreams come true . . .

In blue Hawaii . . . "

Looking Into the Abyss of Other People's Lives

"The moment is dangerous. Democracy is not guaranteed
God's protection; systems and nations end."
Ronnie Dugger, "Real Populists Please Stand Up," *The
Nation* August 14, 1995
"Visibility of behavior, not adherence to values."
Herbert J. Gans, *The War Against the Poor*

'Teledemocracy': On the Promise of Interactive Looking and Responding

Do we interact with TV or do we have to wait for Bill Gates and Microsoft to give us that capability? Right now we don't interact with a TV show if we mean by interacting imputing something into the program and having the program respond. For instance, giving a comeback to one of Roseanne's quips, or warning a soap opera innocent of a soap opera villain, or jumping into a Jenny Jones or Ricki Lake show and scrapping with the guests. CD-ROM hookups, the kind Quentin Tarantino and Steven Spielberg are attempting, will be interactive to the extent that each home viewer can make choices as to what direction they wish a plot to take.[1] Plot options, of course, have to be already programmed and therefore constrained by a prior existing script, albeit a postmodern "garden of forking paths" script. And cable TV offers the opportunity for viewers to signal their responses, the sort of electronic polling Perot envisions. We could then have a total rather than representative democracy as each person votes on every issue. Computer empowered plebiscites on every issue. Say goodbye to Congress and to the wealthy powerbrokers who lobby it. They can't go into every home and lobby every family.

The future of this sort of interaction looks bright, at least in regard to politics. Or does it have a dark side? National health care? Up or down based on TV interactive voting response. The

315

majority of Americans have health care while about forty million
don't. Those forty million might be the same minority who
wouldn't also have interactive TV capability. I witnessed this
plebiscite politics recently here in Lansing, Michigan. Upon the
death of Caesar Chavez, a bill was passed by the State legisla-
ture to change the name of a local avenue to Caesar Chavez
Boulevard. After two years, a grass roots movement brought the
issue to a plebiscite vote where the majority voted to change the
name back again. What it came to was that there were more
whites than Mexican-Americans voting. By the middle of the next
century, that vote may be called again and Chavez may get his
street back. There is a dark side to majority rules, a threat to
democracy that is theoretically countered with the establishment
of the Senate, the Supreme Court, the veto power of the
Presidency, the Electoral College, and perhaps the most potentially effective means of bringing the economically disenfranchised to the table—a progressive income tax. But at a time when
minorities are beginning to argue that "the corrosive notion of a
melting pot confuse[s] our thinking about national identity and
destiny," culture wars are fast turning into an old fashioned fight
for power.[2] "If blacks choose to fight for power," Jacob Weisberg
writes in *New York* magazine, "instead of for justice, the result
will be more of what we saw in the November election—white
America's assertion of its own vastly greater power."[3]

    If we were to have a Perot-ian, electronic town meeting and
vote about a steeply graded progressive income tax to bridge the
gap between rich and poor in this country, (the biggest gap
among the industrial nations according to an August 1995
Luxembourg Income Study), one would expect that an electronic
plebiscite would favor such a tax since eighty percent of the population would not be affected, or only positively affected if the
revenue from the top twenty percent could be brought back to
pre-Reagan levels (the rich had been taxed seventy percent but
Reagan worked it down to twenty-eight percent). However, the
very same industry—telecommunications—that would be ar-
ranging for this electronic plebiscite is owned and operated by
those who do not identify with the bottom eighty percent but
rather with the top twenty percent. Before any home viewer can
interact with the media, in other words, the media has already
interacted with the home viewer. At home, on the job, in traffic,
and in their dreams.

We are indeed daily lobbied in our own homes. Can a huge majority then vote against their own self-interests? Yes, if they have already been "acculturated" to believe that any increase in taxes is bad and that the federal government increases taxes in order to pay for its "give-the-money-away" programs—programs reputed to be ineptly administered and always in the red. Yes, if they have already been "acculturated" to believe that any taxation on the top twenty percent will hamper the "entrepreneurial license" needed to play in the global market arena. If we impede our market "heroes" in any way, the bottom eighty percent will suffer with job loss. The goodies can only trickle down if the twenty percent remain at the top and are treated as national assets, in much the same way we cater to our Olympic Dream Team and to our super-athletes in both commercial and college sports. Don't tax the All-American athlete too heavily in your classes. We have been asked to have double standards when it comes to our rich and we have, as a nation, responded with a "yeah, it's okay." We're just being realistic.

Somehow other, dissenting voices, disturbing questions are being drowned out, although we live with the impression that difference and dissent is too audible, too present and the very cause of our vast cultural and economic woes. Through what cultural filter do the following questions reach us:

> [W]ho says we must always begin at the bottom, taking from those who have least? Why heap more punishment on the losers, the tiny majority of lawbreakers who are dumb enough or unlucky enough to get caught and convicted? . . . Why are patently false cures proclaimed and believed with such passionate conviction? . . . Wouldn't it be better to be swept from the earth while trying to construct a just society, rather than holding on, holding on, in a fortress erected to preserve unfair privilege? . . . What indefensible attitudes are we assuming toward the least fortunate in our society? Isn't shame the reason we are desperately intent on concealing from ourselves the simple injustice of our actions?[4]

Because these questions arise in very few minds today and when they do they meet a "passionate conviction" that disposes of them, I don't have much hope for the electronic plebiscite; minds are already being forged into realities by our cable capabilities. I can imagine how powerful the forging machine will be when fiber optic lines greatly expand that capability and take it to an as-yet inconceivable level.

Venture capital isn't going into interactive technology to extend our representative democracy into a true democracy, although that's a good entrepreneurial card to play with the right crowd. The interactive future looks bright from an economic point of view. And money is being put up in direct proportion to how bright that future looks. The choice now that we can make from home is not a political choice but a market choice. Instead of National Health Care we can choose among hemorrhoidal preparations, or fitness salons, or the latest pasta machine, or a time share in Hawaii, or a lease on a Lexus, or a new roof, or an upgrade of our Wordperfect. And so on and on . . . The promise of interactive TV is that with some sort of remote mouse in our hands, or maybe just by the sound of our voice, we can choose to buy just at the moment when what we are watching has sold us. No delay. It's a done deal in a few electronic clicks. Persuasion and impulse interconnect desire and self-actualization. By the middle of the next century the wealthiest one percent of the world's population will be employing the next nineteen percent to either dun or jail the remaining eighty percent.

This sounds like a sci-fi scenario, the kind that Crow and Tom Servo on *Mystery Science Theater 3000* take apart so devastatingly. Can we really expect eighty percent of the population with the power to register their choices through electronic interaction to victimize and villainize themselves? We have to take a look at the way we are presently looking at each other and who we are viewing as the "other" in order to answer this. We have to turn to TV and popular film.

The "Reality Shows"

> "I'll tell you what I'd like to see . . . [I]t would be good to see Ricki Lake out there atoning too—quietly, if it's not too great a stretch of the imagination. Shoving the cameras away, muttering those words we all long to hear: 'Enough!'
> Patricia Williams, "Different Drummer Please, Marchers!"[5]

Cops, Tales of the Highway Patrol, America's Most Wanted, LAPD, Police Story are on TV almost every evening. Most of the commentary about these shows points out their very pro-police nature: the "starring" officer or officers are patient, courteous and competent when presented with the muck and dreck of the criminal underclass. The "Blue Knight" image seems staged because it is; it's staged for TV presentation. Now the tape of the Rodney King beating was not staged for TV but it found its way there nonetheless. Tales of brutal and brutalizing cops, filled maybe with the sort of racism that Lieutenant Mark Fuhrman has been accused of by O. J. Simpson's lawyers, may draw the biggest share of the TV audience but those will have to be staged totally without police department support. Cameramen on *Cops* don't get to ride along if they're not willing to go along. And American viewers have been going along also. But which American viewers and what are they taking away? Who wants to ride down mean streets that we're trying to escape? Americans can now be divided between those who have retreated "into private schools and gated communities," those who yearn to do so, and those that the rest are retreating from.[6] For the Robert Reichian "symbolic analysts" who have been "assortatively mating" along the lines conjectured by Christopher Lasch, there is more self-respect to be gained by not watching the mean streets circus on TV.[7] There is after all, nothing "cultural" about watching the uncultured. For the one percent who own forty-four percent of the national wealth, "mean street" interests have surely been transcended by what must remain for the rest of us the ineffable protocols of plus-$350,000 per annum incomes. And yet, the top twenty percent wealth-wise in this country, a country which right now ranks dead last in terms of economic equality among the major industrialized countries, have an interest in who is watching these shows, that is, the bottom eighty percent.

TV tales of cops on the beat are tales of violence and the violent, specifically about who the violent are and how our society is able to control them, that is, apprehend them and put them away. These people are dangerous; they endanger the lives, well-being and property of others. But "the moment is dangerous" too, now, because it is a fertile violence–producing moment, perhaps a revolutionary moment. In other words, no matter how much we back a discourse of random violence by psychopaths and sociopaths and a discourse of violence caused by a collapse of "family values," the collapse of any semblance of equality and the deteriorating standard of living of some sixty percent of the population will be, if it not already is, *the* catalytic agent brewing violence in our own time.

These "realistic" TV programs of law enforcement down our mean streets bring to those mean streets a message: if you're not too embarrassed to be one of these low-life, law-breakers that appear on these shows, then note how easily they are rendered powerless, how their defenses are easily broken down, how easily their freedom becomes a thing of the past. And to the diminishing middle class that somehow ignores its own economic plight and continues to identify not with the victims but the victimizers, the message is also clear: you are not a part of this despicable underclass, this horde of losers, boozers, druggies, wife and children beaters, penny ante thieves, low intelligence, morally depraved, welfare dependent parasites on the rest of us. Just at the moment when—if this were a Dickens novel—we would be having great expectations that the plight of those going under the wheel of global market, transnational power would be recognized and rectified, we are "costing out" in every imaginable way this underclass. The nineteenth century parallel and Dickens is even more apt than this. Dickens was countering the efforts of a culture to blame the poor for the excesses of its own blind and precipitous industrialization. "Inborn idleness, irresponsibility, uncontrollable brutish instincts, inferior intelligence, childlike dependence, were attributed to the lower classes."[8] The obtuseness and perversity we show in "costing out" this visible underclass will not stop the gradual descent of others to this level. At the millennium's very beginning, the ranks of those eligible for appearance on *Cops* will have grown considerably: "[S]ince 1973, the number of American children living in poverty has increased fifty percent, so that twenty-two percent now grow up poor, and the number keeps increasing."[9]

I have never seen a "symbolic analyst" treated to a *Cops* show treatment; never a sign of affluence, of high education, of Pat Robertson demeanor, of market player "toughness." The poor are the target. "Money buys privacy and insulation from the sharp eyes of social workers, welfare administrators, and the police."[10] The top twenty percent don't need the money, so they don't turn criminal. Or maybe if they do earn, invest and represent their wealth in illegal as well as legal ways, the cops on this show just don't know how to pick them up. They can't see the crime because it's not a crime on the streets. Maybe it's a boardroom crime, but cops don't go into boardrooms. Maybe what we need is *Tales of* the *Security Exchange Commission* or *Tales of the Justice Department*, shows which focus on the apprehension and putting away of wealthy criminals. And since corporations have been declared "persons" by an 1886 Supreme Court decision, why don't we have cops going after corporations on TV? I would think that Ralph Nader's various litigations would produce interesting TV fare. Cameras could be taken not down mean streets but down elegant streets; cops could drive up to private gatekeepers, show their badges and drive on through. But more importantly, TV cameras wouldn't just be ushered around the homes of the rich and famous so that we could all ogle their toys. Instead they'd follow the rich at play and in the boardroom the way they follow the denizens of the mean streets as if those people lived under glass. Let's see if those whose behavior is now invisible to us signify adherence to William Bennett-sized moral virtues, or whether big gates and gatekeepers are just hiding nasty behavior from us. Let's look into the abyss of wealthy lives for a season or two on prime time so-called documentary verite' TV.

It is ironic that at the same time that we are experiencing a "rising animosity toward the federal government" and its supposed intrusion into the "private sector" and our private lives, we are engaging, via the TV, in a voyeurism of other people's lives.[11] And that audience of voyeurs has led to the commodification of their own private lives. All of this is merely the residue of megacompanies seeking to get government out of their lives. The trick is to entice the majority of the population into dismantling the private sector's only potential chastiser and regulator, the federal government. So joining the "Contract with America" crowd in dispersing governmental power to local and therefore manageable levels is the eighty percent of the population heading for the skids as "stateless" corporations sell them out on the global exchange.[12]

We get into other people's lives these days purely to write them off as deserving their fate at the hands of the "stateless" corporate power structure. We invade their privacy to reassure ourselves that we are not what we are beholding. It is almost an impossibility in this country to turn the camera around and focus it on those who directly benefit from the vilification of the underclass and who hold their own privacy as sacred. Michael Moore's *TV Nation* led the way here but its future is always hanging by a thread. Why?[13] I think because his show reeks of a political agenda (is he one of those Liberals! or worse yet, a Socialist!) while shows like *Cops* seems apolitical, except for the understandable desire to show cops in the best light. But more significantly Moore's TV just can't go where it has to go. There are Private Property—No Trespassing signs stopping him. On the other hand, our mean streets are open streets. No one poor can afford a private life. Their lives make up a cop's day; they are owned by the bureaucracy of surveillance and control. The lives of the rich and famous are never apprehensible nor guilty until proven innocent in this way. We are clearly not set up to televise those who own the cameras; only the poor now become objects of the TV's gaze into "reality."

Clockers

> "Tender and generous, and surprisingly nonviolent given the subject, it's clearly meant to help real people through hard places. How many movies can you say that about?"
> Georgia Brown, "Clocking In," *Village Voice,* Sept. 19, 1995
>
> "[T]he hood movie to end all hood movies."
> Amy Taubin, "Clocking In"
>
> "With the Fuhrman tapes still ringing in our skulls, there's no better moment to lure us into the theatre and give us two hours of prejudice on parade and truth under siege."
> Anthony Lane, "Cracking Up," *New Yorker* September 18, 1995

Mark Fuhrman's racist vituperations must be ringing so loudly in people's ears that they can't hear the film, in this case *Clockers*. Take for example the grand canyon between views regarding Rocco Klein, the cop who won't believe one black man's confession and instead goes after the confessor's brother, a drug dealer named Strike. Anthony Lane, writing in the *New Yorker,* refers to Klein, played by Harvey Keitel, as "a white cop who doesn't care if he leads blacks into trouble or pain, and looks away when they get there." Keitel "doesn't blink at the notion of playing a bastard." Georgia Brown refers to Keitel as "playing a very, very good lieutenant." And Amy Taubin clocks in right in the middle: "Rocco, who's just your average racist—nowhere near the Mark Fuhrman league—is obsessed with proving the truth of his master narrative."

Bastard? Very, very good lieutenant? Your average racist? The inconsistency could be just your usual run of different takes.

Or, it could be an ambiguity that Keitel develops in his portrayal. Or, it could be an ambiguity and undecidableness that drives the film as a whole. Spike Lee might be doing what producer Martin Scorsese did in his version of *Cape Fear*—blur the categories of good and evil, show us how our easy determinations crisscross in a world that always resists the determinate ways we try to mark it. And there is indeed a dialogical narrative style here that Lee adopts, as he did most dramatically in *Do The Right Thing*. No one is ever in total and pure possession of the right thing, or the wrong thing. Morals are muddied, motivations can be narrated from all sides of the street. The camera has to circle and circle swiftly so as not to get drawn into a point of view from any one direction. There is a linear ontology that Lee tries to displace. But for all that, *Clockers* isn't the peak from which the postmodern moral hybridity—coming out of a reality hybridity—can be observed and clocked. The center in this film, unfortunately, is not everywhere but in one place—Ronnie "Strike" Dunham. The fact that he is purely a reactive, much put upon, watchfully defensive center does not exactly decenter him. He is the subject of a documentary-like focus and therefore our gaze is upon him from the outside. What is the point of view that Lee creates for us? Who is doing the looking here and who are the others? And what are the features of their abyss? In spite of the dialogic narration and the circling motion of the camera, this is a fabricated world, a world made by Lee for a particular kind of viewer about a particular kind of life.

We never see Strike strike anyone and it turns out in the end that the murder of Daryl Adams was done by his brother, Victor. But Strike is struck by every other character in the film. Rodney, his drug dealing mentor, knocks him about and shoves a gun muzzle into this mouth. Strike's mother smacks him hard and young Tyrone's mother verbally and physically assails him right on his own turf. The project cop threatens to kill him if he doesn't stop trying to recruit young Tyrone into the drug business. And Rocco Klein harasses him throughout the entire movie, convinced that he murdered Daryl Adams. It's not that Rocco cares who murdered Adams—another stain on the sidewalk is Rocco's partner's comment. What Rocco cares about is the murder making sense to him—it has to fit the way his experience tells him it should fit. It doesn't make a difference that someone has confessed to the murder, namely, Strike's brother Victor. Victor doesn't add up to being a murderer in Rocco's mind. But Strike does.

Strike fulfills the requirements of the law and order film that runs in Rocco's mind. If you doubt that, run a camera on Strike and see how he lives. Which is what Lee does. So we have an answer to the question within whose gaze is this film constructed? Within the gaze of those who know that there are reprobate, drug dealing young blacks and also hardworking, conscientious blacks. And why do we care about sorting out the good from the bad? Because we have to confirm our already existing notion of an underclass and overclass order of things. We can't just arrest any young black as if all young blacks are guilty. Lee wants us to make distinctions because then young blacks can be held to those distinctions. They won't be in a society that blankets them all as innately depraved. In a society alert to the moral worth of its young blacks, there is ample reason for the same young blacks to distinguish themselves morally. To be a victim is to be a Jew in Hitler's Germany where regardless of whether you are a good Jew or a thieving Jew, a Jew of conscience or a Jew of no conscience, you will indiscriminately go to the ovens. There are no victims then in the black world Lee construes. The choice to be a man of conscience or not is a real choice, a choice that has been held out to Victor and his brother, Strike. While Strike has decided to go for the easy money and feed off the addictions of his own people, Victor has decided to work two jobs and take care of his common law wife and their two kids. Lee wants to concoct that order of things, an order not of victim but of underclass, existential hero— to choose to do good in the face not only of mortality but of life in the mean streets of the Brooklyn projects. Thus, Rocco Klein's mission to get the right killer fits in with Lee's mission; they both want to preserve an order of moral distinctions.

Lee and Rocco split up though in regard to the depth of the distinctions they are willing to make. Rocco is a moral dualist; Lee is a moral hybridist. Rocco doesn't view all young blacks as equally guilty—in regard to the moral categories he is color blind. You might say he is a good lieutenant in the sense that solving a murder correctly has nothing to do with race. Getting the right murderer matters, distinguishing good from evil matters. Nonetheless, good and evil are compartmentalized in Rocco's mind, with clear, clean boundaries. They don't run into each other or interpenetrate. You don't ever wind up with a fellow who has hybridized the moral categories. Lee sets up the cameras for these folks, hoping to bring them into a hybridized moral universe. He begins with their point of view and then lateralizes it, stretches it outward and then around until boundaries cross. At the same time, the cameras are set up within the point of view of young blacks who believe they are with Strike in some sort of circle of hell they cannot get out of and this circle is not in the moral universe at all. They are lost in darkness, victims of a white racist order of things that holds goodness and conscience as "Whites Only" possessions. Lee wants to bring them to a beginning level of moral distinction, Rocco's level. What they do can transcend what is being done to them. What they do shapes who and what they become as human beings. They can become moral agents of change, self-conversion and transmutation.

Which view is politically more potent? The conversion of blanket racists to a moral dualism? The conversion of a moral dualist to a moral hybridist? The conversion of the morally self-forsaken to a moral universe which offers hope and self-determination? Within the cultural gaze of the present, these are all features of a visionary politics, the hybridist one smacking of a postmodern moral awareness that itself, if clearly understood by Lee's viewers, would fit nowhere but in the abyss they imagine. Blanket racists do not have to give up their own indiscriminating, racist point of view in order to acknowledge Rocco's mission for the truth. In their view what it comes down to is not conscionable blacks and unconscionable ones but some blacks are more unconscionable than others. After all, for all his goodness, Victor does turn out to be the shooter.

And what of the conversion of young blacks from a victim mode of behavior, (one in which developing a moral conscience doesn't matter), to a moral order, (one in which they can choose to do the right thing?) They don't have to stay in the hood and sell drugs or take drugs. They can do what the kids in *Dangerous Minds* do and get on a bus and go to school. And when they get to that school, maybe they'll meet the lovely Michelle Pfeiffer who cares enough about their lives to visit them there and then walk with them to a new place, a graduating place.

Visionary politics and visions construct reality in a postmodern world. We are, however, living within the construction of a "restore the dream" conservative majority who have already entered Spike Lee's film with the same kind of documentary running in their minds. Except morals don't hybridize, goodness doesn't bleed into badness, and vice versa, the moral categories are not relative constructions, and extreme bad behavior, say, murder, can and should only have an expeditious capitol punishment waiting for it. The only way Lee could have perforated these expectations was by breaking the circle around Strike and striking outward into the culture of moral restoration which he is, after all, in 1995 responding to. He is saying in short, look closely at the black underclass; see distinctions, make distinctions and maintain distinctions, and do so always in a nondualistic but pluralizing way. The abyss is not the neighborhood of the poor, nor are the poor an abysmal congregation. We are however living in a global culture that is economically dualistic and that dualism—rich and poor—is the engine that runs our moral dualism. A culture that increasingly pays no attention to any values but those of wealth and power finds itself unable to attend to anyone, most especially the underclass, in any way other than a way that denies them identity and sets them on a course of identity through cash profits.

By focusing on the black underclass precisely in the way that the dream restorers would, minus the postmodernizing of moral categories, Lee has confirmed the scenes from the abyss they already carry in their heads. That abyss has to be overwritten by a dream in which peace and harmony, stability of order, personal and possession safety are restored to those who have lost it. If that isn't done by century's end, they just might wind up losing their wealth and power. The clock is certainly running . . .

Dangerous Minds

> "A mind is a dangerous thing."
>
> Vice President Dan Quayle, 1990
>
> "He came in without knocking so I refused to see him. They have to learn the rules of the real world. In the real world, we knock before entering an office."
>
> High School Principal in *Dangerous Minds*

"We don't want to continue rewarding bad behavior" expresses the conservative rationale behind current welfare reform. The film the welfare reformists, both conservatives and redeemed newly conservatized liberals, have in mind has a large cast, most of whom we can see in real films like *Clockers* and *Dangerous Minds.* In those films the underclass are selling and taking drugs, killing each other, causing havoc in the public schools, and bitching about their victimization. Since welfare reform is the focus then the plot in the welfare reformers' minds duly focuses on promiscuous, unwed teenagers having baby after baby, getting money from the federal government for doing so, and lying about jobless, using their food stamps to buy everything but food, and generally laughing at the hardworking middle class. In short, they're indulging in bad behavior. And this bad behavior has been fostered by the welfare enthusiasts of the liberal '60s.

When education reform has its turn center stage, a film like *Dangerous Minds* will run its images on every reformer's mind. And the efforts of one teacher, Mrs. Johnson played by Michelle Pfeiffer, to reach these hardcases will, I'm afraid, add up to nothing more than a Hollywoodized, romanticized ending. What doesn't romanticize so easily is the scene she faces when she first walks into that classroom. The regular teacher has had a nervous breakdown and three subsequent replacements have all quit. It will be hard for the Babyboomers now in their majority to see anything more than a scene from the abyss in that classroom. We were educated in the aura of Sputnik, the fear of the Russians getting into space before us, getting technologically ahead of us. Our classrooms were mostly filled with white faces and minds sold on becoming doctors, lawyers and management consultants. Latinos were fewer, blacks weren't being bused, and our cultural mindset could conceive of a "melting pot" synthesis of second and third generation European immigrants but not an in-your-face multiculturalism. Difference was still a bad word; remediation was always called for. My extended family spoke Sicilian which was supposed to be some sort of bastardized, criminalized slang for proper Italian; we went into remediation. I took the longest road—the most deeply repentant, I suppose— and didn't stop until I had a doctorate in the English language. I knew how to treat my teachers and my principals with respect. I always knocked in English.

The principal of Mrs. J's school is a Dickensian Grandgrind type—all protocols and procedures and no humane grasp of what he's in charge of; all civilized and formally educated veneer and no heart, no sensitivity, no awareness except for the legislated order of things. This principal was in the same crowd that thought the Emperor had clothes on, and Mrs. J's the kid who knows the Emperor's naked. The rules don't clothe reality, they don't dress it up or enhance it. The order of things can only pretend to be reality; it marches on in this charade until someone yells out it's naked, it's empty, it's nothing, it's the gossamer of our own fancies.

One of the threads of order that make up this principal's reality weave has to do with knocking before you enter. Not knocking is bad behavior. Emilio Ramirez, a student whom Mrs. J has at long last reached and hopes to save with the help of the principal, is killed on the streets because the principal wouldn't talk to him. And he wouldn't talk to him and hear Emilio's need because Emilio had come into his office without knocking. In the real world, such bad behavior must be punished. Perhaps before Emilio died he learned that lesson about knocking at office doors of principals. I cannot but think that our present welfare reform will teach lessons of this stripe. The order of things will pass its legacy on to the recalcitrant underclass. But we won't save them. And in not saving them, we won't save ourselves.

Michelle Pfeiffer is our eyes in this film. She's physically privileged in our culture: blonde, blue eyed, finely chiselled features, slim body and casual designer clothes to cover it. She's chased out of the class at the first meeting. She doesn't meet the test and she doesn't even know she's taking one or what motivates their testing of her. And since those who are "restoring the dream" at this moment are cornered in her perceptual corner, they don't see anything she doesn't see. They start out in the same cultural film she's in. And, as I say, *Dangerous Minds* doesn't upset that bias in any way that will alter the legislative dimensions of the prevailing "dream restoration" project. What we have are repeated scenes of classroom havoc, educational success tied to drug interpretations of Bob Dylan's lyrics, a success ratio of one academically-suited person—Calley—to a class of forty or so, a recently divorced woman as a teacher who has no personal life at the moment and who becomes an emotional co-dependent of her students, numerous incidents in which these underclass youth show a greater awareness of the real circumstances they are in than the teacher does, and a clear separation of anything that goes on in the classroom from what continues to go on in the violent, underclass "mean streets."

No societal redemption happens here; what happens is that a woman in a post-divorce crisis learns how to become Mother Theresa. In the film *Nell*, Liam Neeson wants to do something that has nothing to do with self-interest for the poor, feral Nell but he is told that even Mother Theresa's altruism is motivated by self-interest. The good Mother can only think well of herself when she is acting like a saint, when she is self-sacrificing. The more she sacrifices herself for others, the richer she becomes. At base, the good Mother is an acquisitive, successful entrepreneur. Michelle Pfeiffer's sacrifice of her own personal life—which at the moment is very slim as she reports to her colleague and friend, George Szunda—becomes the means by which she hooks up with her unruly students. She's willing to give of herself in a personal way, outside the classroom, beyond the traditional "I'm here because I'm paid" connection. It's what wins Emilio to her side and winning Emilio over is the way, Pfeiffer is told by her one academically gifted student, to win the class over. Emilio finds out that she's visited the homes of two of her Chicano students and spoken highly of them to their parents. Emilio nods and tells her "That's cool." Previously he has refused to enter a classroom discussion because the matter is "personal." It's about the meaning of some Dylan lyrics but to Emilio it's about life, about him, about what he feels as well as thinks. And at that moment Pfeiffer is shut out because she's from another world, a world of unconcern, a world of cold protocols, of cash nexus between people. She doesn't care about them and therefore he won't care about what she cares about. He won't show her how he cares because she doesn't deserve to see.

After having heard the principal demand that Pfeiffer follow the curriculum and the lesson plans as laid out—detour her journey toward caring and establishing a link with these students that transcends protocols—we know the world of education Emilio and the others have been experiencing. They have reason to protect what Hawthorne loved to call the privacy and sanctity of the human heart. It's all they have, and although it may be filled with a code of survival on the streets that is different than that code of survival touted by Secretary of Labor Robert Reich, it shapes a personal life-world that, like all such, is protected from violation. Raoul patiently explains this to Pfeiffer. At that moment, she begins to understand that to touch the mind, she has to touch the heart first. And the heart's knowledge is both private and public, a privatization of subcultural values and meanings. Her attention moves then from the outside—never as far on the outside as the Protocol Principal—to the inside and then to the imbrication of inside and outside. What remains impossible for her singlehandedly to change, however, is the

330 Speeding to the Millennium

subcultural, marginalized outside into a presently privileged "restoring the dream" culture.

For the "restoring the dream" legislators her efforts all fall back into a purely personal redemption—hers and not the students nor the society's. Although she tells Raoul that he has been doing college level work in his poetry interpretation, we have not seen anything that personnel interviewers of multinational corporations might cherish. Had she been able to make her students computer literate, or get them into differential calculus, basic accounting procedures, boolean logic, effective business communication, oral presentation skills, management techniques and so on, then her lesson plan could be franchised throughout our troubled public education system. But interpretation of poetry seems to be just that sort of fiscal waste of time in such an underclass classroom that fills the mental screen of our dream restorers. And this disdainful view of what Pfeiffer thinks the proper education focus should be—namely poetry interpretation—is put in the mouth of an aged black woman. "My grandsons don't have time to be reading poetry; they've got bills to pay." Pfeiffer has no response; she's crushed. She walks away and the old lady, filled with the wisdom that underclass life has given her and intent on seeing her grandsons survive in the world as she knows it, sits down and gazes back at Pfeiffer. We know who has the dominant gaze here; we know who has mouthed the words of truth. Of course, they're words flying after that corner of reality that the old lady has spent her whole life trying to hook up with. It's after all her interpretation of things, and the things she has marked in her life are only the byproducts of more powerful, residing interpretations. For instance, a "restoring the dream" interpretation of America will leave her grandsons with an "elephant-is-like-a-snake reality"—like the blind man holding the tail of an elephant, her grandsons will not only mistake the elephant for a snake but will be left with a snake size portion of the world while the dream restorers will be riding the whole elephant. At any rate, it all comes down to reality interpretation and representation, which is what Pfeiffer has been trying to teach her students. She's not as off the mark then as the surface oriented, protocol observers would contend.

Her educational success formula is, however, way off the mark that has been presently drawn in the shifting sands of reality by the "dream restorers". This is what I mean: she discovers that the path to these students's minds is through a personal involvement. She has to get way beyond the "If you don't knock first, I can't let you in or talk to you" mentality. But she also has to get beyond the "self-interest is the foundation for success" mentality. Since, however, this mentality keys the dominant culture (in the form of self-interest leading to competitiveness leading to prosperity leading to a wealthy society leading to jobs and prosperity for all) she is advocating not only a way of attending to the world that is not the dominant society's, but one which misleads these underclass kids. She becomes a model of self-sacrifice, of ignoring time and money and involvement in the lives of others. Mutual aid rather than Darwinian survival of the fittest is her message. And in showing a concern for them on a personal, emotional level, she automatically elevates their feelings, what their hearts know, to a significant level. Inner lives that have been connected to moral depravity and racial inferiority, innate dispositions toward laziness and violence, drug and sex addiction and so on, are reckoned with as only that to those observers who have already denied the importance of anything but the outward trappings of wealth and power. Pfeiffer learns that you can't deal with these kids via the "cash nexus" or the global market metanarrative of self-interest. For her, they matter more than the bottom line at a time when our dream restorers want to re-assert the priorities of the bottom line in a grossly unequal battle with rebel hearts and dangerous minds.

"Observing the Sins of Others: *Seven*"

Just Cause is no more and no less than a portrayal of the underclass as murderous psychopaths, monsters from the abyss, and as a film it has the opportunity to plot its portrayal in a way that the TV cop shows cannot. And plot it does, inveigling itself into a number of current controversies. The film is released just at the moment when the Supreme Court has declared that the federal government should get out of the quota business. Affirmative Action is discriminatory and violates the rule of equality under the law. A young black who has been to Harvard is back home in the south and accused of rape and murder. Education, it turns out, is just a veneer; he's a psychopath. What's going on with all our psychopaths? Ed Harris, who plays another version of an incarcerated Hannibal Lector, says its not a bad childhood or twisted desires that makes him a psychopath. He enjoys it.

In a far more interesting film, *Seven*, Morgan Freeman and Brad Pitt get to arguing over the nature of evil over a few beers. Morgan is the burnt out detective a week away from retirement. He's seen enough mayhem. Apathy, he tells Pitt, (the young man hoping to make a difference), is what is the root of the problem. People not giving a shit has nothing to do with this, Pitt replies. This guy is a psychopath. You can't generalize from the behavior of a psychopath to the general health or ill health of the whole society. Psychopaths don't come out of the cultural flux, they're from Mars. They're genetically crosswired. It wouldn't matter if they were living in Utopia, they'd still go out and do their psychopathic thing.

Kevin Spacey plays the same sort of high IQ psychopath that he played in *The Usual Suspects*, only this time the psychopathic mind's criminal behavior is grounded in religious belief. Spacey wants to bring society to repentance by showing it the bodies of the sinners, from the gluttonous to the wrathful—the seven deadly sins. Is his fixation on sin the product of his derangement, or has the presence of sin fuelled the derangement? Is he like Ed Harris in that he just enjoys what he's doing, in spite of why he says he's doing it? Or, is he just much further along that continuum toward despair than Morgan Freeman, who is about half way down, and Brad Pitt, who has moved from the starting line and has wound up, at film's end, past Freeman? Spacey plots Pitt into his madness in order to bring the world his last two examples: envy and wrath. The envy is Spacey's. He has envied Pitt his normal life—Tracey, (Pitt's wife), with a child on the way and all the love that that entails. But most especially, he envies Pitt his lack of despair, his youthful hope and optimism, his insistence that the world can be made better, that people do care and can be made to care, that sin is not a virus that has invaded the souls of everyone but some sort of genetic, chemical screw up that touches one out of a great many. And Spacey can't have this; he's lost in his drama of revelation through murderous example.

Out on a lonesome highway in the penultimate scene, Pitt receives a package from Spacey: Tracey's head. Consumed by wrath, Pitt shoots Spacey over and over again. The last sin makes the headlines. When asked where he's going in the last scene, Freeman says "I'll be around." He had been ready to retreat to a remote cabin away from this world of apathy but now it seems he's taken a step backward. He's moved in the end closer to where Pitt was at the beginning. He has enough hope now to want to be around. His caring might make a difference. At that moment we see Pitt in the back seat of a squad car. He's one of the victims; one of the gruesome dead bodies but he's alive, physically unhurt. Spacey tortured the gluttonous man for twelve hours; the greedy man for a weekend, the slothful man for twelve months. And Pitt for his whole life. When you become a victim yourself in a psychopath's scenario, the question of root causes, of hope and despair, of the possible effects of caring on the total state of the world—all this becomes inconsequential. It's not even an argument to pursue over beers in a local pub. Conversation and debate are all over.

The film, at any point, winds back to Spacey's mental screenplay. We realize at the end that Spacey has spared Pitt's life earlier in the film because he already knew what part Pitt was to play. He already knew that this was a young man whose anger could be aroused, suddenly and with unthinking results. Here was a young man who could show such quick, targeted wrath that he no longer cared about consequences. Does that volatility come out of a clear sense of offense, of evil, and is his wrath, then, like the wrath of Jesus in the temple among the moneychangers? Or, is such wrath always a breakdown in our caring for each other, a moment when hatred wipes out love, a moment when we fail to see into the life of another and take account of what motivates them. What would be the moment when Spacey realized this about Pitt? When Pitt and Freeman scour Spacey's apartment for clues, they find a photo that had been taken of Pitt at the moment he was kicking the photographer down the stairs. We had our hands on him, Pitt moans. Spacey, pretending to be a newspaper photographer, had shown up at a crime scene to take pictures and Pitt, in an explosive rage, had told him to get away. How do photographers get here so fast? Pitt asks Freeman who tells him that the photographer probably paid some policeman very well for the information. He was just doing his job and one of us was benefitting from it. Pitt then apologizes; he didn't know. He didn't stop to think about the photographer's situation, his mission, his work and his life. Caring, it seems, is not easy.

And yet in Freeman's view, *not* caring has put the world in the sorry shape it's in. Not caring breeds monsters, like Spacey. At the very beginning of the film, when Freeman's boss tries to rouse Freeman out of his despairing funk, Freeman tells him a little story. On his way to work that morning, he had come upon a crime scene. A man had been robbed, but the robber hadn't settled for just taking the victim's wallet. He had poked both the man's eyes out. That action represented, to Freeman, a level of human disconnectedness that went way beyond his rational understanding of thievery. There was no need to blind the man, except if the thief feared being identified at some time in a line-up. Rather than face that possibility, the thief blinded his victim. He took his wallet and his sight. That end justified those means, but Freeman could recall a world in which that end would not have justified those means. Caring, therefore, is on a continuum from brotherly and sisterly concern to total unconcern. Midway most of us, Freeman argues, give up caring what happens to anyone else. And it is that climate in which total unconcern, absolute disconnect, becomes possible. There must be no link between fellow human beings during those moments when Spacey is force feeding the glutton, or cutting off the nose of the vain woman, or forcing the greedy lawyer to cut out his own pound of flesh.

If the film's viewer can disconnect these horrors from ourselves and our culture, see Spacey the way Pitt does right up until the end—as an anomalous freak and psychopath—then our culture's reduction of the caring nexus to the cash nexus remains out of the picture. It has nothing to do with it. What we're looking at is a psychopath who should have been put away a long time ago—a psychopath that is paradoxically both a product of our soft-on-crime posture in the liberal years and a genetic flaw, a chemical imbalance that has no cultural hook-up. If, however, we heed Morgan Freeman's connection; namely, that a spirit of apathy we all share generates a fundamental disconnect between us which ultimately leads to a devaluing and dehumanizing of individual life and society itself, then we're not at a distance watching some psychopath's abysmal life and adventures. Rather, we are each creating the abyss simply by knowing the world in an uncaring, dehumanizing way.

The film has us strung out between looking into the abyss of pure, psychopathic Otherness, the abyss of other people's lives who are clearly *not us*, and an abyss which has something to do with our own insensibility, our own unconcern for others, our own inertness in the face of other people's lives. But since popular film trades in setting up reality in a way in which we are not ontologically unsettled or threatened, the abyss that we see must remain distanced. We are dominating this abyss with a gaze that takes it all in, allocates sympathy and compassion where it is deserved, distinguishes in a clear way guilt from innocence, conscionable actions from unconscionable ones and so on. The film becomes another occasion to view the underclass within the connection our society is intent on privileging: these people lead abysmal lives because they've chosen depravity of various kinds as their way of life. And so on.

The camera is always working its way into dark recesses of the abyss; no apartment we enter seems to have electricity. Flashlight beams perforate shadowy rooms and the camera is always in search of its object, never quite bringing it into focus. It circles the body of the obese man whose face lies in a bowl of spaghetti. The camera pans down to his trunk-like legs and the bloated shackled feet. It's a freak show. Finally we get to see the bloated colossus of dead flesh on the autopsy table. How could a human being let himself get into such a state? *We* could never sink so low, so forget our own humanity, discard all our values and replace them with rapacious appetite. In turn, the camera visits, in the same way, the man of sloth tied for one year to his bed. This is beyond white trash; these are alien creatures. What happens to them is what they deserve; there seem to be so many now that are falling below the status of human. And once they fall below the level of our gaze, they fall out of existence. They fall outside the pale of legislative concern, taxpayer consideration. What a society that seeks to restore its dream must do is first get rid of its nightmares, accelerate the extinction process of those who have absolutely no identity nor hope of identity in a globalized market reality.

What about the greedy lawyer who is forced to cut off his own pound of flesh and thereby over the weekend bleeds to death? And the vain woman who commits suicide rather than accept the loss of her beauty? Do these not come dangerously close to a viewer trying to separate his or her own integrity from the abysmal lives in this film? The lawyer was wealthy because he was successful and he was successful because he won cases and he won cases because he went into the competitive arena and came out a winner. Is this not the preferred route to wealth and success in our own society? And the woman of beauty—is she wrong to think that her life is over when our whole society markets physical appearance as the *summum bonum* of human existence? Consumers consume for self-aggrandizement, for an enhancement of the material existence of their lives but that materiality begins with their own flesh. We need the wealth in order to buy the products that tend to our fleshly image. Psychology and ontology unite under the umbrella of cosmetic being. The death of this vain woman, therefore, cuts right to the heart of that self-interest that propels our economic existence. Self-interest is instantly devalued as selfishness, as self-indulgence. The self-absorbed are besotted, far from love of others and concern for others. Our disinterest in the lives of others branches out from our own self-devotion.

This portrait of the abyss then has us as both distanced observers, superior to what we behold, and has us *in* the portrait, beholding what we have already become.

Notes

1. Kathleen Murphy, "Rebooting the Bard: Hi-Tech Storytelling," *Film Comment* July 1995, p. 42.

2. John Edgar Wideman, "Doing Time, Marking Race," *The Nation* October 30, 1995, p. 505.

3. Jacob Weisberg, "The Truth Card," *New York* October 16, 1995, p. 104.

4. Wideman, "Doing Time," p. 504.

5. *The Nation* October 30, 1995, 494

6. Eric Foner, "The Great Divide," *The Nation* October 30, 1995, p. 488.

7. Christopher Lasch, *The Revolt of the Elites* London: W. W. Norton, 1995.

8. Wideman, "Doing Time," p. 505.

9. Richard J Barnet, "Lords of the Global Economy," *The Nation* December 19, 1994, p. 754.

10. Thomas J Sugrue, "Poor Vision," *Tikkun* v. 10, #5, p. 88.

11. James Ridgeway and Jeffrey St Clair, "This Land is Our Land," *Village Voice*, June 20, 1995, p. 16.

12. See Richard J Barnet, "Lords of the Global Economy," *The Nation*, December 19, 1994, p. 754.

13. See Chip Rowe, "A Funny, Subversive '60 Minutes,'" *American Journalism Review* July/August 1995

Antediluvian Bog

August 3rd
Woods behind County Mental

"Freddie, Freddie, my man!" Kenny called out, turning his new Trekkie Mountain Bike toward a tall, thin man in shorts getting out of his car in front of Morio Saito's house.

Morio Saito came out of his front door and headed toward Freddie.

"You gonna architect the Morio's house, Freddie my man?" Kenny said.

"Sun room," Freddie said as Kenny looked behind and yelled for Pancakes to get to the side of the road.

"You want a picture of Patti and me?" Pancakes said, stopping short in front of Saito and stopping his progress.

"Hey, that'll give the house a look," Kenny said as he leaned back on his bike and studied the front of Morio's house. "But it's gotta fit the historical pattern. This whole section from Woldrich to Sunrise is an official historical district."

"How much is this?" Morio asked Pancakes as he looked at the snapshot of Pancakes holding her doll Patti.

"It's for free," Pancakes said brightly and biked off. Morio nodded and put the photo in his shirt pocket.

"Hey, Morio," Kenny said as Morio walked up to them, "You need a sun room with historical attitude. I mean, like, did they have sunrooms back then?"

"Morio wants something in the back that's a cross between a greenhouse, a sauna, a game room and a veranda," Freddie said.

"Exactly so," Morio replied, nodding.

"I bet they take the sun differently in Japan," Kenny said. "I mean more of a play of light and shadow. More of a yin yang thing."

"I think I can get approval from the town council on this," Freddie said. "History is full of exceptions. And we're adding on in the back anyway."

"It's not like you're gonna do a pagoda front porch," Kenny added, nodding. "I mean what the hell is so sacred about this town's past that we can't change the look. I mean if they did that in the past we'd still be living in caves or tepees. It's goofy."

"Like Woad," Freddie the architect said. "He's taking a bunch of town survivalists out this weekend. The woods behind the County Mental Facility."

"Yeah, I told him I'd go," Kenny said.

"Yeah, me too," Freddie said, shaking his head and smiling.

"He's loaded with poison ivy these days," Kenny said. "I mean what can you learn about the outdoors from a guy slathered in poison ivy?"

"I am able to identify most North American woodland flora and fauna," Morio told them soberly.

"That's how come you became a citizen," Kenny said.

"I want to bike down the hill," Pancakes whined.

"I gotta split. Catch you guys later," Kenny said and biked off with Pancakes following him on a pink bicycle that was a bit too small for her.

Late Friday afternoon, Michael Woad got out of his pick-up and counted and classified the cars already parked at the back of the County Mental Facility. There were old town unemployed and newcomers and those who lived off the newcomers.

When he got all his survivalists gathered around him he told them:

"We'll be out for three days. We pack no food and one canteen of water each. No tents or sleeping bags. We can assume we each got left with a pocketknife. Otherwise nothing but the clothes on our backs. So that means you got five minutes to hoist all that top of the line gear back in your cars."

"What if it rains?" Sally Simmons asked.

"There's ways of capturing the rainwater," Woad told her.

"She means what does she do if she gets her new hairdo wet," Faye Fata, longtime food attendant at the County Mental Facility, said.

"I'm gonna be heading across that field in five minutes," Woad announced.

"Do you know what I think?" Peaches said an hour later when they stopped for their first rest. "It's hot; the mosquitoes are eating us alive; my feet are already killing me, I'm hungry; this water needs some ice cubes. I mean what are we doing in here following Woadie? I mean the guy sleeps in trees and hasn't had a regular job in ages."

"You know, Peaches, I'm willing to give Woadie a chance," Jake Wilcox, the ex-sheriff said.

"Out here is Michael's domain of expertise," Beth Swingle, the mayor, said as she raised her canteen to her lips. "He's the mayor of the woodlands."

"Give the man a chance, Peaches," Jake said, still pissed at Peaches because he had heard that she had voted for his opponent.

"Look, Jake, don't be hustling your balls and be talking to me," Peaches snapped. And then turning to the mayor:

"And what's yours Beth? I mean domain of expertise?"

"Don't fall apart, Peaches," the mayor replied, closing her eyes. "The whole idea of survival is not to fall apart."

"I'll let you do it to the town," Peaches snapped back. "Let it fall apart."

"How about peace in the valley, ladies," Walt Pinsky said, rubbing the sweat from his brow with a large neckerchief.

"Oh, there'll be peace in the valley some day," Lucy Powell sang out. "Some day. No more problems, no more sorrow. Da da da. DaDadAda."

"I'll bet you ain't got woods like these in Japan," Jake said to Morio Saito who was applying some OFF to his legs.

Morio looked around and up and then down and then back at Jake.

"We have mountains with snow."

"No shit," Jake said.

"You know why the Japanese can survive?" Walt Pinsky said. "It's because they're all alike. It makes things easier."

"Hey, where's Woad?" Tony Pinsky said as he came up to them with a roll of toilet paper in his hands.

"He thinks he heard something back in there," Lucy Powell said. "Anybody for a Prozac?"

"Didn't you know Woad had Indian blood?" Peaches said. "He hears things we can't hear. And you can't hear him when he's rifling your garbage in the middle of the night."

Then she looked at Lucy who was swallowing back a Prozac with a hit of water from her canteen.

"I thought this was drug free survival?"

"He shouldn't gone back in there by himself," Jake said, standing up and jacking up his pants. "There was a couple a three weird crimes perpetrated around here years ago. Never been cleared up. I'd better go look see."

"Yeah, you do that Jake," Peaches said as Jake disappeared in the surrounding thicket. "You gotta get lost to find yourself. So get lost."

"You know what I would do if I owned these woods?" Tony Pinsky said.

"You'd cut them down," the Mayor said, not opening her eyes.

"You bet your sweet ass," Tony acknowledged. "No offense, Mayor. I'd do me a sportsman paradise. Golf course, shooting range . . . "

"And bingo parlor," the Mayor interjected.

"Sounds tacky," Sally Simmons said.

"And auto derby," Tony concluded.

"Maybe you won't survive and none of that will happen," Lucy told him.

"Naw, Tony's a survivor," Walt Pinsky said. "You know why?"

"Because you're a survivor and he's your son?" the Mayor asked.

"I ain't a survivor," Walt said. "I got laid off a year and a half ago and all I done since is sell a ninety year time–share on a plot."

"What's a plot?" Lucy asked.

"You know we can talk about that," the Mayor told Walt. "That's one of the reason's I came on this trip."

"You mean it's all a political plot?" Peaches cried out. "I'm out here because I'm part of some federal program for dying towns?"

"As long as there's credit Tony'll survive," Walt told them.

"People should keep spending," Sally Simmons said, peeved at something, perhaps her hiking boots which she had unlaced. "Our economic survival depends on it."

"Can I buy a time-share in your crib of dreams, Sal?" Kenny said, coming out of the woods, followed by Freddie and Woad.

"We got there late," Freddie said, plopping down. "You were already gone and then we got lost."

"Lost your trail," Kenny said. "But we were into another. Freddie my man knows his longitudes and lattitudes."

"Everything basically comes down to geography," Freddie informed them. "What place is this? Is this the place you want to be? Can you change it? What do you want to keep and what do you want to get rid of?"

"Then you hire Freddie to work up a blueprint," Kenny said. "My man is a dream maker."

"You were heading for trouble," Woad told Kenny matter of factly. "There's an antediluvian bog in there."

He pointed back from where they had just come.

Everyone looked.

"It was history calling to me," Kenny said. "Releasing its precious secrets."

"Noah and all the animals were the first survivalists," Lucy informed them.

"Jake went off looking for you," Faye told Woad.

"Jake's waiting for things to open up suddenly," the Mayor said. "Meanwhile he can't get lost."

"Is that a fact?" Walt Pinsky remarked. "He still looking for clues to a couple of murders he should have solved twenty years ago?"

"It's a salve for the mind to be looking," Lucy said. "When you don't have anything to look for, you give up."

"I'll go look for him," Woad said.

They had lost track of time. They sat around the large wood fire that Woad had built and it entranced them. Tree frogs and cicada noise were background to the crackling of the fire. Eyes closed in sleep and then suddenly reopened and followed the words without faces and bodies that drifted up into the darkness.

"I see and hear things in that place."

"What sort of things, Faye?"

"Newborn babies are closer to the womb than we are," Faye Fata responded after a long pause and telling them she didn't know what she meant. "They're closer to what it is before they're born if you know what I mean."

"They had an embryo life," someone said and it sounded like Lucy Powell from far off.

"Even before they're born," Faye said.

"That's eerie," Peaches said, stretched out, her head on Kenny's thigh.

"Old people are closer to where they're going than we are," Faye said.

"Old people give me the *frissons*," Sally Simmons said. "Especially when they fail to take care of their hygiene."

"They're gonna be dead," Jake said.

"The older they get, the closer they get," Faye said.

"You can be young and close to dying," Walt Pinsky said, yawning.

"You're not supposed to be," Faye said. "I mean it's unexpected with young people. They don't have any familiarity. And they absolutely don't show any signs of getting close to death. They're clueless."

"What are the signs?" Lucy asked. "Loss of breath followed by sudden seizure?"

"Those are before the fart occurences," Walt said and then laughed as did Jake and Tony.

"Screw it," Faye said, reaching out toward the fire with a long stick and then poking at the red coals.

"You seen something at the County Mental Facility, right?" Woad asked.

Faye kept poking at the fire and then finally she said,

"In the New Wing," Faye said.

"You designed that, didn't you Freddie my man?" Kenny said. "Cause me and my brother painted it you know. Eggshell base with a blue and purple patina. Gave it a look. You can reach old people through paint. It's an acute artistic sense they develop."

"Oh, yeah?" Walt said. "I heard the world goes flat for you when you get real old. It looks like the way it looks to dogs—all grey and two dimensional and you only hear high pitched sounds like a dog whistle. That's what I heard."

"That how God calls the old and dying to his bosom, Walt," Lucy said. "With a dog whistle. You hear that you should run the other way."

"Somebody don't know toast from toaster over here," Tony Pinsky remarked.

"You know the section I mean, Freddie?" Faye said.

"I do," Freddie said. "I didn't exactly have a rationale for that section. You see, the patients there wouldn't ever be getting up. Architecturally speaking, that means there's no functioning to adapt to. And the occupants were without any particular demands. By and large."

"I was a docent in that wing for awhile," Sally Simmons told them, yawning. "We fixed it up with lithographs and cut flowers. Absolutely no public to deal with."

"You become a patient in a hospital," Walt said, "and nobody gives a shit what you want. Or what you usually want when you're a goddamn human being in your own house every day and night for the past hundred years."

"That's just it," Faye said, pulling her stick out of the fire and holding the flaming end up into the darkness. "They're not sick. But some of them are close to a hundred or older."

She waved the flaming stick in a small circle.

"And they're a sign of someplace else, someplace they're going. I go in there sometimes and it's like I'm an intruder but they don't pay any attention to me."

"It's the antediluvian bog," Kenny chanted.

"That's not living, that's just surviving," Peaches said after awhile. "When I get that old and I'm just lying there shot full of aches and pains, sad dreams and my mind's going in and out like a yoyo I wanna be put out of my misery. Please, call Doctor Death I'll say."

"If I get like that Rico is going to save me," Kenny said.

"I'll bet you won't get like that, Kenny," Mayor Beth said.

"You watch the way Nature dies, you get to know how to die," Woad intoned.

"You're so terribly macho, Woadie," Peaches snapped. "Survival of the fittest except you're not the fittest. You're what's left over after they cut out the suit that fits. Isn't that right, Morio?"

"Who's Rico?" Jake asked.

"Did you see that shooting star?" Tony said, jumping up and pointing to the star–filled summer night sky.

"Yes," Morio said, looking up. "There is a pattern in Nature. But maybe some of us are outside the pattern. All of a sudden like that shooting star."

"That's poetic, Morio my man," Kenny said. "Does it burn itself out after we can't see it anymore or is it surviving someplace else? Shooting across the sky of another galaxy. It's too much of a concept."

"That's it," Faye said. "That's it exactly."

Only a tree frog answered while the cicadas droned on. When everyone seemed asleep, some yawning, some turning and moaning, Woad kept the fire going and Jake kept him company, smoking one Camel after another.

Suddenly Jake's whole body froze and his hand went to his boot where he kept a .22 pistol concealed.

"Did you hear that?" he whispered to Woad.

"One of the night hunters," Woad said, nodding.

"That's how those atrocities were perpetrated," Jake said, getting up slowly and backing away from the fire. "At night. The campers were asleep."

"It's funny how you can't ever forget certain things," Woad said, throwing a piece of wood on the fire.

"I seen them bodies," Jake said, turning now and trying to walk through the circle of sleeping bodies without disturbing them. "You don't forget a thing like that."

Woad watched as Jake slipped into the darkness surrounding them. A little while later he heard the sound of a fall and then a groan and a curse. Almost the same then came from another direction. The sky was getting lighter as a false dawn swept by. Jake would run into the luminous eyes of possums and coons and probably the scent that his own mind and its memories laid down—fearsome things, surviving in the gut, until death vaporized them.

When Woad expressed this view to Mayor Beth the next morning as they trekked further into the woods with all the others straggling far behind, she listened without interruption and then said:

"Jake is stupid and he's traumatized. This town isn't in the same boat."

"If you got no memory how do you know you've survived?" Woad said, bending down to examine an orange–flecked mushroom of considerable size. He took out his buck knife, opened it and cut the mushroom cleanly at ground level. Then he cut it in half and speared a half on his knife and offered it to the mayor:

"Take a chance?"

She pulled it off the knife tip and looked at it.

"You can't keep being what you were," she told Woad. "You can't keep being what you remember you were."

She bit into the mushroom.

"You can't be you unless you remember what you were," Woad said biting into his half.

"There's been sixty million me's," Beth said, sitting down on the ground. "I don't have a Me to arrange them all."

"That's a type of personality," Woad said, sitting down on the ground beside her. "That's the type that eventually wants to dig for memories."

"I rest comfortably in my public persona as mayor of this town," Beth said, closing her eyes.

"All this town offers is unemployment," Woad said, closing his own eyes. "You got to go deeper to survive."

When the others came up to them they were both lying on the ground, their eyes half open, their arms and legs twitching, their faces completely drained of blood. Drool was visible on their chins.

"Think they'll make it?" Peaches said after Jake gave both Woad and the mayor a hasty examination.

Jake looked around and up into the trees above their heads.

"I seen this before," he said. "Spread out and look for strange footprints."

"Yeah, and round up all the usual suspects," Kenny said.

Lucy Powell picked up a bit of uneaten mushroom and looked at it.

"I think they're tripping," she said.

Morio Saito took the mushroom from her and looked at it.

"I remember this mushroom," he said and they all looked at him.

"So?"

"It's better in a salad."

Two days later they returned to where they had parked the cars, behind the County Mental Facility.

"You're getting some color back in your face, Mayor," Walt Pinsky said as he leaned down and looked at Beth Swingle sitting in the driver's seat of her Volvo.

"Sure, the mayor's a real survivor," his son Tony said, coming over to the car.

Beth started up the car and drove off without saying a word.

"I care?" Walt said, putting his arm around Tony. "I sold me a time–share on a Rapid City plot to Morio."

"He wants to be buried in South Dakota?" Tony asked.

"With this check," Walt said, taking Morio's check out of his shirt pocket, "he's got all rights and entitlements to ninety-nine years in the ground."

"And then?" Tony said as they headed toward their own Dodge pick-up.

"Then whatever survives gets evicted," Walt said. "It's the '90s. Nothing's permanent. Time–share's the thing."

"Hey, Woadie, you need a lift?" Walt called out to Woad who was staring at a flat tire.

Woad shook his head, waved and Walt drove off.

"Architecturally speaking, Freddie my man," Kenny said, looking back at the woods they had just come out of, "does Nature have a nice set of bones or what?"

"Gladly not mine," Freddie replied. "Gladly."

Kenny jumped up on the roof of his vintage Buick and spread his arms out:

"Save me, Rico! Save me!" he shouted at the top of his lungs.

Ghosts with Resumes/Vampires as Agents of Change

"Social and political conflict is not now, and in the future will not be, between capital and labor. It will be between the comfortably endowed and the relatively or specifically deprived. This conflict may not be peaceful. When political voice and participation are not available outlets, violence becomes the alternative. The danger is already evident in the United States.

John Kenneth Galbraith, *A Journey Through Economic Time*

Bleeding But Not Bleeding to Death

In the spectacle of the abyss that we are filming for ourselves in the present there are ghosts, ghosts with resumes. "I don't want to be just another one of those ghosts with resumes out there," Michael Douglas' character Tom Sanders says in the film *Disclosure.* Jack says this at the low tide mark in the film as he envisions being fired for incompetence, losing his stock options, his $150,000 per annum salary, and the cruelest blow of all, his place in the race. Tom Sanders connects being-in-the-world with being-in-the race. You recall Gordon Gecko, Douglas's character in *Wall Street,* saying "You're either a player, or you're nothing." He says this to the young aspiring market player, Bud Fox. When Bud responds to Gecko's question as to what he thinks winning is with a "couple of hundred grand a year"—Tom Sander's present salary—Gecko connects and tells him if you don't have millions to play with, you're nothing. When Tom's wife, Susan, responds to Tom's observation that if he gets the VP job, they'll be rich, with the response that they are already rich, Tom says "I mean really rich. Very rich." Crystal clear: if you're not *really* rich or a rung away from it, you have no being; you're a nonentity, an absence, a ghost.

America is now a society filled with ghosts, most of them, in spite of the focus of this film, without resumes. Run a camera on those whose personal histories are not represented on an updated resume but only on their faces and you can't eke out a drop of interest in the audience. Why not? First of all, ghosts without resumes—homeless, unemployed, Mac Job employed, employed and poor, employed in crime and violence, living on welfare, living with someone living on welfare, dropped out, at home and watching Ricki Lake, defeated and dreaming by the window—are already of minimal interest in the new global market order of things. The ghost of Hamlet's father, the murdered King, plays well; poor Yorick is just debris.

When we walk the streets or take the ferry to Seattle from posh digs across the bay, we only see the ghosts with resumes. Tom runs into his corporate counterpart—"I made $150,000 a year—I bet that's what you make, right? and I got 'surplussed'." Tom reaches out and gives the man his card "Call this number. I'll see what I can do for you." He winds up doing nothing for him but he does see him on the ferry once again in the last part of the film. At this point, Tom is too close to becoming a ghost himself; he has been too absorbed in his own fight for his corporate-being to think of helping this ghost with a resume re-enter the world of the living. The ferry then is a sort of Charon's ferry to the netherworld; the successful get off in the land of the living while the losers are fated to ferry back and forth through all time.

Of course, this ghost on the ferry is only adrift from his $150,000 per annum job with stock options. But if the reality he lives within—what I would like to say is the "real" abyss—equates being and non-being, life and death with that salary and those stock options, then he *has* vanished, he *is* a ghost. Neither the film nor America today cares much about seeing how the descent will actually play out—loss of posh digs, loss of stock options, forfeiture of all one's toys, search for an affordable place, perhaps for an affordable wife and family, long waits on the unemployment line, weekly documentation of a job search, looking for a helping hand to climb back up the ladder. The descent, in other words, into what America is now for the working class and what used to be the middle class, namely, the swelling underclass. Whom have I left out? Those in the middle class who have now combined salaries in order to retain or achieve a middle-middle or upper-middle status? Christopher Lasch refers to this as "assortative mating"—"the tendency of men to marry women who can be relied on to bring in income more or less equivalent to their own."[1] Robert Reich has given a name to Tom, the computer engineer and his wife, the lawyer—they are "symbolic analysts." Now we've got the camera on Tom and his family. Symbolic analysts displaying assortative mating. But where do they, the ghosts with resumes and the rest of us, if we don't fit in either category, fit in to the culture right now? Allow me to quote from Lasch's last book:

> People in the upper twenty percent of the income structure now control half the country's wealth. In the last twenty years, only they have experienced a net gain in family income. In the brief years of the Reagan Administration alone, their share of the national income rose from forty-one and a half percent to forty-four percent. The middle class, generally defined as those with incomes ranging from $15,000 to $50,000 a year, declined from sixty-one percent of the population in 1970 to fifty-two percent in 1985. These figures convey only a partial, imperfect impression of momentous changes that have taken place in a remarkably short period of time. The steady growth of unemployment now expanded to include white-collar jobs has doubled since 1980 and now amounts to a quarter of all available jobs.[2]

If Donald Sutherland, the man who owns the company Tom works for, is an average C.E.O., he makes about one hundred forty-nine times the average factory worker's pay. And well he deserves it! the average American of today would say. How do I know this?

A film like *Disclosure* reveals this to me. It's a popular film, which means its market is the widest possible audience. It doesn't mind being touted as a film about a disturbing topic like sexual harassment because sexual harassment has the whole culture mesmerized. What is it? What really goes on? Play it out for us. And so on. What is also assumed, and I think rightly, is that even though the film is about the fear of Reich's prosperous symbolic analysts becoming ghosts with resumes—in other words, losing what most of the country doesn't have and joining the rest of us—we identify with their plight. It's the Tragedy of Tom Sanders, but it has a Hollywood ending, the kind of ending that if applied to the Tragedy of Hamlet would have Ophelia and Hamlet live and marry at the end.

What is behind the ability of those who have themselves been "surplussed" in this society to put aside the real conditions of their own being-in-the-world and worry whether Tom Sanders is going to compete and win, whether he's going to hold on and become "really rich" as he foretold at the film's beginning? How do they suspend their own predicament? Nothing is suspended; all is desire. It is not unbelievable within the present spectacle of America for some eighty percent of the population to believe that somehow Tom Sanders' success accrues to them, that they are a part of it, that they know someone who is a part of it and there's a sort of intermingling going on. This is weird psychology and I want to put my finger on it because it's the pulse of America right now. Have you noticed that no matter how negative the review of Michael Douglas' films may be, how lacking in this or that aesthetic/thematic dimensions, his films are always box office successes? Why? An answer coming out of this or that notion of "high critical ordering" and so on simply attributes the success to its low, seductive, commercial, escapist, sensationalist etc. "values." Put blankly, it's popular because it's popular. A truly good film refrains from being popular and aspires to some spellbinding disentanglement from the flux of the everyday, the transient and superficial that distracts that populace, and touches something eternal, say, like truth and reality and of course, Blah, Blah.

I, on the other hand, attribute Douglas's successes to his ability to pick films that entangle themselves into what our American culture is heatedly and feverishly entangled within. *Fatal Attraction, Basic Instinct, Falling Down,* and *Disclosure* tap into the American abyss and our ways of seeing that abyss so that we can continue to live within it and with ourselves. *Disclosure* can keep the camera off most of what American life is today—except in those wide angle shots of the Asian cleaning woman and the Asian nanny—because no one in the audience wants to look at themselves in a mirror. Since a good number of them are ghosts without a resume, their images, like Dracula's, wouldn't show up anyway. This lack of self image and the rush to lose oneself in the lives of those who have being-in-the-race— Tom Sanders and his crowd—is a sad thing, a tragic thing if it indeed has befallen most of the people in America today. It becomes unbelievably tragic for the country if we move from movie theatre to political arena.

How does it play out there? I mean this annihilation of one's own being-in-the world, one's own acquiescence in one's own "surplussing" in a society that was fabricated to be "by the people and for the people"? Let's use a market approach here and conjecture a hypothetical: if out of ten people able to vote, only two can reasonably be expected to vote for protection of their investments and their net profits and therefore against any of that being taxed away for entitlements or eroded by federal regulations, then their legislative interests would go down to defeat. Eight voters would have no reason to vote against their own self-interest—what market enthusiasts claim to be a genetic prime mover. And their interests would clearly be in getting their share of the pie and also making sure those with the biggest piece paid the biggest freight charges. They might in fact be expected to vote *toward* a re-establishment of egalitarianism, social justice, and human rather than property and corporate rights in this country. Rather than the issue simply being "no more taxes," the issue would be a regaining of a progressive income tax and a sharpened inheritance tax that would close the gap between rich and poor. Rather than the issue simply being "no more government," the concern would be in making the federal government a key player in transnational corporate arrangements that attempt to control communications as well as devastate environment, cities, individual lives and the basic democratic principles of the country.

Having presumed all this, it is now necessary to say that since 1980—except for the Clinton victory in 1992—a majority of Americans have acquiesced and voted for their own extinction, their own "surplussing." We have to go back to the movies to see how this could happen. If you ignore the lives of eight out of ten ticket buyers, treat their existence as ghostly, as incapable of filling the screen in any meaningful way, you have to put in their place an incommensurable but effective dynamic: 1) you have to hotwire your film into the diverse dramas of meaning and value that the majority of Americans perceive as threatening; and 2) you have to hotwire their imaginations into clear-cut battles of good and evil, winning and losing in which both goodness and success are within reach. The first strategy makes the film popular: it plays out the fears and thrills, the nightmares and obsessions of the culture. No dream has potency, or what Jung calls mana value, unless it taps into the deep, lurking levels of the collective unconscious. The transfer to the screen is a transfer of those dark beasts stalking the collective culture. The first strategy guarantees attendance. The second strategy absorbs the sparks generated by the first, but gives no illumination. Rather, the sparks enkindle those desires that have already been stoked by the unrelenting, driving force of market values. Fears are transposed into desires and those desires have already been prefabricated for us. The film in turn gives us an opportunity to see our fears played out on the screen, and—against that tide— plunges us deeper into desires not our own and ultimately dismissive of our being-in-the-world. I mean by this that the desire to have Tom Sanders's truly breathtaking home overlooking the bay, his hip office filled with the latest computer toys, his $150, 000 salary, his stock options, his climb up the ladder to being "very rich"—to desire all this, to convert everything that one is into these desires, leads to one's support of market logic and market values, the very logic and the very values that have already "surplussed" most of the audience.

We extend this confirmation in the movie theater to our vote in the voting booth. And so in this fashion do those who have been "surplussed" accept and indeed design their own ghostly status in the America of today. Our fear of becoming a ghost with a resume is a fear that the film directly presents to us and yet at the same time distances from us. This fellow here is not us. We have no resume. He is not me; the film is not about us. At the same time, the fear is intensified: he *has* a resume and has no job. I don't even have a resume. So the expression "hotwire" is itself too direct and forceful; the film touches a fear of job loss and the total insecurity that such a fear generates in a growing number of Americans, and at the same time puts it at a safe distance from us. But the fear is personal; everyone sitting there must feel it. It cannot be formalized or ritualized or thematized totally away from that personal, direct connection.

Lurking behind the insecurity that the free play of the global market has produced, the downsizing of the viewer's life, work and horizons that global competitiveness has created by placing job, training and experience in jeopardy, is class warfare. I know that the *MacLaughlin Group* will never point to economic inequities as reasons for anything going on in this country, but nevertheless it is only a step or two from the social Darwinism we have adopted to a recognition of the rotten fruit it bears. So the fear of being just another ghost with or without a resume out there is a fear of cinemascopic proportions—it stretches toward social and ontological insecurity and onward to a sense of personal and social injustice.

In its desire for change, the vast majority of Americans are already showing signs of turn-and-lash-out, of some release from this anxious state of witnessing their own imminent "surplussing." It's politically instructive to see how the film gets the viewer on its side. Sexual harassment hooks us. Now sexual harassment is the contemporary hot topic that provides the immediate link with the culture. In fact the film plays out the Clarence Thomas/Anita Hill hearings which left us with just a touch more of that very upsetting postmodern undecidability. *Disclosure* replays that trial and this time we know for sure who is telling the truth and who is lying. The film brings to us that closure and resolution, that determinacy which the real Thomas/Hill hearings denied us. Sexual harassment is not about sex, Tom's lawyer tells him, it's about power. And this film is not about sexual harassment; it's about ghosts attending their own funeral and seeing it as a startling house overlooking Seattle Bay, a $150,000 a year job. With stock options. And a real future.

We're into second strategy tactics here. Sexual harassment, however, cuts into both strategies. Part of that swirl of ever-changing cultural hang-ups and dilemmas, sexual harassment plagues an already uneasy relationship between the sexes. "There was a time when it was a distraction to have a woman on the job," our ghost with a resume on the ferry tells Tom, "but now you have to worry that they're going to take your job." So there are some first strategy sparks here. And then the use of sexual harassment to re-assert our capacity to grasp the real and assert the true. And all that. Very important stuff. Mainly because our vicarious victory in this sexual harassment suit has us applauding Tom's victory, the victory of Truth and Reality, the corporate merger, the "good" woman executive who finally gets the job that Demi Moore (the "bitch" executive), had, the film, the world we are in, our own lives, America, and the market values that have brought us here. Demi Moore's character, then, is not only an Anita Hill exposed as a liar but a Hillary Rodham Clinton in a powerful position who is dethroned. The cultural context of the film has already established a link between Mrs. Clinton, gender tensions, and "angry men . . . bitter about social and cultural changes over the past several decades that they believe have come at their expense." And Mrs. Clinton is the target of much of this anger. "Her symbolic role in the mind of the opposition is unmistakable; the gender tensions that have been boiling for two decades have now spilled on to the presidency."[3]

In other words, my friends, we swallow it all, we go for the whole fairy tale. The ghost with a resume on the ferry? Us without a resume on the subway? Or waiting for the ax to fall? Or waiting tables? Or going through the want ads that promise that if we work forty hours a week we'll make enough to get a credit card that will keep us bleeding but not bleeding to death? That doesn't play anymore. Nobody's interested; not even us.

Am I saying, then, that the whole film, like all popular films, is designed to both upset and seduce eight out of ten in the audience? Yeah. And it proves good politics too. What about the other twenty percent or so? They see a different film. I can only take a wild stab at what they see. Politically, they have no problem voting their interests. They can, of course, vote against their interests: vote for, say, the expansion of government regulation of factory and environmental safety, a more equitable progressive income tax, a raise in the minimum wage, an inheritance tax, increased capital gains tax, anti-trust with teeth and so forth. They could turn their backs on the market logic that has carried them to the top and become Greens, or Socialists or Liberals etc. They could even think that their vote wouldn't matter and not vote at all. I can just barely conceive these possibilities. I take Galbraith's view: "It is the nature of the privileged to take a protective, short-run view of their own position."[4]

What film do they see? Well, the ghost with a resume on the ferry has to get back into the arena and compete, and not look for anyone to lend a hand. Tom Sanders? I'm sure every player in the audience would be playing along with Tom. And playing better. Making smarter moves. Being more aware, more skeptical, harder, tougher. At the film's beginning, Donald Sutherland, the CEO, assures his corporate toadie and snitch that Tom won't fight back. "He's too weak." He's not up to the rough game of social Darwinism these corporate moguls play. Eat or be eaten. Tom's going to be eaten. And when he isn't, when he wins, why then, the whole corporate game is confirmed. America produces winners. If there are any ghosts with resumes in the audience, they should take heed. This is how the game is played.

I want to say something about the virtual reality world that this film also plugs into. Again, both strategies are crossed. I mean, after all, didn't robots take most of the jobs that automobile workers had? Isn't the computer revolution, the semiconductor advance, the basis of our turn from production and manufacture to a service economy? This is our so-called post-Fordism age that is talked about as if it were here rather than just being born on the bodies of the "surplussed." Technology has a well-deserved bad rep: from the machine befouling the garden to the bombs dropped on Japan. The Internet has been greeted as a harbinger of real participative democracy and also as just the sort of technology Big Brother was waiting for. Or, if not Big Brother, then transnational marketing which will electronically enter our biorhythms and neural transmitters and turn us into zombies, couch potatoes who forget to eat their potatoes. We are nervous and apprehensive about this virtual reality that awaits us; it adds to our insecurity.

The profits of the new semiconductor revolution are not to be curtailed by such apprehension. Thus, *Disclosure* moves from tweaking our computer nightmares to allaying them. It does quite explicitly. I mean that at one point we actually listen to part of the merger spin: we can end difference over race, religion, sex, class, and can transcend body and bias, war and hatred by putting everyone into virtual reality where consciousness transmits to consciousness and no harm can ensue. That's a paraphrase. But the fear of this new technology is also transmuted. Once again something that distresses yet draws us is wrapped up in a ready-to-wear package, or, in other words, the simple drama of Tom's struggle to reach the truth and have it recognized. Thus, Tom's path to vindication goes down a virtual reality corridor. The connections are these: something is wrong with the new computer system; Tom is guided throughout by mysterious e-mail messages from "A Friend" and is urged to solve the problem; he does solve the computer problem and then uses the new technology, including a walk into The Corridor, the new virtual reality program his company is creating, to expose Demi Moore as a liar and a sexual harasser. Virtual reality rides in, if you will, on the coat tails of Tom's legal victory. At Tom's darkest hour, the helpful angel of The Corridor appears and leads him to the light, to the truth, to victory over the dark forces.

This hi-tech world that Tom dwells in is sexy, cutting edge, exciting, breathtaking, challenging. It's a new, untravelled frontier. These are the toys of the new class of "symbolic analysts". Never mind that most of the audience will never play with those toys, that those toys promise a walk down The Corridor of virtual reality for those who have already been "surplussed" in the world of bread and sweat, the ghosts with and without resumes.

"Looking at the World Through Vampire Eyes: Blood Sucking and Bleeding Hearts"

I don't want to talk about the Ann Rice novel, *Interview with the Vampire* but the Neil Jordan film, *Interview with the Vampire* except to say that the film, screenplay by Rice, inherits the same weak second half that the novel displays. In the film, the weakness I believe has all to do with the Parisian vampire troupe doing vampire theatre while actually being vampires. This theatricality undermines the sense of realism the film has been desperately trying—mostly successful through the sets and cinematography—to create. The vampire legend exists only cinematically, and for the present viewer most compellingly in the theatrics of Bela Lugosi's performance, now an over the top vampire. The vampire hyperreal is not as Dr. Von Helsing tells us in *Dracula:* "The power of the vampire lies in our disbelief." Rather, once we see this as a costume-and-fangs performance, our disbelief steps in between us and the viewing. The Baudrillardian hyperreal has never been real but nonetheless replaces the real entirely. Armand and his troupe in their theatrical costumes dissolve the atmosphere of the hyperreal. And since the film does not play out any interesting intersections between multiple realities in a deliberate postmodern layering, but diligently tries to envelop us in an unfissured, undispelled sense of vampire realism, the introduction of actors pretending to be vampires undermines our mood and the mood of the film.

I don't ever understand what is going on between Louis (Brad Pitt) and Armand (Antonio Banderas) the leader of the troupe—except to say that once again Louis shows himself to be a bleeding heart vampire. Armand advises him to lose his human conscience, his concern for his innocent victims, and live without self-reproach. Be a survivor, he tells Louis. It's the same thing that Lestat (Tom Cruise) has told him. Armand has shown his survival skills by liquidating (in a conflagration of vampire coffins) his troupe, although Louis is the instrument of this abrupt and fatal termination of his peers. Armand explains that for a vampire to survive he must keep up with the times; he must not fall behind, become an anachronism. In order to feed on the hapless souls of the present, he must remain in the present. In the film's final scene, we see that Lestat, whom we had last seen completely out of sync with the modern world, has indeed survived in the present. More than that, he's a strong player once again. In rejecting both Lestat's and Armand's philosophy of vampire survival, Louis continues on his own path of angst and remorse, of compassion for his victims, his search for an ultimate meaning to his vampire existence. Somehow, even what he has become, must fit into some grand scheme of creation.

The vampire has a part to play that is, Louis must hope, ultimately meaningful and moral and not simply predatory and survivalist. You might say that Louis is a foundationalist, the last modernist in search of ultimate truth and reality through the dark miasma of the contingencies of consciousness and world. There is a flux of everyday vampire life, the endless, meaningless personal history of blood sucking that must be distilled into the stuff of eternal truth, of absolute meaning, determinate origin, universal values. It seems to Louis as if Lestat and Armand fabricate their daily lives, shape a reality that in turn shapes them. And then because the human world outside them moves on and they remain, they thrust themselves into the changed reality and reshape themselves. All vampires must therefore be agents of change and this adaptability, this lack of an essential nature, becomes indeed their nature. Louis wants to find some essential vampire nature that he can submit to, that in turn will provide him with a still center of his vampire existence. He becomes a stubborn seeker of absolute meaning and truth, of one reality from which all truths regarding vampire existence emerge. He remains an Enlightenment Vampire in a postmodern world.

The vampire survives by sucking the blood of his victims; undiscovered, the vampire can survive in this fashion for centuries. Immortality, strengths and faculties beyond the mere human are the possessions of the vampire. It is no wonder that Christian Slater, the one who records Louis' story, wishes, in the end, to be a vampire. He wants to be a survivor, immortal, a winner, a player. He wants to spend eternity feeding on the lives of those who are weaker, the entire human race. He is willing to suck the blood of other people with no grand purpose in mind except his own survival. The future of the lives destroyed—three a night for four hundred years in Lestat's case—do not equal the future of one vampire. This is victimization, exploitation and consumption on a grand scale. Lestat urges Louis to look at the world through "vampire eyes" but it becomes crystal clear to us that this is the way the world has been looking at itself since Reagan and Thatcher.

It is no accident that the conscience-stricken Louis, the bleeding heart liberal, doesn't have a clue as to how to respond. He runs around in a sort of moral desperation: how can he stem the flow of blood? How can he remove himself from this endless round of blood-sucking, of death-dealing, of running through the human flock like a ravenous wolf among sheep? He's a comical figure, although the film isn't played as a tragicomedy nor does Louis ever rise to a level of self-mockery. He is caught in a circling pattern, a solo flight to regret and back again. Sound familiar? I mean why doesn't he become a "New" bleeding heart, a "New" Liberal? Why doesn't he ever reconcile survival according to free market standards with egalitarianism, social justice, community, environment, family values? Why can't he turn his remorse into a liberating, just social agenda? Why can't he prove that market values can be applied to everything: from individual conscience (which torments the hell out of him) to family values? In the end, we grow as tired of what Terrence Rafferty calls his "most persistent case of morning-after-regret" as we are presently—November 1994—tired of Bill Clinton's nebulous, floundering "New" Democrat posture, his so-called "New" Liberalism.

If such a bleeding heart comes across as farce, the blood sucking come across as gruesome and loathsome. The coldness of it gives you the *frissons*. The cold savagery of pure bodily appetite devouring its prey: the female mantis her mate, the rat snake its rat, the python swallowing a whole pig, the bat attached to the throat of a dumb beast falling into even deeper dumbness until stupor is replaced by death. The little pointed thimble device that Lestat wears on an index finger so he can puncture an artery is no more than instrumentation, like the wooden mallet we use to clobber a beef cow. Lestat pops a victim's vein like a can of Coke, a casual act of no real import. He holds punctured wrists over wine glasses as if he were decanting an old wine, making casual conversation all the while. Our stomachs turn; it is we that are being used so, being drained like nothing more than ambulatory food stuff. The scenes are repetitive; we cannot seem to leave the ghastliness and repugnance of all this behind and begin a story, a story in which these scenes are subsumed. And it is vital that they be woven into some narrative pattern that is able to dispel their hideousness. But this does not happen. The film never moves on to a story, although Brad Pitt seems to be

telling Christian Slater a story. He cannot tell him a story that is
only there revealed in those scenes of grisly blood sucking. The
story is there, in the mesmerizing effect the blood sucking has.
We are repelled by the slow devouring of ourselves but we cannot look away. We are being drained, consumed, demolished
while still alive. Our fixed stare at these scenes is itself a gruesome feasting. Because the film never tells a story that puts all
of this out of our mind, we will, in the end, turn on the film. It is
not a good film, we say. And we summon the reasons. But nevertheless we are still there in that film, our entrapped gaze meeting the gaze of those whose lives are slowing ebbing away as a
vampire has his fill of us.

If then the bleeding heart is a sorry, farcical sight, the blood
sucker is a revolting sight, making our stomachs turn. I cannot
help thinking that we now live in a world which has gone on
record supporting an ideology in which a few feast on the many.
And it's okay. No, it is not a good film in the way of allowing us
to surmount or escape ourselves. But it is a film that works its
way through the vampire legend and genre to our own culture at
this moment. It is a version of the vampire legend that only we in
this market oriented reality could have produced. And because
it is a film that represents the horror of our own exploitation of
this planet, our own victimization of three quarters of its inhab-
itants, and the consumption of the many by the few in a feeding
frenzy that must be ever-expanding—because of all this, it is a
good film in the way of mirroring what we have made of ourselves:
vampires and victims.

Lestat's favorite fare is the sybaritic set, the wealthy aristo-
crats who not only feed on the many, but also turn on themselves. It is a game of one upmanship, a sort of market players
game, a struggle in the arena between gladiators. Two go in, one
comes out a loser, one comes out a winner. The New Orleans
winners indulge their appetites in the same way the vampires do.
They do not allow conscience or tremors of remorse to get in the
way. If an elderly husband stands in the way of his elderly wife
having sex with a young man, the young man, wanting to be in
the sybaritic set, wanting to be a winner, a player, will murder
the elderly husband. When Lestat and Louis pay their compliments to this woman, wrinkled and dissipated, and her foppish
teenage lover, we know that these predators will now in turn be
preyed upon. The fop is drained and left like so much garbage

against a tree, and the woman has her neck snapped with one quick, unceremonious twist. Lestat, our hero, our champion. Lestat, our slaughterer, our executioner.

And now on to family values; again no story here but rather living tableaus of alternative family life and values. Because Lestat fears that Louis is about to break up their own strangely linked partnership, he turns a young girl, Claudia, into a vampire. Claudia will keep Louis from leaving. He will stay only because of the child. Otherwise, divorce seems inevitable for this mismatched pair—one a blood sucker, the other a bleeding heart. Claudia learns to feed on the human race with great gusto. She is brought up an amoral monster, not a drop of bleeding heart blood in her. Although Louis thinks he can bring Claudia up better if Lestat were not around, he cannot act. But Claudia can. She arranges Lestat's own gruesome death, offering him twins near death and then throwing Lestat's body into an alligator invested bayou. When it appears to Claudia some thirty years later, that she, still physically a child, will lose Louis, her father-creator-companion, she begs Louis to make a vampire out of a woman who will be her mother and companion.

At first Claudia wants to be like her Dad; this is the puberty stage. Her Dad here is Lestat, the patriarch of their little family. Louis is more like a soul mate, a companion who, like Claudia, is just apprenticing into the vampire life. When Claudia reaches a teenage rebellion stage, Lestat quickly becomes the authority that constrains and suppresses. But beyond that he is the Cruel Creator who has doomed her to life in the body of a child and the appetites of an adult. When Louis admits to being part of her creation as a vampire she turns on him but cannot sustain her anger. Louis remains a fellow victim of Lestat's patriarchy. What is to happen after she kills the father? Is the father the nucleus in the nuclear family? The new father is Louis, but he is more like a brother, even a lover, and most importantly he has no authority. He has no firm sense of who he is or where he is going. He is lost, rebelling against what he is, pissing and moaning about his fate. Instead of being The Father, he is a partner. Will families made up of partners replace the nuclear family? The partner—Louis—may leave and take up with Armand so Claudia seeks a new companion, a woman who would be a companion to her. But these two wind up in a death embrace as the sunlight turns their bodies to dust.

Notes

1. Christopher Lasch, "The Revolt of the Elites," *Harper's Magazine* November 1994, p 41.

2. Ibid, p. 41.

3. Paul Starr, "The Undertow," *American Prospect,* summer 1994, p 8.

4. Galbraith, p. 11.

Acoustic Archaeology

County Mental

"Oh my!" Antony said looking into the bedpan he had just pulled out from under Frank Coletti.

Frank was strapped hand and foot to the bed. Only his head thrashed back and forth on the pillow, eyes closed.

"This is alien shit for sure," Antony told Frank but Frank only thrashed.

Opening the door, Antony walked into former Sheriff Jake Wilcox's belly. The bedpan pressed into Jake's belly.

"How's he doing, Antony?" Jake said, looking as if he had been up all night.

"I think that fella did get himself abducted," Antony whispered. "Look at this alien shit, man."

Jake glanced down at the bedpan.

"The old ladies are looking for you, Antony," a nurse who was passing by called out to Antony. "They're in the Greenhouse."

As Antony hurried down the corridor Jake called out and rushed after him.

"Hey, let me have that, will you, Antony? I think this is evidence."

"That's for sure," Antony said giving Jake the bedpan.

Mrs. Hearder and Mrs. Woad were sitting side by side in deck chairs, blankets covering their legs in the glass enclosed solarium attached to the Mental Facility. Here the temperature was Brazilian and patients believed to be suffering from climate related depression were left in the Greenhouse for at at least an hour a day. Outside the glass, the day was frigid and large snow flakes were wafting toward earth like fragile space crafts.

365

"Not too chilly for you ladies?" Antony asked, taking out a handkerchief to sop up the sweat on his brow..

"Mememto mori," Mrs. Hearder said.

"If we could memento like we used to," Mrs. Woad explained, "we wouldn't need to be out here for Nature's reminder."

"Nature reminds you of something?" Antony said.

"Of death, dear."

"Oh, my," Antony replied, studying a large tropical insect that had just landed on Mrs. Woad's balding head.

"Now, tell us all the hospital gossip, Antony," Mrs. Hearder said.

"It makes us think we still have lives, dear," Mrs. Woad said.

Antony scratched his head.

"Where did I leave off the gossip?" Antony said cagily.

Mrs. Hearder and Mrs. Woad exchanged thoughtful glances.

"Well," Mrs. Hearder said. "A Mister O.J. went somewhere in a white Bronco."

"And Paula Flowers said the President propositioned her."

"Oh, I don't think so, dear."

"Yes, he said to her 'Would you like to see the nice home my boys have'?"

"And that's a proposition, dear?"

"His boys are part of his anatomy, dear."

"Oh, my."

"That's why Mister Daniel Quayle will be the next President of the United States," Mrs. Woad said, as Faye Fata came out. "He doesn't talk about his boys to young ladies."

"Everybody nice and cozy?" Faye said cheerily.

"We're waiting for Antony to tell us the latest gossip," Mrs. Woad said.

"Well, get this," Faye said. "They just caught former Sheriff Jake Wilcox trying to steal a bedpan."

"Oh, my," Antony said. "He was taking the evidence."

"What evidence, Antony?" Faye asked.

"Mr. Coletti's alien abduction."

"That sounds interesting," Mrs. Hearder said and Faye told her as much as she knew about Frank, Jake, a flying saucer hidden behind the Mental Facility, and of Frank's abduction and return in really bad mental shape.

"It's part of that plot by space people," Mrs. Hearder said to Mrs. Woad, who nodded.

"What plot by space people?" Faye asked.

"They're going to resurrect the Earth's dead, dear," Mrs. Hearder said.

"And then turn them against the world," Mrs. Woad added.

"Wasn't that an Ed Wood, Jr. movie?" Antony, who was a great film buff, said. *"Plan 9 From Outer Space?"*

"That's where we learned about it, dear," Mrs. Hearder replied.

"Everything we know about grave robbers we learned at the movies," Mrs. Woad said.

"It's funny how I can remember a whole movie that I saw years and years ago," Mrs. Hearder told them.

"Me too," Antony said.

"And sometimes I have to look at my palm to see what my name is."

She showed them the palm of her right hand where the words "Elizabeth Hearder" were penned, crossed out and then the name "Elizabeth Taylor" printed there.

"I put the ending of one movie on the beginning of another," Mrs. Woad announced. "And visa versa."

"And what about the middle, dear?"

"I get that from wherever I can, dear."

"Well, some people from the FBI took Jake Wilcox for questioning," Faye said.

At that moment former Sheriff Jake Wilcox was sitting across from FBI special agent Knox Muller in the Director's office of the County Mental Facility.

"So you both found what you think was an alien spacecraft," Muller said.

"Smaller than you'd think if you went by what you saw in the movies," Jake replied, wondering why he couldn't stop sweating.

"But it was alien alright. It wasn't an earth vehicle. I was Sheriff of this town for over twelve years."

"You left Mr. Coletti there. Why?"

"To watch it while I went for help."

"You got picked up and driven back to town. Right?"

"Sure," Jake said, running his already soaked handkerchief around the back of his neck. "Is it hot in here?"

"You got some help and went back. What did you find?"

The door opened and a woman with red hair stood there. She motioned to Agent Muller.

"The locals have found a body. In the woods."

"Alien?"

"Local. A guy named Barfield Simmons. Preliminaries look like he was beaten to death with a blunt object. The body was found about three miles from where they found Frank Coletti."

"Tell me about when you got back to where you had left your friend," Knox said, turning back to Jake.

"He wasn't there. And the ship wasn't there. We searched all around. We searched all night. He was gone."

"And then three days later he showed up right outside town?"

"Yeah, he looked like hell. And he didn't know me. He was ranting. 'They took me, they took me', he kept yelling. And then when I said who he looked me straight in the eye and I swear something in there snapped and he wasn't seeing anything anymore. I tell you, Frank's seen things in his life. Frank doesn't fold that easily. Hey, is it hot in here or is it me?"

"We'll talk again, Mr. Wilcox," Muller said and then Jake was alone in the room. He turned his head to the right and left, feeling sort of dizzy. He reached out for his Stetson and it seemed an effort. He made his way slowly to the elevator. Now he was feeling downright nauseous and things were beginning to spin. He hadn't eaten since when? Hadn't slept in a couple of days. Too old and too fat to do the job. The elevator doors opened. Empty. He got in and pushed ground level.

When the doors closed, he slouched to the floor of the elevator. He wondered if he should have told them about that time things opened up for him and Frank.

Frank Coletti opened his eyes and sought the familiar form of his best friend Jake Wilcox. He then tried to get up. He couldn't understand why he was strapped down. Left alone. In a hospital. Something had happened to him. His teeth ached. He felt funny. He was hooked up to some sort of IV. He closed his eyes. There was something keeping the edge off his thoughts. It was like sloshing around in 'Nam, heart racing, going nowhere. Slowed down.

He heard the door open and when he looked he saw an old lady peering in at him.

"Frankie, it's me. Mrs. Woad. Your old fourth grade teacher. Mrs. Hearder is with me. Can we come in?"

"Stay back," Frank said.

"What did he say, dear?"

"Just for a minute, he said," Mrs. Woad told her friend as she advanced into the room and toward Frank's bed. Mrs. Hearder tiptoed behind her. Frank stared at them.

"We just wanted to tell you that we were abducted by aliens too," Mrs. Woad told Frank.

"Aliens?" Frank replied. "Who the fuck was abducted by aliens?"

"What did he say, dear?"

"He said whores are first abducted by aliens," Mrs. Woad interpreted.

"He must be thinking of *Frankenhooker*," Mrs. Hearder said. "You remember, dear. The film where a mad scientist uses the bodies of prostitutes to rebuild his girlfriend who's been cut to pieces in a lawnmower accident."

"And the gardener was somewhat retarded?" Mrs. Woad replied.

"Get Jake Wilcox," Frank cried out, getting frightened.

"He wants us to get him his wool socks," Mrs. Woad told her friend.

"Oh, his feet are bare, aren't they?" Mrs. Hearder said.

"Don't worry, Frankie, we'll get you a nice pair of wool socks."

"The aliens left us naked in Ferris' Apple Orchard," Mrs. Woad told Frank. "We don't remember what things they did to us, do we, Mrs. Hearder?"

"Sexual things, I'm sure," Mrs. Hearder replied. "Joy was born nine months later. She's a doctor now you know."

"Isn't she our doctor, dear?"

"Oh, no. Why would she be our doctor? She went off to Berkeley and became her own woman."

"It was the times, my dear. I'm sure she'll be back."

Frank whose own alien experience was now flashing through the IV preparation asked the old ladies why the aliens would want to take him. Then he remembered he had been guarding the space craft while Jake had gone for help.

"There was a beam of light," he told them. "All of a sudden. No noise. And when I looked up there was something reaching for me."

Saying this, Frank raised his head from the pillow and began to thrash his arms about wildly as if he were doing head and neck aerobics along with Gilad. His head snapped back and forth and something popped out of his ear and rolled on to the floor.

"What are you doing here?" Sunny Powell, Frank's ex, said, coming into the room.

"We're talking to Frank," the old ladies said.

Sunny walked up to Frank who lay rigid on the bed, eyes open and staring at the ceiling.

"Frank?" she called out to him. "Frank? It's me Sunny. Frank Junior is outside and he wants to see you. Frank, can you answer me?"

"Let me see Frankie Junior," Frank said.

"He says he should have seen France sooner," Mrs. Woad told Sunny who replied with "What?"

"He's never been to France," Sunny said.

"Aliens took us to France," Mrs. Woad told her.

"France is just the beginning, dear," Mrs. Hearder told her.

Sunny looked at them dumbfounded and then at the immobile Frank, her ex.

"Of course, one person's beginning . . . " Mrs. Woad began.

"Might be another person's ending," Mrs. Hearder ended, bending down and picking up the device that had fallen out of Frank's ear. She realized that it was the hearing aid she had lost several years ago and deftly inserted it into her left ear.

When the elevator doors opened on the Ground level of the County Mental Facility Mark Wonder made a move to step inside, saw the body of former Sheriff Jake Wilcox lying on the elevator floor, thought about the body and his bid for the mayoralty, turned quickly and headed back to where he had parked his Lexus. In less than two minutes the elevator was summoned up and the doors closed. This time they opened on the lobby floor where Gladys, on her way to the second floor office to apply for a job, took one look at the body, got in the elevator, pushed top floor and then went through Jake's pockets. He had a fat wallet in his back pocket but it was mostly filled with dogeared business cards. When the elevator stopped at the fifth floor she was busy applying CPR to Jake whose face was already a slate blue.

"We need to know all you can tell us about Frank Coletti," Shana Cully, special FBI Agent said to Dr. Joy in Dr. Joy's County Mental Facility Office on the eighth floor.

"Well, Frank was born in this town," Dr. Joy said. "He married his high school sweetheart. They got divorced about two years ago. I think money was the problem. Frank lost his job at the auto plant. Sunny remarried. This time for money. There's a Frankie Junior but Sunny's got him. Frank's been like a lost soul since then. Wandering around with Jake Wilcox. Equally lost since he lost the sheriff's election after being sheriff around here for as long as I can remember."

"Frank ever say he saw a UFO or anything like that?" Muller asked.

Dr. Joy sighed.

"Look, those boys are wrapped in weirdness."

"What do you mean?" Muller said.

"There were strange murders out behind the County Mental Facility years ago. Jake was a deputy sheriff then I think. There were bodies. And some never found. And years before that Frank's father had disappeared on a camping trip. And Frank's dog. Jake and Frank have been scouring those woods every weekend for years looking for clues. Over the years both events have sort of converged in their minds. I did hear that their last theory had something to do with aliens."

"Did Frank think his father was abducted?"

Joy shrugged her shoulders.

"It gets weirder though. Last Spring Frank and Jake took Frankie Junior on a camping trip in those woods and they had some kind of experience. Paranormal experience."

"How paranormal?" Muller said, interest rising at the same time Cully's scepticism was kicking in.

"They somehow relived the camping trip Frank had been on with his own father years before."

"Frank came in to see you about this?"

"Yes, he did. The way he described it was . . . was not very descriptive. He said everything suddenly opened up. He saw himself and his father. He was there. And his dog. Fatima. And then he watched as some strangers hailed the camp. And then the murders. It must have been horrible."

"What about Wilcox?" Cully asked. "Did he see all this too?"

"Corroborated Frank's story to the letter."

"And what did you conclude?" Cully asked.

"Delusional syndrome brought on by years and years of wanting desperately for something to open up in a case that remained frustratingly opaque."

"Is that all?" Muller asked, knowing somehow that there was more.

Dr. Joy hesitated and then laughed.

"What the hell. Look, this town is a breeding ground for the paranormal, if that's what you want to call it."

"How so?" Muller asked.

"There's a kid who was killed in a car accident. While he was on his bike. Further Cooper. He's periodically spotted around town on that same bike."

"So the town is haunted?" Cully said.

"I've seen him," Dr. Joy said flatly and Cully's smile vanished. "Then there's Mike Woad. He's unemployed but always doing something if you know what I mean. He's a kind of Renaissance tinkering genius. I've heard he's found a UFO and has gotten it to fly."

"What?" Muller said.

"It's just a rumor but there have been sightings."

"I'll need his name and address," Muller said. "Is there more?"

"Not if you've had enough," Dr. Joy replied.

Muller and Cully exchanged looks.

At the sound of Little Frankie's voice, Frank opened his eyes.

"Hi, Dad," little Frankie said.

"I'm not crazy, Frankie," Frank croaked.

"Things opened up again, didn't they Dad?"

"I don't know what's going on, Frankie but somehow it's all connected. My father's death back then. The UFO. Now . . . "

"Where did they take you, Dad?"

"I don't know. I don't remember. I just get, like, little snippets of this and that. Voices. Thin, high wire voices that are talking but it's more like computer sounds. I see movement but I don't know what's a face or what's a background. If I try to think more about it, Frankie, I'll go nuts."

"They found another body back there, Dad," Little Frankie said. "Mr. Simmons."

"Barfield Simmons? When?"

"Same night you were out there," Little Frankie replied.

"Listen, here, Frankie. We're gonna solve this. Believe me. We're gonna get to the bottom of this. People thought me and Jake were just wasting our time. But that ain't so. Look at all this now. People'll see that it's really happening."

"Pretend you're okay and all Dad so you can get out," Little Frankie advised.

"I'm gonna do just that," Frank said, nodding. "You watch me."

"Jake Wilcox is dead," Faye said to the old ladies.

"The former Sheriff?" Mrs. Woad asked.

"The former everything," Faye responded. "Major cardio blow-out on the elevator not more than twenty minutes ago."

"Oh my!" Mrs. Hearder exclaimed. "Major Ricardo with a blow-gun in the elevator. Who would of thought of it?"

"Who's Major Ricardio, dear?" Mrs. Woad asked.

"Why, you remember him, dear."

"I don't think so. Do you?"

"No, I don't but I seem to recall your knowing him."

Mrs. Woad thought about it.

"Yes, I think I do now that you mention it. A man of small stature with a face like a bright copper penny?"

"With a distinguished beard, yes."

"Do you ladies have your hearing aids on?" Faye asked.

"I hear about AIDS mostly on the Maury Povitch show," Mrs. Hearder replied. "I wouldn't worry about it dear. You'll reach our age."

"What?" Faye exclaimed, startled by Mrs. Hearder's intuitive grasp of a thought that had just crossed her mind.

"It's usually Colonel Mustard with a pistol in the library," Mrs. Woad called out to Faye as she left the room.

On the fourth floor Office of Human Resources, Gladys sat next to Carl waiting to be interviewed.

"I'm for the custodial job," Carl told Gladys.

"Cafeteria cashier," Gladys replied.

Carl nodded, relieved. He couldn't stand the competition. Not now.

"I lost my prior job," Carl said.

"Me, too," Gladys said.

"I don't think the economy will ever be better for people like us," Carl said. "People who don't play the market and all."

"Gladys Farquarson? Mr. Zowie will see you now."

"Good luck," Carl said as Gladys stood up.

Mr. Zowie was a miniscule man with a hairless, lozenge–shaped face and enormous black eyes.

"You did very poorly on the aptitude test, Ms. Farquarson. You don't seem to have the necessary focus for a cafeteria cashier. There are huge gaps in your numerical intelligence."

"I don't understand," Gladys replied, noting the careful arrangement of every object on Mr. Zowie's desk.

"Well, for instance," Mr. Zowie said, picking up a neat stack of paper and handing it to Gladys. "These are all applications filled out thus far today. I'll give you five minutes to peruse them and at the end of that time I'd like you to tell me every bit of information your mind has absorbed from those applications."

Mr. Zowie took off his Rolex and laid it on the desk.

"Ready, set, go," he said.

Gladys looked down at the first application "Carl Firewoad. Age 28." Mr. Zowie left the room.

In five minutes the Rolex began to beep. Mr. Zowie took the stack of applications from Gladys.

"Okay, Begin."

Gladys recalled that Carl Firewoad had recently worked at Town Towing and Tire and before that at Quickie Lube and before that at Wags and Tails and before that at Grits and Gravy. When she finished Mr. Zowie told her she had absorbed thirteen facts, only four of which were totally accurate.

"Now," Mr. Zowie said, going over to a file cabinet. "In here are ten years worth of applications. Pick a bunch and give me five minutes."

Gladys carefully selected a number of files from different drawers and then handed them to Mr. Zowie.

"Ready, set, go," Mr. Zowie said and then cast his enormous eyes on the files. At the end of five minutes he handed the files to Gladys and while she followed along he summarized the contents of each and every file.

"Now that's a glitch-less mind!" Mr. Zowie exclaimed in triumph when Gladys told him he had been 100% accurate.

"Did you get it?" Carl said when Gladys came out of Mr. Zowie's office. Gladys shook her head.

"Why can't people help other people?" Carl moaned.

Gladys didn't know.

"Maybe I could see you some time?" Carl said. "Gladys Farquarson, right?"

"Carl Firewoad. Mr. Zowie will see you now."

On the way down in the elevator, Gladys inspected Mr. Zowie's Rolex. It probably kept good time. Glitch-less time.

"He's doing something he calls acoustic archaeology," Dr. Joy said in response to the FBI agents desire to hear more.

"What is that?" Cully said. "Acoustic archaeology?"

"I've heard a piece of Grecian urn being played by a laser needle," Muller said. "All the sounds going on when the urn was being made are picked up."

"Like human voices?" Cully asked.

"Human voices, yes," Dr. Joy responded. "Mike Woad told me he heard Elvis' voice coming off an old pink Cadillac steering wheel."

"Okay," Knox said. "Any other paranormal occurences?"

"There is a man who recently came to town who looks exactly like Commander Data from *Star Trek; The Next Generation.* He says he does it as a sales gimmick. People think Data is telling them the facts about his product."

"What is he selling?"

"Some sort of computer surveillance program," Dr. Joy said.

"This is an X-file?" Muller said.

"I've seen him," Dr. Joy said. "He doesn't have any blood. I would bet the farm on that. Or organs."

"He's Data, then?" Cully asked.

"The D I'd pick is Dracula," Dr. Joy responded. "I think he's one of the Undead."

Muller and Cully exchanged glances.

"Got anybody like that in your X-files?" Dr. Joy said, smiling.

"I'm sure Muller does," Cully replied, turning to Muller, who obliged.

"We do know that between the years 1953 and 1957 in a certain part of New Mexico a lot of people ended up as food for the insatiable appetite of creatures unknown for biological enzymes, glandular hormonal secretions. And blood."

"And those creatures unknown could have been vampires?" Cully asked.

"Or aliens," Knox replied. "Those people not used as a food source were abducted and returned with implants that allowed the aliens to control them."

"You think that's what happened to Frank Coletti?"

"I think this Data person may be a genetically engineered human-alien hybrid," Knox said. "Is he mostly hairless with enormous black eyes?"

Dr. Joy shook her head.

"That doesn't sound like anyone around here."

The Call of the Crank: Being Captivated by *Nell*

December 31, 1994

"Cyber-partiers are expected to head out on the information superhighway Saturday night for one of the largest-ever on-line New Year's parties, connecting with an unlimited number of people across the globe or opting for a digital tête-a-tête. . . . .People will tell you what they are drinking and eating and then tell you as they take each drink . . . One thing people like to do is to turn these into costume parties. They sit at the keyboard and tell you what they're wearing, what role they are in, etc."

Chicago Tribune, December 31, 1994

"Look at all this—no running water, no electricity, no phone. Is this reality or what?"

Nell

"Give me a wildness no civilization can endure."

Henry David Thoreau

I.

The real abyss is primordial and it lies in the collective unconscious of humankind, the damp, dark sub-basement and boneshop of species sapien memory. Out of this swampy morass do we rise up, riding the elevator of our ever increasing brainpan size, to the light of . . . of what we are now.

There is nothing essential about this abysmal origin; the genetics get dispersed over millennia; the biology gets shaped and reshaped throughout aeons of cultural processing. Whatever was there in the mud at the beginning gets whipped in a high speed cultural processor so that the blades of cultural difference sever the common pre-adamite roots into a virtual non-existence. Jung says a memory remains, a memory filled with transcultural archetypes that reveal what we are beneath the multilayers of acquired acculturation. And more. We are, each and every one of us, engaged from birth to death in a journey of recognition, of discovery of ourselves as we are personally and as we are collectively. Our personal consciousness is our construction amid the plethora of already existing constructions our present culture has adopted. We shape our consciousness in a world that has already marked the ways consciousness is shaped. We learn to see the world in ways that our present culture has already marked out for us. And by marking the world within these selfsame paths we in turn reproduce the paths, diverging or conjoining, of our culture.

To be a realist is to recognize the myriad ways in which we interact with our culture. We are acculturated products, socialized beings. To mark what we are is to mark the ways we have been culturally stamped. We have even modeled our way out of the note of pessimistic determinism in all this: what we previously called determinants are now clearly seen as culturally-fashioned determinants and therefore not determining at all. They are ours to remodel. And remodel we do—the frenzy of the postmodern age lies in this daily struggle to construct the meanings and values that will in turn construct us. For a time. Till tomorrow. Every faction hopes to secure their own constructions in such a way that the daily bombardment of challenging fabulae can be accommodated and if not accommodated then neutralized, refuted, dismissed with the consent of the majority.

We are also steadily engaged in pointing out to each other what we leave out as we concoct ourselves and the meaning and value of the things around us. We are so fractured into realities and truths now that there is always someone pointing out the limitations within the already existing modes of concocting our present culture has concocted. Yours indeed is a *concoction* while mine is on the path to Truth. Jung's personal unconscious is a reservoir of what we have dismissed in line with the culture's priorities. This is all what we in the course of living have decided not to mark, not to distinguish, not to bring to conceivability in our own lives. Derrida performs the same service in regard to the meanings we attempt to impose: there is no way that such impositions can remain invulnerable to what they seek to exclude. There is no way that what we presence can remain unconfounded by what that presence has pushed into absence.

There seems then to be always more to what we can take note of, and less to our cultural constructions than what lies in the unmarked space of the world and in ourselves. From the very start we have fabricated ourselves and our cultures in diminished, reductive, reified, bureaucratized, objectified ways. We wind up with "I shop, therefore I am." We wind up verifying every aspect of ourselves on-line: if it's not on the hard-drive it can't be retrieved. The Iraqis killed in the Gulf War have no real presence to American TV viewers; their lives and their deaths have been culturally mediated. We want to be realists, then, and acknowledge the ways in which we are culturally imbricated but that cultural imbrication has left us here in the present perceiving the world and the people in it in less real ways than before. Before? When? Was there a beginning in which we were not only more closely attached to reality but we ourselves were all "real stuff?" I mean by this only what we all dream: that we were once "natural" and now we are artificial, that we lived in reality not simulations of the real.

The more the thought of us among Baudrillardian simulacra—indeed our own lives as such simulacra—mesmerizes us, the less able are we to see ourselves differently. Nonetheless, we are easy marks for visions of natural, genuine, artless, unsimulated, innocent, original existence. We become vulnerable to myths of symbolically unmediated life. If civilized culture is a product of such mediation and such civilization perseveres by turning its back on the abyss, then a turning away from both cultural mediation and civilization is a turning back to the abyss. This abyss now is nothing more than the "way we were" before we took the long path that has led us to a postmodern chaos of artifice. The abyss now is not the primitive, instinctual dark morass of atavistic urges but the hyperreal of neural networking that threatens to pull us into a groundless, swirling maze of nonbeing. We abide then nowhere but in our endless fabrications, choosing to leave body and planet behind and be at play with our renderings of both. As we approach the new millennium we doubtlessly see ourselves as furthest from those perennially refashioned signifiers of being "simple and natural," "real and true," "fresh and prototypal." We want not to be replica and live among replica but be archetypal and once again connect with the primary forms of self and world. The fear of virtualization turns us away from a human symbolic environment and *back* to the mythos of natural being, visions of the wild, of existence *au fond*, a mythos that announces itself in the very notion of *going back*. What we hope to find there is what is already conceived here in the present. As in all historical journeys, there is no journey; we manufacture the journey. We get in the car, go no place, get out exactly where we began and think we have gone someplace.

What would we find if we went back to what we were before what we could be would be played out within the frame of what we had already said, practiced and instituted—before, in other words, we were all culturally framed? The question has as much chance of being answered in an empirically verifiable fashion as the question as to what was the one language everyone spoke before Babel. I mean to say it has no interest for the modernist. But for the postmodernist who sees empirical verification as just the present alibi of choice, this question tells us a great deal about how we see ourselves in the present and about what directions we would be taking in altering that perceived reality. Our present interest in an original, bedrock reality out of which we emerged doesn't need to be an empirically profitable interest—it is a shaping interest nonetheless. Interests condition us in the postmodern world—they compose us and our world.

This interest pops up most dramatically with Ronald Reagan's bid for the presidency in 1980. He refers to a golden age America, a hardwon, hardbitten, well-earned reality that we have been led away from by stories of national *malaise,* by stories and poems of the fall of America. Our interest in our primordial stuff takes a decidedly moral turn at the 1992 Republican Conventions: firm moral categories and clear cut moral decisions are back there, the old certitude is something we have strayed from. At that mythic point of beginning, we all knew what was right and what was wrong, what a family was, what love was, what perversion and depravity are, what being anchored in the Lord feels like and so on. And, perhaps, most foundationally, our interest in a timeless time, legends before our fall from fact into fiction, is revealed in our defense of determinate meaning, of the meaning of things fixed forever right at the outset, at the point of origin, by the intentions of the writer or speaker. And if not fixed then, then clearly fixed by a "competent" reader or listener who reconnects signage with message, word and world, signifier with signified.

II.

It is New Year's Eve 1994: November mid-term elections have ousted congressional Democrats in record numbers; this will be the first Republican Congress in forty years. There is nationwide interest in once again changing course. What is this change? America is changing from the premier economic power to an indebted nation, changing from a democracy built on literacy to a nation whose populace needs to be "retrained," changing from a nation in which anybody can become rich to a nation in which no one can get a living wage, changing from a nation with a strong sense of social justice and liberty for all to a nation turning away from its "losers." This is the abridged litany. The point is that if change is what the People want, they also paradoxically want change to end, to be replaced by stability, a stability that is not observable in the present. It is a lost thing; once here but now gone. The rhetoric of change then which seems to be future-oriented is indeed past oriented. We had something but we strayed from it. We have strayed from true meaning and true value; we have strayed from clear definitions and decisive actions. Our consciousness awakens within a war of meanings and values, of endless conflicting interpretations, that belie the rudimentary reality of self and world. We are lost in a whirlwind, drowning in a whirlpool of our own symbolic expressiveness.

Why not future-oriented? Is not every campaigner's promise a promise of a future America? The future, like the past, is no more than a blank slate to be filled in by the present. We drift in and out of attentiveness to historical "facts," "events," "truths." And it is the present like an outboard motor that propels our course, our attentiveness, our valuing. Our present is engaged in multi-dimensional "culture wars" and the Conservatives have just won the mid-term election battle, perhaps what will turn out to be a decisive battle. Put simply the war is over the proliferation of meanings and values. One side holds that we are daily engaged in producing and consuming interpretations of self and world and that every interpretation handily produces its own rationality, its own strategy for "truth correspondence." The other side holds that we are daily engaged in trying to hold on to the truth and reality that we have already discovered and daily engaged in adding to this foundation of truth and reality. In the former, the postmodern view, we are in the present concocting the future out of numerous, diverging articulations, none of whose assumptions are self-evidentially true or self-present. In the latter, the modernist view, we are trying to constrain the articulations of the present by reference to this already established foundation of rationality and realism.

Put blankly, the postmodernist is spinning a future that promises even more instability, more flux, more indeterminacy, more uncertainty, more fabulae and less fact, more life in the buffer zone of symbolic mediation, more negotiating of turbulent seas without the rudder of reason. Nothing in this future has enduring priority, legitimated privilege, perpetual lease, universal justification, innate entitlement, irrevocable warrant. The modernist fears the flux and cites an order of things, perennial, established, reliable, foundational. In this perennial order of things there are meanings and values that have a core, innate resilience to challenges because they reflect what is indeed the nature of truth and reality. There is a vestige of Natural Law theory here but that has no enlightened defense; what we are talking about here is the Western Tradition of Rationality and Realism that has built a foundation of truth that can only be shaken if we adopt the irrationalism of postmodernity.

While the postmodernist *goes back* only to see how a particular mythos has been reified, the modernist goes back to point out the true precedent, the road of truth we have come down, the reason why we should do such and such in the present. We cannot change beyond the parameters that rationality and realism have already established. We can compose the present and the future but only out of the *bricolage* of a rationally legitimated past. The rush to articulate that past—from E. D. Hirsch's *Cultural Literacy* in 1987 to William Bennett's *Book of Moral Virtues* and Harold Bloom's *The Western Canon,* both in 1994— ironically has also exposed those legacies as articulations, as assemblages of views on virtue and lists of "what every American needs to know" and who every American should read in the views of self-proclaimed cultural gurus. Ultimately, one has the feeling that if truth and reality are the possessions of our culture in some abiding and ever-expanding way they would be observable in the culture. We wouldn't have to wait for the word to hit this week's bestseller list. And even more upsetting, we wouldn't be witnessing the fall of our cultural legacy in those same capricious lists. It seems something of a postmodern riposte to see universal moral virtues replaced by a how to get rich quick and not pay taxes guide.

Reports from the Universal and Absolute Truth front are unceremoniously tossed in with other competing narratives of everything under the sun, from the economy to crime in the streets. Every new reminder of core family values, of expedient justice, of clear right and wrong, of determinate gender and sexuality, of species hierarchy, of what identity is and what difference is, of where the center is and where it is not, of what everyone is melting into, of how America is a classless society, of what little Johnny needs to know, of what progress is, of why Americans should feel good about themselves—on and on—every such reminder enters the ring and does fifteen rounds with fifteen contenders. Nothing in this contentious, postmodern age is undisputed. Moses's presentation of the Ten Commandments to a postmodern crowd would have led to stone tablets being turned into open texts.

Not to enter the ring at all will soon seem the wisest course. In Presidential elections, for instance, the incumbent's handlers often advise the incumbent not to respond to a challenger's words because any response will immediately elevate that hopeful while diminishing the aura of the incumbent. To enter the fray is to acquiesce to the notion that what will stand forth as truth will be negotiated here in this exchange of rival narratives. Today all debate, in other words, is held within a postmodern forum. The frustration this causes those who see reality and truth as discoverable and not concoctable propels them down old roads, some of them dark and really scary. Zhirinovsky in Russia is scary; Edward Luttwak's prediction that fascism is the wave of the future is scary; the German's treatment of Turks is scary; California's recent passing of an immigration law; the growing popularity of xenophobic, sexist, racist talk show programs; the preference for prisons and capital punishment over personal and social rehabilitation; the Christian fundamentalism of the 1992 Republican Convention; the "victories" over every form of socialism and the new equation of liberalism with "red" socialism; the vilification of the revolutionary '60s and the important protests of that period; the market's unconcern for the former Yugoslavia, the former Soviet Union as well as the entire continent of Africa; the emergence in 1994 (!) of a racist "bell curve" of intelligence; the total denigration of a liberal welfare economics and the notions of egalitarianism and social justice that inspired them.

Following in the footsteps of *Forrest Gump*, *Nell* takes us into the "dark side" of conservative/modernist frustration with a postmodern world that will not bow to the eternal verities, the innate, indisputable qualities of being, pristine roots and natural rhythms. The war goes on here on the level of dream and magic, of archetypal memories re-awakened, of romantic yearnings

recognized, of urban frustrations released. If we observe someone who does not awaken amid the flurry of our postmodern hul-
labaloo what do we see? If what is essential in our humanity has
in this film a chance to show itself, what will we see?

Out of this innocence made visible to us do we then concoct
the distortions of the postmodern world; obscure what is simple
and vital; push it further and further back until all manner of
simulations contend that they are the real thing. We must feel
that surely what we have now in the postmodern world outside
this theatre is a far cry from where we began. When we go back
and revisit the '60s we have the simple and good Forrest Gump
as our guide; when we go back even further, to our primal beginnings, we find that natural spirit of the wild, Nell. No debate
here; just a clear representation of natural authority: Gump's
mental simplicity is a sort of prophylactic—it protects him from
postmodern dissension; Nell's "wildness" serves the same purpose. What they possess is a bit of the "real thing" untainted by
what we all in the theatre have been tainted by—our own cultural
constructions. We haven't built on or enhanced our original au-
thentic selves but rather have substituted that genuineness with
postmodern simulacra. We've lost our true genetic coding, if that
were possible, our real values, our real beliefs, our real selves.
While Forrest Gump calls us to revise the past so that we can
have a "real" future, Nell calls us back to our own true selves, free
of our dissenting views.

It sounds rather like Hitler addressing his fellow Germans,
Serbs addressing Serbs, Tutus addressing Tutus, Russians addressing Russians, white supremacists all over the world addressing all who have lost track of their own inherent racial
purity. It sounds like all manner of tribalistic, racist claptrap. Or
sexist. There was an aboriginal "iron john" who has been reduced
to the subservient, pliable male of today. It sounds like the advocates of the Gaia principle speaking for the rights of the whole
planet as prior to and greater than anything that goes on in the
human postmodern carnival. It sounds like the advocates of a genetic defense of the free market dismissing all collective action
against global corporations as deviant and regressive.

It sounds like the call of the crank. Who is the crank? The
crank is a person whose views you don't hold—the first response
I got to my question. Since no one's views can prove themselves
to correspond to anything but the sense of realism from which
they emerge, the frame of representation they are in, it makes no

postmodern sense, if you will, to call one's opponents cranks. No, the crank is a crank because he or she positions himself or herself outside or before any quarrel. They hold themselves off from the "contest of narratives." They know something or possess something that merely has to be pointed to in order to resolve all quarrels. The crank has no terms of exchange; language is transcended. A person of faith—any faith—is called upon to take his or her faith into the world and use it as a means of exchange. This faith will grow and change. A crank's mythos is non-dialogic; it is meant to stop the pluralization of meaning by establishing a primal authority from which all meaning and value is causally connected. The crank's chain of signification cannot be challenged; all claims against it, ethical, political, logical, social, aesthetic and so on, are irrelevant.

Offering a moron with limited speech facility as a guide to the most turbulent period of the last half century in the hope that that moron's view will become ours and that we will adopt that moron's philosophy of life as a philosophy to take into the New Millennium is crank work. It tries for a perch above the postmodern strife. Proposing to take us back into an aboriginal setting, into the life of a woman warbling woodnotes wild, in order to show us ourselves in nature, light years away from being "virtualized," is meant to revive a long repressed nostalgia. But for what? For pure individualism? For a vital self-interest not misdirected toward collective and communitarian interests? For a return to our natural and not social selves? For possibly a glimpse at the latent authority of the biological and the natural, an authority that can rule in the postmodern court of endless dissent?

I hear the call of the crank in *Nell* but I am set up to hear it; we are all prepped to hear it. It may be a way out of the abyss; it may be a means to settle our growing fear of the virtualization of our own lives. Here, here is a person unvirtualized; she has never had a remote in her hand. We watch the screen's images to get beyond images to the real.

III.

"[I]deas that draw upon the authority of nature nearly always have their origin in ideas about society."
     Andrew Ross, *The Chicago Gangster Theory of Life*

I saw *Nell* the first time with my oldest daughter who had recently been on an archaeological dig. She went through Nell's cabin and Nell's life in an archaeological fashion. She was disappointed: she wanted to see more of Nell handling her tools, from frying pan to hoe. Nell couldn't be classified as feral because she had been brought up by a mother, an aphasic mother however. One can only speculate as to what horrors aphasic single-parenting might construe in the mind of family values Conservatives. Regardless. Nell is not a feral child. We are not going back to a state of nature where we can supposedly observe foundational self-interest uncontaminated by liberal notions of mutual aid. Nell had had a twin who had died when she was about ten. In short, Nell had been acculturated: she spoke a mix of twin speech and mother aphasic speech; her head was filled with myths implanted by her mother. Nell is hardly the totally natural, wild creature that anthropologists dream of finding. And yet she is wild and natural enough for us. She is sufficiently distanced from our unnatural lives and sufficiently attached to the natural for a critical double-seeing of ourselves and the film. The film is, in fact, multiply coded and therefore finally winds up within the postmodern struggle for meanings and values. In short, we are never quite sure whether we find biological justification for foundational self-interest and possessive individualism or for foundational altruism, mutual aid and community.

Working through the variety of intersections between self-interest and altruism in this film is like working through the same in American culture at the present moment. But—and this is vital—it all passes through the prism of the popular film *and* its interconnections with its own re-working of notions of genetic greed into, in the words of Ronald Colman in *A Tale of Two Cities*, "a far, far better thing." At every turn if you want to argue that the film is in collusion with the market, is a prime example of the "cultural logic of late capitalism" at play, the track you're on gets switched. I mean that this return to a natural and unvirtualized state of existence neither confirms market capitalism's belief in the genetic reality of self-interest nor fails to critique the state of "civilization" that self-interest has wrought. And of course since we do not in fact return to the natural but only to what you can call "aphasic acculturation," Nell is not out of the realm of culturally constructed reality and into reality-before-culture, but simply the product of odd acculturation. Thus, rather than leaving the postmodern clash of narratives and realities, we are led back into it.

The desire to break away and see ourselves before we began our trek toward virtualization remains the underlying desire of the film. It never matters that when we look closely we do not find the bed-rock reality of ourselves. What stays with us is this urge to flee the hyperreal and return to the natural. Let's flee the simulations produced by a postmodern eroding of our confidence. Our confidence in what? Clearly in our capacity to discover the real and the true, being and world before media hype and "difference" hype set in. The "difference" hype? It goes like this: we were one way at the beginning, in a state of nature, responding to one reality. Difference and diversity, therefore, become part of our false turn down the road to virtualization. The point here is that if you go back to the original state of being, you find a survivalist instinct, the instinct to perpetuate one's own existence. In this struggle, difference loses out to the identity that prevails— what prevails establishes identity. Diversity can endure, but only in a hierarchical manner for what has been overwhelmed has been diminished in "being."

Jack London didn't direct *Nell* but the global free market does. However, because the global free market is everywhere and always already itself interacting with the multiple dispositions of our postmodern culture, it can only have a mazy sort of directing style. I mean by this that it has to follow a buck; its concern with the bottom line compels it to not only plug into its own self-preservation (undermine a postmodern contesting of narratives which opposes its own supremacy in all matters) but into that very contesting that leads to a questioning of self-interest as the proper attitude or foundation for an egalitarian democracy concerned with social justice. Of course, egalitarianism and a concern for social justice may be as extinct issues in the view of the global market as nature itself. In any case, films that wind up trashing any of these are hardly obliging the protocols of Hollywood. Hollywood, like Disney, has constructed values that the market itself must value.

Americans in 1994 may be sick and tired of what they see as a bloated welfare system, of the perceived inequities of Affirmative Action, of political correctness and an endless celebration of a difference and diversity that isn't melting down the way past difference had to, of a justice system that can't seem to keep the violent off the streets. And much more. At the same time, Americans live in the mythos of their own generosity; in the mythos of an egalitarianism that a class-ridden Europe could never attain; and a mythos of their own fair-mindedness in judging each other for what they are and not who they are. Corporate board rooms may be the place to run films whose mythos of liberty, equality, justice is cleverly manipulated by and at the mercy of an up-scale '90s social Darwinism. It won't play in Peoria. At least not at the moment.

There is a mythos of self-interest also. The metaphor mechanical: self-interest is the engine driving the free play of the global market. The metaphor agricultural: a society that allows an economy of self-interest to grow will maximize its harvest. The metaphor nautical: generating a rising tide of production and consumption will raise all boats. Richard Libertini, playing the head of a research lab in a major university questions Liam Neeson's desire to help Nell. Even Mother Theresa is pursuing self-interest: she doesn't value her life unless she's devoting it to other people. In other words, everybody is into everything for what they can get out of it, whether fame, fortune or self-denial. Nell becomes a career opportunity for Libertini's whole research staff, including Natasha Richardson, who admits she will probably make full professor for her study of Nell. In pursuing their career interests, they are at the same time increasing the world's knowledge of human personality. Self-interest, therefore, winds up serving a purpose that is beneficial to all. Now Liam Neeson doesn't know what his interest is and Richardson warns him not to screw up her study. In other words, Neeson is motivationally a wild card—in not pursuing his own self-interest he may wind up obstructing the free flow of self-interest. He is liable to break the economic cycle and the reality it creates. Libertini puts it to him in this fashion: if we leave Nell in the woods someone is bound to find her and she'll be plunged into the twentieth century as a talk show curiosity. When Neeson does rescue her from the research lab he takes Nell no further than to a motel where she falls into a sort of catatonic state. There is no real, viable alternative to the free flow of self-interest. It's like Lyndon Johnson's War Against Poverty: the poor and downtrodden were all put on the welfare rosters. And then they went catatonic, dropping out of not only national productiveness but personal as well.

The ending is pure Hollywood: Nell returns to her natural life but now she has neighbors over as friends. She's not a freak in a lab or a wild child in the woods; she's a woman that has found community. Community? She has found a place for others in her life, not ghosts but living people. However, Nell has always been other-directed; her own life has always been shared with her twin, both before the twin's death and after. Self-interest has been genetically multiplied—the self has never really been one. Nell passes this secret of interrelationship on to Neeson and Richardson whom Nell pushes together, forehead touching forehead, after the two have quarreled. It is Nell's example that brings Richardson out of her life-long distance from others and Neeson back into his need to relate.

Nell's attachment to her long dead twin is an attachment to another that goes way beyond the attachment that a genetic self-interest either requires or fosters. I think Nell is clearly not surviving because of an underlying self-interest at work but rather because she is a Blakean mental traveller, living in an ambiance of twin interrelationship that has never abated. At the same time, our cultural expectations at this time have all to do with Nell surviving because she possesses a natural, unacculturated lust for self-preservation and a total detachment from the sort of simulacra and spectacle that has replaced the real in our own lives. As soon as the camera pans the lush growth of the North Carolina forest preserve, the great but simple beauty of lake and woods, we know that we are going back to the way America was before it began to falsify itself with hyper imagining. As a viewer, I must confess that I slip into a crack between a primordial instinct for survival programmed by a basic self-interest, (our most basic instinct), and survival through affiliation with others, preservation of species through community and collectivization, programmed by a subatomic reality in which all is indeed interrelationship. I slip all the way through to what the culture has on its mind, if you will, when community interests face off with self-interests. And it's an economic battlefield.

If you get a bunch of people together who are all out to make a profit by putting out the best car they can, then they will work as a collective. But the worker is in it for the salary, which may be diminished to the point that it does not propel the work but seems merely to be the barest modicum to keep one capable of working. Interrelationship here is thread bare. Group dynamics, management skills, worker motivation, incentive strategies, and organizational behavior clinics are keyed to bolster the one weak link in genetic self-interest: how do you make collective use of people without that collective affiliating beyond, outside and perhaps eventually against the designated corporate goal, which is always to maximize net profits by minimizing labor costs?

Typically within a corporate organization, career interests generate a competitiveness that works against the sort of interrelationship Nell urges Neeson and Richardson into. But when the global labor supply is more than ample, workers's self-interest is totally captivated by finding and holding a job. The necessary corporate interrelationship emerges from this, if not with workers here then with workers there. Rather than the minimum wage in this country rising, it seems probable that it will stay the same for a long, long time, which is the same as saying it will diminish. Global market values are closer to bringing American workers to a Third World wage scale than vice versa. In the same fashion, there is only presently a market-determined relationship between American entrepreneurs and American society. This means that private corporate decisions, say, to pull GM plants out of Flint, Michigan, leaves the city of Flint with monstrous public problems. But the nexus here is limited to a market nexus, so GM goes off pursuing the best global location bottom line-wise. Rather than cities elsewhere on the globe benefiting, what happens is that every city is now competing with every other city to prove to global entrepreneurs that they are the most cost-effective location. They do so by deregulation, lowered taxes, and anti-union legislation. The self-interest of American society, like that of the American worker, is captivated by the incentive to attract business and do anything they can to keep it.

I know the film cannot bear all of this; but the headlines can and the culture does, and any film in 1994 that takes us back to ourselves in a state of nature, before the counterculture took the American dream on a cannabis trip—in Newt Gingrich's view—is hitting all our buttons. And if Nell spoke proper English she would have to enunciate a narrative of genetic self-interest or a narrative of genetic interrelationship or a narrative of undecidability. Any one of these would be adding fuel to the culture wars, the postmodern contesting of narratives. But since Nell is Jodie Foster and the role is an Oscar role and Hollywood has a long tradition of innocence speaking before the multitude, Nell does speak in the final courtroom scene. What does she tell us? She has had her share of pain but she sees more pain in us. We do not look into each other's eyes; we do not interrelate, intersect, interpenetrate. We need each other; we are each other's twin, arm in arm down the same long path of life from birth to death. Old Walt, the good grey poet, casts his shadow over Nell's cabin— we are "Camerado" arms locked going down the road.

Comrades? A bad vibe for a post–Soviet New World Order. There's more than something of the call of the crank here, but it's a sweet note, a Hollywood note. We are enchanted. We are, unfortunately, captivated.

In the Shadow of Elvis and Mildred Pierce

Morio's Basement
> "I . . . will spend . . . my life for you
> Loving you. . . . well, I'll be loving you . . .
> Winter . . . summer, springtime too . . .
> Always be there for you . . .
> Don't make a difference where I go
> Or what I'm gonna do . . .
> You know what I'm saying
> I'll be loving you"

"That is sweet," Kenny said as Morio hooked up his acoustic archaeology laser computer set-up to Elvis's Cadillac steering wheel. "It's like, you know, if you get love past a one night stand . . . "

"Saturday night fever," Woad said, sprawled out on the cot in Morio's lab.

"Love is on the other side," Kenny said, nodding. "The Sunday side."

"I'm ready," Morio said, hitting an enter key.

They heard what sounded like muffled street sounds, car horns, voices, barking, whistling, words in an unknown tongue.

"What are we listening to?" Kenny asked.

"Traffic, I think," Woad said.

"The computer will tighten it up and slow it down," Morio said, typing rapidly at the keyboard. This time when he struck the enter key they heard . . .

"You know I gotta be made a fool of to millions of people or I'm what . . . the Devil?

"Holy shit, that's Elvis!" Kenny yelled.

"You knock on the doors," another voice said, "real loud. So they let you in. Once you're inside, you stop knocking wildly. You let them know you're not really a threat. You let them know you can fit in. You're selling songs, not revolution."

"Who the hell is that?" Woad said.

"Colonel Tom Parker I'll bet," Kenny replied.

"You know, I know who I am. It comes down to that."

They waited but there was no more.

"I don't believe it," Kenny said, shaking his head. "I mean that conversation is on that wheel?"

Morio nodded.

"That is the clearest one," he said.

"But it's like that little conversation is worth a million bucks," Kenny replied. "I mean Elvis says I know who I am? And then he becomes a total sham in those stupid movies? And then in Vegas? Holy shit, this is high tragedy. Captured on a steering wheel."

"The human body and an object interchange subatomic particles," Woad said. "And you've figured out how to pick that up using laser technology and then through the computer reassemble the stored sound energy?"

Morio nodded.

"That is very good," he told Woad.

"Does it make a difference if the object is very old?" Woad asked. "Say, like a hundred years?"

Morio said he didn't know. He hadn't had an opportunity to test very old objects.

"Or like objects from another planet?" Woad asked.

Morio nodded his head enthusiastically.

"You have something of the future?" he asked Woad.

Woad went over to the Elvis wheel and stroked it.

"Now I see why you showed me this," he said. "You believe that stuff they were saying about me finding an alien spacecraft."

"Is it possible?" Morio said, eagerly, eyes entranced by the possibility of playing alien voices on his laser sound system.

"You last worked for Sally Simmons?" Sweeney asked, sitting in his back office, one leg crossed over the other, eyes on the brown and white wing tip balanced on his knee.

"I did," Gladys replied.

"And Abe Fata before that?"

"Thirteen years. Abe and I had a falling out. Personal."

"Hm," Sweeney said, recalling how good a waitress Gladys had been at Fata's. He could use her.

"Let me make a call," Sweeney said. "Why don't you go back to the kitchen and tell Betty to give you a cup of coffee."

When the door closed behind Gladys, Sweeney dialed Sally. Sally sounded as if she had been crying. She had cried all through Barfield's funeral.

"How did the Jean Moreau work for you at the seance?" Sweeney asked.

"Okay. I guess."

"Did you do the Moreau bit with your legs? Black silk stockings? Shapely leg capturing the gaze."

"I . . . I tried . . . but it . . . didn't seem right."

"I see you're still registered at Heartbreak Hotel," Sweeney said sadly. "I heard the seance didn't come off."

"I'm . . . I'm sorry, Sweeney. I have to go."

"Yeah, okay. But can you tell me why you let Gladys Farquarson go?"

"No, I can't."

"Well, she's asking for a job here. If you were me, would you hire her?"

There was a long pause.

"Is this a safe dream of danger part for me, Sweeney?" Sally asked.

"Sure, it is, Sally," Sweeney said.

"Then if I were you I'd hire her," Sally said and then hung up.

Sweeney found Betty Lip and Gladys drinking coffee in the kitchen. As he stood in the doorway the scene before him seemed right out of *Mildred Pierce*, with Joan Crawford, moodily photographed—Gladys Farquarson the star suffering in luxury while

Betty Lip, played by Ann Blyth, sat across from her, the most un-grateful daughter in the history of the movies. Hiring Gladys would be like hiring Mildred Pierce: "The Kind of Woman Most Men Want . . . And Shouldn't Have!"

"What's up?," Mark Wonder called out as Data came out of his door, hesitated and then looked at Mark, who was out walk-ing Ginch, his Rotweiller,

"What?" Data said.

"You look like you got something on your positronic brain," Mark said, smiling.

"If I had one, I'd get the hell out of this town," Data said.

"Hey, don't say that. This town's got a future. All the cards are here. All you need is somebody to deal them."

"Do you know what Stalking is?"

"It's not one of my vices," Mark replied. "Why?"

Do I look like a stalker? For crying out loud, all I was doing was testing that positron brain on the kid's doll. Was I stalking the kid because I had a remote that could operate the doll?"

"Hey, Ginch likes you," Mark said, as Newt slobbered good naturedly on Data's shoes.

"Ginch? Is that his name?"

"Short for Gingrich," Mark said.

"I think that's what I'll call Elvis' hound dog. Ginch."

"What's that supposed to mean?" Mark said, baffled.

"I'm putting together an Elvis hotline over the internet," Data said. "When that catches on, I put the whole enchilada onto CD-Rom and sell it at *Radio Shack.*"

Mark Wonder thought about that.

"Let me run something by you," he said to Data. "I've been in this town less than a year but I haven't been idle. What if I told you there's a guy in town that recovers Elvis' voice from things Elvis touched?"

"I heard that," Data said. "Saito. I know his work in the com-puter application of laser technology."

"He could supply you with a lot of new facts about Elvis," Mark said.

"I suppose so."

"I could bring you guys together in an air-tight partnership," Mark said. "And serve up all the necessary media and marketing promotion you'd need. Fifteen per cent off the top is all I take."

"I'll think about it," Data said, bending down and taking Ginch's monumental head between his two hands. "Hi, boy," he said, rubbing behind Ginch's ears.

"What the hell is that?" Data suddenly said, pointing upward and behind Mark. Mark turned around quickly and as he did so Data pulled out one positron brain chip and slipped in a new one into Ginch's ear canal. It was a sudden inspiration: what if the dog's own brain began to interact with the chip? What if the chip produced a noise that caused the dog's brain to re-organize itself at a higher level in order to receive the chip's transmissions?

As he watched Mark Wonder continue on his walk with Ginch, Data could see the dog's pelvic wiggle ever so slightly, clear evidence that the Elvis Hotline chip was already transmitting. And was being received.

"You've had experiences, bad experiences," the Rev. Aldrich said to the small group of sinners congregated in the model home for the Nouveau Noire Estates.

"There's no color to bad," the Rev. said to the group. "Bad is bad. They may be white bad. Or they may be black bad. Equally bad. It's the only equality you can be sure of in this Godforsaken great land of ours."

"Sister Lucy," the Rev. said to Lu Powell, who had her hand raised.

"It's badder the second time," she told the Reverend.

"What's badder the second time, girl?"

"Well, the first time it's not anything because it doesn't have a special feel to it."

"What doesn't have a special feel to it?" the Rev. said, patience already gone. "Be concrete, girl. Tell us exactly what you're talking about."

"Well, like now. I don't mean like now. I mean the first time we were all here like this and I raised my hand and said "it's badder the second time" and then you said what you just said. Only it was the first time."

The Rev. looked at Rick Monte and Scraps the Loudmouth who had brought Lucy. They both scratched their heads like Stan Laurel.

"SO?" the Rev. boomed.

"Well, that time it was like normal. But now the second time it's a repeat but only for me."

"I think she is talking about déjà vu," Antony, who was sitting in the back next to Doc MacGowan said. "Everything now she feels she has experienced before."

"Yeah, so let's say I did something really bad one time but I didn't feel so bad, but the second time I'd know what was coming and . . . "

"Don't you learn from your mistakes, girl?" the Rev. told her.

"I knew you'd say that," Lu replied, giggling.

"Maybe it happened to her in another life time," Rick Monte put in and then laughed.

"The thing about déjà vu," Doc MacGowan said, "is that you don't choose the experiences to happen. All of a sudden, you realize you've done and said and seen all this before. It's like you're playing a part you've already played. Free will has nothing to do with it. You don't get a chance to choose."

"Maybe God blinked," Antony suggested. "Or farted."

"I'd say stored memories cross or short out," Doc MacGowan said. "My own theory is that it all happens in the eyeball, an optic nerve/brain glitch. It's like a reverse action. The brain throws old images back to the optic nerve. So while you're seeing something again, you're not seeing what's here now."

"So this gal here ain't seeing us all here?" the Rev. said, annoyed at Doc MacGowan for running a science number on them.

"I knew you'd say that," Lu cried out.

"Antony," the Rev. said, checking himself. "The hymn."

"Are you lonesome tonight . . . " Antony began to sing in a high, sweet voice, "Do you miss me tonight? Are you sorry we drifting apart. . . . "

Meanwhile, Kenny, Woad and Morio were listening to the soles of Kenny's track shoes. Most of what they heard was in a foreign tongue but they did a catch a bit of conversation in English regarding the results of the American mid-term elections. Then they played the fillings inside Woad's teeth and with a back left molar they picked up something from when Woad was in the third grade.

"Jeez, it sounds like you were scared shitless," Kenny said as they listened to young Woad pleading with his dentist to be extra careful.

"That was Dr. Berg," Woad said. "You know his son . . . "

"You mean the guy we used to call Whine Berg?" Kenny replied.

"He's a State Senator now where he's whining about privatizing everything from the schools and the post office to garbage and police."

"Private cops? How the hell does that work?"

"Well, a neighborhood gets together and hires as much private protection as they think they need. I mean if they can afford it."

"So you get one cop in South Central LA and about six thousand in West LA," Kenny said, nodding.

"I think we can play organic substance," Morio said, standing over Kenny and looking down into his head of shoulder length hair. "Hair maybe."

"Whoa!" Kenny said, jumping up. "This is turning weird."

"But just think of it, Kenny," Woad said. "You've been growing that head of hair since, when? I mean the tips are like from years ago. Let Morio cut off a sample."

"No way," Kenny said. "Give him some of your hair."

But Morio was already clipping his fingernails which he then placed in line with his laser. Very soon the three of them were listening to Mrs. Saito berate her husband for not getting the eaves troughs cleaned. Morio cut off his own reply.

"Hey, the house!" Woad cried out. "Let's listen to the house. Where's, like, the oldest section, Morio?"

"This house was built in the '50s," Morio said. "Not very old."

Saying this, Morio ran the laser setup along the cement block walls of the lab. Only muffled sounds were produced. Placing his laser on a table with wheels, Morio proceeded out of the room, followed by Woad and Kenny. With their help, he brought the equipment up to the first floor, where again the reception was not good. Finally in the attic, where bare beams were exposed and the walls were covered with thin faded wallpaper they heard the sounds of the '50s. In a great rush, garbled and then as clear as a bell, voices, music, laughter, screams, Ed Sullivan, Ed Wynn, Ed Wood, Jr., Marilyn, Mamie, Jayne, Ike, Roy, Gene, Howdy, Uncle Miltie, Dean and Jerry, Winchell, The Dean, Marlon, Lucy, Desi, Fred, Ethel, the Rosenbergs, Joe McCarthy, Nixon, Dinah, Rock, Doris, Louis, The Bird, the Mouseketeers, Arthur Godfrey, Jack Paar, Mel Allen, Beaver Cleaver, Ozzie, Harriet, Ricky, David, Debbie, Patti, Snookie, Theresa, Pat Boone, Death Valley Ronnie and then, as the three sat there, hypnotized by the sounds—Elvis:

"Ah, you know I can't be found . . . sitting home all alone . . .
If you can't come around . . . at least please telephone . . .
Don't be cruel . . . to a heart that's true. . . . "

After the sinners meeting Rick Monte, Lu Powell, and Antony went to Sweeney's for coffee. As they sat in a booth beneath glossy studio photos of Joan Crawford and Sidney Greenstreet in *Flamingo Road* and Elvis in *King Creole,* Rick told them about his recurrent déjà vu experience.

"I'm in a cherry red '57 Chevy Impala. Top down. Tooling around. I don't know if it's 1957 or 1994 and I'm just driving a '57. See what I mean?"

He looked over his coffee cup at Antony who sat behind an ice cream soda with whipped cream swirls and a cherry at the top. With a long handled spoon designed to reach the very bottom of the glass, Antony was excavating just below and to the right of the cherry. He didn't look up at Rick and Rick went on:

"As soon as I think: 'I'm back here again wondering if it's 1957 or now I know I'm gonna say 1957. And sure enough as I turn a corner I see a girl in a poodle skirt . . . "

"A poodle skirt?" Lu said, sucking on the finger she had just dipped into her coffee to test it.

"Yeah," Rick replied. "They were all the rage about 1957. And there's, like, no cars parked that are even from the '60s. I mean its strictly 1957 and older models I'm seeing. But I know while I'm looking that pretty soon I'm gonna find something from today. And as soon as I find that. Bingo! I know it's really not 1957."

"Sounds like a dream," Antony said, staring at the mixed ice cream, syrup, nuts and cream ore he had just mined. "Not a déjà vu."

"Yeah, but it happens when I'm driving and I know it's got the feel of something I did before and I know what's going to happen but then I free myself of thinking I've been here doing this before and I'm just here. Not thinking I'm repeating what I'm doing and thinking."

Antony worked his spoon, Lucy sipped her coffee and Rick looked around for Gladys, their waitress. He needed something to eat.

"You weren't déjà vuing when you ran Further down, were you?" Antony then said.

"What?" Rick, suddenly pale, said.

"That's what I'd be dreaming about," Lu said. "Over and over and over again."

"Well, I don't," Rick snapped. "And shut up about it. I paid for that."

"Oh, my," Antony said, picking up his half finished ice cream soda. "The man paid for that. Oh, my."

Lu and Rick watched Antony as he took his ice cream soda to the counter where he sat next to Carl who was having tea and an English muffin. Carl was waiting for Gladys to finish her shift so he could tell her the good news.

"I meant I'm paying for it," Rick said to Lu. "That's what I meant. It was an accident. Pure and simple. You think I wanted to run that kid over?"

"I knew you were going to say that," Lu said, her eyes shining and wide with the wonder of it all.

"Big deal," Rick said, grumpily.

"Chariot of Fire," Antony read from the brand new business card Carl had handed him. "Carl Firewoad, Call for Car Service Day or Night. 555-8493."

"What do you think?" Carl asked. "No, keep it. You don't know when you might need me to drive you someplace."

"Firewoad?" Antony said, trying to remember where he had heard that name. It seemed to him that he had lately been someplace and had been reading the name "Firewoad" in red with a white background.

"There were the Woads and the Firewoads that settled this area," Carl informed him as Gladys came over and poured some more hot water in his tea cup. Carl winked at her and she smiled.

"Hey, Gladys," Rick yelled from his booth, "How about some service?"

"Right after the Civil War," Carl said in low, measured tones as he turned on the counter stool to look over at Rick. "The Woads fought with the North. The Firewoads fought alongside Stonewall, standing there like a stone wall. Rebs. Every one of them."

"Oh, my," Antony said, glancing at the card again, noticing the flames shooting off the letters that spelt Chariot of Fire. "What's this little figure over here?" he asked Carl.

Carl looked.

"That's my logo," Carl said.

"It looks like a little midget in flames holding a guitar," Antony said, looking closer.

"That's Elvis," Carl said, still watching the Gladys and Rick exchange. "In *Flaming Star*. Elvis was caught between two worlds in that movie. White and Red. White was for the way things were supposed to be. And red was what happened when things weren't the way they were supposed to be."

"Who's that guy?" Carl said, pointing to Rick who seemed to be doing a Jack Nicholson–with–the–waitress–bit from *Five Easy Pieces* on Gladys.

Antony turned around, and when he did so it seemed to him that he was playing out a part he had played before.

"That's Rick Monte," he said and even his own voice came back to him like an echo.

"Rick. Monte." Carl repeated slowly. "The whole world turned its back on Elvis. And then he stopped trying to make things the way they were supposed to be. Like he did in that film. "

"I have to see the movie," Antony said, realizing that he had let his ice cream melt beyond the point he liked and that the cherry had slid into the melt.

"That's why I picked Elvis as my logo," Carl said. "I'm bringing Elvis out of Hell where his fans deserted him. I'm driving him around so he can get his revenge."

Carl swung back to the counter and his eyes rolled up toward a glossy of Elvis in *Love Me Tender*.

"Elvis was the king," Carl said.

"Oh, my," Antony said, rolling his eyes fearfully upward, knowing he was going to see red flames around the photo, because heat from somewhere had melted his ice cream to a thin liquid.

Antony got up, picked up his check and laid Carl's card down.

"Keep it," Carl said, "You don't know when you might need me to drive you someplace."

"I always walk," Antony said, walking away, toward Betty Lip at the cash register.

"Who *is* that man?" Antony asked Betty, not turning but making eye movements to his right.

"Oh, that's Carl," Betty said, taking the five dollar bill Antony handed her. "He's got the hots for Gladys."

"Hmm," Antony said, taking his change, and shaking his head as if he were chilled. "That man gives me the creeps."

Betty laughed.

"Yeah, well, have a good one."

A good what? Antony said to himself as he pushed through the door and out into the cold February night.

Index

technophobes, 283
telecommunications, and the electronic plebiscite, 316
teledemocracy, 315–18
Terminator II, 301
terrorism, computer, 277, 281
Thelma and Louise, 101
Tikkun, 35–36
time, 104–05; in *Pulp Fiction*, 37–41
Time Cop, 299
Time Machine, 282
Tintern Abbey, 285
Torchsong Trilogy, 249
tough love, 153, 168, 171
transnational marketing, and our insecurity, 357
transnationals, and the Feds, 353
Treasure of the Sierra Madre, 152
true meaning, 271
True Lies, 94
True Romance, 94, 149, 163–67, 233
turbo-charged capitalism, 74
TV, interactive, 315–18; law enforcement programs, 318–20
TV Nation, 321

Unabomber, 14
unconscious, 50, 53; desire, as unthought, 152
Underclass, 98, 99, 142, 225, 326; as violent and dangerous, 160, 168, 170; life, 168–169; and bad behavior, 171; descent into, 350; reaction to O. J. trial, 228
Unthought, 152; desire, contingency and power, 281
Until the End of Time, 284
Usual Suspects, 332

Varela, Francesco, and theory of autopoesis, 46
Vietnam, 20

violence and the violent, 97, 98, 137, 149–61 passim, 163–173 passim, 189–201, 221–29, 319, 349; and economics and politics, 149–61, passim
virtual geography, 96
virtual reality, 271–72, 274–75, 284–85, 300; and our insecurity, 357; fear of, 381; and difference, 389
Virtuosity, 299, 300

Wall Street, 15, 90, 349
War Against the Poor, 169
Wark, MacKenzie, 96
Waterworld, 12, 299–306
wealth, and the wealthy, 96, 97, 136, 140, 142, 144, 335, 319; as a force in *Restoring the Dream*, 246–51; and power, 326; and desire, 352; *see also* money
Weaver, Randy, 139
Weisberg, Jacob, 316
welfare reform, 327, 389
Welles, Orson, 47, 117, 196
Wenders, Wim, 284
Western Canon, 384
white overclass, 170
white trash, 170–71
Wild West Backlash, against the Feds, 173
Will, George, 248
women, in the '60s, 28; liberated, 81–83 as housewives, 100–02
Wordsworth, William, 285
working class, 219–20

youth, 69–74; and popular culture, 191

Zemeckis, Robert, 5
Zhirinovsky, Vladimir, 385